BI 3191602

KV-171-741

This item may be recalled before the date stamped below.
You must return it when it is recalled or you will be fined.

NORMAL LOAN

13/12/17.

KENRICK LIBRARY

PERRY BARR

DOSTOEVSKY AND THE
CHRISTIAN TRADITION

Dostoevsky is one of Russia's greatest novelists and a major influence in modern debates about religion, both in Russia and the West. This collection brings together Western and Russian perspectives on the issues raised by the religious element in his work. The aim of this collection is not to abstract Dostoevsky's religious 'teaching' from his literary works, but to explore the interaction between his Christian faith and his writing. The essays cover such topics as temptation, grace and law, Dostoevsky's use of the gospels and hagiography, Trinitarianism, and the Russian tradition of the veneration of icons, as well as reading aloud, and dialogism. In addition to an exploration of the impact of the Christian tradition on Dostoevsky's major novels, *Crime and Punishment*, *The Idiot* and *The Brothers Karamazov*, there are also discussions of lesser known works such as *The Landlady* and *A Little Boy at Christ's Christmas Tree*.

GEORGE PATTISON is Dean of Chapel at King's College, Cambridge. He has published widely in the field of philosophy of religion and his books include *Kierkegaard: The Aesthetic and the Religious* (1992), *Anxious Angels: A Retrospective View of Religious Existentialism* (1999) and *The Routledge GuideBook to the Later Heidegger* (2000). He has also taught at St Andrew's Biblical-Theological College in Moscow.

DIANE OENNING THOMPSON is Affiliated Lecturer in the Department of Slavonic Studies at the University of Cambridge and has taught Russian literature in the United States. Her book *The Brothers Karamazov and the Poetics of Memory* (1991) was recently translated into Russian and published by the Academic Project in St Petersburg. Her articles on Dostoevsky have appeared in several international collections.

CAMBRIDGE STUDIES IN RUSSIAN LITERATURE

General editor CATRIONA KELLY

Editorial board ANTHONY CROSS, CARYL EMERSON,
BARBARA HELDT, MALCOLM JONES, DONALD RAYFIELD,
G. S. SMITH, VICTOR TERRAS

A complete list of titles in the series is given at the back of the book

DOSTOEVSKY
AND THE CHRISTIAN
TRADITION

EDITED BY

GEORGE PATTISON

AND

DIANE OENNING THOMPSON

CAMBRIDGE
UNIVERSITY PRESS

UNIVERSITY OF
LIBRARY
SERVICES
CENTRAL ENGLAND

PUBLISHED BY THE PRESS SYNDICATE OF THE UNIVERSITY OF CAMBRIDGE
The Pitt Building, Trumpington Street, Cambridge, United Kingdom

CAMBRIDGE UNIVERSITY PRESS
The Edinburgh Building, Cambridge CB2 2RU, UK
40 West 20th Street, New York, NY 10011–4211, USA
10 Stamford Road, Oakleigh, Melbourne 3166, Australia
Ruiz de Alarcón 13, 28014 Madrid, Spain
Dock House, The Waterfront, Cape Town 8001, South Africa

http://www.cambridge.org

© Cambridge University Press 2001

The book is in copyright. Subject to statutory exception and to the provisions of relevant
collective licensing agreements, no reproduction of any part may take place without the
written permission of Cambridge University Press.

First published 2001

Printed in the United Kingdom at the University Press, Cambridge

Typeset in Baskerville 11/12.5pt   System 3b2   [CE]

A catalogue record for this book is available from the British Library

Library of Congress Cataloguing-in-Publication Data
Dostoevsky and the Christian tradition / edited by George Pattison and
Diane Oenning Thompson.
    p.   cm. – (Cambridge studies in Russian literature)
Includes bibliographical references and index.
1. Dostoyevsky, Fyodor, 1821–1881 – Religion.
I. Pattison, George, 1950–   II. Thompson, Diane Oenning.   III. Series.
PG3328.Z7   R4233   2001
891.73′3–dc21   00–065988

ISBN 0 521 78278 3 hardback

UNIVERSITY OF
CENTRAL ENGLAND

Book no. 31916023

Subject no. 891. 733 DOS/Pat

LIBRARY SERVICES

Contents

Notes on contributors

DAVID S. CUNNINGHAM is Professor of Theology and Ethics at Seabury-Western Theological Seminary, Evanston, Illinois. He is the author of *These Three are One: The Practice of Trinitarian Theology* (1998), and the co-editor of *Ecumenical Theology in Worship, Doctrine, and Life* (1999). He recently held the Alan Richardson Fellowship at the University of Durham, where he began work on a project on the doctrine of revelation.

CARYL EMERSON is A. Watson Armour III University Professor of Slavic Languages and Literatures at Princeton University, with a co-appointment in Comparative Literature. Well known as a translator and critic of the Russian literary critic and philosopher Mikhail Bakhtin, she has also published widely on nineteenth-century Russian literature (Pushkin, Dostoevsky, Tolstoy, Chekhov), on the history of literary criticism, and on Russian opera and vocal music. Most recently she is the author of *The First Hundred Years of Mikhail Bakhtin* (1997) and a brief biography of Modest Mussorgsky (1999) in the Cambridge series 'Musical Lives'.

IVAN A. ESAULOV is Professor at the Department of Theoretical and Historical Poetics, Russian State University for the Humanities (RGGU), Moscow. He is the author of numerous articles and four monographs, of which the most recent are *Kategoriia sobornosti v russkoi literature* (*The Category of Sobornost' in Russian Literature*) (1995), and *Spektr adekvatnosti v istolkovanii literaturnogo proizvedeniia* (*The Spectrum of Adequacy in the Interpretation of the Literary Work*) (1997). He is also an editor of the periodical *Postsimvolizm kak iavleniie kul'tury* (1995–). His main area of specialisation is in the poetics of Old Russian and Russian literature, and the philosophy of religion.

ANTONY JOHAE is Associate Professor in the Department of English

Language and Literature, Kuwait University. He has also taught in Britain, Germany, Ghana and Tunisia. His published articles on Dostoevsky include 'Idealism and the dialectic in *The Brothers Karamazov*' (1981), 'Dostoevsky's walls and Holbein's paintings' (1993) and 'Groundwork for a comparative study of Dostoevsky and Kafka' (1997). He has also published articles on Zamyatin and Trotsky as well as Swift, Coleridge, Dickens, Orwell, Soyinka, Kafka, Mann and Grass.

VLADIMIR KANTOR is Professor at Moscow State University, a novelist, philosopher and literary critic whose main scholarly interests lie in the area of the philosophy of Russian history and culture. He is the author of numerous articles, as well as a book on *The Brothers Karamazov* (1983). His two latest books are: '. . .est' evropeiskaia derzhava': Rossiia: trudnyi put' k tsivilizatsii: Istoriosofskie ocherki* (1997) and *Fenomen russkogo evropeitsa* (1999). He is on the Editorial Board of the journal *Voprosy filosofii* (*Questions of Philosophy*). He was awarded the Heinrich Böll Prize in 1992.

IRINA KIRILLOVA is Fellow and Reader Emerita of Newnham College, Cambridge, and Lecturer in Russian (retired) in the Department of Slavonic Studies in the University of Cambridge. She has also lectured extensively on Dostoevsky in Russia. She is presently working on a book on *The Idiot*.

SOPHIE OLLIVIER is Honorary Professor of Russian Literature in the Michel de Montaigne University, Bordeaux, and has also taught at University College, Dublin and the Alliance Française, Dublin. She is the author of many articles on Russian literature. She has lately been working on nineteenth-century Irish history.

GEORGE PATTISON is Dean of Chapel at King's College, Cambridge. His publications include *Kierkegaard: The Aesthetic and the Religious, From the Magic Theatre to the Crucifixion of the Image* (1992) and *Anxious Angels: A Retrospective View of Religious Existentialism* (1999). His most recent book is *The Routledge GuideBook to the Later Heidegger* (2000).

AVRIL PYMAN is Reader Emerita in Russian at the University of Durham. She is the author of *The Life of Aleksandr Blok* (1979–80) and *A History of Russian Symbolism* (1994). She has edited several books, and translated Turgenev's *Fathers and Children*; she has also translated a collection of Russian papers on Shakespeare.

HENRY M. W. RUSSELL is Associate Professor at Ave Maria College, Ypsilanti, Michigan, and is Associate Editor of *The Formalist*. He is presently collecting materials for an encyclopedia of Christian influence in American literature.

DIANE OENNING THOMPSON is Affiliated Lecturer in the Department of Slavonic Studies in the University of Cambridge. She is the author of *The Brothers Karamazov and the Poetics of Memory* (1991) as well as a number of articles on Dostoevsky. Her main interests are in nineteenth-century Russian literature and poetics.

ERIC J. ZIOLKOWSKI is Professor of Religion at Lafayette College, Easton, Pennsylvania. He is the author of *The Sanctification of Don Quixote: From Hidalgo to Priest* (1991) and *Evil Children in Religion, Literature, and Art* (2001). He is also the Editor of *A Museum of Faiths: Histories and Legacies of the 1893 World's Parliament of Religions* (1993).

MARGARET ZIOLKOWSKI is Professor of Russian at Miami University, Ohio, and is the author of *Hagiography and Modern Russian Literature* (1988) and *Literary Exorcisms of Stalin: Russian Writers and the Soviet Past* (1998). She is currently working on a translation of the Life of Boyarynya Feodosya Morozova, a seventeenth-century Old Believer. Her field of specialisation is Russian literature in general, and she has recently been working on the image of women in Old Russian literature.

Acknowledgments

The idea for this volume originated at the conference 'Crime, Punishment and Christ: Reading Dostoevsky Religiously' held at the Centre for the Study of Literature and Theology in the University of Glasgow in 1995. We are therefore greatly indebted to the Centre and to its director, Professor David Jasper. We are also greatly indebted to all who took part in the conference, especially those who contributed through the presentation of papers or participation in discussions to mould the final form of the chapters offered here.

We are especially grateful to our editor at Cambridge University Press, Linda Bree, who has helped steer this collection through many hurdles to final publication. Catriona Kelly read the whole typescript and gave us valuable advice for improving the volume. We should also like to thank Natalya Ashimbaeva of the Dostoevsky Museum, St Petersburg and the Museum itself for permission to reproduce the icon used on the front cover. For help of various kinds we are grateful to Jolita Adomeiene, John Barber, Alan Burns, Bobby Coe, Larissa Fradkin, Teresa Jones, Sue Needham, Nina Perlina, Rosemary Rodd, Natalya Rubenstein and Ray Scrivens. We wish to express our warmest thanks to Caryl Emerson for her stalwart support, for her many helpful comments and for so generously and rapidly coming to our aid with her translation of Vladimir Kantor's chapter.

Note on conventions and abbreviations

All quotations from Dostoevsky's works are, in the case of Russianist contributors, taken from the Academy Edition, *Polnoe sobranie sochinenii v tridtsatykh tomakh*, Leningrad, 1973–90. Volume and page numbers are indicated in brackets; volumes split into two separate books are indicated by volume number, i or ii, followed by page numbers. Translations from the Russian are by the individual contributors.

Contributors using English translations of Dostoevsky's works provide the names of translators and editions in notes, with page numbers being indicated in brackets within the text of their chapters. Contributors' ellipses within quotations are indicated by <. . .>. The transliteration system used has been divided into two parts: (1) the British Standard is used for proper names, hence, Dostoevsky rather than Dostoevskii; (2) the Library of Congress system has been used to transliterate all quotations of Russian words as well as proper names and titles for publications cited or available only in Russian.

Introduction: Reading Dostoevsky religiously

George Pattison and Diane Oenning Thompson

Dostoevsky has emerged as the most provocative writer in Russian literature, the one who speaks most to the modern human condition. His influence on world literature has been immense. Artists working in other media have found inspiration in Dostoevsky for their own translations of his works into opera, drama, film and the graphic arts. He has stimulated writers and thinkers of the most diverse persuasions and callings (philosophers, theologians, marxists, conservatives, psychologists, literary critics). Books, articles, critical debates, comments, allusions abound. His themes of crime, urban alienation, family breakdown, psychic derangement, the decline of religious faith, as well as his penetrating psychological insight and prophetic grasp of the murderous potential of modern totalitarian ideologies and of the social and spiritual chaos spawned by unrestrained capitalism, profoundly resonate with the twentieth century. Other nineteenth-century writers took up these themes; few matched Dostoevsky's psychological acumen, none his ideological prescience.

But what is above all peculiar to Dostoevsky is his genius for eliciting strong pro or contra responses, for tempting us to make global, essentially religious statements. Dostoevsky had a gift, virtually unique among modern writers, for making Christianity dynamic, for subtly forcing the ideological challenges of the modern age to interact dialogically with his Christian vision and for embodying this vision in psychologically compelling characters. To 'read Dostoevsky religiously', then, would mean to engage with this dialogue which runs through his entire post-Siberian oeuvre. This makes those who would rather bypass the religious issues uneasy; they are more comfortable discussing the psychology of his characters and the ideas debated in his fiction. But, given the prominence of biblical motifs and of references to doctrinal, liturgical and devotional elements in the Christian tradition, it is almost impossible *not* to read Dostoevsky religiously. His treatment of the human personality is at once modern – he was a master at conveying the very feel of consciousness, with its acute self-awareness, its tensions between conflicting thoughts, impulses and desires – and biblical, in that he translated psychological complexity into a struggle between good and evil in the human soul. Eric Auerbach attributed Dostoevsky's powerful impact in Europe to the peculiar nature of Russian realism which was based on old Christian realism, complicated by the Russians' 'coming to terms with European civilization', ever vacillating between categorical acceptance and rejection.[1] A brief historical survey may clarify the peculiar concatenation of social and cultural forces which engendered these extreme oscillations and nurtured and stimulated Dostoevsky's singular artistic vision.

THE HISTORICAL CONTEXT

Until the eighteenth century, Russian literature was almost exclusively Christian in form and content (hagiographies, sermons, liturgical works, spiritual verses, religious folk verse). Even the chronicles, heroic folk songs and patriotic epics (*byliny*), though not sacred genres *per se*, served to promote the pre-eminence of Christianity. For example, *The Lay of Igor's Campaign*, the literary masterpiece of medieval Russia, ends with a paen to the princes 'who fight for the Christians against the infidel hosts'. The *byliny* on *Il'ya of Murom* typically extol those 'mighty heroes in Holy Russia' who 'defend the Christian faith'. However, Peter the Great (1672–1725) saw his princely role in quite a different light. His aim was to turn Russia into a great power on an equal footing with the major powers of Western Europe. In pursuance of this goal, Peter adopted the ideology of enlightened absolutism and by sheer force of will drove Russia on a course of rapid modernisation. All institutions were absorbed into the bureaucratic machinery and routine of the state. The Church was deprived of its autonomy and made subordinate to the state, the clergy became, in Georges Florovsky's words 'state servitors'. As Florovsky says, what was most revolutionary in Peter's reforms was not the Westernisation or modernisation of Russia but its secularisation.[2] For along with the modernisation of the state according to Western models, came a massive influx of Western ideas which at that time were steeped in the values of the Enlightenment. The Enlighteners, inspired by the growth in scientific knowledge, placed their faith in reason, rejected traditional authority and revelation, and were largely anti-religious, empiricist, naturalist and materialist. The impact of these ideas in Russia resulted in the bifurcation of Russian society into two different, mutually uncomprehending nations: a small, educated, Westernised elite and the enormous mass of peasant believers who – at least until the mid-eighteenth century – resided in a patriarchal world, shaped by centuries of Orthodoxy and serfdom and scarcely touched by Western influences.

The Petrine reforms also introduced Western cultural forms (primarily French) into Russia on a large scale so that, by the end of the eighteenth century, Russian literature, which was mainly fashioned on French Neoclassicism and the West European baroque, had become almost totally Europeanised and secularised. New secular forms and themes (nature, love lyrics) appeared, and classical allusions, sometimes implying a humanist ideal, became common. Not that Christian themes had disappeared; we have only to recall the devotional odes of Lomonosov and various lyrics of Derzhavin and Zhukovsky to be reminded that religious faith was still the norm. But by the late eighteenth century expressions of Christian piety were mostly cast in secular, literary forms (the lyric, ode, epic, drama, short story and, in the nineteenth century, the novel), and the sacred genres had virtually disappeared from mainstream literature. When, almost a century later, Dostoevsky wrote a saint's life complete with sermons ('The Russian Monk'), into which he poured his most cherished beliefs, he did not publish it as a separate work but boldly incorporated it into a novel (*The Brothers Karamazov*). This was very risky in that the novel, pre-eminently a secular form, threatens to relativise the religious content. 'The Russian Monk' remains, artistically and ideologically, the most controversial part of the great novel. But then, Dostoevsky himself said he wrote Zosima's discourses only 'for the few' (30,105).

The early nineteenth century saw a religious revival largely stimulated by the new secular conditions and the challenge they posed to the religious heritage. The tension between Western European ideas, from the Enlightenment to utopian socialism, and the native religious tradition gave powerful stimulus to a period of extraordinary creativity in literature. After the Napoleonic invasion of 1812, Russian writers broke with French Neoclassicism, and turned for inspiration to the new works of the German and English Romantics as well as to native folklore and the literature of pre-Petrine Russia. The stylistic rules of Neoclassicism had come to seem constraining, artificial, lacking those expressive possibilities which were called for by the new sensibility of Romanticism and, subsequently, realism. The search for new forms and modes of expression became entangled with the question of nationalism as Russian writers sought to discern what was unique about Russia, what was its particular national character. Pushkin entered this debate in an essay of 1822 in which he defined Orthodoxy as the distinctive feature of the Russian national character: 'the Greek creed, different from all others, gives us our particular national character'.[3] However, from the late 1830s, initially under the influence of Russia's first prominent radical critic, Vissarion Belinsky, Russian literary criticism was dominated by the revolutionary democrats who were atheist, anti-religious and materialist. The intelligentsia became progressively polarised between those who urged the adoption of Western ideas as a solution to Russia's problems and those who identified with the people's faith and native traditions, a split which is reflected in Dostoevsky's depictions of his contemporary society and which is still evident today. Dostoevsky is a pivotal figure who gave his allegiance to Christianity and at the same time registered with acute sensitivity the pressures bearing down on it from the imminent modern age.

Belinsky's ideological progeny (N. G. Chernyshevsky, N. A. Dobrolyubov, D. I. Pisarev) of the 1860s, the high point of radical criticism, adopted a utilitarian approach according to which works were judged by their usefulness in the political struggle. Art was treated as a social document, its purpose, to portray objective reality from a socially critical perspective. These ideas were later to have a marked influence on Lenin, a lifelong admirer of Chernyshevsky, and in 1934 hardened into the baleful Communist Party dogma of Socialist Realism. Fortunately the great nineteenth-century writers of the post-Pushkin period (Gogol, Tyutchev, Lermontov, Turgenev, Leskov, Tolstoy, Chekhov) went their own way, paying scant heed to the radicals' call for socio-political relevance, and in the process they created one of the world's great literatures. But it was Dostoevsky who had the most acute ear for the historical implications of the radicals' utopian programmes. His remarkable prescience finds, perhaps, its most succinct expression in *The Brothers Karamazov.*

Towards the end of Ivan Karamazov's nightmare conversation with the devil, the key idea which led to the parricide is finally revealed. Appropriately, it comes from the mouth of the devil, as he taunts Ivan by quoting his most recent work on the imminent advent of a new age which will place its faith in the triumph of science:

The new people [the radicals of Ivan's generation] propose to destroy everything <. . .> Stupid people, they didn't ask me! <. . .> one only needs to destroy in mankind the idea of God <. . .> Once humanity to a man renounces God <. . .> all the former morality will fall away and everything new will begin! <. . .> man will conquer nature without limits by his will and science. (15,83)

Indeed, Dostoevsky's worst forebodings about obliterating 'the idea of God' and constructing society on 'science' were realised in the Soviet period. For the Communist Party went much farther than Peter the Great: its aim was the total obliteration of religion, the total secularisation of Soviet life. The Soviet rulers, determined to impose their militantly atheistic ideology of Marxism–Leninism on the religiously diverse lands over which they ruled, engaged in ruthless, wide-scale attempts to expunge religion (including Judaism, Islam and others) from Soviet life. The Orthodox Church, to which the majority belonged, was (especially after 1929) subjected to whole-sale persecution. Many priests were imprisoned, tortured or murdered, numerous churches were looted, closed or razed, religious education was abolished, seminaries were closed, and religious 'propaganda' was prohibited.[4] Those who openly held to their faith were subjected to ridicule, ostracism or worse. It became totally taboo to discuss religious topics in literature and historiography. At the same time, the State, in promoting its creed of atheism, borrowed the symbols and iconography of Christianity and trans-formed them into its own image.[5] The anti-religious campaign extended to a philistine orthographical censorship; initial capitals designating divine persons were reduced to small-case letters in all publications, including reissues of pre-1917 texts. (Unfortunately, some Western critics citing Soviet editions perpetuate this censor-ship). The Church finally capitulated and agreed to be 'legalised' by the regime. During the Second World War, Stalin, in a cynical effort to drum up patriotism, relented. The Church was allowed to hold services, rebuild its administrative structure and open a few theo-logical schools. During 1959–64, however, these gains were severely curtailed. Khrushchev renewed the persecution of the Church, though more covertly by corrupting it from within. KGB operatives were placed to oversee Church affairs and priests were to report any confessions deemed anti-Soviet. Other faiths also suffered suppression. The Brezhnev era was one of stagnation in all areas of national life. The turning point came in 1988 when, for the first time, a Soviet leader of state, Mikhail Gorbachev, shared a national platform with the Patriarch in celebration of the Millennium of Christianity in Russia. Three years later the atheist state collapsed. This historical situation is reflected in the history of Dostoevsky criticism.

THE VICISSITUDES OF DOSTOEVSKY CRITICISM

Dostoevsky lived at a time when the Christian tradition was far more familiar than it is today, and in a society which shared a common Christian culture. But even then he keenly felt its encroaching erosion. In his notebooks for *The Brothers Karamazov*, there is a sketch for a conversation in which Miusov, Ivan and Fyodor Karamazov mangle biblical quotations, after which Dostoevsky laments: 'No one knows the Gospels', and polemically proceeds to correct his fictional characters' errors (15,206). Nevertheless, during the last decade of his life, he was increasingly hailed as a spiritual guide and prophet. Ordinary readers saw him as a 'teacher of life' and turned to him for consolation, advice and solutions to their dilemmas. While Dostoevsky's works attracted considerable favourable attention in his lifetime, negative responses to his Christianity were occasionally voiced and they came from both ends of the ideological spectrum. Shortly after Dostoevsky's death in 1881, the radical atheist critic M. A. Antonovich published an article on *The Brothers Karamazov* with the title 'A Mystic-Ascetic Novel' in which he condemned it as a 'reactionary' work and perversely identified the Grand Inquisitor's views with those of Dostoevsky. Another critic on the left, N. K. Mikhailovsky, in an article of 1883, pronounced Dostoevsky a 'cruel talent'. Maxim Gorky styled him an 'evil genius' and in 1913 opposed the staging of *The Devils* by the Moscow Arts Theatre. On the conservative side, Dostoevsky was upbraided for being insufficiently Orthodox. The writer Konstantin Leontiev, who died a monk in 1891, took strong exception to Dostoevsky's 'made up' depictions of monastic life and 'rosy' Christianity. More pertinently, Leontiev found his Christianity heretical because he never abandoned the socialist utopian promise of paradise on earth rather than in heaven. Indeed, many members of the Church hierarchy have, with some reason, regarded his Christianity with uneasiness, if not suspicion. Dostoevsky was a confessed Orthodox Christian, but his relationship with official Orthodoxy remains unclear since, unlike some of his contemporaries, notably Tolstoy and Turgenev, he was very private about his own spiritual experience and not given to public personal confessions. Moreover, although his art was nourished by the Orthodox tradition, it also bears significant traces of German Pietism and Protestantism.[6] However, Dostoevsky's literary reputation continued to grow. From his death until 1917 a number of prominent writers, among them, D. S. Merezhkovsky, V. V. Rozanov, A. L. Volynsky, V. L. Komarovich, Viacheslav Ivanov and the religious philosopher Vladimir Soloviev illuminatingly explored the Christian themes in his works.

If negative criticism of Dostoevsky's Christianity did not begin with the Soviet period, at least before 1917 it benignly co-existed with sympathetic evaluations. After the Bolshevik Revolution, however, it began to matter that Lenin, who was held up as the infallible judge in all artistic and ideological matters, had called Dostoevsky 'ultra-repulsive'. He was reported to have pronounced Dostoevsky's writings to be 'trash' and singled out *The Devils* and *The Brothers Karamazov* (of which he read no further than the early monastery scenes) as 'putrid works'.[7] Nevertheless, the 1920s and early 1930s saw the publication of important textological, editorial, biographical and literary studies (L. Grossman, A. S. Dolinin, Iu. N. Tynianov). In 1929 M. M. Bakhtin, Dostoevsky's greatest critic, published his seminal study *Problems of Dostoevsky's Creative Work* (*Problemy kvorchestva Dostoevskogo*).

The 1930s, however, marked a turn for the worse. At the First Congress of Soviet Writers in 1934, Gorky, the keynote speaker, renewed his attack on Dostoevsky, though he allowed that his 'genius was indisputable; perhaps only Shakespeare equals him in power of portrayal'.[8] The mid 1930s to mid 1950s, was a dismal period for interpretative and speculative studies on Dostoevsky. The Soviet overseers of literature proscribed a sympathetic treatment of Dostoevsky's religious themes; if treated, they had to be accompanied by ritual denigrations of the 'cult' of Christianity, and sprinkled with quotes from Lenin or Stalin.[9] Two important studies, V. Kirpotkin's (1946) and A. S. Dolinin's (1947), were submitted for publication, but they came under the censure of A. Zhdanov, Stalin's notorious spokesman for cultural affairs, and were published only after Stalin's death.

In 1955, thanks to the literary 'thaw', some favourable remarks about Dostoevsky reportedly made by Lenin came to light to the effect that he was a writer of 'true genius' who examined 'some sore spots' in Russian society.[10] An official re-evaluation took place that emphasised and approved Dostoevsky's early involvement with socialist utopian ideals, his humanitarian concerns, his anti-capitalist stance and his realistic representations of the poor and oppressed, but condemned his religious philosophical views and routinely warned readers of the dangers of taking them seriously. *Notes from the House of the Dead* was extolled for its exposure of the brutal tsarist penal system. Yet, Dostoevsky's religious concerns were still taboo, to be mentioned only in the context of vilification. The works that came in for the most vehement criticism were *Notes from the Underground*, *The Devils* and *The Brothers Karamazov*. Among those who periodically attacked Dostoevsky's religious views, V. V. Ermilov was particularly vociferous, going so far as to assert that *The Brothers Karamazov* illustrates the 'amorality' of Christianity in that it shows Christ as having purchased the 'right to torment children' because 'he redeemed all men's sins.'[11] Nevertheless, in 1963 Bakhtin's study was reissued in a revised and expanded edition under the title *Problems of Dostoevsky's Poetics*. Bakhtin was profoundly aware of the Christian foundation of Dostoevsky's poetics, but, given the constraints of Soviet censorship and his own precarious position, could never treat it openly. Near the end of his life, he poignantly spoke of his deep regret that he was not able to write 'directly about the main questions', to do justice to what had 'tormented Dostoevsky all his life – the existence of God <. . .> I had constantly to prevaricate <. . .> to keep myself in hand. As soon as a thought came, I had to stop it.'[12]

Dostoevsky studies took a more favourable turn in the 1970s. In 1973 the first volume of the Academy Edition of Dostoevsky's complete works appeared. The late Academician G. Fridlender, in a heroic feat of editorship, saw the whole project through to its completion in 1990. This outstanding work of devoted scholarship, to which some of the best scholars in Russia contributed, suffers from one serious flaw which was not the fault of the editor and contributors; namely, they were not allowed to use Dostoevsky's capitals for divine persons. Evidently, this was one factor which prompted V. N. Zakharov to undertake a new complete edition in the old orthography in which Dostoevsky wrote his works.[13] This is not just nitpicking pedantry. In 1928 Dmitry Likhachev, the distinguished Russian medievalist, in response to the 'particularly merciless attacks on the Church' during 1927–28, wrote a paper ('half in jest, half seriously') in which he mounted a spirited attack on the alphabet reform imposed by the Bolsheviks in 1918, and defended the old orthography on linguistic, historical, aesthetic and Orthodox grounds.[14] He declared that the imposition of the new orthography was 'the act of an anti-Christ power', and a further rupturing of the Russian language from its Church Slavonic roots which, because the abolished letters were spiritually symbolic, drained Russian of some of its most Orthodox features.[15] For example, he decries the loss of the common letter *iat'*, whose shape symbolises the Church with a cross on top. Within days Likhachev was arrested and sent to the notorious camp of Solovki. This paper was used as evidence against him. The loss of the old letters and the abolition of initial capitals for divine persons affect interpretations. The Grand Inquisitor's speech is replete with capitalised pronouns for his addressee, and *iat's* as well as other old letters abound, a feature totally lost in translation. Here it becomes visible that the Grand Inquisitor is defeated even orthographically by Christ.

Given this situation in their native country, it was left to the Russian emigrés to pursue the religious dimension in Dostoevsky's writings. Here too his works attracted an outstanding group of literary critics and religious philosophers, among them K. Mochulsky, N. Berdyaev, L. Shestov, M. Slonim, N. Trubetskoy and N. Lossky. Some read Dostoevsky perhaps too religiously, seeing him as a prophet and messenger of God to the exclusion of some of the complexities of his work. Berdyaev concluded his well-known book on Dostoevsky with what may be the most exalted tribute ever paid to a writer of fiction: 'So great is the worth of Dostoevsky that to have produced him is by itself sufficient justification for the existence of the Russian people in the world; and he will bear witness for his countrymen at the Last Judgment of the nations.'[16] Given that such a vital part of Russian life was under violent attack in their native land, it was understandable that they looked to Dostoevsky as a refuge and repository of Orthodox spirituality, as, in Berdyaev's words, a 'spiritual homeland'.

At present we are witnessing in Russia a great upsurge of interest in religion and a revival of the Orthodox Church. This has created an atmosphere favourable to religious readings. Held back for decades by Soviet censorship, Russian scholars are freely exploring the religious themes in their literature. Since the collapse of the Soviet regime, Dostoevsky studies in Russia have entered a particularly active phase. Symposia, seminars, exhibits, meetings and studies by young as well as established scholars are proliferating, among them V. E. Vetlovskaya, V. N. Zakharov, B. N. Tikhomirov, I. A. Esaulov, N. Ashimbaeva, L. I. Saraskina, to mention a few.[17] The publication of previously forbidden emigré critics, thinkers and philosophers of religion as well as seminal Western works have greatly enriched debates and scholarly work within Russia.[18] If just occasionally there is an exaggerated emphasis on Russian Orthodox concerns, this is only part of the process of restoring to Russia its cultural memory, of salvaging its best and of coming to terms with its worst, with those events which should be remembered but never repeated. Russia is a traumatised nation, deeply scarred by the horrific events of the twentieth century. This is not always sufficiently appreciated by those who live in stable democratic societies. We have only to imagine St Paul's Cathedral in London being turned into a museum of atheism, Notre Dame de Paris being replaced by a swimming pool, or the Vatican being closed to the public and occupied by an atheist government to gain some idea of what it must have been like for many to witness helplessly (to protest was futile or dangerous) such vandalistic desecration of their religious heritage. As the Russians search for new values, or rediscover old ones to fill the moral vacuum left by the collapse of the Soviet regime, Dostoevsky's works have acquired fresh relevance, as the contributions of Esaulov and Kantor to this volume demonstrate. This gives renewed impetus to the question of what it may mean to read Dostoevsky religiously now.

Two main tendencies can be discerned, each corresponding to the two main senses of 'religiously'. Neither is new. The first adopts a reverential attitude towards Dostoevsky's creative writings, turning them into a springboard for 'co-philosophising' or sermonising. This runs the danger of 'monologising' them, of forgetting that they are works of the imagination subject to aesthetic judgment and rhetorical analysis. However, Dostoevsky's prophetic and spiritual insights resonate beyond the concerns of aesthetics, rhetoric and literary criticism. To read him religiously in the sense of seeking spiritual illumination is a common and potentially rewarding approach. As Caryl Emerson observes in her 'Translator's afterword' *apropos* Vladimir Kantor's reflections, rereading Dostoevsky may make Russia wiser in confronting contemporary moral, spiritual dilemmas, and thus better able to guard against future catastrophes. The devout approach, then, is not necessarily illegitimate. St Augustine's remark that there are some things which one understands only when one believes is not to be dismissed. Believers, and especially those who come from within the Orthodox community, can offer insights and perspectives unavailable to or remote from the views of 'outsiders'. Sympathy with Dostoevsky's Christian aspirations does not entail succumbing to his political and nationalist prejudices, to what Bakhtin called 'the small Dostoevsky'.

The second approach takes 'religiously' in the sense of faithfully, conscientiously and scrupulously disclosing, analysing and interpreting the Christian basis of Dostoevsky's art, its themes, ideas and symbols. This does not require allegiance to Dostoevsky's ideals or beliefs, but it does entail taking account of them, and making an effort to understand them on their own terms, as best we can from our increasing historical distance. Readings which denigrate or trivialise the Christian dimension in Dostoevsky are impoverished; those which wilfully ignore or excise it are mendacious. To read Dostoevsky without reference to his Christian beliefs is the same as to deny the paramount role of Christianity in Dante, to reduce the *Divine Comedy* to a struggle in Florentine politics. To interpret past writers exclusively within the horizon of present concerns is to overlook the possibility that they knew some things we do not know, or have forgotten. On the other hand, the scholarly, analytical approach does not preclude sharing Dostoevsky's Christian beliefs, but it does require a modicum of critical distance, of openness to new perspectives on literary analysis, and an awareness of the problematic nature of his work. Of course, any reading bears traces of an interpreter's own responses which Dostoevsky so pre-eminently provokes. This is as inevitable as it is legitimate since there is no such thing as an absolutely objective reading. Probably the way to get the most out of Dostoevsky is to read him dialogically, probing, interrogating and challenging him. Perhaps this is to read him religiously in the fullest sense.

DOSTOEVSKY AND THE RELIGIOUS CRISIS OF THE WEST

The reception of Dostoevsky's work in the English-speaking world is, of course, a topic that goes far beyond the scope of this introduction. Even if we limit ourselves to his impact on religious thought we risk getting entangled in the criss-crossing threads of a *Rezeptionsgeschichte* that, although not vast in scope, is extraordinarily complex in its detail.

This complexity has a number of sources. The first is simply the variety of responses to Dostoevsky's writing, ranging from those that see in it a thinly-disguised avowal of atheism to those that see Dostoevsky as one of the great prophets of Christian faith for a post-Nietzschean world. The second has to do with the fact that, by the 1940s, Dostoevsky had become identified for good or ill (and in varying degrees) with existentialism – precisely in the period when existentialism was not only the most fashionable but also the most controversial of European philosophical movements. Questions as to whether Dostoevsky was or was not 'a good thing' and whether his work was or was not compatible with Christianity became inseparable from analogous questions about existentialism in general. Third, there is the difficulty (or, better perhaps, the challenge) that, whilst theologians and religious writers are very often also readers of novels and are often ready to acknowledge the influence of novels on them, this influence is often only fleetingly acknowledged in their work.[19] It is really only in the relatively recent past that the study of literature has come to be seen as a *bona fide* pursuit for a professional theologian. Connected with this is the fact that theologians and religious writers are also capable of reading critical literature that is not primarily theological, with the result that the view of Dostoevsky found in theological writing is often (though not invariably) dependent on critical appraisals that theologians themselves are not (or have not regarded themselves as being) competent to judge. Fourth – and by no means least importantly – we need to have a sense for the extreme complexity of the routes by which Dostoevsky entered into the English-speaking religious consciousness. In part this follows from what has already been said about the relationship between literature, criticism and theology. So, for example, Dostoevsky was discovered and became fashionable in literary circles in Britain in the period 1912–21, whereas his impact on religious thought probably peaked a generation later, from the mid-1940s onwards. The theologians' 'image' of Dostoevsky was thus already impressed with a significant history of interpretation. But the situation is still more complex, since this history included not only the previous British literary reception of Dostoevsky, but the theological, philosophical and literary reception of his work in Germany, France and elsewhere (including, of course, Russia itself) – and, as we shall see, theologians elsewhere had made a significantly earlier start than those in Anglo-Saxony. Here we also have to take into account the different confessional interests that play a part in the story: the English-speaking Protestant world was, of course, most receptive to the kind of Dostoevsky interpretation associated with Barth and dialectical theology, whereas others would come to see him more as a paradigmatic representative of Orthodoxy.

We cannot, therefore, hope to construct any simple linear narrative history: all we can aim to achieve here is to signal some of the main reference points that any such history would need to incorporate.

It has already been noted that the first wave of Dostoevsky reception in Britain (and we shall focus on Britain rather than on the United States here) can be dated to the period 1912–21, partly because this was the period when Constance Garnett's translations of the novels and short stories was appearing, and although these were not the first translations to appear, this was *the* publishing event that first allowed English language readers to grasp the full scope of his fiction. These translations were complemented by a critical reception that included works by J. A. T. Lloyd, John Cowper Powys and John Middleton Murry. Middleton Murry's *Dostoevsky: A Critical Study* (1916) was in many ways paradigmatic of the 'Dostoevsky cult' of that time.[20] According to Middleton Murry the final significance of Dostoevsky's work is a 'desperate and courageous fulfilment of humanity', produced by one who 'ventured against the unknown with no other armour than human personality'.[21] Implicit in this acclamation, however, is the judgment that, in his novels, Dostoevsky has transcended what Middleton Murry regarded as the constraints of Christianity. Thus Alyosha, whom Middleton Murry judges to be the very epitome of Dostoevsky's ideal of human personality, 'is not a Christian. He has passed beyond the Christian revelation <. . .> for his knowledge of the great Oneness needs no belief in God for its support, and the beast which he knows within him is no more a beast. He has transcended these sublunary things. Their names are but earthly and blunted symbols for the reality which bears within him [sic]'.[22] Dostoevsky is no apologist of the old faith but a prophet of the new, pointing the way to a post-Christian humanism (albeit a humanism of a different kind from that of positivistic science). Is it merely coincidental that he almost sounds like Nietzsche's Zarathustra?

If this kind of Dostoevsky-reception created an image that almost inevitably repelled religiously-minded readers, a very different kind of reception was developing in the German-speaking world. Karl Barth's commentary on St Paul's *Letter to the Romans* signalled his own indebtedness to Dostoevsky as an aid in reading the New Testament.[23] Barth also acknowledges a debt to Eduard Thurneysen, a friend and colleague who had introduced him to Dostoevsky's work. Thurneysen's own Dostoevsky book, although not published in English translation until 1964, gushingly expounds the kind of view of Dostoevsky that Barth built on and that became standard amongst those influenced by Neo-Orthodoxy (in this context, of course, Protestant and not Russian Orthodoxy). Dostoevsky's achievement, according to Thurneysen, is to call into question everything human in such a way and to such a degree that the only possible remaining answer is God. Like Middleton Murry, Thurneysen envisages Dostoevsky as standing at the very outermost edge of the old order, experiencing and transcribing its collapse and pointing to a radical overcoming of its contradictions – only this time the transcendence is said to be exclusively and decisively religious since humanity is powerless to bring about its own transformation: 'the dawn of the new day which is visible in Dostoevsky's work breaks forth only in the deepest night of human uncertainty'.[24]

This view of Dostoevsky as the prophet of the religious horror of a life without God is concentrated in an extraordinary panegyric that is worth quoting at length, because it is so characteristic of the important line of theological Dostoevsky interpretation first found in Thurneysen.

Whoever comes to Dostoevsky from the regions of secure humanity, of the pre-war period for instance, must feel like one who has been looking at such domesticated animals as the dog and the cat, the chicken or the horse, and then suddenly sees the Wild before him, and without warning finds himself face to face with the yet untamed animal world, jaguar and puma, tiger and crocodile, the slithering of the snakes and the fluttering of the wings of the eagle and the condor <. . .> He has been led out past the farthermost border posts, past the limits of known humanity; with pounding heart he looks on the unknown face of a man who shares with him the common name of 'man', and who yet appears to live beyond all the concepts tied with this name, beyond good and evil, wisdom and folly, beauty and ugliness, beyond even state and family, school and church. And just as one who returns from the wilderness to domesticated animals rediscovers in the four-footed creatures who share his house, and whom he had previously regarded sympathetically, the traces of original wildness, and sees himself even in his own four walls confronted at a stroke with dangerous, unsuspected slumbering possibilities, so there proceeds from an encounter with the world and the men of Dostoevsky something of hidden trembling and fear.[25]

A major event in the English-speaking reception of Dostoevsky was the publication in 1934 of a translation of Berdyaev's enormously influential study – published in London, interestingly, by Sheed and Ward, a Catholic publishing house. Perhaps the most significant contribution Berdyaev's book made to the theological understanding of Dostoevsky in the West was his emphasis on the abyssal freedom of the individual. Whereas the Neo-Orthodox view saw in Dostoevsky's novels a revelation of the profound bondage of the human will, desperately seeking and longing for redemption but utterly incapable of self-deliverance, Berdyaev argued that Dostoevsky's religious teaching was inseparable from his insistence on the freedom of the human spirit. He wrote that 'those of [Dostoevsky's] characters who deny this freedom deny God, and inversely. A world in which goodness and righteousness reign by compulsion, whose harmony is ensured by undeniable necessity, is a godless world, a rationalised mechanism, and to reject God and human liberty is to push the world in that direction.'[26] Both the interpretation of Dostoevsky brought into focus by this quotation and the interpretation of Christianity offered by Berdyaev could not be further removed from that of Thurneysen and the Neo-Orthodox.

Berdyaev was widely perceived in the 1940s and 1950s as a 'Christian existentialist' and there is no doubt that his advocacy of Dostoevsky helped both to strengthen the perception of Dostoevsky himself as being some kind of Christian proto-existentialist as well as to stir the debate as to whether there could indeed be any such thing as 'Christian existentialism'. Certainly he provided a significant line of defence for Christians who did not wish to cede the entire territory of human freedom to Sartrean atheism, although that line had simultaneously to be defended against the Calvinism of Barth and his followers.

Curiously, given his extremely difficult relationship with the Orthodox hierarchy (in 1914 he was awaiting trial on a charge of blasphemy), Berdyaev's involvement with the YMCA and with the ecumenical movement in the 1930s meant that he was often called upon to represent the Orthodox voice at theological and Church conferences. For many Western Christians he was one of the defining voices of Russian Orthodox spirituality. In this respect he was widely linked with Sergy Bulgakov, who also reflected the influence of Dostoevsky.

A study by L. A. Zander in 1942, published in English by the Student Christian Movement Press in 1948, drew a number of links between Dostoevsky and Bulgakov. The Dostoevskian theme of 'the life-giving power of the earth and its mysterious bond with man'[27] is said both to be an 'ancient mystical teaching' of the Russian Church and to find philosophical articulation in Bulgakov's sophiological doctrine. Here the thought of humanity's unity with nature is contextualised in a larger picture of the cosmic unity of all beings within the divine Wisdom or Sophia. A 'Sophian' dimension is also seen by Zander in Dostoevsky's female characters and in the various 'humble ones' who people his novels. Finally, Dostoevsky's vision of human destiny culminates in the promotion of active love, the 'deeds', as Zander calls them, of 'faithful service, loyalty, marriage', deeds in which 'Christ overtakes the human soul and the Holy Spirit comes to dwell in it, so that "the servant" becomes "a friend", the creature – a temple.'[28] In similar terms Zander sees Dostoevsky's understanding of human destiny as drawn from the imagery of the New Testament: becoming 'the friend of the Bridegroom' (an image that is once more said to be central to Bulgakov). The 'limits' of Dostoevsky's thought are in this way not pictured as bordering on a future of radical humanism, nor yet as requiring recourse to 'grace alone', nor even revealing our abyssal freedom, but as 'the gates leading to an Orthodox world-conception.'[29]

But this is by no means the end of Dostoevsky's very varied appearances as a religious thinker.

One element singularly lacking (or at least significantly under-played) in the interpretations examined so far is any Christological reference. This was, however, provided by Henri de Lubac in his study *The Drama of Atheist Humanism*, a drama in which Dostoevsky emerges as the prophet (once more) of a kind of Christian faith that has taken the measure of modern atheism and lived to tell the tale.

'[Dostoevsky] was present at the "death of God". He saw the murderer springing up into the saddle for a stupendous career,' but, seeing the implications of this death he turned away. In this 'he forestalled Nietzsche. He overcame the temptation to which Nietzsche was to succumb.'[30]

At the heart of the 'new dimension' that Dostoevsky's work discloses is a vision of Christ. In the image of Jesus in *The Grand Inquisitor* Dostoevsky, according to de Lubac, 'reveals the depths of his heart'. Even Ivan is 'impressed with the majesty and the truth of Christ.'[31] Nor should this be taken as implying that Dostoevsky's focus is exclusively on the human Jesus. His Christ is not simply an ideal human being, but the One who has been brought, through death, to resurrection and by this means has become the prototype of our own eschatological future. 'Dostoevsky is the prophet of the *other life* <. . .> the prophet of the resurrection, which presupposes experience of death.'[32]

In rooting Dostoevsky's faith in the incarnate and resurrected Christ, de Lubac is thus rebutting a view that had found expression in a critical response by Derek Traversi to Berdyaev's Dostoevsky. Traversi's objection was this: that 'there is no place for the Incarnation in Dostoevsky's theology, except, perhaps, as an impalpable abstraction on some distant metaphysical plane.'[33]

If, by the early 1950s, 'Dostoevsky' seemed to be in danger of dissolving into whatever the interpreters wanted to make of him, there were a number of constants, or at least convergences, in the theological literature. Above all he was widely seen, at least by those who regarded him as in some sense a religious writer, as one of the few who had experienced the sting of contemporary nihilism in his own person and had nonetheless succeeded in passing through the 'crucible of doubt' to a renewed faith 'beyond the wasteland'. His work was therefore a vital resource for all who saw that it was not enough to respond to modern atheism by reiterating the dogmatic formulations or advocating the devotional practices of a pre-modern age. But if it could be agreed that Dostoevsky was uniquely gifted in depicting the agony of atheism and the spiritual predicament of humanity without God, disagreement set in when it came to saying just what kind of faith he envisaged emerging from under the rubble of nihilism: faith in a spiritualised humanity? or radical dependence on the Wholly Other God? or the awakening of radical freedom? or participation in the divine Sophia? or trusting discipleship of the incarnate Christ? (Or some combination of these?) And perhaps the suspicion still lurked that, as for Middleton Murry and D. H. Lawrence (and as the atheist existentialists also maintained), Dostoevsky rather too frequently gave all the best lines to the Devil, and his attempt to create a positive image of the Christian life was repeatedly defeated by his own unflinching honesty in face of the abandonment of the human situation.

It is to this position that William Hamilton returned in his essay 'Banished from the Land of Unity: Dostoyevsky's Religious Vision Through the Eyes of Dmitry, Ivan and Alyosha Karamazov', included in the controversial collection he wrote with Thomas Altizer *Radical Theology and the Death of God*, the defining text of the 'death of God' theology of the 1960s. In his essay Hamilton enlisted the support of Dostoevsky for this influential but perhaps inevitably short-lived theological movement. Hamilton recognised the difficulty or even the folly of any attempt to pin Dostoevsky down to a one-line theological position, since 'He bequeaths at once deep insight and inner division.'[34] Nonetheless his verdict seems to be that, with some qualification, the evidence of *The Brothers Karamazov* contradicts Dostoevsky's own claim that in it he had provided a definitive answer to the denial of God. If one half of Dostoevsky is indeed a believer, the other half is a no less passionate unbeliever. Hamilton takes both his conclusion and the title of his essay from Stefan Zweig: 'At one and the same time he is the truest of believers and the most arrant atheist <. . .> He loves both the servant of God and the man who denies God, both Alyosha and Ivan <. . .> In the very presence of God, Dostoyevsky remains banished from the land of unity.'[35] And Hamilton continues in his own words that, although Alyosha is intended to represent the kind of faith that emerges from the crucible of doubt, we cannot receive him as such, 'whether it be Dostoyevsky's unclarity or our blindness' that is to blame. We can, however, 'receive Ivan with a terrible kind of delight. Here is a true gift to us all, perhaps Dostoyevsky's supreme gift. Ivan's picture of himself we immediately recognise as self-portrait; the God that is dead for him is dead for us; and his Karamazov-God of tension and terror is often the only one we are able to find.'[36]

Whatever we make of Hamilton's argument, it does perhaps illustrate the profound difficulty that theology has had in coming to terms with Dostoevsky and in deriving any clear or consistent teaching from his work. The material itself seems resistant to theology's chosen instruments and methods, selected and developed in order to maximise logical and conceptual consistency within the material bequeathed by scripture, tradition and religious experience. And if it is true of many great novelists that their work helps us to see and to articulate those complexities and obscurities of lived action and experience that reduce philosophy and theology to an embarrassed silence, this was all the more true of Dostoevsky. The outcome, then, is that, in the period up to and including the theology of the death of God, Dostoevsky, although frequently alluded to by theologians and religious writers, remained more of a name to conjure with than the representative of a single definable position. To say 'Dostoevsky' was to offer surety for having 'plumbed the depths' of the crisis of modernity, and yet to be resolved to go on believing.

The fading of existentialism from the late 1960s onwards almost inevitably involved a diminishing of interest in Dostoevsky amongst theologians. At the same time, however, a number of works suggested the possibility of new approaches that would allow richer, more nuanced and less doctrinaire religious readings to emerge. Many of these were not connected with each other, and cannot easily be forced into any common mould. Taken together, however, they do suggest that there are many possibilities for theological interpretations of Dostoevsky that the crises and controversies of the mid-twentieth century did not exhaust.

René Girard's theory of the role of violence in the origin of religion and culture, and his privileging of the gospel narrative as a means of demythologising the ideological underpinning of violence, have become highly influential in the study of religion in the last decade. Surprisingly, his early (1963) study of Dostoevsky, *Dostoïevski: du double à l'unité*, has only recently been published in English.[37] To those who have read the Dostoevsky study it is clear that many of the key elements in the later theory of violence, used by Girard to explain a wide variety of ethnological and cultural data, are in fact derived from what he learned in reading Dostoevsky. This is by no means surprising if we consider the significance that Girard ascribes to the gospels, since he claims to do no more than to articulate in a systematic manner what is already present there in a narrative form. However, despite the fashionableness of Girard's theory of violence, Girardian readings of Dostoevsky are generally unfamiliar in the world of theology and religious studies and it is likely that there is useful work to be done in this area.

A very different approach is to be found in the work of Stewart Sutherland. A philosopher of religion with a firm grounding in the Anglo-Saxon tradition of philosophy, Sutherland has put Dostoevsky to philosophical use on a number of occasions, most extensively in his study *Atheism and the Rejection of God: Contemporary Philosophy and 'The Brothers Karamazov'* (1977). Here Sutherland argues that Ivan's famed 'acceptance' of God is not to be taken at its face value. The God Ivan accepts is the God of 'the Russian boys' talking in a pub, that is, a 'God' whose existence can be discussed over a glass of beer in a pub. His 'acceptance' in fact satirises the view that this is an appropriate way of treating religious belief – and the implication is that philosophers in armchairs are no better off in this respect than Russian boys in pubs. Such belief is 'cheap'. Appealing to Wittgenstein's recommendation that language games can only be properly understood if they are contextualised in their corresponding form of life, Sutherland goes on to argue that the life of Father Zosima does just that: it shows how notional belief works when embedded in a lived life. However, this is not finally satisfactory and, picking up on a point made by Rush Rhees, Sutherland suggests that if we are to make sense of the language of belief we have to see it working in more than one context. But this point too is anticipated in the novel, in Zosima's requirement that Alyosha should leave the monastery and live in the world. If Zosima's faith is to be credible, it must be able to make this transition – but we do not see it achieve this within the compass of the novel. Sutherland's conclusion is therefore necessarily inconclusive: 'All [Dostoevsky] offers is hope, freedom, and a warning.'[38]

In his contribution to the 1983 collection *New Essays on Dostoyevsky*, Sutherland returns to *The Brothers Karamazov*, this time with regard to the question of freedom. He begins by looking at *Notes from the Underground*, where he finds Dostoevsky to be successful in arguing against a deterministic view of human nature. However, both *The Notes* and *Crime and Punishment* also illustrate the problem that freedom is won at the price of social isolation, in varying degrees both the Underground Man and Raskolnikov become incomprehensible to those around them and even to themselves. That '*isolation* and spiritual suicide' are the price of radical freedom is stated by Father Zosima, and Sutherland sees this recognition as leading to Dostoevsky's attempt in *The Brothers Karamazov* to exemplify the contextualisation of freedom within social solidarity (as in the ideal of *sobornost'*).

The outcome is that, over against those who see Dostoevsky as unqualifiedly committed to the promotion of a doctrine of abyssal freedom, Sutherland sees Dostoevsky as both arguing for freedom but also demonstrating its problems and limitations.[39]

In his *God, Jesus and Belief,* Sutherland's main references to Dostoevsky are in connection with *The Idiot* and the problem (which he here relates to the problem of the historical narratives of the gospel as testimony to the divine Sonship of their subject) concerning the representation of 'goodness incarnate'. As Sutherland understands it, the failure of Dostoevsky's attempt to portray a perfectly good man is not so much to do with a failure of Dostoevsky's literary art as with the necessary incognito or ambiguity of the Incarnate One such that there can be 'no distinctive form for the manifestation of man's telos or perfection'.[40] He is however critical of Dostoevsky for believing that the attempt could be made, contrasting this with Kierkegaard's clear emphasis on the necessity of the divine incognito.

The significance of Bakhtin for a religious or theological interpretation of Dostoevsky has only gradually worked its way into the literature. This is not only due to the fact that Bakhtin was only comparatively recently translated into English, but also to do with the widespread impression that a polyphonic reading is bound to be a- or anti-religious – an impression that betrays the prior assumption that religion is inherently monological and cannot admit a plurality of voices. This assumption is plausible to the extent that many believers do insist on an ideal of doctrinal truth that is strictly univocal and that admits of no deviation or equivocation. On the other hand, the religious life itself is often experienced and often portrayed as requiring an ever deepening awareness of life's complexities and ambiguities, and an acceptance of the insuperable tension between the finality of eschatological truth and the inconclusiveness of all human actions, sentiments and judgments. As Kierkegaard said, even if the universe is a system for God it is not and cannot be for us, constrained as we are by the limitations of finitude and, many would add, of sin.

Sutherland's work already provides insight into ways in which a religious reading can not only admit but even require ambiguity or polyphony, and a not dissimilar approach is provided in A. Boyce Gibson's *The Religion of Dostoevsky.* This was one of the first religious readings of Dostoevsky in English to take on board the burden of Bakhtin's work (although Gibson does not recognise a religious motivation at work in Bakhtin himself). If it is the 'special accomplishment' of the polyphonic novelist 'to insinuate himself into the unique predicament of a character', it is also 'the business of Christians to put themselves in all manner of people's places'.[41] The Christian novelist is in any case not immediately concerned with God, but with characters attempting to live the Christian life, and must therefore submit to the situation that 'every Christian carries the weight of imperfectly Christianized impulses which are liable under stress to take an anti-Christian direction'; moreover, even the Christian impulse itself is chronically prone to be diminished or misdirected under pressure from a character's other motivations and commitments.[42] 'Even Bunyan', Gibson writes 'who dealt allegorically with types and generalities, used them to discredit typical and generalised morality in favour of the pilgrim.'[43] How much more the novelist who sets his or her scene in the midst of a realistically conceived world.

On this basis Gibson's study in fact emerges as one of the best fruits to date of an approach that manages to be both literary and theological (and at the same time to be accessible to the non-specialist – an increasingly rare quality). His discussion of the situation of the Christian novelist points forwards to the kind of easing of disciplinary boundaries over the last twenty-five years that have made such studies more widely acceptable in the academic study of religion and in Christian theology. Such cross-fertilisation is not entirely new,[44] but it has now gained added momentum and substance. It is no coincidence that the papers collected here are selected from those presented at a conference held under the aegis of the Glasgow Centre for the Study of Literature and Theology. Also, the existence of the Centre itself (not to mention the considerable number of publications it has generated, including the journal *Literature and Theology*) testifies to the vitality of both research and debate occurring at this particular interface.

We have, then, a number of new contexts and possibilities for reading Dostoevsky religiously that have survived the decline of existentialism and the image of Dostoevsky-the-prophet associated with it. These do not necessarily cohere, but they converge at a number of points. Above all they converge in the recognition that neither religion nor philosophy nor literature are well served by the privileging of monologue at the expense of complexity. Reason is not identical with a reductive rationality, and one does not make of

Dostoevsky an irrationalist by refusing to subject his authorship to the demands of a narrowly conceived logic. Equally, religion is not identical with conscious adherence to a propositionally-defined message and still less with occult knowledge of hidden laws of history or psychology, and one does not make of Dostoevsky an atheist by declining to elevate him to the rank of teacher of the faith or prophet. Reading Dostoevsky religiously is more interesting and more rewarding than it ever was. This situation is not only fruitful for the understanding of Dostoevsky, however: it is also fruitful for growing, through the study of Dostoevsky, towards a fuller and deeper understanding of religion itself.

OVERVIEW OF THE PRESENT VOLUME

Dostoevsky is a broad church, and in selecting the papers for this volume we aimed to reflect this extraordinary amplitude by bringing together a wide range of perspectives on his Christian themes. We also thought it essential to give the reader a sample of present-day Russian responses, now freed from censorship, to the religious dimension in Dostoevsky's works. This collection, accordingly, includes Dostoevsky scholars, a comparativist, Russianists and theologians from all the major Christian confessions, and two scholars presently active in Russia. Several contributors focus on particular features of Russian Orthodoxy and their reflections in Dostoevsky's works. Ivan A. Esaulov highlights the opposition between the two theological categories of Law and Grace in Dostoevsky's poetics. His selection of various key passages from the major novels provides persuasive illustrations of his thesis that in Dostoevsky's fictional worlds Grace predominates. Sophie Ollivier discusses the icon of the Mother of God in *The Landlady*, and briefly traces this image through Dostoevsky's subsequent fiction, uncovering its importance for his Orthodox religious sensibility. Irina Kirillova offers a theological perspective on Dostoevsky's reading of the Gospel of St John, gleaned from the marks he made in his copy of the New Testament. Grouping his marked passages under several major theological themes, she relates them to his biography, fiction and Christocentric vision. Margaret Ziolkowski explores the kenotic ideal in the Russian monastic tradition and its various reflections in *The Devils* and *The Brothers Karamazov*. She pinpoints the salient features in the lives of three historical Russian saints, and examines the extent to which

Dostoevsky incorporated their traits into his fictional monastic and kenotic figures of Tikhon, Father Zosima and Zosima's brother Markel.

Avril Pyman emphasises Dostoevsky's debt to Eastern and Western Christianity and thus suggests a broader way to read him religiously. Whilst she finds Dostoevsky to be firmly within the Christian tradition, she argues that he never succeeded in completely vanquishing his doubts, and gives an interesting interpretation of polyphony as 'a tragic form of *sobornost'*' which remains 'unresolved'.

In a close analysis of the complex dialogic relationship between Smerdyakov and Ivan Karamazov, Vladimir Kantor offers fresh insights into the fine moral boundary between an intention and its execution. He finds that, contrary to long received opinion, Smerdyakov is not just the helpless tool of Ivan, but an active manipulator who bears primary responsibility for the parricide. This means we have to rethink the meaning of temptation in Dostoevsky's last novel. Caryl Emerson responds to these issues in her 'Translator's afterword', paying particular attention to Kantor's treatment of evil doubles, the strengths and dangers of unfinalisability and indefiniteness, and the points where Kantor's interpretation of temptation differs from Bakhtin.

Two papers are concerned with Dostoevsky's Christian poetics. Antony Johae elucidates the relationship between symbology and realistic fiction in *Crime and Punishment*. Incorporating iconographical symbolism in this novel, Dostoevsky, he argues, was able to transcend the secular, mimetic mode of Western realism, which is structured on a horizontal temporal continuum. Diane Oenning Thompson's contribution was prompted by Bakhtin's observations on the pervasiveness of irony in Western civilisation. Indeed, we live under the tyranny of irony to the extent that it has become a universal and virtually obligatory term of praise. Since Bakhtin's thought was significantly inspired by Dostoevsky's art, it seemed worthwhile to consider Dostoevsky's use of irony and his attempts to transcend it through his poetic use of the biblical word.

Theological categories are prominent in several of the contributions. Henry M. W. Russell sees a number of the key characters of *Crime and Punishment* as exemplifying the application of the spirit of apophatic (i.e. negative) theology to the human condition. This is revealed in the characters' search for humiliation. This can either lead to despair or, in the cases of Sonya and Raskolnikov, to Christ.

For Eric J. Ziolkowski the key theological category is incarnation, and he relates this to the motif of reading aloud, as found in several of the major novels. Such reading aloud is shown to reinforce – and is indeed demanded by – the incarnational thrust of Dostoevsky's theology. David S. Cunningham's concern is with the multitudinous reflections of trinitarian theology in *The Brothers Karamazov*, where triadic patterns abound. This is seen to heighten the significance of Bakhtin's concept of polyphony, and to point towards a metaphysical vision in which subsistent relationality takes precedence over individual consciousness.

George Pattison's chapter looks at the long tradition of reading Dostoevsky and Kierkegaard together. Recognising the limits of the existentialist way of seeing them as representatives of the anguish of modernity, it is argued that the current situation allows for fruitful new readings that are able to explore further the real convergences between these two highly original religious writers. Bakhtin and René Girard are linked to suggest the outlines of a possible interpretative framework for such a new collection.

The problem of reading Dostoevsky religiously begs the general question of reading a poetic work theologically. It has long been important for theology to get across its meanings through poetry. Some of the great theologians did precisely that. St Gregory of Nazianzus, for example, refused to isolate theology from poetry and rhetoric in his sermons and orations. In this he was following the Christian tradition from its very origin. Christ often spoke in parables. The Gospels are not a set of dogmas and doctrines – this was the systematising work of the Church – but comprise four stories or versions, of the life of Jesus, each with different emphases and theological implications. The religious meanings incorporated into an artistic text are not dogmatic, not doctrinal and can be easily rejected as heretical by the official church. One is reminded of the reservations some Orthodox readers have about Father Zosima.[45] Theology may be read out of Dostoevsky, but it is a creation: in writing his fiction he was creating a new theology. The Gospels, which were generically supremely important for Dostoevsky, served as literary models for his own version of the novel.

The variety of responses to Dostoevsky included here testifies to the continuing vitality of his art. Should the questions raised with such urgent passion by Judaism and Christianity ever come to seem irrelevant, solved or arouse only indifference, then religious readings of Dostoevsky will recede into the history of Russian literature and cease to engage the future. However, over the last two millennia these questions have exhibited stubborn staying power. On the threshold of the third millennium, they continue to circulate in 'great time', with no end in sight.

NOTES

1 Erich Auerbach, *Mimesis: The Representation of Reality in Western Literature*, trans. Willard R. Trask (Princeton, NJ, 1974), 521–24.
2 Archpriest Georges Florovsky, *Ways of Russian Theology*, Part 1, *Collected Works of Georges Florovsky* vol. 5, ed. Richard S. Haugh, trans. Robert L. Nicholas (Belmont, MA, 1979), 114–16.
3 A. S. Pushkin, 'O russkoi istorii XVIII veka', vol. 7, *Sobranie sochinenii* (Moscow, 1962), 194.
4 For a detailed history of the Church under the Soviet regime see Dimitry V. Pospielovsky, *A History of Soviet Atheism in Theory and Practice, and the Believer*, vols. 1–3 (London, 1987, 1988) and his *The Russian Church under the Soviet Regime 1917–1982*, 2 vols. (Crestwood, NY, 1984).
5 See Orlando Figes and Boris Kolonitskii, *Interpreting the Russian Revolution: The Language and Symbols of 1917* (New Haven, CT, 1999), especially 100, 102 and 150–52.
6 See Ludolf Müller, 'Der Einfluss des liberalen Protestantismus auf die russische Laientheologie des 19. Jahrhunderts', *Kirche im Osten*, 3 (1960) (21–32).
7 See N. Valentinov, *Vstrechi s Leninym* (New York, 1953), 85.
8 Quoted in Vladimir Seduro, *Dostoevski's Image in Russia Today* (Belmont, MA, 1975), 9.
9 This was *de rigeur* during the 1930s–1950s but even in 1971, *Neizdannyi Dostoevskii (The Unpublished Dostoevsky)* had as its sole epigraph a quote from Lenin and three references to him in the text, a practice hardly conceivable nowadays.
10 Vladimir Seduro, *Dostoevski's Image in Russia Today*, 16–18.
11 V. Ermilov, *F. M. Dostoevskii* (Moscow, 1956), 271. Ermilov introduces this distortion by playing on the common root *kup* in the verbs *iskupit'* (to redeem) and *kupit'* (to buy). Quoted in Seduro, 225.
12 S. G. Bocharov, 'Ob odnom razgovore i vokrug nego', *Novoe literaturnoe obozrenie*, 2, 1993 (70–89), 71–72.
13 The first three volumes of this edition, F. M. Dostoevskii, *Plonoe Sochinenii: kanonicheskie teksty* (Petrozavodsk, 1995–), ed. V. N. Zakharov, have already appeared. The edition contains Dostoevsky's first published work, his 1844 translation of Balzac's *Eugénie Grandet*, which was not included in the Academy Edition.
14 D. S. Likhachev, 'Tezisy doklada o staroi orfografii. 1928', *Stat'i rannikh let* (Tver', 1993) (6–14), 12–14. This paper originated in a student

discussion group which called itself, 'as a joke', 'The Cosmic Academy of Sciences', 6.

15 In view of Dostoevsky's anxieties about the radicals of the 1860s–1870s (expressed most vividly in *The Devils*), it is striking that Likhachev dubbed the Bolsheviks' enforcement of the new orthography 'an idea of demonry (*besovshchina*) ever since the [18]60s', 13. On the impact of that crucial decade on Dostoevsky's art and thought, see Joseph Frank's excellent account in his two volumes spanning the period 1860–1871. It is also pertinent that even in the late 1960s Likhachev got into trouble for using the traditional term 'Church Slavonic' instead of the pre-scribed 'Ancient Slavonic'.

16 Nicholas Berdyaev, *Dostoievsky*, trans. Donald Attwater (London, 1934), 227. The Russian reads somewhat differently, though the sense is almost the same. Berdyaev's capital letters have been restored.

17 See, for example, the journals *Dostoevskii i mirovaia literatura*, *F. M. Dostoevsky: Materialy i issledovania*, *Dostoevskii i mirovaia kul'tura*, and the Bibliography.

18 See especially the collection *Vlastitel' dum: F. M. Dostoevskii v russkoi kritike kontsa XIX do nachalo XXI vekov*, ed. N. Ashimbaeva (St Petersburg, 1997).

19 Thus Dostoevsky features in John Hick's *Evil and the God of Love* (the standard text book on theodicy for theological students for thirty years) merely in a footnote attached to a section entitled 'Some Residual Problems', where *The Brothers Karamazov* is said to give 'a powerful underlining' of the question as to whether 'an endless heavenly joy' could 'ever heal the scars of deep human suffering'. See J. Hick, *Evil and the God of Love* (London, 1968), 386.

20 The fullest account of the early reception of Dostoevsky in England is Peter Kaye, *Dostoevsky and English Modernism 1900–1930* (Cambridge, 1999). For a more theologically oriented account of this phenomenon see C. Crowder, 'The appropriation of Dostoevsky in the early twentieth century: Cult, counter-cult, and incarnation' in D. Jasper and C. Crowder (eds.), *European Literature and Theology in the Twentieth Century: Ends of Time* (Basingstoke, 1990), 15–33.

21 J. Middleton Murry, *Dostoevsky: A Critical Study* (London, 1916), 260, 262.

22 *Ibid.*, 258–59.

23 See G. Pattison, this volume.

24 E. Thurneysen, *Dostoevsky* (London, 1964), 14.

25 *Ibid.*, 7–8.

26 N. Berdyaev, *Dostoievsky*, 87.

27 L. A. Zander, *Dostoevsky* (London, 1948), 38.

28 *Ibid.*, 131.

29 *Ibid.*, 137.

30 H. de Lubac, *The Drama of Atheist Humanism* (London, 1949), 171–72.

31 *Ibid.*, 185, 186.

32 *Ibid.*, 245.

33 Quoted in Crowder (1990), 30.
34 W. Hamilton, 'Banished from the land of unity: Dostoyevsky's religious vision through the eyes of Dmitry, Ivan and Alyosha Karamazov', in T. J. J. Altizer and W. Hamilton (eds.), *Radical Theology and the Death of God* (Harmondsworth, 1968), 91.
35 *Ibid.*, 93–94.
36 *Ibid.*, 94.
37 R. Girard, *Resurrection from the Underground* (New York, 1997).
38 S. R. Sutherland, *Atheism and the Rejection of God: Contemporary Philosophy and 'The Brothers Karamazov'* (Oxford, 1977), 139.
39 Sutherland, 'The philosophical dimension: Self and freedom', in Malcolm V. Jones and Garth M. Terry (eds.), *New Essays on Dostoyevsky* (Cambridge, 1983).
40 Sutherland, *God, Jesus and Belief* (Oxford, 1984), 159.
41 W. Boyce Gibson, *The Religion of Dostoevsky* (London, 1973), 68–69.
42 *Ibid.*, 52–53.
43 *Ibid.*, 56.
44 As witness Martin Jarrett-Kerr's chapter on Dostoevsky in his *Studies in Literature and Belief* (London, 1954).
45 For example, see Sergei Hackel, 'The religious dimension: Vision or evasion? Zosima's discourse in *The Brothers Karamazov*', *New Essays on Dostoevsky*, eds. M. V. Jones and G. Terry (Cambridge, 1983), 139–68.

PART I

Dostoevsky and the practice of Orthodoxy

CHAPTER I

Dostoevsky and the kenotic tradition

Margaret Ziolkowski

In an often cited letter that he wrote in August 1879 to the editor Nikolai Lyubimov, Dostoevsky declared about the character of Zosima in *The Brothers Karamazov*:

He could not express himself in other language or in another spirit than that which I gave him <. . .> I took his person and figure from the Old Russian monks and prelates: together with deep humility [they had] limitless naive hopes for the future of Russia, about its moral and even political predestination. Didn't St Sergy and the metropolitans Pyotr and Aleksy really always, in this sense, have Russia in mind? (30,i,102)

Dostoevsky's remarks to a large extent echo, both in general and in particular, comments made a decade earlier by the renowned nineteenth-century historian Vasily Klyuchevsky in a review of a new edition of saints' Lives. Klyuchevsky was convinced that such writings demonstrated the tremendous role played by holy personalities in Russian history:

not only the notorious Moscow Ivans gave the state such vitality <. . .> their material creation was also served by the best moral forces of the people, in the form of Pyotr and Aleksy, Sergy, and many others. Perhaps we would look more seriously at ourselves and at our future, if we knew and appreciated better these moral forces that laboured for us in the past.[1]

Dostoevsky and Klyuchevsky regarded the symbiosis between medieval Orthodoxy and princely circles bent on the unification of the Russian lands in a decidedly romantic light. The saints they both adduce in support of their rose-tinted view of the growth of Muscovite power – Pyotr, Aleksy and Sergy – were united in their commitment to the struggle waged by fourteenth-century Russian princes against Mongol occupiers, but from a purely religious standpoint they represent a curious triumvirate. The nature of this paradox and its implications for an appreciation of Dostoevsky's fictional creations Zosima and Tikhon of *The Possessed* are the major

31

subject of this discussion. Both characters are in many ways products of an enthusiasm for longstanding Russian monastic traditions, but their precise contours have been influenced by late nineteenth-century concerns about Russia's future shared by Dostoevsky and others.

Pyotr and Aleksy were both metropolitans of Russia and saints of the Russian Church. Pyotr died in 1326, Aleksy in 1378. During Pyotr's tenure as head of the church, the metropolitan's see was moved from the ancient city of Vladimir to nearby Moscow. The union between Pyotr and the Muscovite princes was to their mutual advantage. Both gained materially and in influence. Aleksy, too, helped to further the cause of Muscovite power, consistently supporting the princes of Moscow against their political rivals. At the same time he consolidated the ecclesiastical authority of the metropolitanate. While both Pyotr and Aleksy were recognised for their piety, their major achievements reflect a canny political sense and administrative talent. By no stretch of the imagination can either serve as a fitting symbol of Old Russian spirituality, unless that spirituality is construed in a narrowly nationalistic manner.

The best known of the trio of ecclesiastical figures mentioned by Klyuchevsky and Dostoevsky is Sergy of Radonezh, who died in 1392 and has arguably remained Russia's most popular saint. The Holy Trinity Monastery he founded in the wilderness north of Moscow is still a major site of pilgrimage. Dostoevsky himself frequently travelled to the monastery as a child, and when he returned from exile in 1859 he visited it again. The appeal exerted by Sergy for innumerable generations of Russian believers has very different roots from the admiration sometimes elicited by Metropolitans Pyotr and Aleksy. Sergy was a friend of Aleksy, but unlike his contemporary, he spent his entire life, at least according to hagiographical accounts, resisting or refusing ecclesiastical honours. Aleksy hoped Sergy would succeed him as metropolitan, but the saint declined. To accept would have meant violating the deeply held spiritual beliefs of a lifetime.

In contrast to Aleksy and Pyotr, Sergy is an outstanding representative of a dominant trend in Russian monasticism and Russian spirituality in general. In his book *The Russian Religious Mind*, George Fedotov defines this trend as kenotic, that is, imitative of Christ's extraordinary humility. The notion of kenosis is based on a statement made about the incarnation of Christ by Paul in Philippians

2:6–8: 'His state was divine, yet he did not cling to his equality with God but emptied himself (*ekenosen*) to assume the condition of a slave, and became as men are; and being as all men are, he was humbler yet, even to accepting death, death on a cross' (Jerusalem Bible). In speaking of the influence of the act described by Paul on the Russian monastic tradition, it is important to distinguish between the concerns of modern kenosis theology and the kenotic stance embraced by many Russian monks from the eleventh to the nineteenth century. Especially in the nineteenth century a number of European theologians sought to define the extent to which Paul's statement may suggest Christ's renunciation of his divine nature. In contrast to traditional patristic exegesis, which viewed this text as 'a scriptural proof of the divinity of Christ, of his real and complete humanity, and of the unity of His Person', kenotic theories of the incarnation question the simultaneity of Christ's divinity and humanity.[2] Such concerns play no role in the medieval Russian kenotic tradition, perhaps – at the risk of sounding condescending – because of what the theologian Georges Florovsky called 'Russia's ancient, enduring, and centuries long intellectual silence', by which he meant in part its often superficial attention to exegetical questions.[3] The theological issues that might be raised by the second Letter to the Philippians seem to have eluded Russian monks. Instead, they were attracted to the potential model for spiritual behaviour that Paul suggested, namely, unceasing self-humiliation as a means of transcendence, and they took to heart the apostle's directive in Philippians 2:3–5:

There must be no competition among you, no conceit; but everybody is to be self-effacing. Always consider the other person to be better than yourself, so that nobody thinks of his own interests first but everybody thinks of other people's interests instead. In your minds you must be the same as Christ Jesus.

The earliest monastic exemplar of the Russian kenotic tradition was the eleventh-century abbot of the Kievan Cave Monastery, Feodosy of Pechersk, whose popular Life was one of the seminal works of Russian hagiography. In his *Life*, the kenotic ideal finds full expression both ideologically and pragmatically. The author of the Life declares of his subject: 'he possessed true humility and great meekness, for in this he imitated Christ, the true God, who said: "Learn from me, for I am gentle and humble in heart" (Matthew 11:29). Contemplating such humility, he therefore humbled himself and considered himself the last of all.'[4] As represented in the Life,

Feodosy's quest for humility is all-encompassing, affecting his dress (his ragged clothing causes him on occasion to be mistaken for a beggar), his activities (even as a child, he enjoys menial tasks inappropriate to his social background) and his attitudes (he happily endures ridicule and resists honourific recognition).

In the context of previous hagiographical tradition, neither Feodosy's humility nor its often stereotyped expression is original. What distinguishes Feodosy's saintly persona and becomes the hallmark of many later accounts of Russian monks is the centrality of the kenotic ideal. This is very apparent, for example, in the Life of Sergy, in which the saint, dressed once again in tattered clothing, performing chores others disdain, repeatedly tries to subordinate all other considerations to a vision of self-humiliation. He at first refuses to become abbot of the monastery he has founded, inviting the reproach by his bishop that he has acquired all virtues except obedience. As I have mentioned, however, in a typically kenotic act of renunciation Sergy does succeed in avoiding the honour of being installed as metropolitan.

The kenotic model by no means dominated medieval Russian monasticism. From the earliest period of Russian Christianity, and especially from the fifteenth century on, an alternative approach existed that tended to privilege ascetic demonstrations over idiosyncratic expressions of self-effacement, and ritualistic subordination to communal rule over individualised commitment to humility. A devotion to kenoticism persisted, however, and in the eighteenth and nineteenth centuries was exhibited in both the statements and actions of monks like Tikhon of Zadonsk, a contemporary of Catherine the Great and the primary model for Dostoevsky's Tikhon, as well as one of the models for his Zosima, and the three great elders of the monastery of Optina Pustyn', the last of whom, Amvrosy, was visited by Dostoevsky and had a profound impact on the genesis of Zosima's character. Tikhon's famous response to the nobleman who angrily slapped him when the retired bishop dared to remonstrate with him about his mistreatment of his serfs is a classic demonstration of extraordinary humility; Tikhon fell at the nobleman's feet and begged his forgiveness for 'having led him into such a temptation'.[5] Tikhon's writings too are filled with an emphasis on humility, as, for example, in his request in one of the short prayers he produced, 'Give me eyes to see thy humility and to imitate it.'[6] Similarly, the elder Amvrosy's contention that 'we must humble ourselves before everyone considering ourselves the worst of all' is a quintessentially self-deprecating remark.[7]

The kenotic model available to Dostoevsky had, in the course of several centuries, acquired a number of reasonably well defined traits, some of which developed logically from the notion of self-humiliation, like the avoidance of ecclesiastical honours and a reluctance to flaunt one's spiritual authority. Other qualities, although not inherently related to kenosis, had often come to be associated with kenotic saints. Unlike Feodosy of Pechersk, Sergy of Radonezh appears to have enjoyed a number of mystical experiences, and from Sergy on, a mystical bent often characterised Russian kenotics; this is certainly true of his nineteenth-century spiritual descendants. Perhaps related to this mystical tendency is a phenomenal insight into human psychology that may border on clairvoyance. Such understanding also does not stem organically from an emphasis on humility, but seems implicitly to derive from the spiritual awareness attained through adherence to kenotic thinking. A number of these conventional qualities are exploited by Dostoevsky in his portraits of Tikhon and Zosima.

As a character, Tikhon is much less fully developed than Zosima and plays a less central role in the novel in which he figures. Zosima comes equipped with an entire biography and philosophy of existence, both of which exhibit many kenotic features. Tikhon appears in only one episode in *The Possessed* and we gain an impression of his character largely through his reactions to Stavrogin and this moral monster's ugly confession; the systematic delineation found with Zosima is lacking here. Yet Dostoevsky clearly viewed Tikhon as no less an exemplar of a specific spiritual type than he later did Zosima. While working on *The Possessed*, he wrote to the publicist Mikhail Katkov: 'For the first time <. . .> I want to touch upon one category of characters, still little touched by literature. As the ideal of such a character I am taking Tikhon of Zadonsk' (29,i,142).

Dostoevsky's Tikhon has many points of similarity with his historical model. Both are retired bishops who do not enjoy the confidence and support of their abbots and some of their fellow monks because of what is perceived as their spiritual laxity. Both Tikhons are noteworthy for the comparative intellectual broadmindedness that distinguishes them from their conservative fellows. For example, Tikhon of Zadonsk occasionally engaged in discussions of military operations with the noblemen who visited him, while

Dostoevsky's Tikhon is even more unconventional, having in his possession a book on the last war and a map on which he traces its major campaigns.

In his encounter with Stavrogin, Tikhon's essentially kenotic spirit is communicated through occasional explicit remarks, certain oddities in his behaviour, and his awesome insight into Stavrogin's twisted motivations. When Stavrogin demands to know whether Tikhon's faith is capable of moving mountains, the prelate replies, lowering his eyes: 'God will command, and I will move it' (11,10). Such insistence on the total dependence of one's own spiritual achievements on God is typical of kenotics. Later Tikhon unintentionally provokes Stavrogin's irritation by telling him that he will forgive Stavrogin if Stavrogin forgives him: 'For what? What have you done to me? Ah, yes, that's a monastic formula, isn't it?' (11,26). Stavrogin errs in condemning Tikhon's request as empty rhetoric; the spirit of humility evidenced by these words is the wellspring of Tikhon's existence. Ironically, this is borne out by the ways in which Dostoevsky's Tikhon most departs from his historical model, namely, in touches of eccentric behaviour that underscore his kenoticism – odd smiles, bashful looks and an occasional halting manner of speech. Such peculiarities recall the type of the holy fool, which in its radical emphasis on self-humiliation as the path to spiritual salvation overlaps to a great extent with the type of the kenotic monk; historically many kenotic monks did exhibit patterns of behaviour also associated with holy fools. In the case of Dostoevsky's Tikhon, his slight air of mental incompetence throws into relief his startling insight, the insight that so angers and frightens Stavrogin and elicits his bitter but astute parting comment: 'Damned psychologist' (11,30).

With Zosima, we are permitted a glimpse into the character's spiritual development, as well as extended exposure to his theology and ethics. Unlike the traditional account of a saint's life, Zosima's story is not presented in strict chronological order in *The Brothers Karamazov*. However, the elder's autobiographical reminiscences contain a number of realisations of hagiographical topoi, some of which are connected with pivotal moments in his biography. One of these involves his brother Markel, a sometime agnostic who immediately before his premature death is transformed into an iconic embodiment of exultant religiosity, the tenor of which is profoundly kenotic. Markel's transformation prefigures that of Zosima. His acceptance of God is accompanied by constant joyful reiterations of his own inconsequentiality. To the family servants he declares: 'Dear, darling people, why are you waiting on me, and do I deserve to be waited on? If God had mercy and left me among the living, I myself would begin to wait on you, for all should wait on one another' (14,262). He assures his mother that 'everyone of us is guilty of everything before everyone, and I more than everyone', and he explains his begging forgiveness from the birds by saying: 'I feel like being guilty before them <. . .> for I don't know how to love them. Though I am culpable before everyone, yet everyone will forgive even me, and that's paradise' (14,262,263). It is not difficult to see why many Orthodox readers found Dostoevsky's Christianity suspect, and yet Markel's attitudes are profoundly, if idiosyncratically, kenotic. Moreover, the insistence on his own insignificance and his concomitant achievement of spiritual happiness validate the link between humility and righteousness.

In the context of Zosima's existence, Markel serves as a hagiographical model. Many years later, when the future elder is a self-centred young officer, the pitiful reactions of his orderly Afanasy to Zosima's savage blows force him to confront the evil of his present existence. Markel is directly implicated in this spiritual resurrection, for Zosima suddenly remembers his brother's questions to his servants and assertions of communal responsibility; he concludes: 'In truth, perhaps, I am more responsible than everyone for everyone, yes and am worse than all people in the world' (14,270). This epiphany marks the beginning of the kenotic way adopted by Zosima. When he meets Afanasy in the course of his later wanderings, he responds to his former orderly's request for a blessing for his children by saying: 'Is it for me to bless them <. . .> I am a simple and humble monk, I will pray to God about them' (14,287). This refusal to take spiritual credit, which, as I mentioned above, also finds expression in the remarks of Dostoevsky's Tikhon, is a familiar topos. Zosima remains committed to this idea throughout his monastic career. When a visiting monk asks him about his possible healing of a young woman, the elder replies: 'if there has been something, it is by no one's power except God's will. Everything is from God' (14,51).

Like Tikhon and many monks of the kenotic tradition, Zosima is distinguished and revered for his remarkable insight. Just as Tikhon has an acute understanding of Stavrogin's complex motives, so Zosima easily divines the psychological make-up of the various

Karamazovs, from Fyodor's shame and buffoonery to Ivan's tormented quest for faith. In the case of Dmitry, Zosima's famous bow, which he later tells Alyosha was meant to recognise the eldest brother's 'great future suffering' (14,258), reflects a combination of perception, humility and compassion typical of kenotically inclined monks. Alyosha's friend, the seminarist Rakitin, scoffs at Zosima's act, telling Alyosha: 'With holy fools it's always like that: they cross themselves at the tavern and throw stones at the temple. Like your elder: [he drives] away a just man with a stick, and [makes] a bow at the feet of a murderer' (14,73). While Zosima's behaviour generally does not exhibit the particular traces of eccentricity typical of holy fools, Rakitin's comment is significant, for it points once again to the fluid boundary between holy foolishness and kenotic humility, a boundary that Dostoevsky certainly seems to have crossed easily and repeatedly in his fictional creations.

Unlike Tikhon, Zosima is given extended opportunities to discourse upon his beliefs. The importance of humility, although not expressed with specific reference to the New Testament, occupies a central position in his remarks. In Zosima's conception, humility is the guiding force of the monastic way: 'When [a monk] realises that he is not only worse than others, but that he is responsible to all men for all and everything, for all human sins, general and individual, only then the aim of our seclusion is attained' (14,149). Indeed, in Zosima's conception, humility is a powerful transformative force: 'Loving humility is marvellously strong, the strongest of all things and there is nothing else like it' (14,298). The saints' Lives which the elder suggests as being especially suitable for reading aloud to the peasants are those of Mary of Egypt and Alexis, the Man of God, a figure repeatedly evoked in *The Brothers Karamazov*. Both of these Lives are noteworthy for their endorsement of unceasing humility. No Russian saints are named by Zosima, but Sergy of Radonezh is recalled through the elder's reference to a well-known episode from his Life involving feeding a bear.

Where Zosima departs most dramatically from the kenotic tradition narrowly defined is in his overtly nationalistic interests. Kenoticism is inherently apolitical, supposedly concerned with its practitioner's spiritual perfectibility and not with participation in worldly activities. Yet Sergy of Radonezh – and such actions in a sense provide the ideological bridge between Sergy and the Metropolitans Pyotr and Aleksy – gave his blessing to Prince Dmitry

Donskoy of Moscow in his successful confrontation with the
Mongols at the Battle of Kulikovo in 1380 and even sent two monks,
both former boyars and skilled warriors, to aid the prince. Pierre
Kovalevsky observes that the author of Sergy's Life 'brings out the
humility, mercy and monastic poverty of [Sergy], but he is markedly
reserved in speaking about his national actions'.[8] In the case of the
Kulikovo episode, this means that the blessing is described, but not
the mission of the two monks. Yet it was precisely this kind of
partisan involvement in Russian political events that contributed to
Sergy's recognition not only as an exemplar of kenoticism, but as a
kind of patron saint of Russia. Hence his linking, by both Dostoevsky
and Klyuchevsky, with Pyotr and Aleksy, an association founded
upon extra-kenotic factors and one essentially contrary to a focus on
self-humiliation.

Tikhon and Zosima are not rabid nationalists. In the case of
Tikhon, the only hint of secular concerns is provided by the
reference to his interest in recent military history; his book and his
map symbolise his possible preoccupation with Russia's fortunes.
With Zosima, a devotion to Russia is made more explicit. Indeed he
suggests that it is kenotic monks who offer some hope of salvation for
Russia. While acknowledging the prevalence of monastic corruption,
the elder believes that there are many 'humble and meek' monks
who may provide 'once again the salvation of the Russian land'
(14,284). Undoubtedly with Sergy of Radonezh in mind, he declares:
'from among us in the old days came popular leaders, why can't they
now as well? The same humble and meek fasters and monks who
have taken the vow of silence will rise up and set out for the great
cause' (14,285).[9] The precise nature of the cause – presumably the
resurrection of Orthodoxy's political role and the defence of traditional values against radical assault – is not defined, but the latent
political tenor of Zosima's declaration is evident.

The Brothers Karamazov is set in the late 1860s. It was written a little
more than a decade later (1878–80), however, near the end of the
Russo-Turkish War (1877–78), a war in which Pan-Slav sentiments,
with their emphasis on the need for militant preservation of the
international Orthodox community, played a significant role. The
novel was completed in 1880, the quincentennial of the Battle of
Kulikovo. Dostoevsky's conservative political sympathies and
endorsement of the Orthodox establishment are well known. In the
late 1870s especially he repeatedly expressed chauvinistic sentiments

in *The Diary of a Writer* about the need for Russia to act as an aggressive leader within the Orthodox world; 'sooner or later, Constantinople must be ours', he declared (25,65).

In the context of contemporary events and his own attitudes, Dostoevsky's infusion of the character of Zosima with vaguely nationalistic ambitions is not surprising. The kenotic tradition finds moving expression in Dostoevsky's elder, many of whose actions, reminiscences and observations bespeak the 'deep humility' to which Dostoevsky refers in his letter to Lyubimov. At the same time Zosima expresses the 'limitless naive hopes for the future of Russia' that Dostoevsky claimed were associated with medieval Russian monks and prelates, but which should probably more properly be attributed to the author himself. In capturing the essence of Russian spirituality, Dostoevsky could not ultimately rest content with a purely religious message. In Zosima he embodies, but then transcends, the kenotic tradition, with its numerous adherents who fled secular involvement as if it were the devil's own handiwork.

NOTES

1 Vasily Klyuchevsky, 'Velikie minei chetii, sobrannye vserossiiskim Mitropolitom Makariem', *Sbornik statei*, 3 vols. (Petrograd, 1918), III: 10.
2 *New Catholic Encyclopedia*, 17 vols. (New York, 1967–74), s. v. kenosis.
3 Archpriest Georges Florovsky, *Ways of Russian Theology*, Part I, *Collected Works of Georges Florovsky*, vol. 5, ed. Richard S. Haugh, trans. Robert L. Nicholas (Belmont, MA, 1979), 1.
4 Dmitrij Tschiževskij, ed., *Das Paterikon des Kiever Hohlenklösters*, 2nd edn (Munich, 1964) (reprint of *Kievo-Pechers'kii paterik*, ed. D. I. Abramovich (Kiev, 1930), 46. On the role played by kenosis in Feodosy's existence, see George Fedotov, *The Collected Works of George Fedotov: The Russian Religious Mind* (I), vol. 3 (Belmont, MA, 1975), especially 128.
5 'From the Memoirs of Ivan Yefimov', in *A Treasury of Russian Spirituality*, ed. George Fedotov, *The Collected Works of George Fedotov*, vol. 2 (Belmont, MA, 1975), 211.
6 Cited in Nadejda Gorodetzky, *Saint Tikhon of Zadonsk: Inspirer of Dostoevsky* (Crestwood, NY, 1976), 99.
7 Cited in Sergius Bolshakoff, *Russian Mystics* (Kalamazoo, MI, 1977), 191.
8 Pierre Kovalevsky, *Saint Sergius and Russian Spirituality* (Crestwood, NY, 1976), 62.
9 Joseph Frank observes that 'it was certainly of St. Sergey that Dostoevsky was thinking' when Zosima makes these assertions. See Joseph Frank, *Dostoevsky: The Seeds of Revolt, 1821–1849* (Princeton, NJ, 1976), 47.

CHAPTER 2

Dostoevsky's markings in the Gospel according to St John

Irina Kirillova

Unlike his great contemporaries Turgenev and Tolstoy, whose early religious education was perfunctory, Dostoevsky was steeped in church life and Orthodox spirituality from an early age. His mother was a very devout woman who lived her short life according to the precepts of her faith. She was greatly loved by her children and inspired in her son Fyodor a lifelong sense of the living significance of the Bible and of the New Testament in particular. He accompanied his mother on her yearly pilgrimage to the great churches and monasteries in and around Moscow, and never forgot the profound impression the Lenten readings of the Old Testament Book of Job made on him. In a letter to his wife from Ems, dated 22 June 1875, when he was working on *The Raw Youth*, Dostoevsky wrote: 'I am reading the Book of Job, and it provokes in me a sense of painful excitement <. . .> it was one of the first books to make a profound impression on me' (29,ii,43). It influenced his whole thinking on a major theme in his work, that of innocent suffering, and key passages in *The Raw Youth* and *The Brothers Karamazov* are marked by this text.

However the most important spiritual experience of Dostoevsky's whole life – even during a youthful loss of faith in the sacramental life and mystical teaching of the Church – was his constant awareness of the figure of Christ, Whom he venerated throughout his life as both perfect Man and God. Christ for Dostoevsky was the incarnation of divine love for man and a teacher whose vision defines the writer's belief in absolute moral and spiritual values. In his notebooks for 1880–81, Dostoevsky wrote: 'Moral ideas exist. They grow out of religious feeling, but can never be justified by logic alone.'[1] They rested in the authority of Christ alone. When Dostoevsky was imprisoned pending his trial for political sedition, he wrote to his brother asking for certain books, and in particular for a book of the Gospels. This particular volume was later lost, but on the long march to the Siberian penal colony the prisoners were each presented with a Gospel by the wives of earlier conspirators, the Decembrists, living in exile in Siberia. From then on till the very end of his life Dostoevsky was never parted from his copy of the Gospel. Rather than reading it consistently he regularly consulted it, reading selectively and covering it in markings of every kind in ink, pencil and indentation with a finger nail, as he singled out passages of special significance for him. The forcefulness of many of the markings testify to the absorption and commitment of his reading. The importance of the figure of Christ and the Johannine 'theology of love' ('theology' is here used in the Eastern Orthodox sense of mystical theology) meant that the greatest number of markings comes in the Gospel of St John and its companion text the First Epistle of John. Dostoevsky shows a marked preference for these texts over the Sermon on the Mount. In the Gospel of St John the number of markings is fifty-eight, in St Matthew, twelve, in St Luke, seven, and in St Mark, two. The Book of Revelation has sixteen markings.[2]

There is a direct correlation between the Christological thrust of St John's Gospel, Dostoevsky's lifelong veneration of Christ and the number of markings. This is all the more significant in that the image of Christ for Dostoevsky was not a stable, clearly defined, unchanging image.

In the 1840s, under the influence of a Romantic, Utopian 'New Christian' and historico-anthropological 'humanisation' of the figure of Christ, Dostoevsky refers to him as the 'ideal man', 'the ideal of humanity'. After his 'change of convictions' (*peremena ubezhdenii*), his conversion in Siberia (soberly recorded in *Notes from a House of the Dead*, in a fictionalised form, however thinly veiled), Dostoevsky not only reverts to the Gospel image of Christ, the Son of God, he knew in his childhood and early youth, but places the figure of Christ at the centre of his intellectual, spiritual and aesthetic reflection. Dostoevsky refers to Christ as the 'touchstone' (*proverka*) of any proposition, particularly in the moral-ethical field, but he still has to struggle to confess his unconditional faith in Him as the Son of God, the God-Man. This struggle is reflected in the remarkable declaration at the end of his letter to Natalia Fonvizina written from Omsk in February 1854: 'if someone were to prove to me that Christ is outside of the truth, and it were truly so, that the truth was outside of Christ, I would prefer to remain with Christ, rather than with the truth' (28,i,176). The truth here signifies the 'arguments to the contrary' (*dovody protivnye*) of mid-nineteenth-century natural science (28,i,176). Dostoevsky's statement is intellectually provocative, but testifies to what he knew in terms of the 'knowledge of the heart' (I refer here to the Orthodox Patristic teaching on the heart as the seat of Communion with God) and finds its resolution in Christ's words: 'I am the Way, and the Truth, and the Life' (14:6), clearly marked by Dostoevsky. To the end of his life Dostoevsky found it difficult to accept the totality of the Church's teaching. In an entry right at the end of his notebooks for 1880–81, he notes: 'All Christ's ideas can be contested by the human mind and appear inapplicable in practice <. . .> Christ was mistaken – that has been proved! <. . .> but I would rather remain with error, together with Christ' and concludes 'it is not as a child that I believe in Christ and confess Him. My hosanna has passed through a great trial of doubt.'[3] In 1854 he had spoken of himself as a 'child of the century, as a child of unbelief and doubt', but he never betrayed what can only be called an ecstatic faith in Christ, which remained an absolute certainty in his heart, whatever the 'arguments to the contrary' (28,i,176).

Dostoevsky's markings begin after 1850, the year he was given the book of the Gospels by one of the Decembrist wives, in exile in Tobolsk. It was then that he developed his lifelong habit of not only 'dipping' into the text continuously, but also of opening it at random and seeing providential guidance in the passages that presented themselves in this way. The markings multiply after the 'change of convictions', and reflect not only Dostoevsky's preference for certain aspects of the Gospel teaching, but a dynamic evolution in the affirmation of his faith, and a developing personal vision of the figure of Christ and the teaching which is refracted in all his novels. This vision and the teaching it inspires provide the redemptive vision – a vision rarely if ever made explicit, other than in didactic form in *The Brothers Karamazov*, but which illumines with soteriological poten- tial the tragic moral and metaphysical landscape of the novels. The redemptive vision, which for Dostoevsky is totally centred in the person of Christ, as man's only hope of life, is like a light, the source of which remains invisible, but which illuminates and brings to life and into focus a dark, stained-glass window.

Dostoevsky is a very private man where his intimate spiritual life is concerned. He confesses his doubts and later his faith. He does not discuss them, even in his Notebooks. The letter to Natalya Fonvizina is a rare exception. The markings in his Gospel are all the more valuable in that they enable us to check and validate – through their refraction in his writing – the nature and thrust of his spiritual reflection which organises his fictional universe, his concept of man and of man's relationship with God. Dostoevsky's markings lend themselves to commentary under a number of headings: the image of Christ, His Sonship and Oneness with the Father; the nature and conditions of faith; the darkness and perdition that come with loss of faith; the question of innocent suffering, and of redemptive suffering; the resurrection of each one of us; the 'theology of love' (taken in conjunction with markings in the First Epistle of John).

Taken all together Dostoevsky's markings 'highlight' his whole conception of man's vision of God and relationship with Him. They are also a very personal, revealing testimony which deepens our understanding of his otherwise rare, laconic but always deeply felt confessions of faith.

The greatest number of markings – nine – relate to the question of the divinity of Christ which in St John's Gospel is affirmed through the repeated assertion of the Son's Oneness with the Father. After his 'change of convictions' Dostoevsky clearly felt the need to affirm the divinity of Christ. In his heart he was already convinced of it, as his Confession of Faith minutes before the execution he was expecting demonstrates. In almost ecstatic excitement he said to the Jacobin, atheist Speshnev, standing next to him in line: 'Nous serons avec le Christ' (quoted by Joseph Frank in his *Years of Ordeal*), a phrase hauntingly reminiscent of Christ's words on the Cross to the righteous robber: 'Verily I say unto thee, today thou shalt be with Me in paradise' (Luke 23:43). Dostoevsky's confessions of faith in Christ the Son of God are rare, but when they occur, they are forceful. Christ is 'an infinite miracle', 'the source of all', and in the *Diary of a Writer* (1877) he proclaims that 'God is one and there is no other God like Him' and that 'Christ is the true God, was born of God the Father, and made incarnate of the Virgin Mary' (25,167). But as his markings testify, Dostoevsky still appears to feel the need to 'exorcise' the mirage of the Utopian Christ – the ideal human being. The image of the humanised Christ is always seen in isolation from God the Father. The Jesus figure has no need of a divine Father, there is and cannot be any Holy Trinity. In repeatedly marking the passages on Sonship and Oneness, Dostoevsky is reaffirming emphatically both the divinity of Christ and the mystery of His Oneness with the

Father: (8:19) 'I do nothing of Myself, but as the Father taught Me.' (10:30) is heavily underlined by Dostoevsky. 'I and the Father are One.' (10:34) 'I said I am the Son of God.' (10:38) is marked NB – 'The Father is in Me, and I in the Father.' Several further reaffirmations are emphatically marked and NB-ed, and the series concludes with the valedictory (16:28) marked NB: 'I came out from the Father, and am come into the world: again I leave the world, and go unto the Father.'

The next group of markings highlights particular emphases in Dostoevsky's veneration of Christ, and his faith generally. In (2:22), (3:12,13) and (2:18) Dostoevsky marks passages that address the question of wavering or imperfect faith. There is a dialectical tension between these passages and the letter to Natalya Fonvizina, in which every affirmation of unbelief is countered by a despairing *de profundis*. In these passages, Dostoevsky seeks to re-affirm his faith in the Christ he venerated whatever the 'evidence' to the contrary. Characteristically, Dostoevsky seeks this re-affirmation through images that belong to the realm of revelation, and are known through faith: (2:22) 'When therefore He was raised from the dead, His disciples remembered that he spake this; and they believed the Scripture, and the word which Jesus had said.' (3:12) is a rebuke to Dostoevsky's own wavering: 'If I told you earthly things, and ye believe not, how shall ye believe if I tell you heavenly things.' As is (3:18) 'he that believeth on Him is not judged: he that believeth not hath been judged already, because he hath not believed on the name of the only begotten Son of God.' (3:13) opens up the theme of resurrection – of Christ and of man. In his faith Dostoevsky was drawn strongly to the question of man's moral regeneration and spiritual resurrection. The question of bodily resurrection troubled him deeply, and he seeks Gospel authority in this matter: (3:13) 'And no man hath ascended into heaven, but He that descended out of heaven, even the Son of Man which is in heaven.'

Dostoevsky as a religious type is a Thomas the Doubter, who needed to confront Christ in his own way, and to articulate his need for physical conviction, even while recognising Him and worshipping Him with the words 'My Lord and My God.' Dostoevsky marks the last phrase of (20:29) with an NB, but significantly omits verse 28: 'Jesus said unto him, because thou hast seen Me, thou hast believed: blessed are they that have not seen, and yet have believed.'

Dostoevsky marks a series of passages that speak of faith rejected.

They suggest a spiritual landscape which prepares the surreal landscape of evil in *The Devils*, and Dostoevsky's evocation of the spiritual desert that is a Russia losing its faith: 'and this is the judgment, that the light is come into the world, and men loved the darkness rather than the light; for their works were evil. For everyone that doeth ill hateth the light, and cometh not to the light, lest his works should be reproved' (3:19,20), and in (5:44) and (8:43) he marks passages which articulate his question: 'How can ye believe <. . .> and the glory that cometh from the only God ye seek not?' and 'Why do ye not understand My speech? Even because ye cannot hear My word.' This last sentence is underlined and marked by an exclamation mark. In (8:45) and (8:47) the words are of judgment: 'But because I say the truth ye believe Me not', and 'he that is of God heareth the words of God: for this cause ye hear them not, because ye are not of God.'

The inevitable consequence of turning away from Christ is made clear in (8:24): 'ye shall die in your sins: for except ye believe that I am He, ye shall die in your sins.' Dostoevsky underlines '*that I am He*', stressing both the uniqueness of Christ and that there is no salvation without Him. But the promise and the light I (3:21), as in (6:5), is the spiritual landscape of Zosima and Alyosha: 'But he that doeth the truth cometh to the light, that his works may be made manifest, that they have been wrought in God' (3:21), and 'everyone that hath heard from the Father, and hath learned, cometh unto Me' (6:45). In (7:18) Dostoevsky marks the 'profile' of the righteous believer – 'he that seeketh the glory of Him that sent Him, the same is true and no unrighteousness is in Him.'

A whole group of markings testify to Dostoevsky's preoccupation with resurrection. In marking these passages, Dostoevsky goes beyond the moral exhortation to good and proclaims the faith that is revealed. 'He that eateth My flesh and drinketh My blood hath eternal life, and I will raise him up at the last day' (6:54). During his Utopian/Petrashevsky Circle period, in the mid-1840s, Dostoevsky had stopped taking Holy Communion. In Siberia he again began to do so. These passages are primarily concerned with the question which so troubled Dostoevsky, that of bodily resurrection: 'When ye have lifted up the Son of Man, then shall ye know that I am He' (8:28) – and again: 'And I, if I be lifted up from the earth will draw all men unto Myself' (12:32). Verses (8:51) and (8:52) set out the conditions for life eternal, and are marked with multiple NBs.

'Verily, verily I say unto ye, if a man keep My word, he shall never see death, and if a man keep My word, he shall never taste of death', and 'If a man keep My word, he shall never taste of death.' Dostoevsky returns to the same theme in (11:26) and underlines the last three words, as though checking and reaffirming his own faith: 'whosoever liveth and believeth on Me shall never die. *Believest thou this?*' Dostoevsky's markings emphasise again and again that belief and life – a 'living life' (*zhivaia zhizn'*) and life eternal were inseparably linked. Life was not possible without faith – a conclusion Dostoevsky came to after much travail, though a transcendental belief in life eternal did not come easily to him. These markings testify to the conclusions he *does* eventually come to.

This group of markings culminates in the near complete narrative of the Raising of Lazarus – central to both *Crime and Punishment* and to Dostoevsky's personal faith. It is interesting to note that he omits to mark the last two verses, and stops at the words: 'that they may believe that Thou didst send Me' – i.e. at the all important affirmation of Christ's divinity and Oneness with the Father. Dostoevsky's marking of this narrative is totally in the spirit of the Church's understanding of this text, perhaps the most startling of Christ's miracles – it is a reminder of the promise that each one of us is called to resurrection, and that Christ, the Son of God, is the One and only One who will raise us. In *Crime and Punishment* this promise is refracted in psychological terms which encode its spiritual significance. Raskolnikov is spiritually dead, and only a miracle overruling natural, psychological law can save him. It is this knowledge which prompts him to ask Sonya to read him the Raising of Lazarus.

The final, smaller groups of markings relate to aspects of Christ's teaching. Two single verse markings highlight two major themes in Dostoevsky's work: that of freedom – in the Eastern Orthodox understanding of freedom as God's most challenging and tragic gift to man – and that of innocent suffering. (8:32), marked by an NB, states: 'And ye shall know the truth, and the truth shall make you free.'

That truth is Christ. (9:3) provides a clear but difficult answer to the problem of innocent suffering. Concerning the man born blind, Christ says 'Neither did this man sin, nor his parents: but that the works of God should be made manifest in him.' From the evidence of his work, Dostoevsky sought a somewhat different answer to this question.

Markings on several groups of verses stress two further major themes – Christ's judgment on the world, and the teaching on love. Dostoevsky interprets Christ's judgment in his own characteristic way – 'those who see not' are those who do not accept Him. Dostoevsky marks (9:39) with an NB: 'And Jesus said, For judgment I came into this world, that they which see not may see; and that they which see may become blind.' And the Pharisees, the blind and the arrogant ask (9:40) 'Are we also blind?' In (9:41) 'Jesus said unto them, if ye were blind, ye would have no sin: but now ye say, we see: your sin remaineth.' Is this a judgment on the Grand Inquisitor?

Dostoevsky marks Christ's use of the figure of the Good Shepherd, but his markings suggest not so much a humble, caring figure, as a Royal figure, a figure of Royal Priesthood, dedicated to those He has come to save, but also a figure of authority and judgment. (10:1) and (10:2) – 'Verily, I say unto you, he that entereth not by the door into the fold of the sheep. . .the same is a thief and a robber.' But 'He that entereth in by the door is the shepherd of the sheep.' In (10:8) the first phrase is underlined by Dostoevsky: '*All that came before Me* are thieves and robbers. . .' In (10:11) 'I am the Good Shepherd: the good shepherd layeth down His life for the sheep.' (10:17) follows in the same conceptual register – not only is it the duty and the vocation of the king and the priest to lay down his life for those for whom he has care, but for Dostoevsky this is the duty and the privilege of *every* believer. We have to note the significance he ascribes to the story of the soldier who chooses to be flayed alive rather than apostacise his Christianity for Islam (*Diary of a Writer*). 'Therefore doth the Father love Me, because I lay down My life, that I may take it again.' Dostoevsky is not afraid to stress that martyrdom is the gateway to life eternal. Dostoevsky also marks emphatically (NB) (10:16) 'And other sheep I have, which are not of this fold: them also must I bring, and they shall hear My voice; and they shall become one flock, one shepherd.' *The Diary of a Writer* provides ample evidence of Dostoevsky's conviction that Orthodoxy alone was faithful to the Divine Plan for man, and though he does not speak of conversion in specific terms, he sees Gospel confirmation, in words such as these, of his vision of Orthodoxy as the only true fold for the flock of Christ.

A number of verses relating to Christ's rejection before His Passion, by those who do not recognise Him again evoke the metaphysical, surreal landscape of evil in *The Devils* – the landscape in which Dostoevsky sets those who reject Christ: (11:8) 'if a man walk in the day, he stumbleth not, because he seeth the light of this world' (compare Christ's words 'I am the Light of the world'), and (10:10) 'But if a man walk in the night, he stumbleth, because the light is not in him.' The image of Christ that Dostoevsky's markings of St John's Gospel bring out is that of a magisterial, even stern Christ, the Pantocrator, whose vision is projected into eternity as an absolute, and one which is not adapted to historic, human time. It is as though Dostoevsky *needs* the authoritative word of God to support him in his striving and in his observation of a fractured, increasingly unbelieving world. However, it is important to note two other markings, which underline the figure of a kenotic Christ, of humility and service, rather than judgment. In (8:50) Dostoevsky underlines the words 'But I seek not Mine own glory', and marks (13:14) 'If I then, the Lord and Master, have washed your feet, ye also ought to wash one another's feet.'

This leads on very naturally to the last group of markings, those relating to the teaching on love which is so central to Dostoevsky's redemptive vision, which illuminates *Crime and Punishment* through the figure of Sonya and the salvation held out to Raskolnikov, and which although tragic and broken, nonetheless makes *The Idiot* so haunting, and which is made explicit in *The Brothers Karamazov.* Taken in sequence, and amplified by verses from the First Epistle of John, these verses create a theology of love which informs the text of Zosima's teaching: (13:34) 'A new commandment I give unto you, that ye love one another; even as I have loved you, that ye also love one another.' (14:23) is heavily marked with NBs and underlinings '*If a man love Me*, he will keep My word: and My Father will love him, and We will come unto him, and make our abode with him.' (14:24): '. . . he that *loveth* Me not keepeth not My words. . .' and again (15:12,13) 'This is My commandment, that ye love one another, even as I have loved you.' In (15:13) 'Greater love hath no man than this, that a man lay down his life for his friends', and the price to be paid in this world is stated in (15:19) 'If ye were of the world, the world would love its own: but because ye are not of the world, but I chose you out of the world, therefore the world hateth you', a warning reinforced in the following verse. Dostoevsky was painfully aware that a Christian vocation, faithfully fulfilled, made its disciples 'fools for Christ's sake' and martyrs, and he marks (16:33) 'These things have I spoken unto you, that in Me ye may have peace. In the world ye have tribulation [in Russian *skorb'* – sorrow, lamentation] but be of good cheer [*muzhaites'* – be strong]. I have overcome the world.' The theology of love proclaimed in the First Epistle of John reaches its fullness in (4:7) and (4:8) 'Beloved, let us love one another: for love is of God, and everyone that loveth is begotten of God, and knoweth God. He that loveth not knoweth not God; for God is love.' Dostoevsky also marks successive verses: (4:12,19,21) and (5:4), that expand and affirm this proclamation. In (19:21) he inserts the word *by* to denote '*should* love', thereby making the verse a commandment: 'And this commandment have we from Him, that he who loveth God love his brother also' (4:21), which Dostoevsky amends to '*should* love his brother also'.

The Gospel of St John has particular significance for Dostoevsky because, more than any of the other New Testament books, it enables him to affirm his faith in the divine Son of God through the affirmation of Christ's Sonship made manifest in the 'theology of love' that is so central to both the Gospel of St John and the First Epistle of John. Dostoevsky's profession of faith had to overcome not so much the claims of nineteenth-century Natural Science as the tragic, insoluble contradiction between belief in an omnipotent and merciful God and the cruel, bleak reality of innocent suffering. The luminous revelation of love in the person of Christ enables Dostoevsky to believe that it is possible to resolve the terrible antinomy of innocent suffering and divine mercy through faith in Christ, the God Man, Who is both innocent victim and Redeemer.

NOTES

1 *Neizdannyi Dostoevskii: Zapisnye knizhki i tetradi 1860–1881*, ed. V. R. Shcherbina, *Literaturnoe nasledstvo*, 83 (Moscow, 1971), 625.
2 The first English translation of the New Testament passages marked by Dostoevsky was published by Geir Kjetsaa in *Dostoewsky and his New Testament* (Oslo, Atlantic Highlands, NJ, 1984). The finger-nail markings since revealed were not available to Kjetsaa at the time he published his work. For all indications of finger-nail and other markings by Dostoevsky I am indebted to Professor Nikolai Zakharov of Petrozavodsk University, Russia, who made available to me an unpublished photocopy edition of Dostoevsky's New Testament.
3 *Neizdannyi Dostoevskii*, 696.

CHAPTER 3

Icons in Dostoevsky's works

Sophie Ollivier[1]

Dostoevsky's world is full of icons. The one which appears most often is the icon of the Mother of God.[2] In the novel *A Raw Youth* there is an icon representing two saints but we are given no information about them. Sometimes, indeed, the icon is left without a name. Icons are generally located in a church, on the iconostasis[3] or on the walls, in a monastery, in a house,[4] over a bed.[5] They can be removed from their consecrated place, change ownership, go from hand to hand. The presence of icons is never fortuitous in Dostoevsky's works and it is therefore important to determine their role in the plot, and the relationships established between them and the characters. Face to face with the icons the latter reveal their inmost selves, and the effect which the icons will have on them will derive mainly from that attitude. This chapter is a preliminary study which may prepare the ground for a wider and more thorough examination of the so far rather neglected topic of the icons in Dostoevsky's fiction.

There has, of course, been considerable interest in the West in recent years in Russian icons, both as works of art and as epitomising some of the characteristic and most attractive aspects of Orthodox spirituality. Despite this interest, it is probably advisable to remind ourselves of some of the chief aspects of the history and meaning of icons in the Russian Church.

The word 'icon' (Russian *ikona*) itself derives from the Greek *eikona*, meaning image or portrait. In Russian the word *obraz* ('image') is frequently used together with the word *ikona*. The tradition of icons originated in Byzantium, their production being officially authorised by the Church in the late fourth century. This ratified a widespread practice. The Quinisext Council of 692 asks the artists not to paint Christ in a symbolic manner but to show his human aspect.[6]

In the seventh century the icon became part of the Christian way of life in Byzantium. Systematic hostility towards icons broke out in the eighth century, however, and the iconoclastic controversies dominated a whole period of the Empire (725–843). Under Constantine V, the Council of Hiereia (754) declared that the making of icons was to be regarded as unacceptable, and, indeed, idolatrous. The promulgation of the decree led to persecution, torture, exile and pillaging. The second Nicene Council (787) re-established the cult of icons and asserted their legitimacy in the strongest of terms: to reject icons is to reject the Incarnation. The image is the object of veneration and not of adoration, which is reserved for God. But since the veneration of an image is addressed to the prototype, veneration becomes transformed into adoration. Iconoclasm became active again from 813 to 842, and the persecution continued. Finally on 11 March 843, the Empress Theodora rehabilitated the second Nicene Council.

After the conversion of Russia in 988, workshops of icons began to develop under the leadership of the Greeks. Very soon Russian iconography acquired its own language. It reached its peak at the end of the fourteenth century and in the fifteenth century when the monastery of St Sergius was founded north of Moscow, and Russia rose from its ruins after the victory over the Tatars at Kulikovo in 1380. The famous icons of Andrei Rublev, whose master was Theophanes the Greek, reflect the inner history of the religious and national consciousness of Russia, its spiritual rebirth. In the seventeenth century, however, the art of the icon declines. Ornaments of various kinds, in silver, precious metal and precious stones were used to cover the icons – a detail that is, for example, alluded to in *The Devils*, where the convict Fedka steals such jewels (see below).

Like the Greek icon, the Russian icon represents and expresses the divine. As it displays the glory of God in this world, it raises the spirit and the soul of man to the upper world. The function of the icon is a contemplative one: it is an object of long and deep contemplation and requires spiritual concentration from the one who contemplates. The believer loves the archetype and awaits a miraculous help from it. But the Russian icon has its specific qualities. It expresses the deepest roots of the culture of ancient Russia, the faith in the national genius of the Russian people, the sensitivity of a country which has endured long sufferings and has finally defeated the enemy. Russian features appear on the faces of God, Christ, the Mother of God and the Saints. Russian life, habits, clothes also make their appearance on the icons.

The work of Dostoevsky in which the role of the icons is most apparent is *The Landlady*. The story was written in 1846–47 and followed *Poor Folk* (1845), Dostoevsky's first novel, *The Double* and *Mr Prokharchin* (1846). Belinsky, the leader of the 'natural' (that is to say realist) school, who at that time was at the centre of cultural life in St Petersburg, was enthusiastic about *Poor Folk* in which he saw the social novel he was waiting for. But when Dostoevsky started to portray psychological cases and insisted on the responsibility of the individual, Belinsky could not accept such a shift from the poetics he advocated. His reaction to *The Landlady*, where Dostoevsky overused gothic and romantic conventions, was particularly hostile. He wrote to P. V. Annenkov that the story had no meaning. Today the story is often regarded as a minor work and sometimes as an artistic failure.[7]

Whatever the literary verdict on *The Landlady*, however, it remains of great interest with regard to the question of icons, and it is in this connection that I concentrate on it here. It has been asserted that in the 1840s Dostoevsky 'moved away from the Church if not from Christ'[8] and that he 'meant *The Landlady* not only as a symbolic critique of Slavophilism but also of Orthodoxy, so far as he, like Belinsky, then saw the latter as a religion of fear or terror'.[9] Given the prevalence of the view that Dostoevsky, or at least the post-Siberia Dostoevsky, is a profoundly Orthodox writer, such assertions pose a sharp critical challenge, and one which is most directly addressed by focusing on the role of the icons in the story, since this enables us to see how Dostoevsky viewed both the Russian people and Orthodoxy at this time. He emphasised the contradictory yearnings of the people, experiencing the lure of evil, on the one hand, and the desire for purification, on the other, and he accentuated the essential role that Orthodoxy has to play in the reconstruction of Russian society.

The icon of the Mother of God appears three times in *The Landlady*.[10] The first is at the very beginning of the story when the central character Ordynov, a young man of noble origins, enters the Church:

The rays of the setting sun were pouring through the narrow windows of the dome and flooding the side aisle with a bright light; but the brightness was growing dimmer and, as darkness pervaded the vaults of church, the brilliant glittering of the golden adorned icons stood out unevenly, illuminated by the flickering glow of the lamps and candles. (1,267)

The motif of the slanting rays of the setting sun is a recurrent and ambivalent one in Dostoevsky's works. It may be linked with sorrow and death but also with joy, eternal life and Christ. Here the rays that flood the Church are gradually fading, then the darkness that pervades the church is illuminated by the glittering of the icons. As it is written in the Book of Revelation (21:23) about the holy City of Jerusalem: 'It had no need of the sun neither of the moon to shine in it for the glory of God did lighten it and the Lamb is the light thereof.' The rays of the setting sun are a cosmic icon of the divine presence in the Church.

Ordynov cannot bear the brightness of the icons, and hides in a dark corner, losing consciousness for a while. When he comes to, he sees Murin, an older man of Old Believer background (to whom we return below), with a young companion and witnesses a very strange scene:

> The old man stopped in the middle of the Church and bowed in all three directions though there was not a single soul in the Church; so did his companion. Then he took her hand and led her to a large local icon of the Mother of God who protected the Church: by the altar the icon was suffused by the dazzling blaze reflected by the gold and gems the cope was adorned with. (1,268)

Dostoevsky confronts his hero, a nobleman, with the common people. The encounter is taking place by the light of the icon of the Mother of God. One might have thought it was the icon of the Intercession because at the end of that scene Murin takes the veil which is hanging at the foot of the icon to cover Katerina's head (the word *pokrov* means both 'veil' and 'protection'). But as the icon is set in the iconostasis, on the left side of the Holy Gates, there is no doubt that it is the icon of the Hodigitria (which means in Greek 'the guide'), who is shown standing and holding the Infant Jesus on her left arm while pointing at Him with her right hand. She is the one who shows the way of the truth to the three characters in the story and it is not by chance that they meet by the light of the icon. Dostoevsky is faithful to the Byzantine conception of the icon which is founded on the dogma of the Incarnation: every holy image is linked to the archetype and is one of the deepest ways of religious expression. Through their attitude towards the icon the three characters of the story reveal their attitude towards the Mother of God, their attraction towards the divine, the nature of their faith or their lack of faith.

That Ordynov's experience takes place in a Church is highly

significant. Ordynov's character is a typically romantic one: the type of the dreamer who lives a secluded life far from reality. But Ordynov differs from the usual type of dreamer because of his passion for 'science'. In the context of the 1840s the word could mean philosophy and could also be a reference to utopian socialist theories. One can assume that Ordynov was very much attracted towards utopian socialism since he was working on a 'system' (a term usually associated with utopian socialism), and at the end of the story we learn that his work was connected, like many works of utopian socialism, with the history of the Church. In 1846 Belinsky had rejected utopian socialism but Dostoevsky was still very much interested in a doctrine which set the *New Christianity* (such is the title of the famous book of Saint Simon written in 1825), based on the religion of Christ, in opposition to the 'false' religion of the established Church. According to Saint-Simonism, the former was a religion of light and hope, the latter was a religion of fear and eternal damnation. While investing his hero with his own ideas about changing society and creating a social life based on justice and love, Dostoevsky blames him for having let himself be so devoured by his passion for 'science' that he cut himself off from other people and for having ignored Orthodox religion. After his banishment Dostoevsky convinces himself, during his journeys through Europe and by exploring the new revolutionary movements in Russia, that the socialists of the 1840s are completely responsible for the nihilistic doctrines that, according to him, reject Christ and announce the reign of the Antichrist. As the philosopher Zenkovsky writes, 'he did not separate his passionate faith in the establishing of justice on earth from his faith in Christ', and 'his enthusiasm for Socialism was related to his religious searchings'.[11] Ordynov seems to have lost the faith of his youth, but his entering the church proves that he unconsciously longed for it.

We noted before that Ordynov did not pray. Murin does not pray either. The attention of the two men is focused on the young woman who is fervently praying. Ordynov is greatly moved by her sobbing. His first religious experience in the story takes place through the contemplation of a suffering woman of the common people. But he is a passive observer whereas Murin seems to serve as a mediator between the Mother of God and Katerina. The young woman is the only one to offer up prayers to the Mother of God as if asking her for forgiveness.

Another large and very old icon of the Mother of God is seen when Ordynov is welcomed by Katerina to her house. Against his will the old man has to accede to her request. Again Ordynov's gaze is not focused on the heavenly Mother but on the earthly Katerina. In every Russian house there was at least one icon, and one had to bow before it when entering the room where it was hung. Ordynov neither bows nor crosses himself when he enters the room. But the presence of the icon is significant. By its light he is allowed to live in Katerina's lodgings (she is the eponymous 'landlady') and in a spiritual world which was hitherto unknown to him. It is in its light that he is going to live in this room. He is under its protection and it is by its light he is tended by Katerina when he falls ill.

There is a third icon in Katerina's lodgings. In the room where she lives with Murin, 'an icon was hung in a corner, as old as the one which was in his room: before the icon a lamp was lit' (1,280). By its light Murin reads aloud from a book, and Katerina listens to him 'with an inexhaustible curiosity'. When, spurred by curiosity and jealousy, Ordynov bursts into the room, Murin wants to kill him and then falls into an epileptic fit. The icon sheds light on the three characters of the story and the evolution of their feelings: Katerina is enraptured by Murin, the two men love her and hate each other. Through the icon as witness to these human passions two worlds are brought together: the spiritual and the earthly. By its presence the motionless icon asserts the possibility of redemption, it announces the Kingdom of Heaven. But in order to realise this possibility it must become the object of contemplation and prayer.

In that scene no one regards it in this way, but in Katerina's story the same icon appears again and there it is essentially an object of contemplation and prayer. Katerina tells Ordynov that Murin instilled a sense of culpability in her by convincing her that she sold her soul to him, that man is doomed to do evil and will be judged and condemned by God. His words are very ambiguous as he induces her to pray to the Mother of God while persuading her that her prayers will not reach the saints. But her real grief is that she began to enjoy her enslavement: 'My shame and disgrace are dear to me' (1,299). And, out of a deep sense of sinfulness, she keeps on praying: 'I pray,' she tells Ordynov, 'until the sovereign Lady looks at me with more love from the icon' (1,294). Of course, the contemplative gaze must become a combative one. By contemplating the icon, Katerina should overcome the temptation, go beyond it and destroy

the enjoyment she finds in her degradation. The well-known special-
ist in icons, Evgeny Trubetskoy, writes: 'As long as we are tempted by
the pleasures of the flesh, the icon will say nothing to us.'[12] But the
fact that she is endowed with 'the gift of tears', which is often the
privilege of the saints, proves that she deeply feels the purifying
power of suffering, and that through suffering she strives to find the
truth of God.[13] Torn between a strong personality and a 'weak man'
(this is how Murin characterises Ordynov),[14] Katerina is an expia-
tory victim in the story. She is the one who can save both of them.

Through Katerina, Murin strives towards redemption. His conception of a terrible punishing God, of the irrevocability of man's
fate is linked with the schism, *raskol* in Russian, that took place in the
middle of the seventeenth century in reaction to Nikon's reforms.
The Old Believers stood up against the established Church and were
persecuted. Some of them joined the Orthodox Church in 1868.
Murin is the first Old Believer in Dostoevsky's works. Later on, in his
article 'Two camps of theoreticians' (1862), Dostoevsky speaks of the
raskol as a 'significant event in Russian history' (20,20). Through
Myshkin's words in *The Idiot*, he expresses his conviction that the Old
Believers are the real bearers of the Russian spirit and that the
striving for inextinguishable suffering is the main feature of the
Russian people. But in the same novel, Rogozhin, who is linked with
the Old Believers – in fact with their extreme sect, the Castrates – is
ruled by a passion which leads to crime. The house of his father, who
'had great respect for the Castrates' (8,173), looks like a 'cemetery'
and contains a reproduction of Hans Holbein's *The Entombment of
Christ* about which Myshkin and another character of the novel,
Ippolit, said that, by looking at it, one could lose one's faith in
God.[15] In choosing an Old Believer as a character for his story, then,
Dostoevsky would seem to have wanted to penetrate the historical
consciousness of the Russian people.

Dostoevsky repudiates the idealisation of the people which was
characteristic of the Slavophiles and the utopian socialists, but he
also rejects the view of Belinsky, for whom the people were something coarse and godless. In the figure of Murin he shows that the
Russian people were more complex than either the Slavophiles or
Westernisers thought. Russians have a dual character: like Murin,
they may not pray to the icons, and yet be believers. They may
plunder, kill and repent their sins, being both sincere and hypocri-
tical at the same time. In Murin's soul the divine element is closely

linked to a kind of diabolical grandeur, which makes him resemble
the Grand Inquisitor. His eyes 'burned like coals', he is tall, and his
face emaciated. Katerina often likens him to the Devil: 'the unclean
spirit gained possession of my soul', 'and at times I feel as though he
were my enemy and satan' (1,295,294). The word *murin* means 'a
black person', a 'moor' or an *efiop* (i.e. 'an Ethiop' in the archaic
sense of a 'negro'), which in earlier Russian was often used as a
synonym for the Devil.

Yuri Marmeladov offers an interesting interpretation of the image
of Murin, in whom he finds many features of the prophet Elijah:
epilepsy, a blazing stare, a knife, thunder (compare Murin's thun-
dering gun), the ability to foretell people's destiny, as well as the
surname 'Murin', which Marmeladov associates with the name of a
fourth-century saint, Moses Murin. This saint is sometimes represented in icons next to the prophet Elijah.[16] It would therefore be
misleading to think of Murin as simply a demonic figure. It should
be remembered that Dostoevsky put into the mouth of this character
his own condemnation of 'the weak heart' and the intellectuals:
'You've read an awful lot of books, sir; I'd say you'd gotten to be
awful clever; or, as we muzhiks say in Russian: your mind is gone
ahead of your reason' (1,316). With these cunning words Murin
establishes his affinity with the people and, moreover, emphasises the
difference which separates him from Ordynov, who leads a life far
removed from that of the people. Condemning the young Ordynov
for reading too many books, he implies that he should read different
books and read in a different way. Murin here explicitly hints at
Holy Writ.[17]

Murin's incapacity to pray to the icon reveals his lack of compassion and mercy. He probably feels the divinity on the face of the icon
but it is significant that he cannot look at it. Murin deeply needs
Katerina's prayers. As for Ordynov, he began to pray after he left
Katerina and acquired 'the gift of tears'. With her attentive and
sorrowful eyes, she became for him an iconic image. But he is still a
solitary dreamer and, as Bem pointed out, he 'has not understood
himself, has not created his philosophy of the underground and is
therefore helpless in the face of reality.'[18]

In *The Idiot* (1868), an icon is mentioned in the 'Necessary
explanation' of Ippolit, the consumptive intellectual who wants to
commit suicide in order to defy death. He relates how, at night,
when he was thinking about the picture representing the dead

Christ which he has seen in Rogozhin's house,[19] the latter came into his room and sat under the icon. Rogozhin is 'illuminated' by the little lamp that is burning before the icon, 'as the tarantula had been by the candle' in Ippolit's delirium.[20] Dostoevsky confronts 'the eternal force' of nature (according to Ippolit's own words), incarnated in the tarantula and closely linked to the two characters, with the divine light. The possibility at being raised up to the world of God is there, but neither Ippolit nor Rogozhin is aware of it. They neither contemplate the icon nor pray before it and it has no effect on them.

In *The Devils* (1871) along with the icons of the Mother of God there is another icon, that of the Saviour, associated with Kirillov who meditates, like Ippolit, on the dead Christ and wants to become the saviour of humanity. This icon appears twice. It is first present at the time of Stavrogin's visit. We learn that it is Kirillov who lights the lamp and prays before the icon. The same icon is present again, and its presence is of crucial significance in the dramatic scene which precedes the suicide. In a moment of exaltation Kirillov points it out to Peter Verkhovensky, the petty demon, who is, as a result, infuriated. Torn between his heart which is full of compassion for mankind and his reason which persuades him that God does not exist, Kirillov wants to kill himself to show that men should not fear death. He is the false saviour looking at the true one. It is no accident that his suicide does not take place in the room where the icon is located. Kirillov's suicide excludes him definitively from the sphere of the divine.

The attitude of Dostoevsky's characters towards the icon, proto-type of the divine, is often ambiguous. The escaped convict Fedka can do evil and remain a believer. For the first time Dostoevsky deals with the theme of the desecration of the icon. Fedka steals jewels encrusted on icons and yet continues to believe in God: 'but I only took the pearlies off, and how do you know, maybe that same moment my tear, too, was transformed before the crucible of the Almighty for some offense against me, since I'm just exactly that same orphan, not even having any daily refuge' (10,428).[21] We find a similar attitude in the story he relates about the shopkeeper who wept as he stole a pearl from the nimbus of the Mother of God. The shopkeeper returns the money, placing it right at her feet and a miracle happens: 'and our Mother and Intercessor overshadowed him with her veil before all the people' (10,428).[22] The case of the second lieutenant, who throws out two icons and replaces them with German books before which he lights candles, is totally different. Here, the sacrilege is the act of a nihilist and the expression of the rejection of God. The refusal of the transcendent dimension of the world implies the divinisation of man's power, symbolised by the books of German materialist writers. The link is obvious between the axe used by the mad officer to destroy one of the icons and the axe designed on the top of the revolutionary proclamations.[23]

The theme of the desecration of the icon reaches its culmination in *A Raw Youth* (1875), when one of the central characters of the book, the nobleman Versilov, smashes an icon against the corner of the tiled stove so that it breaks in two. We learnt before, through his son Arkady, that Versilov, 'had no feeling for the ikons in their inner meaning and religious significance'.[24] In the drawing room there were two old-fashioned icons. One had 'a gilt-silver setting', and the family had, at one time, wished to pawn it. (This theme is developed in *The Meek One.*) The other, an icon of the Mother of God, has 'a velvet setting embroidered in pearls' (13,82). Versilov sometimes complained that the little lamp that was lighted under the icons hurt his eyes but he did not prevent Sofia from lighting the lamp.

The icon which features in the scene of the desecration is not Versilov's. It had belonged to Makar Ivanovich, the old gardener who had married Sofia when she was eighteen. She ran off with Versilov, their landlord, who bought her freedom from her husband. Makar then became a pilgrim, a penitent. The icon had belonged to his ancestors and he had never parted from it, believing it to be miraculous. It was 'a plain antique icon, with halos on the heads of saints, of which there were two' (13,407).[25] According to Versilov, it is a schismatic's icon.[26] The two saints could be the disciples of St Sergius, Zosima and Sabaty, who founded in 1430 the Solovetsky Monastery on an island in the White Sea. This monastery played an important part in the history of the schism, when the monks rebelled against Nikon's reforms, although it is the case that other pairings of saints occur on popular icons – Boris and Gleb, and Sergy and German being two examples.

The icon was long ago bequeathed by Makar to Versilov. After his death, Sofia intends to give Versilov the icon of her lawful husband, whom she has always honoured and who has magnanimously pardoned her. The role of the woman is again essential. She is the intermediary between the two men, Makar, the saint, and Versilov, who is torn between faith and atheism, Orthodoxy and Catholicism, Russia and the West, his love for Sofia and his passion for Akhmakova. Sofia's name is highly significant and suggests that the meek and humble peasant woman embodies divine wisdom. 'Burdened with her sin, she realises her guilt in relation to her husband <. . .> Versilov knows that she possesses a spiritual power, and that this power comes from the people.'[27] Like Makar, she embodies the religion of the Russian people. For Konstantin Mochulsky, she is 'the image of a humble and suffering mother, almost an icon.'[28]

Versilov arrives after Makar's funeral at which he has not been present. It is a solemn moment. The icon is lying on a small round table. It is not an object to be venerated, since Sofia does not want to stand it up against the wall and light the lamp before it.[29] The icon is to become Versilov's property, and he has to decide what he is going to do with it. When he notices it on the table he takes it up and looks at it intently. It reminds him of his sin but suggests the possibility of redemption. During his last visit Makar had asked him to marry Sofia, and Versilov is quite aware that he must do so. He feels the presence of the old man in the room: 'I believe he is here somewhere in the room' (13,408).[30] In a way one could say that Makar is a witness of the desecration. Versilov's attitude is very strange. He seems delirious but at the same time he analyses very acutely his state of mind. He brought Sofia a nosegay of fresh flowers on her birthday (it is not by chance that the breaking of the icon takes place on this day) and feels an irresistible longing to 'throw it in the snow and trample on it' (13,408).[31] The symbolism is clear: he wants to destroy the purity of his act. The temptation to do evil is even stronger when he is holding the icon.

'It was five o'clock in the afternoon', notes Arkady. Versilov is at a turning point of his life, on the verge of temptation. Three women and his son are gazing at him. Before the desecration he gives them a long explanation of his mental state: 'Yes, I am really split in two mentally, and I'm horribly afraid of it. It is just as though one's second self were standing beside one; one is sensible and rational oneself, but the other self is impelled to do something perfectly senseless, and sometimes very funny' (13,408).[32] So the breaking is viewed as an irrational action. It could also symbolise his split personality. But it could also have other symbolic meanings. Versilov himself seems to hesitate between two possible explanations: 'Don't take it for a symbol, Sonya, it is not as Makar's legacy I have broken

it, and anyway I shall come back to you, my last angel! You may take
it as a symbol, though' (13,409).[33] By breaking the icon Versilov
rejects Makar's heirloom. It signifies not only 'a rejection of the
religious Russian heritage, but also a repudiation of God's image.
Repudiating the divine icon, Versilov repudiates the faith of the
people.'[34] It is also a way of rejecting a possibility of expiation. But
he asserts that he will come back to Sofia. As Berdyaev remarked in
The Russian Revolution: 'one cannot commit sacrilege against an
ordinary piece of matter <. . .> The man who commits sacrilege not
only makes a mockery of what others deem holy, he himself enters
into a special relationship with the sacred objects he mocks.'[35]
Versilov's act does not – and, if we follow Berdyaev – cannot sever
the links binding him spiritually to the world of the icon, even if he is
bound against his own will and inclination.

After his spiritual crisis, Versilov, like Ordynov, acquired the gift of
tears. Will he attain spiritual unity through Sofia's intercession?
Alhough he will not leave her and knows that she is his sheet-anchor,
the question remains unanswered. For Pierre Pascal, 'the matter is
uncertain.'[36] For Mochulsky, Versilov 'undergoes a spiritual
renewal'.[37] As it is often the case in Dostoevsky's fiction, the hero is
left on the threshold of change.

In the story *The Meek One* (*The Diary of a Writer*, November 1876)
the icon of the Mother of God is once more associated with a young
woman. The icon of 'The Mother of God with the Infant', 'an
ancient, family household icon, in a gilt-silver setting', belongs to
'the meek one' of the title (24,8).[38] When it is pawned the icon seems
to lose its religious character. It changes from a sacred object into a
commercial one. But the pawnbroker puts it with his other icons in
the icon case (*kiot* in Russian), a glass-fronted cabinet, surmounted
by a pediment from which a small lamp is suspended, and which
enshrines the icons. Since the day he opened his shop, the pawnbroker has always kept an icon lamp burning. In this way the icon
acquires an ambiguous status, it is at one and the same time a
commercial object and an object of veneration.

Before committing suicide (the icon appears twice, at the beginning and at the end of the story) 'the meek one' recovers the icon,
removes it from the pawnbroker's world, puts it on the table after
praying before it and leaps out of the window, pressing it to her
bosom. The icon is a witness, a companion, a sheet-anchor. It is a
way of neutralising, of sublimating the taking of life condemned by

the Church. According to the Orthodox custom, an icon is placed on the body of the deceased before the funeral. 'The meek one' seems to have anticipated this moment so that, even though she has committed suicide, she is buried with her icon.

After her wife's suicide, the pawnbroker begins to understand that he wanted to destroy the divine principle in her and realises that he loved her. He remembers Christ's commandment: 'Love one another', but forgot who had said it (24,35). Like Versilov, he is perhaps at the threshold of a new life.

Another woman is linked with the icon of the Mother of God in Dostoevsky's works: another Sofia, Alyosha Karamazov's mother. Like Katerina, she is depicted praying. But she does not pray for herself, she prays for her two-year-old son. The scene is remembered by Alyosha and remains alive in him 'for all life':

> That is how it was with him. He remembered one still summer evening, an open window, the slanting rays of the setting sun (he recalled the slanting rays most vividly of all); in a corner of the room the holy image, before it a lighted lamp, and on her knees before the image his mother, sobbing hysterically with cries and shrieks, snatching him up in both arms, squeezing him close till it hurt, and praying for him to the Mother of God, holding him out in both arms to the image as though to put him under the Mother's protection . . . and suddenly a nurse runs in and snatches him from her in terror (14,18).

In her book *The Brothers Karamazov and the Poetics of Memory*, Diane Oenning Thompson with great acuteness pointed out 'the atemporality' of Alyosha's 'sacred memory' and the iconographic nature of the scene.[39] A mortal mother holding her mortal child is praying to the icon of the Mother of God: one becomes what one looks at. She is a sorrowful mother, foreseeing the sufferings of her child. But here are also striking differences. Alyosha's mother is going to die, the Mother of God is immortal. The first one is supplicating and shrieking, the second one suffers with serenity. Nevertheless what most endures in Alyosha's memory are the slanting rays of the setting sun which portend for her suffering and death, and also his mother's face, 'frenzied but beautiful'. As far as he can remember, his attention as a child was focused not on the icon but on his mother's face; in the picture which will remain engraved in his memory, Alyosha's inner glance will always be focused on his mortal mother, who is for him a venerated image, an icon. Like Arkady's father, Alyosha's father does not venerate icons. He tells his sons how once he wanted to spit on their mother's icon of the Holy Virgin in order to knock her mysticism out of her and how she covered her face with her hands and fell to the floor. Struck by Alyosha's 'extraordinary resemblance' to his mother (he does what she was said to have done in reaction to Fyodor's threat of desecration) and moved by his tenderness towards him after he was beaten by his elder son, Mitya, Fyodor offers him the icon of the Mother of God. So the icon worked miracles, as Alyosha's mother believed. It aroused love in the heart of a great sinner as well as a sense of guilt towards his second wife, another 'gentle creature' (compare 'the meek one') in Dostoevsky's works. Fyodor felt that the holy image should not be in his house and that it belongs to the only one worthy to have it, the one he calls 'angel'. The desecrated icon becomes, then, an instrument of expiation. Moreover, when he gives Alyosha the icon, he allows him to return to the monastery, whereas previously he had forbidden him to do so. It is an implicit way of dismissing a paternity he never assumed and of recognising Zosima's spiritual paternity and the bond uniting the elder and his novice. This offering is a crucial moment in Alyosha's life. The icon, which belonged to his mother, becomes his. With the protection of the Mother of God to whom he was consecrated by his mother, Alyosha is ready to begin his way of the Cross.

It has to be noted that Alyosha is never depicted praying to the icon. Only women pray before the icons in Dostoevsky's works. By contemplating the icon of the Mother of God, they become very much like its divine archetype. Women do not act, do not change the world. They represent the iconic image of redemption in a world threatened by idols.

On the threshold of the rediscovery of icons at the end of the nineteenth century (as previously noted the art of the icon fell into disuse at the end of the seventeenth century) Dostoevsky's interest in icons brings him close to such great Russian thinkers as E. Trubetskoy, L. Uspensky, P. Evdokimov and others. According to them, the icon testifies to Russian Orthodox faith, protects the Russian people from evil and expresses the renewal of creative forces which can be fulfilled only through great sufferings.

For Dostoevsky the icon also has a national character. His conception of national culture is linked to Orthodoxy, but, unlike the Slavophiles, he does not idealise the pre-Petrine past and does not seem to consider the Russian spirit as being immutable. On the contrary, he shows, especially in *The Landlady*, that it undergoes a constantly changing process. The Russian common people have not yet found the truth but they are aiming at it. As for the noblemen, they will reach the truth by getting closer to the Russian common people and by trying to understand the religious and moral essence of the Russian nature and its contradictory aspects. In an article 'On love for the people: The necessary contract with the people' in *The Diary of a Writer* of 1876, Dostoevsky expresses similar views: in the Russian people the Christian spirit co-exists with the capacity to do evil, to dominate others and to enjoy one's own cruelty; nevertheless, 'diamonds' must be sought in 'the filth' (22,43). In the story *The Peasant Marey*, which appears in the same issue of his *Diary of a Writer*, he recalls how in his childhood he was soothed and blessed by Marey when, wandering in the forest, he thought he heard some-body shouting: 'A wolf is running about!' and he was terrified (22,48). With his 'maternal' smile and love, his name close to Maria, Marey is a luminous iconographic image. Though he is not an invented character, he was recreated by Dostoevsky's artistic memory, and his feminine tenderness allies him quite closely to the women characters referred above.[40] Unlike Katerina, Arkady's mother, *The Meek One* and Alyosha's mother found the truth. But all of them are purified by the contemplation of the icon of the Mother of God. They are the embodiment of the Russian spirit which, according to Dostoevsky, is founded on love and compassion.

NOTES

1 This chapter is a somewhat expanded version of: Sophie Ollivier, 'Dostoevskii's *The Landlady* and the Icon of the Mother of God', in *Cultural Discontinuity and Reconstruction*, eds. Jostein Børtnes and Ingunn Lunde (Oslo, 1997), 202–16.
2 The Virgin is almost always called Mother of God in Russian (*Bogoroditsa, Bogomater'*).
3 The iconostasis is a sort of screen, decorated with icons, which separates the nave from the sanctuary where the priest officiates.
4 They are located in the icon corner, called in Russian *krasnyi ugol* which means red corner. In Old Russian, in popular speech, *krasnyi* means 'fair', 'beautiful'. The red corner generally faces towards the south-east. In the church or house there is a small lamp (*lampadka*), always or nearly always burning before the icon. The domestic icon is often of small dimensions.
5 In his house the dying person is placed beneath the icons, and therefore

to be lying under the icons means to die. In *The Brothers Karamazov* little Ilyusha is lain beneath an icon when he becomes very ill.

6 Alain Besançon, *L'image invisible* (Paris, 1984), 167.

7 For an analysis of the story, see Joseph Frank, *Dostoevsky: The Seeds of Revolt 1821–1849* (Princeton, NJ, 1976) and Victor Terras, *The Young Dostoevsky (1846–1849)* (The Hague, 1969).

8 Jacques Catteau, *La création littéraire chez Dostoïevski* (Paris, 1978), 99.

9 Frank, *Seeds of Revolt*, 341.

10 There are many icons of the Mother of God: the icon of Consolation, of Tenderness, of Incarnation, of Sorrows, of Intercession, et al.

11 Vassili Zenkovsky, *A History of Russian Philosophy* (London, 1967), 416, 417.

12 Eugène Troubetskoy, *Trois études sur l'icône* (Paris, 1965), 35.

13 According to Rudolf Neuhäuser, the main allegorical theme of the story is the enslavement of the Russian soul, unable to free itself from national and religious traditions and enjoying its own humiliation (Rudolf Neuhäuser, 'The Landlady: A new interpretation', *Canadian Slavonic Papers*, 10, 1 (1968): 57). It is true that when entering the church, Ordynov enters in contact with the Russian people. The whole story may be interpreted as an encounter between an intellectual and the Russian people. Through Katerina, Ordynov discovers their capacity for suffering and love, but also for enjoying their own degradation. Through Murin he discovers their capacity to do evil, their despotism. Katerina is a victim, the maiden of the Russian folk-tales. But in my view, she is also Dostoevsky's first attempt to represent the Russian woman as the only one who can save the Russian people.

14 Ordynov is a 'weak heart', like Vasya Shumkov in Dostoevsky's story entitled *A Weak Heart*.

15 Richard Peace very accurately notes that Rogozhin 'is the embodiment of a strain of religious fanaticism, peculiar to the Russian common people' (Richard Peace, *Dostoevsky*, London, 1992, 86; first published 1971; paperback edn 1992). Peace notes all the ambiguous allusions to the Old Believers such as the names of Rogozhin and Nastasia Filippovna (and Myshkin's inheritance). See Peace, 84, 86, 318. Dostoevsky's character Ippolit embodies his own reaction to the picture of Holbein. When he was in Basel in June 1867 he stood for a long time in front to the picture and told his wife that one could lose one's faith by looking at it.

16 Iu. I. Marmeladov, *Tainyi kod Dostoevskogo: Il'ia-prorok v russkoi literature* (St Petersburg, 1992), 84, 85.

17 Ollivier, 'Dostoevsky's *The Landlady*', 211, 212.

18 A. L. Bem, 'Dramatizatsiia breda (*Khoziaika* Dostoevskogo)', *O Dostoevskom*, 1 (Prague, 1929), 78.

19 See above, note 15.

20 See Peace, *Dostoevsky*, 319.

21 F. M. Dostoevsky, *The Demons* (London, 1994), 560.

22 *Ibid.*
23 In his well-known book, *The Icon and the Axe*, James H. Billington has united 'two artifacts of enduring meaning to Russians': 'The two objects were traditionally hung together on the wall of the peasant hut in the wooded Russian north <. . .> They serve to suggest both the visionary and the earthy aspects of Russian culture.' The axe was 'the principal weapon' used by the tsars against the rebellions and by the peasants during the rebellions. In the nineteenth century it 'lived on as a symbol of rebellion'. See James H. Billington, *The Icon and the Axe: An Interpretative History of Russian Culture* (New York, 1970), 27, 28. In *The Devils*, Dostoevsky modelled Verkhovensky on Nechaev who set up a secret 'society of the axe' in the late 1850s. In the episode of the officer destroying the icon, he highlighted the iconoclastic spirit of the revolutionaries.
24 F. M. Dostoevsky, *A Raw Youth* (New York, 1950), 94.
25 *Ibid.*, 501.
26 In a note to this passage in the Academy of Sciences edition it is said that Makar was not an Old Believer and that Versilov just meant that the icon was very old. A reference is made to Zosima's ancient icon, which was painted before the *raskol* (xvii,390). We agree with R. Peace who emphasises the link between *raskol'niki* (schismatics) and *raskoloti'* (to split in two). Peace, *Dostoevsky*, 303.
27 Ollivier, 'Dostoevsky's *The Landlady*', 213.
28 Konstantin Mochul'skii, *Dostoevskii: Zhizn' i tvorchestvo* (Paris, 1947), 429.
29 The lighting of an icon is a very important gesture. There is a lighted lamp before Zosima's icons. In Tikhon's cell there is an icon case with silver and golden icons but there is no mention of a lamp. It is to be noted that Stavrogin is indifferent to their presence. Other male characters have a lamp lit before their icon: Murin, Ippolit, Kirillov, the revolutionary Dergachev in *A Raw Youth* (Dostoevsky took the fact from reality, slightly changing it: the revolutionary Dolgushin had a crucifix in his room), the pawnbroker in *The Meek One*. The lighted lamp could mean that there is a possibility of redemption for them.- When Zosima's brother, Markel, who is very ill, urges the servant to light the lamp before the icon, it means that a great spiritual change had come over him: 'Light it, dearest, light it, it was monstruous of me to forbid all of you to do so before. While lighting the lamp you pray and watching you with delight I pray. That is we both pray to the same God' (xiv,261,262).
30 *A Raw Youth*, 502.
31 *Ibid.*
32 *Ibid.*, 503.
33 *Ibid.*, 504.
34 Ollivier, 'Dostoevsky's *The Landlady*', 213.
35 Nicholas Berdyaev, *The Russian Revolution* (London, 1931), 47.

36 Pierre Pascal, *Dostoevski* (Paris, 1969), 64 (English edn 1963; French edn 1969).

37 Mochul'skii, *Dostoevskii*, 432.

38 xxiv,8. The pawnbroker wants to remove the setting, which is worth about six roubles, and give back the image to her. But he changes his mind and puts the icon with his other icons.

39 Diane Oenning Thompson, *'The Brothers Karamazov' and the Poetics of Memory* (Cambridge, 1991), 74–84.

40 See Robert Louis Jackson's excellent article on this subject: R. L. Jackson, 'The triple vision: *The Peasant Marey*', *Yale Review* (Winter 1978), 225–35.

CHAPTER 4

Problems of the biblical word in Dostoevsky's poetics

Diane Oenning Thompson

Dostoevsky is hailed as a great Christian writer and a profound, innovatory depictor of the modern human condition. Precisely this combination raises intriguing problems for interpretation. In notes written towards the end of his life, Bakhtin observed:

> Irony has penetrated all languages of modern times (especially French); it has penetrated into all words and forms <. . .> Irony is everywhere – from the minimal and imperceptible, to the loud, which borders on laughter. Modern man does not proclaim; he speaks. That is, he speaks with reservations. Proclamatory genres have been retained mainly as parodic and semi-parodic building blocks for the novel. <. . .> The speaking subjects of high, proclamatory genres – of priests, prophets, preachers, judges, leaders, patriarchal fathers, and so forth – have departed this life. They have all been replaced by the writer, simply the writer, who has fallen heir to their styles <. . .> Literature has been completely secularised.[1]

This, paradoxically, is both true and untrue for Dostoevsky. He was a master of irony, of the word spoken with reservations, but his works are hardly 'completely secularised'. The Christian worldview permeates and shapes all Dostoevsky's post-Siberian works, from the large narrative structures of his redemptive plots, whether failed, realised or suspended, to single words charged with Christian significance. By 'the biblical word' is meant any saying, image, symbol or thought whose source can be traced to the Bible. It is by his use of this word, with its distinctive content, stylistics and emotional tonalities, that Dostoevsky belongs to Christian art. Proclamation is a mode of speech characteristic of biblical style used to transmit sacral messages and divine commands, either directly (God speaks), or by witnesses to the divine acts and words who, as messengers of the word of God, claim to speak with the utmost authority. The proclamatory word of the Bible may be veiled, mysterious, but it does not dissimulate, it does not say one thing, but give us to understand the contrary. It is a direct, fully convinced word, spoken without reservations, that urgently strives to transmit its message in as true a way as possible because universal salvation depends on its widest dissemination.

But it was a style no longer available to Dostoevsky in its pure form. The Christian meanings he wished to explore had, by his time, to be conveyed in secular forms (the novel, the short story) which arose from popular and profane genres. The very language in which he wrote had already been largely determined 'by a lengthy and complex process of expunging <. . .> the sacred and authoritarian word'.[2] Moreover, during his epoch, new Western political, social and scientific ideas were driving deep rifts in the Russian consciousness, relativising the claims of Christianity to universal truth. This historical situation is reflected in the speech of Dostoevsky's divided heroes, plagued by 'double thoughts'. The 'sideward glance' at another's word, so characteristic of his ideological heroes, betrays their anxiety about the semantic stability of their own word. Indeed, as Bakhtin has shown, double-voiced discourse, of which irony is one variety, predominates in Dostoevsky's fiction. Such discourse is simultaneously directed towards the referential object of speech and towards someone else's speech, towards another's response. This means that the biblical words Dostoevsky variously incorporated into his works undergo refraction and testing by the pervasive medium of double-voiced discourse. But in Dostoevsky it also means that double-voiced words manifest the impress of the biblical word. The result is an intense struggle and it is on this turbulent boundary, where the biblical word interacts with double-voiced words, that Dostoevsky's dynamic art lives.

What chance the biblical word, then, against the new secular ideologies, the undermining word of irony 'that with one eye looks two ways at once', and the subversive forces of evil so powerfully represented in Dostoevsky's fiction? Does it hold its own and emerge with its semantic authority intact? What are targets of the author's irony? For irony is a double-edged sword; it may support the biblical word by exposing lies, deflating overweening pride, confounding theoretical certitudes or evil intrigues. Irony may also serve as a contrastive device whereby the biblical word, and the ideal it expresses, emerge from the double-voiced context all the more purely, provided that it is not ironised to the annihilation of its essence. Then, too, there are situations, such as tragedy, the suffering of children, the betrayal of innocence, to which irony is an inappropriate or repugnant response. With these questions in mind, we consider various passages from Dostoevsky's post-Siberian works, taking them in chronological order.

CRIME AND PUNISHMENT

The biblical word first sounds in a seedy tavern where Raskolnikov meets Marmeladov, the down-and-out drunk who seeks 'sorrow and tears' in drink, and who now has 'nowhere to go', 'no one to go to' (6,14). Seeing in Raskolnikov a sensitive, educated man, Marmeladov proceeds to tell him his sorrows, during which it emerges that he does have somewhere to go, someone to go to. For while Marmeladov chooses Raskolnikov as his interlocutor in the here and now of the story, at the same time he addresses his 'superaddressee' (*nadadresat*), 'an ideally true, absolutely just, responsive understanding'.[3] 'Behold the man', exclaims Marmeladov, quoting the words of Pontius Pilate before he delivered Christ up to be crucified (John 19:5) (6,14). At the very mention of the divine prototype, Marmeladov, as if keenly aware of his own unworthiness, berates himself: 'I have the image of the beast <. . .> I'm a brute by nature' (6,14–15). He then gives a vivid account of his family's desperate plight and his daughter Sonya's self sacrificial act of taking up prostitution, concluding with the challenging query: 'Well, who will take pity on a man like me? <. . .> I should be crucified!' (6,20) With this, his speech rises to a crescendo as he unreservedly turns himself over to Christ for judgment: 'He's the only One, He is the Judge' (6,21). As Marmeladov strives to approach Him, he imitates proclamatory biblical style, interweaving biblical quotations with his own speech. In so imitating the biblical word, he takes it seriously, merges his voice with it and makes it familiar. He shapes all his words in the expectation of ultimately being heard, understood and mercifully forgiven by Christ. Not expecting justice and compassion in this world, his speech culminates in an impassioned appeal to eschatological mercy in which he projects himself and Sonya to the Last Judgment and creates his own version of Christ. It is consonant with Dostoevsky's poetics and his extraordinarily powerful feeling for the Incarnation, that Christ is not only a 'superaddressee', but a superaddressor, a personal Christ Who talks to people, Who understands them, knows their sufferings, forgives their wrongdoings and accepts them all. So intensely attuned is Marmeladov to this highest voice, that he envisages Christ as being present and impersonates His voice calling to Sonya:

He will come on that day and will ask: And where is the daughter who sacrificed herself for an unkind and consumptive stepmother, for another's little children? Where is the daughter who took pity on her earthly father, an obscene drunkard, not fearing his beastliness?' And he will say: 'Come! I've already forgiven thee <. . .> Thy many sins are forgiven thee even now because thou hast loved much . . .' And He will forgive my Sonya. (6,21)

Next he imagines Christ addressing not just him personally (here is his genuine humbleness), but calling the whole collective of the world's Marmeladovs to Him:

And when he has finished with everyone, then He will say to us: 'Come forth', He will say, 'ye also! Come forth ye drunkards, come forth ye weaklings, come forth ye shameless creatures. Ye are swine! who have the image of the beast and bear his stamp. Yet come ye also unto Me! <. . .> I accept these because not a one of them ever considered himself worthy of it'. And we shall all go forth without shame and stand up. And we shall weep . . . and we shall understand everything <. . .> Lord, Thy Kingdom come! (6,21)

Marmeladov's interaction with the biblical word gives birth to a vibrant new word, a radical sermon transposed from the solemn liturgy into his milieu of 'slum naturalism', into his contemporary context of destitute, humiliated people. A drunkard enjoys a carnival freedom from decorum; he can proclaim and he can scandalise. We may detect here a hidden polemic with official Christianity whose respectable adherents would find in this scene a gross and shocking travesty of the Gospels. This carnivalised situation is in complete accord with the Christian spirit; Christ lived among the lowest classes, mingling with sinners, social outcasts, the poor, the down-trodden and humiliated.[4] The whole meaning of His mission would collapse were He not present here, in the Petersburg misery. The spectacle of a drunkard grandiloquently impersonating Christ has overtones of comedy. However the element of laughter is tempered by the suffering of Marmeladov's family and the pathos of his image of Christ. For although most of the words he puts into Christ's mouth are his own, they do not violate the spirit of the canonical word, or Christ's divine status. (In fact, Dostoevsky was never again to make up words for Christ.) Marmeladov appropriates Holy Writ not to travesty it (as did the liturgies of drunks in the *parodia sacra* of the Middle Ages), but to hold it before him as the focus of his highest hopes. His carnivalesque performance enables him momentarily to transcend himself, to be liberated from his misery, into that 'larger fellowship' of all those who will be called to the Kingdom.[5] Marmeladov's oration is a nineteenth-century variation on an old Christian style, the *sermo humilis*, which lends dignity to any theme or speaker, no matter how lowly, humble or comic, because it combines them with the most sublime and serious of topics, Christian salvation and redemption.[6]

Throughout this scene, Raskolnikov does not join the chorus of mockers in the tavern, but 'listens attentively'. Thanks to her father's words, the image of Sonya forgiven by Christ because of her self-sacrificial love and fearless compassion for others, no matter how 'unkind' or 'beastly', here enters Raskolnikov's consciousness. After his beastly murders, he will seek her out and she will remain with him to the end of the novel and beyond, mediating through the Gospels his 'resurrection'. Thus, from the kernel of this meeting grows the novel's plot of a redemption eventually accomplished.

THE IDIOT

In *The Idiot* the treatment of the biblical word is radically different. Of the twenty-six or so biblical allusions in the novel, the majority concern the Crucifixion, followed by the Apocalypse.[7] Most occur in Ippolit's 'My necessary explanation' where he discusses Holbein's painting of Christ, depicted just after the Crucifixion, the signs of 'infinite suffering' graphically visible on His face and body (8,339). No word can issue from this broken, tortured corpse ever again. The Word is dead, defeated by 'the laws of nature'. Ippolit invokes two of Christ's most nature defying miracles, the raising of Lazarus and Jairus's daughter, only to call His divinity into doubt. And he brings in the Holbein as a pictorial way of trying to confirm (and overcome) his despairing doubts, posing them as polemical interrogations of the Gospel account: How could His followers, seeing His corpse, believe that He would rise? If even He could not overcome the 'laws of nature', how can anyone believe in Him? If He could have seen this image, would He have ascended the cross? However, the mortally ill young man's composition is an accusation, a protest against the injustice of his own imminent death which, while addressed to those present, is implicitly addressed to some unidentified higher power.

He receives no answer or consolation from the assembled company, including Myshkin, nor from the author, who soon drops him. Ippolit's reading of his 'Explanation' is followed by his attempted suicide.

But Ippolit has left out the other half of the Passion narrative – and so has the author. On the threshold of death, he can only see the corpse of a human Jesus as depicted by Holbein and not the resurrected Christ. This cruel realism corresponds to the pitiless realism of the Holbein Christ. Indeed, the Holbein painting is not an Orthodox icon but a masterpiece of Western naturalist art, devoid of any iconographic signs of His divinity. As Julia Kristeva remarks, Christ is depicted utterly alone, forsaken, in a cramped tomb whose low ceiling presses down on His corpse 'without any prospect toward heaven'.[8] Myshkin's response, and it is the same as Ippolit's – 'looking at this picture some people may lose their faith' – expresses the central problematic of the novel (8,182). The anguish and despair this image provokes in *The Idiot* bespeaks Dostoevsky's own anxiety, of which the Holbein is a graphic image, that if Christ was not divine, then His sacrifice 'has lost its meaning' and consequently so has the whole Christian tradition.[9] The social consequences of this loss are reflected in the rampant greed and pervasive cynicism depicted in a Russian society which has fallen prey to the corrupting influence of Western ideas and is, according to Lebedev's and Nastasia Filippovna's reading of Revelation, on the verge of Apocalypse.

There is another image of Christ in the novel: Nastasia Filippovna's fantasy picture, also 'different' from the 'Gospel stories' (8,381). Her image, superficially reminiscent of Bible story illustrations for children, is overshadowed by disturbing features. Significantly, her picture is not of a Christ Who speaks, but Who is silent and alone, save for a small child (a surrogate of her once innocent self) to whose babble He has ceased to listen. A strange air of profound melancholy suffuses the entire image. His hand absently rests on the child's head, His 'sad face' abstractly gazes into the distance. The child, mirroring His mood, falls into a pensive silence, but intently watches Him, as if waiting for Him to speak. But He has retreated into 'a thought great as the whole world' which 'lies (*pokoitsia*) in his look', where the unusual verb *pokoitsia* designates the 'repose' of the dead (or their ashes) in the grave. Nastasia's picture projects a solitary, powerless figure, withdrawn into an incommunicable sorrow. The whole scene is illuminated by the 'setting sun', a symbolic prefiguration of His death. Nastasia Filippovna, sexually abused throughout her lonely orphaned adolescence, and now 'in a state to ruin herself irretrievably', seeks communion with the Christ of her fantasy (8,28). But from this mournful conception she cannot draw sufficient strength to save herself. Indeed, she will soon give herself up as a sacrificial victim and, as if in imitation of His premonition of death, she closes her picture with the prophecy: 'I shall soon die', expressing, perhaps, with this, her wish to be with Christ, with Whom alone she can be restored to innocence (8,381). The Christ Who does not speak comes back in Ivan Karamazov's poem, only to be dialogically countered by the last novel's overarching affirmation of His word and image. In *The Idiot*, communion with Christ is precluded. One cannot have a dialogue with a Christ contemplating His death, nor a corpse which is the organising symbol of the novel's tragic vision. But, the Holbein is not a canonical image of Christ any more than Myshkin is a true *imitator Christi*.

In fact, it is the particular omissions of the biblical word in *The Idiot* that are most telling. Here, as opposed to Dostoevsky's other novels, there are no readings or faithful interpreters of the biblical word, no prayers, no heavenly visions, no biblical epigraphs, no references to the Kingdom, and no one moves towards redemption or renewal through the Word. Significantly, both the doomed Ippolit and Myshkin quote the same phrase from the Apocalypse – 'there will be no more time' (Rev. 10:6) – the one in suicidal despair, the other describing his epileptic aura. In neither case is their invocation of the biblical word transformational. The Word is not so much ironised as disabled, rendered impotent, like the epileptic idiot hero, because it is not invested with sufficient countervailing force to resist, let alone stem, the avalanche of avarice, lies and malice which prevails in this novel's world.[10] Christian virtues cannot function in *The Idiot* because they lack adequate embodiment and an adequate spokesperson.[11] They also lack full-fledged symbolic representation. As Jostein Børtnes points out, Dostoevsky provisionally associates Myshkin to three Christian prototypes (Don Quixote, the holy fool and Christ) only to fracture each one by 'a process of de-symbolization', whereby the symbol is successively shorn of its constituent features.[12] This persistent diminishing of Myshkin's salvific potential casts a parodically distorting ripple over his image. In parody two voices with opposing semantic intentions, one of which is hostile to the other, meet in one utterance. There are initially just enough similarities in Myshkin's image to establish a connection with Christ. However, his Christological attributes are progressively offset and undermined by qualities which render him impotent and are therefore inimical to them. His compassion degnerates into pity, his humility into weakness, his penetrant word disintegrates into incoherence and his attempts to reconcile those he loves provoke only hurt and rivalrous hatred. His word changes nothing, and even causes unwitting harm. Only Kolya, the boy who admires and loves the prince, may carry into the future the ideal he so imperfectly exemplifies, though this remains little more than a hint. Myshkin resolves into a tragic parody of Christ, a failed kenosis without the backbone of the Word. *The Idiot* moves us by the tragic spectacle of goodness defeated, of innocence corrupted, of a great promise come to naught.[13] Myshkin sinks into permanent darkness, bereft of speech, as impotent in the living death of his incurable idiocy as the Christ of Holbein's painting.

There is one other executed corpse depicted with pitiless naturalism, Nastasia Filippovna. Laid out on Rogozhin's bed, covered with a sheet, depriving her of 'any prospect toward heaven', the signs of her mortality made visible by the hovering fly and phials of disinfectant to mask the smell of her decomposing body, Nastasia Filippovna is now with Christ, not the Christ of the Gospels, or her child-like fantasy, but the figure of the dead Christ of Holbein, 'emptied of its divine content'.[14] This similarity makes her the most tragic person in the novel. Moreover, if He was not resurrected, then she and all humanity are without hope of resurrection. This image and its sombre implications haunt the whole novel, making *The Idiot* Dostoevsky's bleakest work, a claustrophobic tale of unmitigated tragedy for all its protagonists.

THE DEVILS

For all the demonic mayhem represented in *The Devils*, there is, in the novel's penultimate chapter, 'The last wandering of Stepan Trofimovich', one instance of conversion and final reconciliation. Resolving at last to cast off his parasitic existence at Varvara Petrovna's, Stepan Trofimovich Verkhovensky sets out on the 'great road' 'to raise the banner of a great idea (*znamia velikoi idei*) and to die for it' (10,480). The narrator, however, calls it a 'pilgrimage', and his term is telling. For Stepan Trofimovich's last wanderings are conceived as a journey to a spiritual transformation, thanks to his new, revelatory apprehension of the biblical word. It is his last journey on earth. His spiritual rebirth, mediated by the itinerant bible seller, Sophia Matveevna, the eponym and literal bearer of divine wisdom, is counterpointed by the symptoms of his approaching death.

The chapter detailing Stepan's last wandering is divided into three parts, forming a triptych which represents his ascending comprehension of the Word concomitant with his shedding the false layers of his self. In the first part he is the man he has been so far: a Westernized liberal of the 1840s, a vain poseur who speaks in a mélange of French and Russian, who ludicrously imagines himself a dangerous revolutionary and is the butt of the narrator's irony. When Sophia offers him the New Testament, Stepan, the Frenchified Russian, exclaims: 'Eh . . . mais je crois que c'est l'Evangile <. . .> Je n'ai rien contre l'Evangile, et . . . I've long wanted to reread it . . .' (10,486). At this point the narrator reports the unspoken thought that flashes through Stepan's mind: 'he hadn't read the Gospels for at least some thirty years and only about seven years ago he had recalled a little bit only from reading Renan's *Vie de Jésus*', an appropriate guide for a liberal atheist (10,486–87).[15] But now, the very appearance of the Gospels prompts in him for the first time a fleeting realisation that he has been speaking falsely.

In the second part, this awareness intensifies. Greatly taken with Sophia, and apparently having already forgotten the 'banner of a great idea', Stepan enthusiastically proposes to her that they preach the Gospels together: 'The common people are religious, c'est admis, but they still don't know the Gospels. I will interpret it to the people . . . In an oral interpretation one can correct the mistakes of this remarkable book, for which I have, of course, the utmost respect' (10,491). Stepan knows neither the common people nor the Gospels. These are the lies he has long been telling himself and believing.

Coincidentally, however, a quite different attitude begins to appear. Riding with Sophia to Ustievo, Stepan declares: 'I want to forgive all my enemies immediately <. . .> Oh, let us forgive everyone and always . . . Let us hope that we will be forgiven too. Each and every one is guilty before others' (10,490–91). A precept of Christ is taking root in his heart, imparting tones of humility and reconcilation to his speech. His last phrase anticipates word-for-word Father Zosima's central teaching in *The Brothers Karamazov.*

But Stepan quickly reverts to his first self. Settled at the inn, he insists on telling his life story to Sophia, because his 'genius must no longer remain a secret to her' (10,494). What follows is a long 'dissertation' of romantic fantasies, lies, half-truths and grandiose, self-deluding inventions. This is his sham confession and belongs to the shallow facade of his initial image.

The turning point comes on the same night when he falls seriously ill. Now his speech becomes self-confessional in earnest. 'I – I'm a scoundrel!', he tells Sophia, 'Oh, all my life I've been dishonourable. Everything I just told you was a lie. I've been thinking only about myself' (10,496). The efficacy of his 'self-judgment' emerges at once when he suddenly reproaches himself for forgetting about Liza. And now, realising how he has wronged Varvara Petrovna over the years, another key teaching of Christ slips into his speech: 'I'll turn the other cheek to her comme dans votre livre' (10,496). Now, feeling the inadequacy of his own word to express what is beginning to stir in him, he seeks a word greater than himself, asking Sophia to read to him from the New Testament: 'I haven't read it for a long time . . . in the original. What if someone asks and I make a mistake?', this from the man who a short while ago thought of 'correcting' the Gospels (10,496).[16]

Sophia chooses Christ's Sermon on the Mount (not given in the novel's text) from which he has just quoted. After she finishes, he makes a crucial confession: 'I've been lying all my life. Even when I spoke the truth (*pravda*). I never spoke for the truth (*istina*), but only for myself' (10,497). Stepan's own truth, *pravda*, which usually designates earthly truth or justice, is now opposed to *istina* (verity), a common biblical term and a synonym for Christ. Next to the true word of Christ, Stepan's convictions are now exposed to him as lies. Never having loved nor spoken for *istina*, he has mispent his words, and his life. Now, trusting to a higher guidance, he asks her to select a passage at random. Her eyes fall on Rev. 3:14 (reproduced *in toto*) which is addressed to the lukewarm Church of the Laodiceans. 'That . . . that too is in your book <. . .> I never knew this great passage!' (10,497–98). The lukewarm are the condescending liberals of Stepan Trofimovich's stamp who are 'prepared to have the utmost respect' for the Bible.

Finally he chooses a passage he wants 'to remember literally', the novel's epigraph on the Gadarene swine (Luke 8:27–36), the 'biblical thematic clue' which announces the 'higher theme that explains the hidden meaning' of the 'earthly events related' in the work (10,498).[17] Dostoevsky inserted verses (32–36) where the devils go out of the demoniac, enter the herd of swine and throw themselves into the lake, culminating in the healed man sitting at the feet of Jesus. The 'miraculous passage' that was a 'stumbling block' for Stepan all his life now comes as a stunning revelation. When he interprets the ills infecting Russia, his own and his son's generation, as an enactment of this passage, and a prophetic sign for their healing, he has divined the true meaning of the novel's events. And when he at last humbly recognises the harm he himself has caused – 'I, perhaps, first of all at the head of them [the devils]' – his healing can begin (10,499). These insights have a spiritually transforming effect on him.

Dostoevsky's finest poetic effects are often caught in small symbolic details which speak more subtly, more eloquently than even his most brilliant dialogic exchanges, thanks to the power of symbolic representation to convey 'semantic *depth*' and expand 'contextual meanings'.[18] When Stepan first enters the room where he is soon to die, the narrator appends a seemingly casual remark: 'he didn't even look out the window at the huge lake' close by the hut (10,492). With this extraordinary lacuna in Stepan's visual field, the author symbolically conveys his blindness to spiritual truths, to everything but himself, his ideas, his wish to impress Sophia. Shortly after his interpretation of the passage from Luke, Stepan sinks into a delirium which faintly mimics the ravings of the demoniac. On the morning of 'the third day' he wakes in his full mind and suddenly 'wants to look out the window'; he marvels: 'Tiens, un lac! – ah, my God, I hadn't seen it before' (10,499). Across the lake lies Spasov, a name bound to remind the Russian reader of *Spas* (the Saviour). The 'third day' in this context is reminiscent of the Resurrection, and the lake which has to be crossed to reach Spasov is symbolic of a journey of purification. Thus, the lake in the Gospel and the lake outside a nineteenth-century Russian peasant hut here come together in a similarity relationship of poetry. On the threshold of leaving this world, there opens up for Stepan Trofimovich a prospect to *Spas*ov, to the Saviour. '[T]out le monde va à Spasov', exclaimed Stepan earlier (10,487). This is the destination to which Dostoevsky hoped Russia, and perhaps all humanity, were making a pilgrimage.

In the third part Dostoevsky takes his hero still farther. After Stepan finally declares his love to Varvara Petrovna and takes the

sacrament, he, 'firmly and with great feeling', launches into a speech
in which he says things 'directly contrary to many of his former
convictions' (10,505). Here, when he reaches the highest stage of his
transformation, he passes beyond himself and Russia's malaise to
universal themes, his language taking on the accents of biblical style.
Stepan discovers his need to love ('what is more precious than
love?'), his need for 'God, the only Being one can eternally love'
(10,505). The last words of the former deist, who once declared he
was 'not – a Christian' but rather an 'ancient pagan, like the great
Goethe, the ancient Greek', are a sermon on love, the gift of life and
immortality, one that could be almost seamlessly incorporated into
Zosima's sermons (10,33).[19] A sermon is the word of the converted.
The initial catalyst was Christ's word (Mat. 5:39) which Stepan
repeats, now as an assimiliated idea: 'When I understood . . . this
turning of the other cheek, I . . . I then and there understood
something else' (10,505–06). If, as Bakhtin says, understanding is
always dialogic, then Stepan's dawning comprehension of the truth
about himself, Russia, the human condition and God, is a result of
his internal dialogue with Christ's teaching. Indeed, at the end,
'transformed into an image of the possessed healed by Christ', he
alone realises the final stage of the biblical epigraph.[20]

In this sequence of events, we may discern arresting parallels to
one of the great prototypes of the European novel, Don Quixote, a
figure Dostoevsky thought 'of the beautiful characters in Christian
literature [to be] the most perfect' (28,ii,251).[21] They share many
carnival motifs, but most important is the common pattern which
shapes their ends. Both heroes are in their fiftieth year when they
suddenly decide to leave behind their familiar world, their habits,
comforts and former identities, and set out on the open road to
realise a deluded image of themselves as ardent champions of their
ideal, gleaned from their long immersion in bookish dreams and
ideas.

But there takes place a reversal when, nearing the end of their
lives, each realises that his quest is illusory. What happens is a
process which has become a tradition of the picaresque novel
whereby the fool or buffoon, who has been living in the grip of an
illusion (engaño), falls into a state of disillusionment (desengaño).[22]
Then, on his deathbed, when, in Don Quixote's words, 'a man must
not jest with his soul', he suddenly awakens to the truth. And in the
light of this truth, the illusion by which he has hitherto lived is

discredited, rejected, seen for what it is. The hero repents his folly, makes peace with others and just before dying entrusts himself to God. Thus, Don Quixote, despondent over his defeat by the Knight of the Moon and his melancholy realisation that Dulcinea will never appear, falls ill and takes to his bed. His liberation from his delusion occurs suddenly, after a deep sleep, when he awakes blessing 'Almighty God' and 'his mercies'.[23] He finally sees the lunacy of his chivalric quest and, his sanity restored, his judgment 'clear and free', he abominates the 'profane', 'detestable books of chivalry' with their 'absurdities' and 'deceits'. He repents his foolishness, asks to be confessed, takes the sacrament, begs pardon from Pancho Sanza for leading him astray, rejects his self-styled sobriquet of Don Quixote de la Mancha, and just before death he becomes the hidalgo he always really was, plain Alonso Quixano the Good. And so it is with Stepan Trofimovich. From being Varvara Petrovna's 'puppet' (*kukol*) whom she fashioned to resemble the minor poet Kukol'nik, the idol of her youthful infatuation, Stepan Trofimovich throws off this false *imitatio* in which the miasma of his old ideas held him captive and, his wanderings over, returns at the end of his life to the faith of his native land, to that man who was always within him, to the 'divine image hidden in his heart'.[24]

True to psychological realism, Stepan's former self has not totally fallen away. It surfaces even at the end when, casting his affirmation of the biblical word in the speech genre of the revolutionary slogan, he exclaims 'Long live the Great Thought' (10,506). But what is important is that the Word has entered his heart and that Dostoevsky gave it to Stepan Trofimovich to make that 'comparison' between Luke and Russia which drives the whole novel. Stepan Trofimovich takes his final leave of ideology, the 'great idea' (*velikaia ideia*), and dies affirming faith, the 'eternal Great Thought' (*vechnaia Velikaia Mysl'*). The listener to the canonical biblical word has become its interpreter. The biblical word has become his word, and in Dostoevsky's dialogic art this is the summit of responsive under-standing. This process Dostoevsky embodied in a character whom he called 'the cornerstone of everything' in his novel (29,i,184).

Cervantes wished to divert his readers and discredit the outmoded chivalric romances. Dostoevsky was, however, concerned with the future of Russia, with great historical trends; he meant to expose the new ideas from the West as harmful illusions by illustrating their lethal effects in Russia. Don Quixote's illusions have neither harmed

nor helped anyone. Stepan Trofimovich's illusions, however, are not
so innocent; his 'great idea' comprises a whole complex of ideas
espoused by generations of the Russian intelligentsia. As the negli-
gent father of his malevolent natural son and the teacher of
Stavrogin from whom the 'devils' got their ideas, he has much more
to answer for. Dostoevsky aimed to show that the liberal, atheist
idealist fathers of the 1840s gave ideological birth to their radical,
materialist nihilist sons of the 1860s; that the fathers misled the sons
and thus brought ruin on the younger generation, and it is through
Stepan's conversion that he makes this connection.

Don Quixote, we are told, died 'in so calm and Christian a
manner'. Similarly, Stepan Trofimovich 'did not in the least fear
death' and 'calmly passed away'; the inscription on his tombstone
'was postponed until spring' (10,504,506). We could hardly find a
more succinct expression of Stepan Trofimovich's transformation at
the end of his last wandering than the closing lines of the epitaph on
Don Quixote's tombstone: 'He had the luck <. . .> to live a fool, and
yet die wise'.

In the following three years Dostoevsky published three 'fantastic'
stories, each a kind of modernised parable told by a first-person
narrator, two unnamed, whose particular point of view he uses to get
other perspectives on the biblical word.

BOBOK

The narrator of *Bobok*, a mediocre journalist, has lately been
haunted by 'not exactly voices, but as if someone nearby were saying
"*bobok, bobok, bobok*"' (*bobok* is 'a small bean') (21,43). Going out in
search of amusement, he happens upon a funeral, after which he
remains alone in the cemetery, a place bound to provoke reflections
on the afterlife. He suddenly becomes aware of an underground
conversation of the utmost banality going on amongst the recently
dead. All their earthly vanities have been transposed to their coffin
existence. A certain 'philosopher' among them explains the situation
thus: 'the remains of life are concentrated but only in consciousness,
life goes on as if by inertia for two or three months' (21,51). The
corpses agree to spend their last days of consciousness amusing
themselves by dispensing with all shame in their speech: 'Let's bare
ourselves! <. . .> The main thing is that no one can forbid us <. . .>
living [*zhizn'*] and lying [*lozh'*] are synonyms' (21,52). This is con-

fession as a cynical game, without repentance, without any consciousness of a higher 'voice' to whom one is accountable, a variation, as Bakhtin notes, on Dostoevsky's theme of 'everything is permitted if there is no God and immortality for the soul'.[25] The object of the author's satire is his contemporary rotten society populated by the living dead who, having lost all capacity for 'wonder', 'respect', and any sense of higher values or 'other worlds', profane every word they utter. One corpse in an advanced state of decomposition 'now about every six weeks will still suddenly mumble one word, of course, nonsensical, about some kind of *bobok*, but this means even in him life is still glimmering with an imperceptible spark' (21,51). We are here presented with the relentless distintegration of language, the final extinguishing of all words, human and divine. For these dead souls in the netherworld there is no redemption, no resurrection, only a limbo existence ending in decay, '*bobok*' and extinction.

But Dostoevsky does not allow the empty perspective of these underground dead souls to dominate as a metaphor for the absurdity of the human condition, an attitude which modernism has made all too familiar. For even here, among the voices in this chorus of cynical debauchery, one voice, that of a shopkeeper called 'simpleman', sounds quite a different note. In words couched in an archaic style studded with Church Slavonicisms and liturgical rhythms, he intermittently intones: 'before God's judgment [we] are equal in sins'; 'May our *sorokoviny* come quickly; then I shall hear tearful voices over me, my wife's lament and the soft weeping of my children'; 'verily the soul is going through the tribulations [*mytarstva*]' (21,45,46,53).[26] These reverent formulae from the Orthodox tradition manifest the simpleman's 'bond with the common people and their faith'.[27] He alone amidst this cynical company has retained the view of death as a sacrament ('*Smerti tainstvo*'); he alone sees his present predicament as a transitory passage to a higher existence (he awaits the *sorokoviny*), even though the macabre situation inevitably lends a note of black comedy to his words. Whilst these are not quotations of the Word *per se*, their origins in the Christian liturgy causes a shadow of the divine to move across the whole tale.

Crucial to Bakhtin's master concept of dialogism is his idea of the utterance as 'a real unit of speech communion'.[28] Every utterance has an author and presupposes a listener. Every individual's utterance signifies his or her semantic position which seeks a response.

Every utterance is an individual's unique, unrepeatable creation forming a link in a complex chain of utterances which simultaneously draws on past utterances and anticipates a new one. Consciousness, expressed in utterances (anticipation and response), is our connection to others, to the whole life of the word and to life; and in Dostoevsky, to the Word and thus to eternal life. In *Bobok* this chain is debased and almost ruptured. Here he imagines a situation in which words cease to be utterances, the repeated '*bobok*' to which all those corpses who have not taken the consciousness of God with them into the grave will soon be reduced, save the simpleman. '*Bobok*' would seem to be a sound cut off from any social communion, reduced to nonsense by compulsive repetition. These mutterings – appropriately emitted from an almost totally disembodied corpse who is apparently not responding to anyone or expecting any answer – cannot, it would seem, be a vehicle for the Word.

And yet, *bobok* is an utterance. For in Dostoevsky's poetic universe, as long as even 'a spark of life' is still glimmering, a person's word seeks to communicate to someone. Concealed in *bobok*, where the stress falls on the second syllable *-bok*, the first *bo-* being weakly articulated, is the word *Bog* (God), pronounced *Bok*. This suggests a reading of *Bobok* as a kind of parable built on an inversion of John (1,1): in the end there is no Word, hence no God; in the end *Bog* (*Bok*) is just *bo-bok*, a small bean. This further suggests that the corpse, now absolutely alone, all trivial words having fallen away, is struggling to call to God, but can only articulate *bobok*. He receives no answer. This *is* the ultimate hell; in Bakhtin's words 'there is nothing more terrible than a *lack of response*.'[29] No wonder the narrator leaves the cemetery, hoping to 'stumble across something comforting' (21,54.).[30] Lest this anticipation of modernism seem too fanciful, an English speaker, encountering Samuel Beckett's highly idiosyncratic 'Godot' in *Waiting for Godot*, could hardly help thinking of 'God', even without knowing that 'Goddot' is an archaic corruption of 'God wot' ('God knows'). But Beckett has no 'simpleman'.

THE MEEK ONE

As the narrator of *The Meek One* struggles to understand why his young wife killed herself only a few hours ago, he 'speaks to himself', says the author in his preface, 'but addresses, as it were, an invisible listener, a kind of judge' (24,6). From the hero's recollections it emerges that he drove her to suicide by his sadistic 'system' of using silence to break her spirit. To attempt to reduce a person to a voiceless object is a kind of murder. Only towards the end does he feel overcome by remorseful longing to make up to her for his maltreatment. Only then, sitting by her corpse, does he talk to her as he should have done when she was alive: 'Paradise was in my soul, I would have planted it around you!' (24,35). Feeling utterly alone, he meets only silence in response to his agonising questions. 'People on earth are alone <. . .> I shout <. . .> and no one answers. <. . .> They say the sun gives life to the universe <. . .> but look at it, isn't it a corpse? Everything is dead and everywhere there are the dead' (24,35). But in the last lines, as if in answer, the 'invisible listener, a kind of judge' finally speaks. The words 'People, love one another' drift into his consciousness. 'Who said it? Whose commandment is it?', he asks, and gives no answer (24,35). But the reader can. This is a quotation of Christ's commandment (John 15:12,17) which the hero has so fatally failed to live by. He cannot connect the word with the speaker because he has never acknowledged the truth or authority of another's word.[31] His silence was a barrier to keep others' words from his consciousness. 'I'm a master at speaking silently', he says, 'I have spent a lifetime speaking in silence and I have lived through tragedies by myself and in silence' (24,14). Thus, no one else's word could penetrate his heart. The story presents the tragic consequences of trying to live as a solitary consciousness without loving communion with others. This is the truth the hero now painfully begins to grasp. And the highest expression of that truth is Christ's commandment dialogically addressed to the hero's own consciousness. This is the truth Dostoevsky meant when he said that the hero's reminiscences 'irresistibly bring him at last to the truth (*pravda*); the truth irresistibly ennobles his heart and mind. The truth (*istina*) is revealed to the unfortunate man quite clearly and definitely, at least sufficiently for him himself' (24,5). In Dostoevsky's poetics, this is sufficient to open up at least a potential salvation.

THE DREAM OF A RIDICULOUS MAN

The narrator of the *Dream of a Ridiculous Man* proclaims at the outset that he alone has 'found the truth'. But before revealing it, he recounts the events which led him to it; his terminal indifference to life, his planned suicide, his meeting with the little girl who saved his life and his fantastic dream journey to an Edenic world. There, after an initial period of bliss, he tries to make the inhabitants of this paradise recapitulate salvation history. First he performs the role of Satan; he corrupts the innocent dwellers by teaching them 'to love the lie'. He thereby plunges their world into a strife-torn history which is a mirror image of earth's, almost. Horrified at his success and its terrible consequences, he then tries to play the role of Christ by pleading to be crucified, to no avail. Assailed by intolerable grief, yet he wakes up affirming life, convinced he has seen 'the living image of truth' which could direct the building of paradise on earth in 'one hour', and which he resolves at once to preach to the world. But he does not 'know how to convey it in words' because after his dream he 'lost the words' (25,118). However, he has found one person's word. The truth he has finally understood is 'an old truth', in fact, a quotation of Christ's second commandment (Mk. 12:31, Mat. 22:39): 'Love others as yourself <. . .> That's all' (25,119). He too does not identify the speaker, but what is a dawning apprehension for the narrator of *The Meek One*, is for the Ridiculous Man an assimilated truth. But the 'living image of truth' is not in the Edenic world. For the paradise he visited, and the history he brought into being by corrupting it, is without the unique event of Christ. Therefore the fallen paradise will never be redeemed. But the earth may, and this is why he returns regenerated. Implicit is the idea that he would rather be in this fallen world where the event of Christ has occurred than in a paradise without redemption and immortality. He would rather preach Christ's cardinal teaching on love in the here and now of our world because through it alone the world may be redeemed and heaven attained. For the paradise the Ridiculous Man visits lies in a pagan Golden Age of classical mythology, in a world completely severed from the biblical word. It is, in consequence, one of the most equivocal and melancholy of Dostoevsky's recurring motifs. Stavrogin (*The Devils*), the criminal, and Versilov (*The Adolescent*), the 'philosophical deist', relate an almost identical dream, but unlike them, the Ridiculous Man rejects the Golden Age and makes the transition to the Word as a revelation of truth. As Bakhtin remarks of this tale, 'what dominates <. . .> is not the Christian but the ancient spirit'.[32] Indeed, it is a Golden Age fantasy, modernised with scientific and socialist utopian elements, that Ivan Karamazov composed and which the devil quotes back at him in mockery.

THE BROTHERS KARAMAZOV

The Brothers Karamazov is saturated with the biblical word. Here we consider Ivan, who, in his struggle with the biblical word, commands what is arguably the most subtle range of the double-voiced word in Dostoevsky's fiction.

The first erosion of Ivan's openly expressed convictions takes place during the family gathering in Father Zosima's cell. After hearing Ivan's theory of 'all is permitted', Zosima counsels Ivan through the biblical word; they are the most important words about Ivan in the novel:

For the time being from despair you too amuse yourself with magazine articles and worldly arguments, yourself not believing your dialectic and with pain in your heart mocking at it to yourself. In you this question [faith or atheism] is not decided and in this is your great grief <. . .> But thank the Creator that He gave you a higher heart capable of suffering such torment, 'set your thoughts on heavenly [*gornii*] things, seek heavenly things, for our dwelling is in heaven'. (Phil. 3:20, Col. 3:2) (14,65–66)

Had Ivan accepted Zosima's word, there would have been no murder. Which is to say, had Ivan set his thoughts on heavenly things, he would have been able to counter the evil within and, thus strengthened, overcome the evil tempting him from without.[33] But later, after the murder, Ivan is no longer amusing himself with 'worldly arguments', nor is Smerdyakov devising Jesuitical travesties of the Bible. During their last meeting, Smerdyakov, in a state of suicidal despair, has grown sick of the 'comedy' of playing the clever man's game of talking in hints, and Ivan is compelled at last to face the truth. We consider the moment just after Smerdyakov openly accuses Ivan:

– You are the main murderer <. . .> I did it following your word <. . .> Ivan turned cold <. . .> Something seemed to explode in his brain and he began to shiver all over with a cold quivering <. . .> – You know what: I'm afraid that you're a dream, that you're a phantom sitting before me.
– There's no phantom here, sir, only us two, sir, – and a certain third person. Without doubt he's right here now, that third person, he's here between the two of us.
– Who is he? Who's here? Who is the third person?', Ivan Fyodorovich said, frightened, looking around, his eyes hastily searching for some one in all the corners.
– This third person – is God, sir, it is Providence itself, sir, it's right here now beside us, only don't you look for it, you won't find it.

– You were lying, [when you said] that you killed [him]!, – furiously yelled Ivan. (15,59–60)

Here, in a totally unexpected reversal, Smerdyakov feels 'the presence of the living God', whereas for Ivan the 'third person' is the devil.[34] However, after Ivan has heard all the details from Smerdyakov and the truth has become incontrovertible, he himself, for the first and only time, directly appeals to that 'third person' invoked by Smerdyakov. Vowing to take him with him to 'answer' in court, Ivan shouts, raising his hand upwards: 'God sees <. . .> maybe I was guilty too, maybe I really had a secret wish that . . . father would die, but I swear to you I was not as guilty as you think, and maybe I didn't incite you at all' (15,66–67). And so it turns out that God is not so far away, that He is not indifferent, that He has not absconded into the infinitely remote regions of non-Euclidean space, but is right there, 'between the two' of them. The revelation of the truth coincides with an awareness of God's presence. The author's irony is not at the expense of God, but of the two participants in murder who now express a belief quite contrary to the ideas they asserted before the murder. And this is not because they are the victims of the tragic irony of circumstances beyond their control. Rather it is a criminal tragedy they talked themselves into, but one which proves impossible to talk themselves out of. Forced to acknowledge a higher instance to whom they are accountable, their belief in the immunity of clever men to moral judgment is shattered. This is what Bakhtin calls a 'hidden dialogue' in which there is an invisible speaker whose word, while not reproduced, deeply influences the word of the present speakers. The 'third person' does not speak, but the consciousness of His presence 'right here now beside' them, of His judging word, structures this whole dialogue.

The primary meaning of *logos* is 'account' or 'reckoning', and thus presupposes a higher witness and judge. As soon as a witness and a judge appear, says Bakhtin, the whole sense of human existence changes radically.[35] What one is conscious of does not coincide with all that is conscious. The surplus of consciousness belongs to the witness and judge of the whole person whom Bakhtin calls the 'supra-person' (*nadchelovek*), or the 'supra-I' (*nad-ia*). In Dostoevsky's poetics, such a persective can only belong to God. Calling on God as his witness, Ivan implicitly acknowledges Him as his ultimate standard of truth and judgment and repudiates his idea that 'everything is permitted'. However, the consciousness of God's presence lasts only a moment. Instead of going at once to the police, Ivan, still drawn to the diabolic, goes home to meet his devil. The question of his guilt is not resolved so easily or directly.

When Ivan says he is not as guilty as Smerdyakov thinks, he is right. Smerdyakov fatally misreads him because, as Kantor and Emerson point out, he is incapable of seeing Ivan's noble qualities; or, in Bakhtin's terms, of hearing that 'first voice' in Ivan's inner dialogue which really does not wish for his father's death and is deeply repelled by Smerdyakov's villainy.[36] Nevertheless, when Ivan says 'maybe I was guilty too', he is also right. The whole story of the parricide is structured to implicate Ivan in the murder, to show that he is 'guilty too', psychologically and ideologically.[37] The very fact that Ivan judges himself 'a scoundrel' when he abandons his father and suffers torments after his murder is evidence both of his participation in the crime and of his 'deep conscience'. It is an established legal principle that those who know that a murder will be committed and, being in no danger themselves, do nothing to prevent it but, what is more, clear the way for its commission by removing themselves from the scene, and subsequently promise to keep quiet about suspicious facts, are considered accessories to the crime, not to speak of morally culpable. All of this applies to Ivan, and it is virtually impossible to prove in a court. Only Ivan can know this in his conscience whose workings are in essence dialogic, struggling between the contending voices of Alyosha and Smerdyakov, his 'angel' and devil.

What makes Ivan vulnerable to Smerdyakov's manipulation is his contemptuous hatred for his father and his brother Mitya, and his wish that Mitya bring about Fyodor's death. Ivan's ideas may be undecided, but there is nothing indefinite about his lethal hatred; it is intensely felt, violently expressed and noticed by others besides Smerdyakov.[38] Of Mitya, he exclaims: 'I hate the monster <. . .> let him rot in hard labour!' (15,88). After his first conversation with Smerdyakov, he turns to Alyosha for 'the truth': 'But didn't you think then that I was precisely wishing for "viper to eat viper" – that is, precisely for Dmitry to kill father, and the sooner the better . . . and that I myself was not even against helping it along?' Alyosha replies: 'Forgive me, I did' (15,49). The very wish for another's death, and for 'precisely' another to do the killing, is in Christianity deemed a sin. For Ivan to 'permit' Smerdyakov or to 'help' Mitya carry out his own murderous wish, even though only part of him wished for Fyodor's death, is by any ethical standards base. And Ivan knows it, though he does not want to see it. Ivan's desire to remain '*internally* uninvolved' in his own deeply held evil wishes without incurring any 'external' involvement is, as Dostoevsky meant to show, a dangerous self delusion.[39] Ivan's refusal to be his brother's keeper, to live by one of the novel's central biblical precepts, to be concerned about those near to him and not only those who are dead, far away or unknown to him, is an inalienable factor in the tragedy. Fyodor *is* a bad father, but this does not mean that he deserves to be murdered.[40] On the contrary, the love Alyosha inspires in Fyodor is an eloquent counter example to Ivan's hatred and contempt. The Christian injunction to love one's neighbour, no matter how unworthy, is as close to a categorical imperative that Dostoevsky comes. It also applies on a larger scale.

Dostoevsky was convinced that Russia's Europeanised atheist intelligentsia was corrupting its semi-literate, half-educated compatriots (the Smerdyakovs) with nihilistic, hence demonic ideas alien to Russian values. Nothing compromises a general idea more than the proof that it has led to a 'catastrophe'. If Smerdyakov was seeking a rationale to avenge his own resentments, Ivan irresponsibly supplied it with his talk of 'there is no virtue' and 'everything is permitted if there is no God or immortality'. True, Ivan does not really want to believe in his idea, but others may. True, he did not and would not kill, but others will, and some of them are not as stupid as he (and the intelligentsia) think. Dostoevsky was intent on establishing a tight connection between nihilistic ideas and social mayhem, on showing that one cannot amuse oneself with nihilism without courting disaster. The Smerdyakovs of the world will pick it up and run with it.

And what of Smerdyakov? He is indeed despicable, but even his story has tragic elements and multilevelled meanings in which the biblical word plays a shaping role. Disillusioned to despair with Ivan's word, Smerdyakov has evidently been seeking a higher word for guidance. Esaulov draws attention to the significance of what was apparently Smerdyakov's last reading, *The Homilies of Our Holy Father Isaac the Syrian*, and pertinently remarks that Smerdyakov's soul right up to his suicide also becomes a 'battlefield' where 'the devil struggles with God'.[41] Indeed, if he remained nothing but a thoroughgoing lackey, why did he not take the three thousand roubles for which he killed and with which, he says 'in a trembling voice', he had hoped to fulfil his 'dream' of begining life in Moscow, or abroad, and clear out? (15,67). Evidently, even Smerdyakov cannot 'begin life' on blood money. The Word, which he used to mock, has apparently sufficiently penetrated his soul to reveal to him the evil within. However, he has not the spiritual resources to overcome it, nor can he live with it any longer, and so he condemns himself to death. As Esaulov suggests, behind the story of Smerdyakov lies the shadow of Judas. Like Judas he betrays his master for money (the three thousand roubles are a poetic equivalent of the biblical thirty pieces of silver), devises a prearranged 'sign' (Mt. 26:15), rids himself of the 'price of blood', and hangs himself in despair if not with remorse (Mt. 27:3–8). Utterly alone, he now realises that Ivan, the only person he 'took it in his head to respect', whose 'praise' he sought, loathes him: 'you considered me a midge' and 'not a human being' (14,122,118) (15,67). Smerdyakov's resemblance to the Grand Inquisitor has been noted by others. Perhaps, had Ivan imitated his own Christ figure and not contaminated his word by entangling it with Smerdyakov's, but offered love instead, Smerdyakov would never have become a murderer.

This is just what Ivan cannot do. The reason for his reservations may be sought in his ambiguous attitude to Christ, most graphically portrayed in his Grand Inquisitor poem, though in fact it is implied in all his words.[42] Ivan, in his pride, composes his own heretical text which he uses, through his Inquisitor, to put Christ to the sharpest *anacrisis* in modern fiction in order to expose the ineffectualness of His word in the face of human weakness and history.[43] In so doing, Ivan stresses His human nature, presenting an essentially kenotic Christ. However, too exclusive an emphasis on Christ's kenosis, by which He voluntarily renounced His divine nature (Phil. 2:7), easily leads to a humanised Jesus, to the great man or idealist typical of nineteenth-century thought, and consequently to a negation of Christianity. The core question tormenting Ivan is: if Christ was only human, then there can be no God nor immortality, and then the world is nothing but a 'devilish chaos' (14,209). Thus, Ivan cannot set his thoughts on heavenly things, only on earthly evils. Hence, Alyosha's sorrowful query 'How will you live, with what will you love <. . .> With such a hell in your heart and head is it possible?' (14,239). This is because Ivan approaches the Word intellectually, as an idea refuted by historical evidence, and not dynamically, as God ever present in the Logos, independently of historical contingencies. Theologically the Word is understood to comprise a thought subject to reason as well as a dynamic energy felt by those who readily receive it; the Word manifests its truth by its power to transform the lives of those who actively appropriate it. For Ivan, the Word has no power to transform one's life on earth, no further revelations to offer. His invention of a silent Christ-like figure may indicate his respect for what He has already said, but it also imprisons His Word in history, seals off it from the future.[44] Unlike Marmeladov, Ivan has no personal Christ to Whom he speaks and Who speaks to him; he can only speak about Him, which is to say, Ivan, lacking humility and gratitude, cannot pray. If Christ was only human, prayer is useless, if not absurd. The Word Incarnate is a moving reminiscence, but not a present power, though he wishes it were. This is why he cannot establish a relationship with Christ, only with Jesus, morally triumphant but hopelessly earthbound, defeated again by worldly powers.

Yet, Ivan's 'higher heart' subtly defeats the intention of his intellect. In silence (molchanie), notes Bakhtin, 'somebody does not speak', which is to say, silence presupposes the presence of a person.[45] Silence, word and pause constitute a 'special logosphere', an 'open (unfinalised) totality'. The Grand Inquisitor strives to occupy all verbal space, to silence his Prisoner, as he bombards Him with his accusatory words. But the Inquisitor's words do not consititute the whole logosphere of Ivan's poem. The silence of Christ is an extraordinarily pregnant silence, laden with the words He has already spoken. It is a silence 'fraught' with the 'background' of the Logos-sphere which evokes an overwhelming, multifaceted sense of His presence. Over this sphere Ivan and his fantasy Inquisitor have no control. Readers familiar with the Gospels will be creatively swept into the dialogue by supplying, through memory, Christ's words and acts, which is to say, they will be stimulated to use their own interpretations of the Logos to answer the Inquisitor. Moreover, the very fact that the Inquisitor addresses Him as 'Thou', that he avidly seeks His responsive understanding, that after a lifetime of lying, he freely and trustingly reveals himself to Him alone, creates a sphere of intimate contact which subtly undermines his overt, ideological harangue. It is in these ways that Ivan's poem becomes a work, as Alyosha says, 'in praise of Jesus, and not a reviling' of Him (14,237). The logosphere created by the Inquisitor and Christ constitutes Ivan's internal dialogue, wavering between faith and atheism.

When the novel ends, the 'decision' of Ivan's 'heart' hangs in the balance. However, Zosima has divined in him a great spiritual potential. It was evident in his early youth, in the 'anecdote' he composed about the atheist philosopher who, after death was condemned for aeons to 'walk in darkness' to paradise, but after one glimpse of the stupendous vision, cried 'Hosannah'. The Voltairian overtones are unmistakable, but so are the biblical reminiscences (Is. 9:2, Jn. 8:12) and the heavenly direction of his aspirations. Later, it emerges in his impassioned preoccupation with questions of faith, suffering and justice in his dialogues with Alyosha, his young Christ-like brother whom he cannot help loving. To paraphrase Zosima, if Ivan cannot yet accept Christ in his head, he will never reject Him in his heart. In Dostoevsky's poetics, therein lies his salvation.

Alyosha's encounter with the biblical word is transformational. While praying by Zosima's coffin, Alyosha hears Father Paisy reading the miracle at Cana of Galilee in liturgical Church Slavonic. 'I love that passage', he says (14,326). As the sonorous ancient words, ever new, speak to his young soul, all the hatreds and dissonant words rending the Karamazov world recede and give way to serene joy, to a dream which culminates in the appearance of the resurrected Zosima in heaven, pointing to the radiant vision of 'our Sun' (14,327). For Alyosha, the Jesus Who celebrated the wedding at Cana is the same as the Christ Who invites everyone to the banquet in heaven. In his hero's experience, Dostoevsky presents Jesus Christ in the fullness of His Godhead, fully human and divine, conjoining earth and heaven. After glimpsing the beatific vision, Alyosha takes possession of his true voice and goes 'into the world'. Here, rarely, irony is transcended by the sublime as the secular language of modern times achieves dialogic harmony with the sacred language of the biblical word.

CONCLUDING REMARKS

Seeking to forearm Alyosha Karamazov against the 'learned ones of this world' who, by their 'cruel analysis' are demolishing 'the holy books bequeathed from heaven', Father Paisy proclaims:

Meanwhile, the whole stands before their eyes unshakeable as before and the gates of hell shall not prevail against it <. . .> Even in <. . .> the souls of those very atheists who have destroyed everything, it lives on as before, unshakeable. For those who have renounced Christianity and rebelled against it <. . .> are of the same image of Christ, such they have remained, for to this day neither their wisdom nor the ardour of their heart have been able create another higher image for man and his dignity than the image shown in ancient times by Christ. (14,155–56)

This may be taken as a concise expression of a belief which informs Dostoevsky's entire post-Siberian oeuvre. Indeed, the most extraordinary thing about the biblical word in Dostoevsky is that it remains what it is, 'unshakeable', that it retains its semantic integrity and distinctive features. How is it that the biblical word does not become denatured or dissolve in the predominant double-voiced discourse? We may attempt several answers.

Dostoevsky's feeling for the dynamic aspect of the Logos was exceptionally strong, as was his gift for making it a living rejoinder in the great dialogue of his works.[46] He never seals off the biblical word from other words, from the life depicted in his works, but makes everyone, from deniers to affirmers, respond to that word, thus maximising its sphere of contacts and opening it up to further development, and further revelations. Dostoevsky disseminates his characters' and his own deeply subjective responses to Christianity through every word he writes, turning them into the utterances of their internal and spoken dialogues. In Bakhtin's terms, Dostoevsky aimed to reanimate the authoritative word of conventional Christianity, grown calcified through formulaic repetition, by making it internally persuasive, and thus authoritative at a deeper level of psychological and spiritual complexity. He never objectifies the biblical word, he never reifies it as an inert specimen of typical features, as a word impenetrable to other's meanings, intentions and aspirations. Nor is it ever the passive, mute object of the author's superior understanding. The biblical word becomes a life-giving word for there is no renewal in Dostoevsky except through that Word. All the high turning points in his characters' spiritual dramas pivot on affirmative responses to the canonical words and acts of Christ. Dostoevsky consistently follows the Christian conception of the Logos: to encounter the truth in Christ leads to a transformation by which one turns away from old lies and orients one's life to the Word. When the truth of the biblical word, usually as a quotation, penetrates the consciousnesses of his charcters, their lives begin to change. As they assimilate it to their own inner words, they feel the need to acknowledge their lies and wrongdoings, to forgive their enemies. In consequence, their words about themselves, about others and the world become truer, more honest. (This never happens in *The Idiot*.) Since the hero's insight into the truth about himself coincides with his apprehension of the truth of the biblical word, we receive a doubly reinforced sense of truth. The truth of the person merges with and verifies the truth of the Logos which, in turn, ennobles and magnifies as it humbles and chastens. To make way for the true word, lies must be acknowledged and expunged. This can happen because, according to Dostoevsky, the Logos, of which Christ is the Incarnation, is in everyone, even the most unlikely persons; one has only to discover Him. All the major crises in his fiction are designed to lead to this discovery.

In *Crime and Punishment* the Word never enters Raskolnikov's consciousness as revealed truth through an open dialogic exchange. We may infer its influence when he asks Sonya to read the Lazarus miracle. But it is Sonya's love and not the Word *per se* which is most decisive. This may account for a certain lack of convincingness about his 'resurrection'. In *The Idiot*, the *living* Word is absent. By the 1870s, beginning with *The Devils*, Dostoevsky is moving more boldly in the direction of introducing the Word directly into his characters' consciousnesses which, with great subtlety, he turns into scenes of dialogic interaction between the human and divine words.

According to Christian theology, when we speak the word of God, God is with us. Similarly, when Dostoevsky's characters speak the biblical word, His presence is evoked (from quotations to hidden dialogues). As a result, they enter the Logos-sphere and their words acquire a significance larger than themselves. Even when the Logos merely hovers on the edge of consciousness as a vaguely remembered word, it exerts an exceptional power, and always in the direction of its own meaning. Double-voiced discourse (irony, parody) is inherently ambivalent, and thus semantically unstable. This is why the biblical word can never be finalised by an ironic word. But the converse does not hold. The ironisers of the highest truth themselves become ironised by the irresistible claims of that truth. Only the Logos offered Dostoevsky an unassailibly serious word from which one can at critical moments 'cast off irony'.[47] Those who try to live without it, to undermine or destroy it, to change its essence, are either compromised or meet with tragedy. However, despair is never absolute in Dostoevsky; inscribed in all his works (minimally in *The Idiot*) is a saving Grace whose source is always the biblical word.[48] Dostoevsky consistently aligns his characters' highest aspirations towards divining the biblical word. Acutely listening to the logos-sphere in which we live, he discerned the utterances of the Logos-sphere to which he makes the human word ultimately answerable. The final aim of his dialogues is to bring his characters into a dia-Logos.

Whenever we respond dialogically to an utterance, we personify the one who uttered it.[49] For Dostoevsky the Logos is personified since Christ is the Logos Incarnate. Because he composes such a wide diapason of responses to Christ, the richest, most various image of Him builds up within each work and across Dostoevsky's entire post-Siberian oeuvre: from the suffering Christ at the Crucifixion to the raiser of the dead and the merciful Judge at the Last Judgment, Christ, emptied of His divinity, Whose suffering was for nought in an irredeemably fallen world, Christ the teacher and healer of the demoniac, Christ as a faint reminiscence bringing hope in the grave, Christ the bearer of the message of love, Christ, reduced to His human nature and defeated by secular powers, and Christ in Glory presiding over the joyous feast in heaven. The works of Dostoevsky comprise the greatest body of representations of Christ in modern fiction. Despite all the batterings of polemic, distortion, parody and irony, the Logos glimmers through in its inviolable holiness, intermittently penetrating the fraught medium of discordant voices like a shaft of light, illuminating it from within. I do not know of a single writer since who has achieved this.

NOTES

1 M. M. Bakhtin, 'From notes written in 1970–71', *Speech Genres and Other Late Essays*, trans. Vern M. McGee, ed. Caryl Emerson and Michael Holquist (Austin, TX, 1986), 132.
2 Bakhtin, *Speech Genres*, 132–33.
3 *Ibid.*, 126.
4 On the natural carnivalicity of the Gospels, see the chapter, 'Christian motifs in Bakhtin's carnival writings', in Ruth Coates's *Christianity in Bakhtin: God and the Exiled Author* (Cambridge, 1998), 126–51.
5 See Alexandar Mihailovic's observations on the christological motifs of carnival in *Corporeal Words: Mikhail Bakhtin's Theology of Discourse* (Evanston, IL, 1997), especially 15 and 184–86.

6 See Erich Auerbach, 'Sermo Humilis', in *Literary Language and its Public in Late Latin Antiquity and in The Middle Ages*, trans. Ralph Manheim (Princeton, NJ, 1993) (27–66), 35–36.

7 David Bethea in *The Shape of the Apocalypse in Modern Russian Fiction* (Princeton, NJ, 1989) and Robert Hollander in 'The apocalyptic framework of Dostoevsky's *The Idiot*', *Mosaic*, 6 (1974), 123–39, making a somewhat different emphasis from mine, find the Apocalypse to be the shaping subtext of the novel.

8 Julia Kristeva, *Black Sun: Depression and Melancholia*, trans. Leon S. Roudiez (New York, 1989), 112–13, 115. Robert Louis Jackson makes some strong but different points on the relationship of images to the religious in *Dialogues with Dostoevsky: The Overwhelming Questions* (Stanford, CA, 1993), 52–53.

9 Jostein Børtnes, 'Dostoevskij's idiot or the poetics of emptiness', *Scando-Slavica*, 40 (1994), 5–14, 13.

10 Peter Stern similarly argues that Myshkin is a defective *imitatio*, for his meekness is 'unsupported by an equal spiritual strength'. See J. Peter Stern, *On Realism* (London, 1973), 16, 18.

11 As Robin Miller has shown, even the narrator gradually gives up on his hero. See Chapter 4 in her study *Dostoevsky and 'The Idiot'* (Cambridge, MA; London, 1981).

12 Børtnes, *Ibid.*, 10–11.

13 Joseph Frank makes a similar point in his *Dostoevsky: The Miraculous Years, 1865–1871* (Princeton, NJ, 1995); see especially 341.

14 Børtnes, *Ibid.*, 13

15 Dostoevsky pronounced Renan's book 'full of atheism' (21,11). See also (9,396–99).

16 See Bakhtin on 'the search' for a word 'larger' than oneself in M. M. Bakhtin, *Estetika slovesnogo tvorchestva* (Moscow, 1979), 354.

17 Riccardo Picchio, 'The function of biblical thematic clues in the literary code of "Slavia Orthodoxa"', *Slavica Hierosolymitana*, 1 (Jerusalem, 1977), 1–31, pp. 5, 9.

18 Bakhtin, *Speech Genres*, 159–60.

19 Mitya Karamazov makes the same transit through classical Greek and German pre-Romanticism to the biblical word. See my *'The Brothers Karamazov' and the Poetics of Memory* (Cambridge, 1991), 275–77.

20 Jostein Børtnes, 'The last delusion in an infinite series of delusions: Stavrogin and the symbolic structure of *The Devils*', *Dostoevsky Studies*, 4 (1983), 60.

21 See Eric Ziolkowski's discussion on the relationship between Don Quixote and Myshkin in this volume.

22 Relevant studies on the picaresque novel are: Alexander A. Parker, *Literature and the Delinquent: The Picaresque Novel in Spain and Europe, 1599–1753* (Edinburgh, 1967); Hans Gerd Rötzer, *Picaro-Landstörtzer-Simplicius* (Darmstadt, 1972); and Goffredo Jommi, *Realität der irrealen*

Dichtung: Don Quijote und Dante (Hamburg, 1964). I thank Jostein Børtnes for drawing my attention to these sources and for discussing this theme with me.

23 Quotations are taken from the edition: Miguel de Cervantes, *Don Quixote*, trans. J. M. Cohen (Harmondsworth, 1950), 935–39.

24 *Ibid.*, 59–60.

25 M. Bakhtin, *Problems of Dostoevsky's Poetics*, ed. and trans. Caryl Emerson (Minneapolis, MN, 1984), 144.

26 The *sorokoviny* are the prayers offered for the remembrance of the dead forty days after their death at which time they enter a new existence. The *mytarstva* are the trials by evil spirits the soul undergoes as, spiritually purified, it ascends heavenwards.

27 Bakhtin, *Problems of Dostoevsky's Poetics*, 145.

28 Bakhtin, *Speech Genres*, 67.

29 *Ibid.*, 127.

30 Similarly, Raskolnikov, after hearing Svidrigailov's black fantasy of eternity as a filthy bathhouse hung with spider webs, exclaims: 'couldn't you think of something more comforting and more just than that!' (6,221).

31 Bakhtin puts essentially the same point: 'he does not acknowledge any higher judgment on himself'. *Problems of Dostoevsky's Poetics*, 154.

32 *Ibid.*, 149. As Robin Miller notes, 'we can see a biblical (and Christmas) resonance to the bright star that leads the ridiculous man' to the '"poor child"' and to salvation'. Robin Feuer Miller, 'Dostoevsky's "The Dream of a Ridiculous Man"': Unsealing the Generic Envelope', *Freedom and Responsibility in Russian Literature: Essays in Honor of Robert Louis Jackson*, ed. Elizabeth Cheresh Allen and Gary Saul Morson (Evanston, IL, 1995), 99.

33 See Vladimir Kantor's insightful analysis of temptation in this volume.

34 See Ivan Esaulov's discussion in this volume. Ivan's looking 'in all the corners of the room' for the 'third person' chimes with Lise Khokhlakova's dream in which devils lurk 'in all the corners' of her room ready to seize her (15,23). Ivan, with whom she shares the opinion that everyone 'secretly loves it' that his father was killed, has exacerbated her derangement (15,23). See my article, 'Lise Khokhlakova: *shalunja/ besenok'*, *O Rus!: Studia litteraria slavica in honourem Hugh McLean* (Oakland, CA, 1995), 281–92.

35 Bakhtin, *Speech Genres*, 137–38.

36 See Kantor, *ibid.*, and Caryl Emerson's incisive pinpointing of the fundamental issues he raises in her 'Translator's afterword'. In fact, Bakhtin says that Smerdyakov hears only Ivan's second voice, the one that wishes for his father's death. See Bakhtin, *Problems of Dostoevsky's Poetics*, 258.

37 See Dostoevsky's letter quoted in Kantor's chapter where he states that Ivan 'saw and had a clear presentiment of' the 'evil deed' Smerdyakov

was planning, but 'intentionally' refrained from 'clearly and categorically' expressing his revulsion.

38 As V. E. Vetlovskaya rightly points out, Ivan's hostility towards others has reached almost 'pathological proportions'. *Poetika romana 'Brat'ia Karamazovy'* (Leningrad, 1977), 75–76. See also her sharp analysis of Ivan on pages 84–85.

39 In Bakhtin's words, Ivan wishes to 'remain not only externally but even *internally* uninvolved in' the murder. *Problems of Dostoevsky's Poetics*, 258–59.

40 Vetlovskaya makes a similar observation, *ibid.*, 113.

41 Esaulov, *ibid.* See also Victor Terras's perceptive comments in *A Karamazov Companion* (Madison, WI, 1981), notes 257, 383, pp. 382 and 384 respectively.

42 An analysis of Ivan's flawed image of Christ can be found in my study on memory in *The Brothers Karamazov, ibid.*, chapter 8.

43 The heretical nature of Ivan's discourse has been elucidated by Ellis Sandoz in *Political Apocalypse: Dostoevsky's Grand Inquisitor* (Baton Rouge, LA, 1971) and Nina Perlina in *Varieties of Poetic Utterance: Quotation in 'The Brothers Karamazov'* (Lanham, 1985).

44 Malcolm V. Jones gives a different gloss to this silence in his article 'Silence in *The Brothers Karamazov, 'Die Brüder Karamasow': Dostojewskis letzter Roman in heutiger Sicht,* ed. Horst-Jürgen Gerigk (Dresden, 1997), 29–46.

45 Bakhtin distinguishes silence (*molchanie*) from quietude (*tishina*) where 'nothing makes a sound'. *Speech Genres*, 133–34.

46 Dostoevsky's dialogic art has deep roots in the Christian tradition. Commenting on the Christian style of oratory, Auerbach notes the 'directness' with which it 'speak[s] to each individual soul', and 'its power to express human brotherhood'. Auerbach, '*Sermo Humilis*', 53, 57.

47 Bakhtin, *Speech Genres*, 147.

48 See Ivan Esaulov's paper in this volume on the primacy of Grace in Dostoevsky's poetics.

49 In Bakhtin's words: 'A dialogic reaction personifies every utterance to which it responds.' *Problems of Dostoevsky's Poetics*, 184.

Dostoevsky and Christian theology

CHAPTER 5

Dostoevsky in the prism of the orthodox semiosphere

Avril Pyman

One of the most astute and enlightened Orthodox readers of Dostoevsky wrote of him in the 1930s:

> Dostoevsky dreamt of Russian socialism, but what he saw was a 'Russian
> monk'. And that monk had neither the intention nor the wish to build
> 'world harmony'; he was in no way a builder within the historical process.
> It is clear, therefore, <. . .> that Dostoevsky's dream did not coincide with
> Dostoevsky's vision. Dostoevsky's place in the history of Russian philosophy
> belongs to him not because he worked out a philosophical system, but
> because he opened up and deepened actual metaphysical experience <. . .>
> and Dostoevsky shows more than he argues.[1]

To read Dostoevsky religiously it is not 'necessary to put everything
in its proper place so that everything can be reconciled' as,
according to Sergei Averintsev, the Neo-Thomist 'theology of art'
tends to do.[2] Dostoevsky is no Dante, but a nineteenth-century
writer whose 'dreams' are influenced not by Christian theology but
by secular European Utopianism and Romanticism, though his
vision and his 'metaphysical experience' are Christian and, indeed,
in many ways specifically Russian Orthodox Christian. One can
only accept these contradictions, and work from within the paradox.

Most great art reflects the world as chaos and this is particularly
evident in Russian art. Dostoevsky, in his novels, reflects religious
dereliction and aspiration and is capable of 'showing' profound
insights, 'metaphysical experience', even Grace, but these are seen
from within 'the sphere of our sorrows', glimpses not to be
reassembled according to any all-embracing concept of hierarchy
and order. In his notebooks for 1880–81, Dostoevsky speaks of his
'Hosannah', having passed through a furnace of doubt (27,86). I
think, however, that one has to accept that, throughout his life in
literature, this furnace was kept well stoked. After all, if we are to
believe Ivan Karamazov's devil,

they don't want to let me in on the secret, because if they did I dare say that, having cottoned on to what was really happening, I might forget myself and yell 'Hosannah!' and then the essential minus would disappear and good sense would prevail throughout the world and that would be the end of everything, even newspapers and journals, because who the hell would want to subscribe to them any more? (15,28)

Again and again, Dostoevsky's characters pronounce their 'Hosannah' or strike up their underground hymn, and again and again their songs of praise are drowned out by the thunder of history, stamped back into earth by jack-booted realism, extinguished by doubt. His gift, almost unique in secular literature, is that the reader remembers and cherishes and wants the 'Hosannah' but, because 'Hosannah' belongs to Eternity and Art to time, it can neither be retained and possessed within the context of Dostoevsky's writing, nor can it be entirely isolated from that context. It is necessary to accept both the Hosannah and the furnace, or, of course, to seek the Hosannah beyond literature.

There is, however, a different way of reading Dostoevsky religiously. The attempt is made, with increasing frequency, to apply to the novels a decoding strategy based on Eastern Orthodox semiotics.[3] Whereas it was at one time accepted wisdom in literary criticism that 'all we have is the text', in recent years the late Yuri Lotman's creative thinking about the 'semiosphere' has restored the cultural environment and the 'sign-system' as a legitimate field of study.[4] To define the semiosphere of Dostoevsky's novels is, however, a delicate process. As for the majority of nineteenth-century Russians, the objects, traditions, bedside books, manners and customs which surrounded Dostoevsky in his youth and first triggered the associative process of his authorial imagination were polygenic. The researcher has to take into account layer after layer of entangled 'sign-systems' without damaging or dismissing any in the process. A roughly formed semiotic master-key will thus give access to the outer rooms only. No literary tool is an open sesame.

Before interpreting works of Russian secular literature on the assumption that they were written by and for people fully conversant with the semiotics of Orthodox theology as expressed through ecclesiastical art, liturgical text and the formulations of the Creed (the 'Symbol of Faith' in Russian), scholars should make sure that such familiarity truly existed and, if it did, among which classes of the population, at what stages of the authors' intellectual development, at what specific periods of Russian history? There is a tendency to stress the differences between 'Eastern' and 'Western' mentality and to draw lines either along the Germano-Slavic divide, or (more acceptable to some because less overtly racist) along the Eastern borders of Lithuania, Poland, the old Austro-Hungarian Empire and Croatia, where Roman-Catholicism gives way to Eastern Orthodoxy (whether Greek, Serbian, Bulgarian, Romanian or 'of all the Russias') and beyond which, until comparatively recently in European history, dominion was held not even by the Orthodox, but by a pagan or, later, Muslim, non-European East. Generalisation about spiritual geography should be rigorously sifted. All boundaries of the spirit should be tested at every step. In art we have a language which leaps such boundaries. Literature, although trammelled by language, is also a form developed from earliest time through a process of cross pollination and grafting and through translation. In the case of Russian Orthodoxy this process was initiated when Cyrill and Methodius received the blessing of Rome on their mission to the Slavs and began the labour of translating the Greek text and, before that again, when the Hebrew and Aramaic Scriptures were rendered into Greek and Latin and the early church adopted these languages.

Nevertheless there is now a growing tendency in Western analysis of Russian literature to attempt a 'theological' semiotic approach by stressing such features of Eastern Christian Orthodox worship as the veneration of icons, the emphasis Orthodox tend to place on Incarnation, Transfiguration and Resurrection (that is on contemplating the cosmic majesty and kenosis of Christ rather than on expounding His moral teaching), and the tendency to make more of 'image' than of 'likeness'. One corollary of this last concept is 'Godmanhood' (important in the thought of Dostoevsky's younger friend and interpreter Vladimir Solovyov, where it appears as the religious answer to the fascination of Nietzsche's superman or of Dostoevsky's 'man-god'). There is also much discussion of the Aristotelian term, 'mimesis', and whether this should be taken to mean the willed 'imitation of Christ' or the 'passive' '*stiazhanie Dukha Sviatogo*', the ascetic endeavour to become the vessel of the Holy Spirit and thus to resemble Christ inwardly. The first is sometimes thought of as 'Western', the second as 'Eastern' Christianity, but the active and the passive ways have surely been held legitimate throughout the history of Christendom.

The question we have to examine, then, is how Orthodox was Dostoevsky, the writer? The sinful man and believing Christian soul is not our province. It is legitimate, however, to look carefully at the cultural environment of an author educated in the home of a Moscow doctor and at the Military Engineering Academy in St Petersburg in the second quarter of the nineteenth century. It is also legitimate to ask how Orthodox was his reading public? How Orthodox, for example, were the critic Vissarion Belinsky and the publisher Nikolai Nekrasov, who discovered Dostoevsky at the outset of his career and whose approbation confirmed him in his rejection of the safe job of draftsman-engineer for which he qualified in 1843? Was it natural for the young author to regard men and women as icons or, for that matter, to regard icons as works of art which might inspire even the secular artist to catch at some refraction of the divine?

The answer to these questions would appear to be no, at least not entirely. Possibly influenced by a gentle and devout mother, Dos-toevsky early conceived a personal devotion to Jesus Christ which outlasted and outshone his doubts as to His divinity.[5] Yet for most of his life the great novelist seems to have been a man of the Book rather than of the Church.

Of course, Dostoevsky was brought up as an Orthodox Christian to pray to and love Christ, to read the Bible and to venerate icons (probably produced in craftsmen's ateliers and certainly thought of at the time as cult objects rather than works of art), and to practise his religion, as Russian school-children were expected to do, as part of the curriculum and their civic duty, a practice which, in common with many of his free-thinking contemporaries, he relaxed and almost forgot about as a student and young writer.[6] In 1873, he was to recall the impression made on him by the Moscow Cathedrals and we know he was taken once on a pilgrimage to the St Sergius Monastery of the Holy Trinity but, in the *Diary of a Writer*, he claims that 'in spite of' this traditional Russian Christian upbringing it was hard for him to convince himself of the superiority of these values 'to all that we at home considered light and truth', i.e. to something which was the opposite of this tradition: enlightened agnosticism (21,134).

The 'sub-texts' on which Dostoevsky drew unconsciously, as all artists draw on the impressions of childhood and early youth, were largely pre-schism (the common Christian Greco-Judaic heritage,

The Book of Job, the Gospels, the Fathers, liturgical texts and the Greek and Latin classics) or Western European. His knowledge of the Russian classics began with the Sentimentalist Karamzin, the Romantic Zhukovsky, Pushkin, Griboyedov, Lermontov and the 'naturalistic' Gogol of Ukrainian legends and the Petersburg Tales: all examples of Westernised, post-Petrine, post-Enlightenment Russian culture. Gogol, it is true, wrote a rather Baroque piece, *Meditations on the Divine Liturgy* and, in his *Selected Passages from Correspondence with Friends*, exhorted Russians to return to the Orthodox fold, but it was for reading out Belinsky's impassioned attack on this publication that Dostoevsky and his friends were arrested. Moreover, though the young author was reduced to tears by Belinsky's rejection of Christ, he deeply appreciated the consumptive critic's devotion to Christian fraternity as expounded by Charles Fourier and other French utopian socialists. Later he may well have modelled Ivan Karamazov's return of his ticket to paradise on Belinsky's paradoxical statement that the present deprivation and ignorance of the least of our brothers in Christ was too high a price to pay for any future individual enlightenment.[7] The high Romanticism of Schiller was Dostoevsky's original inspiration in Western European literature, but he was also brought up on Shakespeare, Molière and Cervantes. As a young man he was an avid reader of Eugene Sue and George Sand. Chateaubriand, it seems, was the author who first suggested to him the possibility of a Christian aesthetic capable of embracing secular culture. Dickens and Balzac influenced his later work, and apprenticeship to Balzac began early with his translation of *Eugénie Grandet* (published in 1844).

A young man who can compare Jesus Christ to Homer, as Dostoevsky did in a letter to his brother Mikhail of 1 January 1840, can hardly then have been thinking of the Russian people and the Russian Christ (28,1,69). N. Lossky, whose book *Dostoevsky and his Christian Understanding of the World* gives a detailed account of the great novelist's religious development, tells us that only shortly before his arrest did Dostoevsky show signs of resuming practice as a communicating Christian under the influence of an Orthodox friend, and that before the 'execution' he refused confession though he did kiss the cross.[8] We know of the comfort he received in prison from the gift of the New Testament and from the Passion Week services. Here too, he formed an intense admiration for the stoicism of the common prisoners which, he felt, came from their Russian

Orthodox faith and, in *Notes from the House of the Dead*, there is eloquent evidence of his gratitude for the non-judgmental charity of women and children (4,18–19).

It was in prison that the foundations were laid for the truth which illumines the great novels, 'the truth which appears more clearly in misfortune', the simple creed which he confided in a letter of February 1854 to a friend:

to believe that there is nothing more beautiful, more profound, more likeable, more reasonable, more courageous and perfect than Christ and not only is there not, but I tell myself with jealous love that there cannot be. More than that, if it were proved to me that Christ is not in truth and it were really so indeed, that the truth is not in Christ, then I would wish rather to remain with Christ than with truth (28,i,176).

Here we have the first formulation of that love which, in Dostoevsky's works as in St Paul's epistle (1 Cor. 13:13), greatly exceeds faith and hope.

We also know, however, that Dostoevsky read the Koran in prison and was absorbed in the study of criminal psychology, and that when he was released he avoided the 'Siberian priests', who were too closely connected with the secular authorities to inspire confidence in a man anxious above all things to return to life and creative work in the capital.[9] His private life after his return was not that of a penitent. It was many years later, partially in revulsion against contemporary Europe and partially under the influence of the priest Yanichev and of Anna Dostoevskaya, his unobtrusively devout second wife, and thanks to his involvement in the structured joys and sorrows of family life, that 'middle sphere' which many find lacking in his work, that Dostoevsky came consciously to embrace the Orthodox Church in his own life. It is a moot point whether this should be confused with his Russian 'Messianism', basically another 'dream' founded like that of the Slavophiles, on Schlegel's romantic concept of national destiny. He dared to hope that the Purpose of history, in the temporal process, was 'Union in Christ', which would lead 'without doubt to a righteous State of Social Union'.[10] More consonant with the resumption of Orthodox practice is Dostoevsky's *pochvennichestvo*, the search for 'firm ground', the desire to come in from the cold outsider's stance of privileged, educated Westernism and to get involved, to rejoin the communion of the Church.

In *A Raw Youth*, the eponymous hero's father, the enigmatic Versilov, an educated 'Westerner' who, for all he shares the doubts of his communist European friends, is profoundly offended by the brutal ingratitude with which they reject Christ and feels that, as a Russian, he still has a choice. As Versilov had once sought union with the Russian people through a physical relationship with a peasant woman, so now he plunges into ascetic life in an attempt to regain simple faith. He does not succeed, and remains a sceptical outsider. Even as Ivan Karamazov tells the story of the Grand Inquisitor, so Versilov tells his son his vision of the end of the world, seen in terms not of a fresco of the Last Judgment but of a favourite picture: the setting sun in a landscape by the seventeenth-century French artist Claude Lorraine (17,389).[11] In the last throes of hopelessness, the capacity for love not dissipated by religious adoration, people feel more kindly towards one another, aware of the precious brevity of human life on earth, resigned to a loving last farewell. All is set for a secular Apocalypse, but in the glorious light of the sunset, here, at the end of all things, Christ reappears and asks: how could you forget me? And the Universal Hosannah rings out in a hymn of unadulterated joy. Neither Versilov nor Dostoevsky nor, it is implied, Russians as such, could do without Him, but in Versilov's story He comes of Himself as Saviour rather than Messiah and is recognised by all.

Like Versilov, Dostoevsky sought to resolve his doubts in the company of believers, notably his younger friend the Christian apologist and ecumenical dreamer Vladimir Solovyov, who is said to have served us the model not for Alyosha but for Ivan Karamazov. He also visited places of pilgrimage popular with the people (and the Slavophiles), notably the elders at the monastery of *Optyna pustyn'*, where he sought comfort after the death of his son Alyosha in the spring of 1878. There can be no doubt, however, that, for Dostoevsky, the conscious effort to put down roots in his native soil and his native faith was precisely that: a conscious effort. It was, nevertheless, pivotal not just for the writer, but for his future readers.

The Orthodox Church, not at that time noted for interest in secular culture, began to take a serious interest in Dostoevsky's works only some twenty years after his death.[12] Under the influence of these works, on the other hand, the secular reading public began to take an interest in the Church, seeing it as he had done: as the way back into Communion with their own people, their own *pochva* (ground, soil). The Godseekers – Merezhkovsky, Shestov, Bulgakov, Berdyaev and the symbolists Andrey Bely and Vyacheslav Ivanov –

were, as Berdyaev pointed out, among the first to have the kind of
soul capable of distinguishing Dostoevsky from the mainstream of
naturalism and critical realism.[13] His work was re-examined and re-
interpreted in journals like *Mir iskusstva* (*The World of Art*, 1898–1904),
Novy put' (*The New Way*, 1903–04) and *Voprosy zhizni* (*Questions of Life*,
1905). From this re-examination sprang the Intelligentsia's attempt
to contact the teaching Church through the Religious-Philosophical
Meetings in St Petersburg (1901–03). 'Knowledge', Merezhkovsky,
the prime mover in the convening of these meetings, wrote in Sergy
Diaghilev's *World of Art*, 'exposes the relativity of every religious
truth; love reveals the truth of every religious convention <. . .> The
combination of knowledge and love is our new religion, the religion
of Dostoevsky.'[14] The Orthodox Church, not surprisingly, felt it had
been around for some time before Dostoevsky and did not quite
know what to make of such statements. Bishop Sergy, Chairman of
the Meetings, had actually run a discussion group at the St
Petersburg Theological Academy for the study of Dostoevsky and
Tolstoy. This, however, was for the elite, the very few. The ideas of
the great novelists were considered dangerous. Indeed 1901, the year
the first Religious-Philosophical Meetings were convened, was the
year of Tolstoy's excommunication. Yet here were the 'godless
intelligentsia', who had made a cult figure of Dostoevsky, that
essentially Petersburg author, caught between two cultures and
troubled by all the sicknesses of their world, knocking on the doors
of the Church. It seemed to them that: 'When such a man, hearing
the confession of our hearts, nevertheless forgives us, when he says
"Believe in good, in God, in yourselves", this is more than aesthetic
delight in beauty and greater than the arrogant sermonising of an
alien prophet.'[15] This was the period, twenty years after Dostoevsky's death, when the Westernised Russian intelligentsia, in his
name, began to explore the mind and traditions of the Orthodox
Church, to become aware of its aesthetics and semiotics (as well as of
its spiritual riches). It was also the time when Churchmen, looking
deeper than Leontiev's intemperate accusations of Father Zosima's
Christianity as rosy and pantheistic, began to examine both Dostoevsky and secular culture with a friendlier eye, the time when
secular culture and the Church began to learn each other's language
and to partake in that *sobornost'* which is indeed a feature of Russian
Orthodoxy, and which is perhaps best translated into English by the
Anglican Charles Williams' term: 'coinherence'.[16]

In Dostoevsky's novels, however, it is not coinherence or *sobornost'*, but the allied yet not identical concept of 'polyphony' which prevails. This Bakhtinian concept is accepted with gratitude rather than dismay in Florovsky's critique of Dostoevsky's work.[17] Florovsky is aware that all the theologian will find in the great novels are disjointed voices, insights into psychological depths and glimpses of metaphysical heights: and that the rest is 'dream', passion, laughter, gossip, politics, crime, voices rising up *de profundis* to light and joy and sinking back into tittle-tattle . . .

Dostoevsky, Florovsky states, was 'too sensitive a seer of the secrets of the human soul to stop at organic optimism'.[18] But, in listening to the 'voices' of his teeming novels, the theologian is able to grasp and show the inherent religious import of an ongoing 'polyphony', which attains no true finale but breaks off amidst notes for an unfinished novel – *Atheism*. Florovsky maintains that Dostoevsky's Christian insights emanate precisely from the perceived *reality* of the dialogue between his characters, not merely from their 'discourse', from the ideas they advocate. It is, after all, the coinherence of the characters, from the paranoid criminal to the near-saint, and the interweaving of voices which constitutes the 'action' of Dostoevsky's novels. The reader is involved in the author's perception of his protagonists' absolute need for Redemption, a need shared not just by the great tragic heroes and tormented heroines of his books but by the man from the Underground, the absurd schizophrenic Golyadkin, the drunkard Marmeladov, the vituperatively moribund Ippolit, the irresistibly comic Lebedev and the peripheral feminine characters, obsessed no less than the men by this need for 'an absolute'. Through dialogue, through the living, individual voices of his characters, Dostoevsky imparts this longing for the experience of repentance as a turning about towards the light of God and a rejoicing in this Earth 'as in Heaven'. Even when this remains only readiness (Shatov's 'I will believe in God') then 'readiness is all'. The saintly characters who have achieved the experience (Tikhon, Zosima) do not advance the action. Neither do they move or develop within the time-span of the novels. Zosima's teachings are an inset to the drama of *The Brothers Karamazov*, the chapter 'At Tikhon's' is an epilogue to *The Possessed*.

In the light of this awareness of the different attitude to time implicit in the sober stability of such characters, of the Russian monk's groundedness in the acceptance of Christ's 'one oblation of

Himself once offered', Florovsky perceives the key to Dostoevsky's *pochvennost'*, the firm ground that, increasingly, he came to find in the reality of the Russian people and the Orthodox Church. Dostoevsky's ambition, as a novelist, to create a 'positively beautiful character', keeps breaking and failing against the other dimension, the *uniqueness* of Christ who 'came', as Dostoevsky once said himself:

so humanity might know that the nature of the human spirit could appear in such heavenly glory indeed and in the Flesh <. . .> There is only one positively beautiful face in the world – Christ, so that the manifestation of this one immeasurably, infinitely beautiful person is already, of course, an ongoing miracle (the whole sense of the Gospel of John is this; for him the whole miracle is in the incarnation alone, in the appearance of the beautiful alone). (28,ii,249–252)

Figures such as Myshkin and Alyosha glow with some inner presence but can scarcely be said to attain 'positive beauty'. In the novels they act as catalysts; they precipitate action but do not partake in it, at least until Alyosha shoulders responsibility for his boys. Nevertheless, they go further than any characters I know in the nineteenth-century novel as a whole to make the 'good' attractive. This is precisely because they are never allowed to lose touch with the underground people who act out all the sinful impulses they and we recognise as our own. Far from seeking, as Strakhov suggested to Tolstoy after his erstwhile 'friend's' death, 'to prove that all kinds of filth can be accommodated with nobility of character', Dostoevsky depicts a reality in which 'no man living can be justified', but where 'the one positively beautiful face' is remembered, loved, desired – not as a 'dream' but as ultimate reality.[19]

This reality can only be shut out by the individual who has lost the ground from beneath his (or her) feet, who has become a spiritual 'wanderer', an 'outsider'. Such a one is Stavrogin; such are Svidrigailov, Smerdyakov. Totally withdrawn into self, indifferent to others, amnesiac towards the need for the absolute, the loss of the 'positively beautiful', they move inexorably from dialogue to monologue to self-destruction. Yet these, too, are extreme cases rather than exceptions. Rogozhin is almost one of them, so are Nastasia Filippovna in *The Idiot* and Katerina Ivanovna in *The Brothers Karamazov*, both of whom provoke their own destruction, even if they neither kill nor commit suicide. Perilously close are Dmitry, Ivan, Grushenka, even Aglaya. Myshkin and Alyosha understand and *love* them all, not just as biological units, 'infusoriae', as Captain

Lebyadkin puts it, but as immortal souls, each linked to all (10,106). Florovsky again uses the Bakhtinian concept of polyphony: the voice of 'the other' which can weave its way into the melody to suggest the interrelationship of all these individual, unique human souls – as when Alyosha answers the question Ivan asks himself: 'it was not you, not you, you did not kill him', or when Sonya's voice reads Raskolnikov the longed-for story of the raising of Lazarus.

Unlike his synthesising friend and interpreter, Vladimir Solovyov, Dostoevsky presents this polyphony, this dramatic, artistic, tragic form of *sobornost'*, as *un*resolved. He 'never gave the last synthesis', Florovsky writes, but adds, 'the feeling remained clear and firm for him always: "And the word was made flesh" <. . .> Truth was revealed in *this* life <. . .> Dostoevsky believed from love, not from fear'.[20]

This, coming from a priest of the Orthodox Church, seems to be a truer and more catholic (in the sense in which the word is used in the Orthodox *and* Anglican as well as in the Roman Catholic Creeds) summing up of the religious significance of Dostoevsky's witness than any attempt to interpret him through refinements of specifically Orthodox doctrine.

NOTES

1 Archpriest G. Florovskii, *Puti russkogo bogosloviia*, 2nd edn, intro. Archpriest Meiendorff (Paris, 1981), 300.
2 Sergei Averintsev, 'Zhan Mariten, neo-tomizm i katolicheskaia teologiia iskusstva', *Religiia i Literatura* (Ann Arbor, MI, 1981), 138.
3 An example of an intelligent and moderate application of 'drawing on semiotics and theology' to decodify Silver Age literature is Stephen C. Hutchings', *Russian Modernism: The Transfiguration of the Everyday* (Cambridge, 1997).
4 Yuri M. Lotman, *Universe of the Mind: A Semiotic Theory of Culture*, intro. Umberto Eco, trans. Ann Shukman (London and New York, 1990), Part 2, 'The semiosphere', 123–216.
5 For a discussion of the early Christian influences on Dostoevsky, and his mother in particular, see Irina Kirillova's article in the present volume.
6 The icon as a work of art was rediscovered in the late nineteenth and early twentieth century in Russia, when the Church was persuaded by specialists such as Igor Grabar to allow some of the great twelfth to sixteenth century icons to be cleaned from the blend of dark varnish (*olifa*) and candle-smoke which, for centuries, had obscured the colours even of those images that were not hidden (all but for hands and faces) behind metal frames (*oklady*). In Britain, the British Museum merely reflected the attitude of many cultivated Russians when, as late as the

1920s–1930s, it passed up opportunities provided by sales of Church property during the Russian Revolution, stating proudly that it did not collect 'peasant artefacts'. In the early nineteenth century, Andrei Rublev would have been thought of as a devout monk rather than a great artist – if indeed, the name was known at all. The pictures which made the most profound impression on Dostoevsky's imagination were, as we know, Raphael's Sistine Madonna, Holbein's dead Christ, and a picture of Acis and Galathea by Claude Lorraine which, when staying in Dresden, he regularly contemplated on his daily visits to the city gallery and called, for himself, 'the Golden Age' (17,389). In the Moscow home of his contemporary, Count Leo Tolstoy, one finds icons only in the children's and servants' rooms 'pour les pauvres et pour les enfants'.

7 Belinsky made several statements to this effect during the period of his rejection of Hegel in his 1841 correspondence with his friend Botkin. The passage I have in mind is long and occurs in a letter of 8 September 1841. See V. G. Belinsky, *Izbrannye sotchineniia* (Moscow, 1941), 647. Other scholars have perceived 'the original inspiration for Ivan's eloquence' in a passage from Herzen's dialogue *From the Other Shore:* 'Do you truly wish to condemn all human beings alive today to the sad role of caryatids supporting a floor on which others someday will dance?' A. I. Gertsen, *Sobranie sochinenii v deviati tomakh* (Moscow, 1955–58), vol. 3, 261–62. See also Nina Perlina, 'Herzen in *The Brothers Karamazov*', *Canadian–American Slavic Studies*, 17, no. 3 (1983), 349–61. This kind of argument was common currency during the reaction against Hegel, and Dostoevsky may have had other sources, but Belinsky's passionate style ('What is it to me <. . .>? Away from me, bliss, if it is only for me alone among thousands! I don't want it, unless I enjoy it in common with my lesser brethren <. . .> with those, who should be my brothers in humanity, my neighbours in Christ') is a great deal closer to Ivan's than Herzen's classic caryatids. It is a fair assumption that Dostoevsky heard similar sentiments from Belinsky's own lips – though possibly without reference to Christ – during the year of their greatest intimacy in 1845. For the relevance of Belinsky's argument to Ivan Karamazov's rejection of 'his ticket' see also (15,470).

8 N. O. Losskii, *Dostoevskii i ego khristianskoe miroponimanie* (New York, 1946). The edition I have used is the reprint in the collection N. O. Losskii, *Bog i mirovoe zlo* (Moscow, 1994).

9 The source for this statement is the reminiscences of Baron Wrangel quoted by K. Mochul'skii, *Dostoevskii: Zhizn' i tvorchestvo* (Paris, 1947), 130.

10 Compare Losskii, *Dostoevskii*, 233.

11 Claude Lorraine's picture is also mentioned in Stavrogin's Confession in *The Devils* and in *The Dream of a Ridiculous Man*. See also K. Mochul'skii, *Dostoevskii*, 458.

12 An early study by a churchman, who perceived Dostoevsky as one of

the few modern writers with a sense of original sin and as a great interpreter of the Parable of the Prodigal Son, was Metropolitan Antonii Khrapovitskii, *Pastyrskoe izuchenie liudei i zhizni po sochineniiam F. M. Dostoevskogo* (Kazan, 1898).

13 N. Berdyaev, *Dostoevsky*, trans. Donald A. Attwater (New York, 1957), 14.

14 D. S. Merezhkovsky, 'Khristos i Antikhrist v russkoi literature', *Mir iskusstva*, no. 7 (1901), 22. See also Avril Pyman, 'Dostoevsky's influence on religious thought in the Russian Silver Age', *Canadian–American Slavic Studies*, 17, no, 3, (1983), 287–325.

15 D. S. Merezhkovskii, 'O *Prestuplenii i nakazanii* Dostoevskogo', *Russkoe obozrenie*, 2, no. 3 (1890), 155–86. Here quoted from Vladimir Seduro, *Dostoevsky in Russian Literary Criticism 1846–1956* (New York, 1958), 43.

16 See Charles Williams, *The Descent of the Dove* (London, 1939) and, particularly, 'The way of exchange' in *The Image of the City and Other Essays* (Oxford, 1958). The *Oxford Russian Dictionary* translates the word *sobornost'* as 'collectivism' or (in the ecclesiastical and philosophical sense) as 'conciliarism'. Donald Rayfield, in *Reference Guide to Russian Literature*, ed. Neil Cornwell (London, 1998), 477, translates it as 'congregationality'. The root *sobor* or *sbor* does indeed mean 'council' or 'assembly', but the term as used by Khomyakov and other Russian religious thinkers means rather the metaphysical interaction of all members of the body of the Church. Williams captures this wider metaphysical subtext underlying the Russian word *sobornost'* when he writes: 'The doctrine of the Christian Church has declared that the mystery of the Christian religion is a doctrine of co-inherence and substitution', *The Image of the City*, 152.

17 See Florovskii, *Puti*, 235 for an appreciative reference to Bakhtin, whom he must have read in Bakhtin's first study of Dostoevsky published in 1929 under the title *Problems of Dostoevsky's Creative Work*.

18 Florovskii, *Puti*, 300.

19 N. N. Strakhov to L. N. Tolstoy, dated 26 November 1883. Quoted from Losskii, *Dostoevskii*, 32.

20 Florovskii, *Puti*, 300.

CHAPTER 6

The categories of Law and Grace in Dostoevsky's poetics

Ivan A. Esaulov

The opposition between law (*pravo*) and Grace (*Blagodat'*) in Dostoevsky's poetics can be traced back to the Old Russian Orthodox opposition between Law (*Zakon*) and Grace first enunciated by Metropolitan Hilarion more than nine centuries ago.[1] In Western theology the opposition between justification by works of the law and justification by faith (Luther) or grace (Calvin) was one of the decisive issues in the Reformation disputes between Roman Catholicism and early Protestantism. As Luther and Calvin in particular insisted, this opposition is firmly rooted in the epistles of Paul, and the letters to the Romans and to the Galatians were particularly important sources of proof texts for their polemics. However, this same opposition appears in the Orthodox tradition in quite a distinctive form, and it was this tradition which nourished Dostoevsky's art and thought.

The history of original Russian literature begins with the famous, eleventh-century *Sermon on Law and Grace*, a seminal work of Russian homiletics and spirituality, by Hilarion (Ilarion), an outstanding preacher who became the first Russian Metropolitan of Kiev in 1051.[2] Medievalists differ on the exact date when the *Sermon* was preached, but, more important for us, are its sources and position in the annual Orthodox cycle, and on this point scholars are virtually at one: it was 'based on a New Testament text' and was given only on Easter.[3]

From his first lines, Hilarion speaks 'of the Law of Moses given to him by God, and of the Grace and Truth which has appeared in Jesus Christ, and of how the Law has departed'.[4] Hilarion then sets out a series of metaphorical antitheses between the Law and Grace based on contrasted opposites, laying particular stress on the universality and permanence of Christianity and the two natures of Christ. Hilarion identifies the Law with the Old Testament, in particular with the Pentateuch, whose prophecy, from the Christian point of view, has already been completely fulfilled, and therefore must be replaced, and has already been replaced, and transferred into a different, Christian system of ethical coordinates. The abrogation of the Law does not at all mean that it is useless or unnecessary. On the contrary, the Law was necessary 'for the preparation of Truth and Grace', in so far as 'the Law was the precursor and the servant of Grace and Truth'.[5] Thus, the Law appeared as a necessary historical stepping stone for ancient humanity on its path towards Grace: thanks to the Law, 'human nature turned from bowing down to polytheistic idols to faith in the one God'.[6] But precisely this stepping stone must be overcome in full measure, having fulfilled its predestined role. For if not, it becomes a hindrance, a ballast dragging one down to what is 'earthly' and turning one away from the 'heavenly'.

Hilarion distinguishes two possible ways of a person's orientation in the world: *self-assertion* in earthly life and *spiritual salvation* for the achievement of which it is necessary to free oneself from the 'slavery' of earthly cares. Grace is understood as a result of the Salvific influence of the Holy Spirit on man. It is traditionally juxtaposed to the law as a supra-legal category and therefore as one proleptically 'rescinding' all legal relations. In the tradition of Eastern Christianity, the 'mechanical' observance of the law without Grace is understood as servile submission to necessity; as commandments which come not from God, but have been 'invented' by man (for example, 'Roman law' and the general idea of 'legal space'); as the formal frames of an abstract 'norm', incapable of providing for the variety of life's concrete conflicts; as a 'dead letter', killing life and hindering spiritual salvation; as something opposed to the Kingdom of God. For this reason, liberation from all the 'shackles' of the law is usually understood as a kind of ideal orientation point (based on Grace) for Russia, despite never having become an historical fact. One can say that the supra-legal relationships of Grace are more characteristic of the ideal space of 'Holy Rus'' than historical Russia.

In his detailed analysis of this text, V. N. Toporov finds 'in this literary monument the first formulation of the "Russian idea"', its chief features being the notion of 'spiritual succession' and of 'holiness as the highest moral ideal of behaviour, of one's life position, more exactly, of a special type of holiness understood as sacrifice, as the hope for another world, for values which are *not of this world*.[7] The main purpose of the *Sermon* was, most likely, 'to glorify the conversion of Rus'' and to affirm Russia's equality with all Christian peoples.[8]

There is yet another notable circumstance for Russian culture. For many generations of Russians the main means of assimilating the Bible came from hearing the liturgy and not domestic reading. Therefore, it is especially important that the central value-laden opposition of Law and Grace is intended for the Orthodox Easter liturgy, and that the first Gospel reading on Easter eve begins with the first verse of St John's Gospel ('In the Beginning was the Word') and concludes with the seventeenth verse in which the Law of Moses and the Grace of Christ are opposed: 'For the law was given by Moses, but grace and truth came through Jesus Christ' (John 1:17). Thus, for the world's Orthodox believers, the first Easter liturgy gave rise to a kind of semantic unity of the gospel text they were hearing, whose limits were bound by the Johannine Word and the super-session of Law by Grace. And precisely this final stress on the Easter triumph of Christ is an indubitable fact of the consciousness of every Orthodox believer. The semantic unity of this liturgical segment from John's gospel gives a special horizon of expectation to Ortho-dox Christians on the whole church year in that the moveable calendrical cycle begins with Easter day.

For Orthodox theology and Orthodox consciousness, the oppo-sition between Law and Grace has by no means been relegated to the Church's historical past. Almost a millennium later, the Ortho-dox theologian, N. Afanasiev, applies the same demarcation when he describes Grace as the antipode of 'legal space':

By its very nature, Grace excludes the law (*pravo*) just as Grace, having overcome it by fulfilment, excluded the Old Testament law (*zakon*) <. . .> The end of the Old Testament law (*zakon*) is at the same time the end for the secular law (*pravo*) <. . .> Christianity proclaimed the surmounting of law in human relationships in a new life in Grace <. . .> This was not a new Law based on new legal principles, since what Christ said in the Sermon on the Mount does not and cannot be fitted into a concept of law <. . .> The acknowledgment of law (*pravo*) is a rejection of Grace by which the members of the Church live in Christ <. . .> [it] is a *return to the law* (*zakon*), and if there is justification by law, then Christ died in vain.[9] [my emphasis, I. E.]

Of course, one may not agree with a certain 'harshness' in this opposition, since for the contemporary, secularised legal consciousness, the exact fulfilment of legal obligations is a most important, if not the main, value of the world order; it has in fact become the axiology of 'civil society'. Afanasiev, however, is only explicating an utterly essential opposition for Russian Orthodoxy which had a powerful influence on Russian literature and culture as a whole, and in particular on Dostoevsky's poetics.

The twentieth-century Russian philosopher B. P. Vysheslavtsev interprets the Law in a very broad sense: 'as the fundamental holy precepts (*sviatynia*) of the whole antique world, as the basic principle of pre-Christian and non-Christian ethics'.[10] In his opinion 'the opposition between Law and Grace, Law and love, Law and the Kingdom of God' is 'a fundamental principle of Christianity' which 'runs through the entire Gospels'.[11] According to Vysheslavtsev, who bases his thought on St Paul and Orthodox axiology, the antinomy of Law and Grace is the antinomy of 'two great systems of values' which are 'incompatible', in that they temporally exclude each other, 'the one supersedes the other <. . .> the Law is transient and Christ is the end of the Law'.[12] For 'the Law shows what is a sin, and forbids sin, but it is powerless to fight against sin <. . .> the Law cannot love the sinner, but Christ can'.[13]

In Dostoevsky's novels, the heroes' orientation towards 'legal space', as a rule, inevitably presupposes a retreat from moral criteria. The narrator in *The Brothers Karamazov* remarks: 'The majority of the men were positively wishing for the criminal's punishment, except for the lawyers who cared not about the moral aspect of the case, but only, so to speak, its contemporary legal aspect' (15,91). Also, Dmitry Karamazov says about his father: 'legally he doesn't owe me anything <. . .> But morally he surely owes me something' (14,111). Therefore, the ideas of law and Grace are not simply *different* by their nature, but are in a certain sense antinomical.

It is far from chance that, according to a popular Russian conception, which also finds its reflection in the poetics of *The Brothers Karamazov*, *ablakat'* (a colloquial pronunciation of *advokat* ('lawyer')) is a 'hired conscience' (14,220). Nor is it by chance that chapter XIII, Book 12, in which the defence lawyer sums up his case, has the title 'An Adulterer of Thought' (*Preliubodei mysli*) (12,XIII). Although for the actualisation of strictly *legal* relations, the lawyer, of course, is one of the most important and irreplaceable figures in society.

Legitimacy and legality, according to Dostoevsky, are by no means the discovery of Catholic civilisation, a notion that is sometimes ascribed to him. On the contrary, for Dostoevsky, the predominance in human relationships of juridical (legal) criteria to the detriment of relations based on Grace as understood in the Gospels, is an unfruitful and dangerous return of humanity to the pre-Christian state of the world.

The essence of the Grand Inquisitor's reproaches to Christ consists precisely in the fact that the Saviour effected a transition from 'the firm foundations for the appeasing of human conscience' to the freedom of the New Testament, a substitution of 'the hard ancient law' (the Old Testament) by the New Testament (14,232). In other words, there occurred a rejection of the Old Testament *hierarchical* division of humanity into those who are worthy of freedom and those who are not. The Grand Inquisitor openly demonstrates his 'correction' of Christ's great deed and a return to a pre-Gospel situation when he states: 'people rejoiced that they were again led like a herd' (14,234). One finds the same cruel division of humanity into two unequal parts in Raskolnikov's theory (the 'extraordinary people' and all the rest), and in Shigailov's project (the elite *we* and *they*, everyone else). The common totalitarian 'anthill' formed as a result of these divisions has one essential difference from its pre-Christian analogues: to reject God already *after* Christ's arrival in the world means, in the words of the Grand Inquisitor, to be with the devil: 'We haven't been with Thee [Christ] for a long time, but with *him* [the devil]' (14,234).

It is interesting that both liberalism and, paradoxically, revolutionary radicalism, fully subscribe to the idea of 'legal consciousness'. This particular feature of *The Brothers Karamazov* is revealed even in the most seemingly 'neutral' fragments of the text. Thus, the minor character, Miusov, a vain, Europeanised Russian liberal, who 'personally knew Proudhon and Bakunin and especially loved to remember and talk <. . .> about the three days of the February Revolution in Paris in forty eight [1848]', 'considered it even his civic and enlightened duty to initiate a lawsuit with the "clericals" [with the monastery]' (14,10–11). In *Crime and Punishment* we find another example. Pyotr Petrovich Luzhin, the bullying exploiter and pompous scoundrel who basely plants a 100-rouble note on Sonya in order to incriminate her before Raskolnikov, 'wants to open a public law office in Petersburg. For a long time he has been busy conducting various actions and lawsuits and the other day just won an important case' (6,32). At the same time this character 'decided immediately on his arrival in Petersburg to find out what was going on <. . .> and if necessary, to anticipate developments and ingratiate himself with "our young generation"', since he heard, 'that there existed, especially in Petersburg, some progressists, nihilists, denouncers, and so forth and so forth', 'powerful, all-knowing circles, who despised and denounced everyone' (6,279,278). Finally, we should not forget that the rebel himself, Raskolnikov, is a law student who has written an article in which he attempts to found a legal (although immoral) 'right (*pravo*) to allow one's conscience to overstep <. . .> certain obstacles', that is, the *right* of 'extraordinary' people to commit crimes (6,199).[14] In his verbal duel with the detective, Porfiry Petrovich, the hero remarks: 'I speak in my article about their [the exceptional people's] *right (pravo) to crime*. (You will recall, we actually began with the *legal question*)' (6,200) [my emphasis, I. E.]. However, Raskolnikov's mother explicates another side of her son's law studies in her letter to him:

Dunya <. . .> for several days already has simply been in a kind of fever and has already worked out a whole project by which you can later on be the colleague and even the partner of Pyotr Petrovich in his legal business, all the more since you yourself are studying on the law faculty. (6,32–33)

We see that legalism, according to Dostoevsky, does not contradict revolutionary radicalism. However both contradict the idea of Grace insofar as they are based on external, that is, on formal legal principles and criteria.

The apocryphal text, *The Mother of God's Descent into Hell*,[15] to which Ivan alludes in his conversation with Alyosha just before reciting his Grand Inquisitor 'poem', occupies, from the point of view of our problem, a key place in *The Brothers Karamazov*. It is hardly by chance that Ivan Karamazov *twice* refers to Dante in his 'preface' to 'The Grand Inquisitor':

You see, my action takes place in the sixteenth century, and then <. . .> it was quite common practice in poetic works to bring heavenly powers down to earth. I do not speak about Dante. <. . .> In our monasteries they also translated, copied and even composed such poems, yes, even as far back as the period of Tatar rule. There is, for example, one little monastery poem (of course, from the Greek): *The Mother of God's Descent into Hell*, with scenes of a boldness not inferior to Dante. (14,224–25)

This passage has three features worthy of note. First is the broad historical, philosophical perspective sketched by Ivan: although the action of 'The Grand Inquisitor' 'takes place in the sixteenth century', his first literary reference is to Dante, who lived in the thirteenth and fourteenth centuries. Second, the denominational origin of the 'little monastery poem' is specially emphasised ('of course, from the Greek'). Third, the Orthodox text is directly compared by Ivan to the *Divine Comedy*, whereby he insists on a kind of equivalence between Dante's great creation and the anonymous translation from the Greek: 'with scenes of a boldness not inferior to Dante'.

In the mytho-poetics of Dante's cosmos, every sinner *hierarchically* receives what he 'deserved' in life. Although Dante's work is an extremely original artistic creation, it is, at the same time, a kind of poetic encyclopedia of the medieval Catholic worldview, not a dogmatic view, but a poetic reflection of Catholic eschatology.[16] But in Dostoevsky, contrary to Dante, the circles of Hell, with their hierarchy of the tiers of sinners, disappear. The Mother of God 'begs for mercy for everyone in hell <. . .> without distinction', and 'orders all the saints <. . .> to pray for mercy for everyone without discrimination' (14,225). Mercy 'for everyone without discrimination', which is based on an essentially non-legal idea, is a supremely important characteristic of the Russian Orthodox mentality, and it also permeates Dostoevsky's poetics.

One may also recall the 'fable' of the 'little onion' which Grushenka tells Alyosha at a time of spiritual crisis in their lives. It is about a 'wicked woman' who, having died and left no good deeds behind her, was seized by devils and thrown down to the burning lake of hell. God tells her Guardian Angel that if he can think of one good deed the woman did, she may be saved. The Angel remembers that she once gave an onion to a beggar woman, whereupon God tells the Angel to take the onion and if he can pull her out with it, she can enter paradise. The Angel throws her the onion and starts to pull her out of hell with it. When other sinners see this, they grab onto her so as to be pulled out too. But the woman kicks them away whereupon the onion snaps, and the woman remains in hell 'to this day' (14,319). The woman in Grushenka's fable is sinful through and through and is deservedly punished by the 'devils' because, so to speak, of the 'sum total of facts' of her sinful life. She is punished not because she was 'wicked', but because she left 'not a single good deed behind her'. The 'devils' embody, in an exaggerated form, the idea of justice: the punishment is adequate to the crime, that is, the

devils enter into a complete correspondence with a formally understood conception of justice: 'the devils seized her and threw her into
the burning lake'. One could interpret the *dramatis personae* of this
fable allegorically, in a juridical context: the woman is the accused,
her iniquitous life is her crime, the devils are the executors of the
sentence, the Guardian Angel is the defence lawyer, and God is the
chairman of the court. However, such a 'juridical' interpretation is
flagrantly inadequate to the very meaning of Grushenka's story. The
woman's guilt is clear from the beginning and is not subject to doubt
or dispute. However, God embodies *Grace*, and not *law*, and therefore, in spite of the obvious legal incommensurability of one single
'onion' (one good deed) and a mass of wicked deeds, the woman can
be *saved* by Divine Grace, regardless of the fact that by her life she
fully deserved the 'burning lake'. What is striking, but at the same
time very characteristic of the Orthodox mentality, is that in the final
analysis it is not a long series of personal transgressions which is the
woman's undoing, but her pretension to chosenness, her egoism and
her setting herself against other sinners, her hope only for personal
and not communal salvation ('they're pulling me out, not you, it's
my onion and not yours'). And so, as soon as she utters this, 'the
onion snaps', not because the other sinners 'grab onto her', but
because the sinner herself pushes them away. Nevertheless, even
after this wicked act of the woman, her 'Angel' feels pity: 'he wept
and turned aside' (14,319).

   In Dostoevsky's poetic cosmos, the image of this 'little onion'
strikingly and paradoxically places on an *equal* footing – as potentially open to salvation by grace and not by a legal court – both the
'wicked woman' without even one good deed and the most exalted
characters. Thus, Grushenka says about herself: 'I myself am this
wicked woman <. . .> only here's what, Rakita, although I am
wicked, still, I gave an onion <. . .> *All* I ever gave was just one little
onion in my whole life' (14,318–319). Alyosha, in his turn, says to
Grushenka: '"What have I done for you? <. . .> I gave you an onion,
one tiny little onion, that's all, that's all!" And saying this, he himself
began to weep' (14,323). However, even this tiny little onion of grace,
given to an Other, can, in Dostoevsky's world, save this Other. Thus
Alyosha, who almost 'against my God rebelled', says to Grushenka,
who gave him an onion: 'You restored my soul just now' (14,317,318).
And Grushenka announces about Alyosha's 'onion': 'he turned my
heart . . . He was the first one to take pity on me, the only one, that's

what!' (14,323). Shortly thereafter, Alyosha hears in his dream vision
his dead elder Zosima, now dwelling in Paradise, saying to him:
'Why are you surprised at me? I gave an onion, that's why I am here
too. And many are here only because they gave an onion, only one
little onion' (14,327).

This 'fable' told by Grushenka is vitally connected with the
apochrypha *The Mother of God's Descent into Hell*; each demonstrates
that in Dostoevsky's world the possibility of salvation even from Hell
is allowed. This possibility follows from the absence, significant for
the Orthodox tradition, of an intermediary dimension between Hell
and Paradise, i.e. the absence of Purgatory.[17] 'If you pull her [the
sinner] out of the lake, then let her go to paradise' (14,319). Of
course, the possibility Dostoevsky allows of an *instantaneous* transition
from the 'lake' of hell directly to paradise also has an Orthodox
subtext of meaning.

Let us observe here that Yuri Lotman, whilst convincingly juxta-
posing a binary model of Russian culture with a West European
ternary system, omitted only one, but in my view the most important, point which gives rise to this profound typological difference
between two images of the world, namely, the significant absence of
the idea of Purgatory in Orthodox culture.[18] Although Lotman and
B. A. Uspensky's joint article makes a distinction between the
Catholic conception of three sacral realms beyond the grave and the
Orthodox idea of two, this distinction is characterised as merely one
of many particular examples of Russian 'binarism', as just one
'particular case'.[19] This 'particular case' disappears (as being not
fundamental) in the book later written by Lotman. However, it is
precisely in this distinction that one can detect the most important
archetypal source of subsequent general cultural differentiation. The
absence of Purgatory, consequently, sharply brings together the
opposite sacral spheres of Heaven and Hell. Thus, in Dostoevsky we
find the possibility allowed for every character of an *instantaneous*
transition from the realm of *sin* to the realm of *holiness* and back. For
example, Grushenka, wishing at first to 'swallow up' Alyosha, in the
end 'saves' him; Katerina Ivanovna, on the contrary, although
initially wanting to 'save' Dmitry in court, 'ruins' him. Dostoevsky's
famous and frequent use of the word 'suddenly' is another artistic
refraction of this specifically Orthodox spiritual tradition,which is, I
suggest, the necessary 'forcing-bed' for the understanding of these
particular features of Dostoevsky's poetics.

We recall the 'rebellion' (*bunt*) of Alyosha, who had doubted Providence after his elder's corpse emitted 'an odour of corruption', which culminates, however, in his being 'open to the mystical vision' of 'Cana of Galilee'.[20] And then, spiritually transformed, his soul is also open to a visitation by Divine Grace:

It was as if the threads from all those numerous worlds of God came together at once in his soul and it was all trembling 'as it came into contact with other worlds'. He wanted to forgive everyone and for everything, and to ask forgiveness, oh! not for himself, but for everyone, for all and everything, and 'for me others are asking too', – resounded again in his soul. But with each moment he felt clearly and almost tangibly, something as firm and unshakeable as this heavenly vault *descend into his soul* <. . .> 'Someone visited my soul in that hour', – he used to say afterwards with a firm faith in his words. . .' [my emphasis, I. E.]. (14,328)

Thus, in Book 7, the hero first experiences the Karamazovian sensuality on his way to Grushenka's, and then, after keeping vigil by Zosima's coffin, his soul 'trembles' in the mystical experience of a sensation of the Divine unity of the world, when the invisible 'threads' join into one the 'stars', the 'flowers in the flowerbeds', and the 'golden cupolas of the cathedral' (14,328).[21] The hero's 'soul full of ecstasy' becomes the point where, by the author's will, the 'heavenly cupola' (the beginning of Dostoevsky's paragraph) and the 'earth' (the end of the paragraph) merge into one (14,328).

On the other hand, there is an implicit lexical convergence between the most repulsive and the most exalted characters. Smerdyakov (whose surname derives from *smerdet'*, 'to stink') and the elder Zosima converge, even if only in the phenomenon of stinking: Zosima's body unexpectedly stinks (*smerdit*) after his death, just as Smerdyakov's soul does in life. However, the latter's birth from a 'holy fool' (*iurodivaia*), 'whom it seemed everyone even loved', is also significant (14,90). The images of the saintly Zosima and the stinking holy fool correspond within the limits of one system. Fyodor Pavlovich Karamazov, having fathered Smerdyakov, intrudes into this system not as a holy fool, but as a 'buffoon', and thus becomes the cause of its fluctuation.[22]

In Smerdyakov's handing over of the three thousand roubles to Ivan, one can observe not only a situation behind which flickers the Gospel invariant of the return of the silver by Judas, but other connotations which give evidence of the multi-faceted significance of Smerdyakov as well. And in him there is displayed the sharp rapprochement of two opposite sacral spheres characteristic of Orthodox axiology; and his heart too – right up to his suicide – is a 'battlefield' where the 'devil struggles with God'. One cannot but notice that in the conversation with Ivan, Smerdyakov experiences the presence of the living God: 'Without a doubt, He is here, this third person, right between the two of us. Who is he? Where is he? Who is the third person?' – said Ivan Fydorovich in fright, quickly looking around all the corners of the room' [the 'third' person for Ivan is, of course, the devil, I. E.]. 'The third person – is God, sir' (15,60).

The intentionally macaronic combination of money and the book *Isaac the Syrian* (which Smerdyakov had possibly been reading before his death) is one of the textual manifestations of a fluctuation which may signify the continuation of the struggle for Smerdyakov's soul. Smerdyakov 'took from the table the thick yellow book, the *only* one lying there <. . .> and pressed the money down with it [my emphasis, I. E.]. The title of the book was: *The Homilies of Our Holy Father Isaac the Syrian.* Ivan read the title mechanically' (15,61). Then, once again the name of the saint sounds, not as the title of a book, but as the *name* itself: 'Smerdyakov removed Isaac the Syrian from the bundle of money and laid it[23] aside' (15,67). Let us not forget Ivan's ironic supposition, when, turning to Smerdyakov he says: 'So now you've come to believe in God, since you're returning the money?' (15,67). However, Smerdyakov's rejection of the money testifies not to his newly acquired real faith in God, but to his lack of faith in Ivan's atheistic doctrine. This is yet another one of the manifestations of the system of fluctuations most vividly appearing in this character.

Within the limits of the theme I have raised, the way in which Dostoevsky's favourite heroes understand the subsidiary importance of the cult of earthly deeds ('what are our deeds?', says Zosima) for the salvation of the soul is very important (14,327). In Dostoevsky's artistic world, where both instantaneous salvation and instantaneous ruin are possible, one cannot count on a *register* or long list *of deeds* for the attainment of Grace. One cannot earn Grace, one can only *receive* it.

In Dostoevsky one can discover a non-legal concept of guilt and punishment even for the servants of Themis: 'the Russian court', says the prosecuting attorney in *The Brothers Karamazov*, 'does not exist only for punishment (*kara*), but also for the salvation of the fallen man! Let other nations have the letter and the punishment, we have the spirit and the meaning, the salvation and the regeneration of the fallen' (15,173). To be sure, this is not a description of a *real* Russian court, but a posited *ideal* situation based on the fact that 'Russian criminals are still believers' (14,60). Thus, *guilt* and *punishment* are virtually taken out of the sphere of 'legal space'. So, in *Crime and Punishment*, Sonya urges Raskolnikov:

Go right now, this very minute, stand at the crossroad, bow down, first kiss the earth which you have defiled, and then bow down to the whole world [and not legal officials, I. E.], to all four corners and say to everyone, aloud: 'I killed!' Then God [and not a court of law] will send you life again. (6,322)

Sonya insists on the grace potentially conferred by suffering as opposed to juridical retribution for a crime. 'Accept suffering and redeem yourself with it, that's what you have to do' (6,323).

Even the investigator Porfiry Petrovich has a certain distrust of formal juridical limits, of the letter of the law, of strict legal form. Consequently he attempts to turn the interrogation of Raskolnikov into an informal and almost friendly conversation: 'I'm so glad that you've finally come to us . . . I receive you like a guest' (6,257). 'Why you also recently referred to form as regards, you know, this little interrogation, sir <. . .> Yes, why follow form! Form, you know, in many cases is nonsense, sir, sometimes it is more advantageous just to have a friendly talk' (6,260). Thus, even the character who is obliged according to his professional duty to adhere to legal frameworks, declares their secondary importance. However, in this case Porfiry Petrovich's deviation from legal norms is a trap and Raskolnikov senses it. Porfiry's behaviour is not a manifestation of grace, although it does reveal the inadequacy of legal limits alone. As he observes to Raskolnikov:

after all, the general case sir, the case on which all legal forms and rules are devised and from which they are calculated and noted down in books, does not exist at all, sir, because every case, every, at least, for example, crime, as soon as it happens in reality at once turns into a quite particular case, sir; yes, and sometimes into one which is absolutely unlike anything that has happened before. (6,261)

Here, in his juxtaposition of 'books' and 'reality', the investigator himself opposes the dead paragraph of rules written down in 'little law books' and the living life which cannot be accommodated in these formal criteria of legal norms. It is much easier for Raskolnikov, as a law student, to fight with Porfiry precisely on a strictly legal field: 'Arrest me, search me but be so good as to use the proper procedure' (6,269). Whereas for Porfiry Petrovich, on the contrary, it is more important to move away from strict procedures into the realm of the suspect's conscience: 'Don't you worry about the proper form, – interrupted Porfiry – <. . .> I invited you here, old man, informally, completely in a friendly fashion' (6,269). Raskolnikov's torment and guilt can not by any means be reduced to the legal sphere: 'Of course an illegal act has been committed; of course, the letter of the law has been broken and blood spilt, well, take my head for the letter of the law – and that's enough!' (6,417).

From the viewpoint of the Orthodox consciousness, the primary guilt of Raskolnikov does not consist in the fact that he committed a murder, i.e. that he committed a legal crime. His true guilt lies in the fact that he has forfeited Grace, that he has fallen out of the communal unity of people and set himself against other people, self-wilfully trying to define the 'value' of his and others' lives. The legal crime is only one of the *consequences* of this guilt. Moreover, this consequence (i.e. the destruction of legal space) may or may not take place. Dmitry Karamazov, from the juridical point of view is not a criminal who has transgressed the bounds of legal norms: that is why Book 12 has the title 'A Judicial Error'. Ivan also does not abandon the boundaries of legal space proper. However, just as in the case of Raskolnikov, Dostoevsky applies another measure to these heroes – the presence or absence of Grace.

Therefore it is not surprising that, in Dostoevsky's world, rational *calculation* – the *calculating* of a possible advantage from acts performed – is sometimes a synonym for *baseness*. For example, concerning the money he received from Katerina Ivanovna, Dmitry Karamazov announces to the surprise of others: 'I set it [half of Katerina's money] aside out of baseness, *that is*, out of calculation' [my emphasis, I. E.] (14,443). Thus, calculation and baseness form a single semantic series.

It is necessary to note the problematical character of blaming the Other. In one of his sermons, Zosima asks: 'Can one be the judge of one's fellow creatures? <. . .> For <. . .> this judge <. . .> is just such a criminal as the one standing before him, and he himself is, perhaps, most guilty of all for the crime of the one standing before him' (14,291). Indeed, Zosima's key teaching is a succinct expression of this idea: 'every person is guilty before everyone and everything' (14,275). This is to say that in Dostoevsky's artistic world, the idea of *communal (sobornoi)* guilt and *communal salvation* dominates. The most important definition of Alyosha Karamazov is: 'he did not want to be a judge of people, he would not want to take judgment on himself and not for anything would he condemn' (14,18).

From the impossibility of *judging* the Other follows another particular feature of Dostoevsky's poetics: the problematical nature of the *finalisation* of the Other. When Lise Khokhlakova responds to Alyosha's prediction that Snegirov will eventually take the money proffered to help him with the remark: 'isn't there contempt towards him <. . .> in the fact that we are dissecting his soul', she is expressing a reluctance to pass a *final* judgment on a person (14,197). Alyosha's reply: 'we ourselves are the same as he <. . .> everyone is the same as he is' expresses an ethical directive which can be understood as the Christian orientation in the world of Others.

Believing that he has killed his father's old servant Grigory, Dmitry Karamazov rushes off to Mokroe to see Grushenka before the law catches up with him. On the way, he asks the simple coachman who is taking him there whether he 'will end up in hell or not' (14,372). The coachman's reply: 'the Son of God <. . .> went down from the cross directly into hell and freed all the sinners who were in torment', and Grushenka's conviction: 'If I were God, I would forgive all people' (14,397) are highly revealing for Dostoevsky's cosmos. Dostoevsky's world is sustained by an orientation towards mercy and Grace, and not towards the law and legal justice in so much as, to cite Zosima's words: 'there is not a sin and cannot be one on all the earth that the Lord would not forgive to the truly penitent <. . .> Could there be such a sin which would exceed God's love?' (14,292). Thus, Ivan Karamazov ironically relates to Alyosha the contents of a pamphlet in 'a French translation about how in Geneva <. . .> they executed a certain evildoer and murderer named Richard, <. . .> who had repented and converted to the Christian faith right before the scaffold' (14,218). The story of Richard is projected onto the Gospel subject of the prodigal son (Luke 15:11–32). However, 'philanthropic and pious Geneva' does not forgive the sins of its repenting prodigal son but, on the contrary, leads Richard, on whom 'had descended grace', onto the legal, juridical plane (14,218). The prodigal son Richard is condemned – in accordance with legal criteria – just because he is prodigal; because he broke the juridical norms of the Law before his repentance: 'but you have shed blood and must die' (14,219). 'And so, – says Ivan ironically, – brother Richard was dragged up to the scaffold, placed on the guillotine and his head was fraternally chopped off [in fact according to legal norms, I. E.] because even on him grace descended' (14,219). This formal and exact fulfilment of the law, according to Dostoevsky, is, of course, absolutely devoid of grace and negates the very spirit of Christian mercy, of Christian love for man.

In late Dostoevsky, the extension of a person's *external* rights, alienated from the salvation of the soul, is not of primary importance. Therefore Rakitin's advice to Dmitry Karamazov 'you'd <. . .> do better to worry about extending man's civil rights, or at least about not letting the price of beef go up' is not by chance placed by the author in a rather comic context (15,32). This is a marginal vector of the Russian tradition. For Russian spirituality the construction of a 'legal space' alienated from a foundation in Grace is a typical utopia, it is the theoretical and practical negation of the positive significance of the very roots of Russian Orthodox culture and its system of values as 'incorrect' in the name of – to use an expression of M. M. Bakhtin, – an imposed 'theoreticism', that is, *a priori* notions about what constitutes a 'proper', 'just', 'correct' civilisation.[24] I emphasise that it is not a question of using legal criteria for the perfection and development of Russian culture, but of the utopian hope for a complete mutation of the nucleus of Russian civilisation and Russian Orthodox spirituality, for replacing it with ideas and principles devised in a completely different historical context and originating in other models of civilisation. It is not surprising, therefore, that in carrying out a violent 'reformation', alien to the Orthodox values of Russian society, precisely a destructive and not a constructive component frequently prevailed. When the political, ideological and social ideas and principles, introduced from outside, collided with the Russian cultural environment, they were not adapted to its environment but, on the contrary, the Russian cultural model itself was rejected as irrational, as a phenomenon of a low order.

In Dostoevsky's artistic cosmos, there is a different conception of human freedom relating to the realm of right and to the sphere of the spirit. In the elder Zosima's words:

the world says: 'you have needs, therefore satisfy them, for you have the same rights as the noblest and richest men. Do not be afraid to satisfy them, but even increase them' – this is the current teaching of the world. And in this they see freedom. (14,284)

Thus, according to the logic of a world without Grace, freedom is the satiation of needs, and the achievement of a formal (juridical) equality from the position of a right. However, this is far from being the universal understanding of freedom. It is not by chance that Zosima speaks about 'their freedom' (14,284). For example, in *The Devils* the cautious Karmazinov (the 'great writer' who is a parody of Turgenev) prudently attempts to find out when the revolutionary disturbances in Russia will begin so that he can get out of the country in good time. There is no doubt that freedom of travel relates to the domain of the legal freedoms of man. However, even Pyotr Verkhovensky (the unscrupulous manipulator and instigator of the catastrophic events in the novel) takes this legal right of Karmazinov as a despicable escape from a sinking ship (Russia). After visiting him, Pyotr Stepanovich thinks to himself: 'you'll get out of the ship in time, rat!', and then characterises him as 'just an escaping rat; such a man won't inform on us!' (10,289). In this novel an undisguised 'right to dishonesty' presupposes above all freedom from Christian conscience, freedom from God and His Grace as the chief 'right of man' (10,288). However, in *The Brothers Karamazov*, Zosima already indicates the possible result of replacing freedom in Grace of spirit for a juridical freedom of right: 'They think they are establishing a just order, but, having rejected Christ, they will end by drenching the world in blood' (14,288). Russian history – and not only Russian history – has proven the utter validity of this prognosis of Dostoevsky.

Translated by Diane Oenning Thompson

NOTES

1 Whereas both *pravo* and *zakon* mean 'law' as defined by human institutions (international law, legal acts, codes, statutes), only *zakon* is used to denote a law beyond human control or agency, as in 'God's law' or the 'laws of nature'. Additionally, *pravo*, unlike *zakon*, means 'right', as in the vote, civil rights, and so on. Thus, *pravo* relates exclusively to the secular sphere, whereas *zakon* comprises the secular (legal, scientific) and the religious. Historically, *pravo* has sources in Roman law, whereas *zakon* and *Blagodat'* (Grace) are of biblical origin: the Law dominates in the Old Testament and Grace in the New Testament. (Translator's note.)

2 For an English translation of Hilarion's *Sermon*, see *Medieval Russia's Epics, Chronicles and Tales*, ed. Serge A. Zenkovsky (New York, 1963),

78–81. For an analysis of Hilarion's text, see J. Fennell and A. Stokes, *Early Russian Literature* (London, 1974), 41–60, and Ludolf Müller, *Die Werke des Metropoliten Ilarion (Forum Slavicum,* no. 37) (Munich, 1971).

3 See N. N. Rozov, 'Sinodal'nyi spisok sochinenii Ilariona – russkogo pisatelia XI v.', *Slavia,* 32 (Prague, 1963), 147–48; A. N. Uzhankov, 'Kogda i gde bylo prochitano Ilarionom *Slovo o Zakone i Blagodati'*, *Germenevtika russkoi literatury.* Sbornik, 7, chast' 1 (Moscow, 1994), 102.

4 Hilarion, *Slovo o Zakone i Blagodati* (Moscow, 1994), 29.

5 Hilarion, *ibid.,* 31, 33.

6 Hilarion, *ibid.,* 31.

7 V. N. Toporov, *Sviatye i sviatost' v russkoi dukhovnoi kul'ture,* vol. 1 (Moscow 1995), 264–66.

8 Fennell, *ibid.,* 59 and Serge Zenkovsky, *ibid.,* 78–79.

9 Nikolai Afanasiev, 'Vlast' liubvi: K probleme prava i blagodati', *Trudy Pravoslavnogo Bogoslovskogo Instituta v Parizhe* 14 (Paris, 1971), 13–15.

10 B. P. Vysheslavtsev, *Etika preobrazhennogo erosa* (Moscow, 1994), 34.

11 Vysheslavtsev, *ibid.,* 17

12 Vysheslavtsev, *ibid.,* 26–28.

13 Vysheslavtsev, *ibid.,* 38–39.

14 I thank Diane Oenning Thompson for drawing my attention to this point.

15 The more literal translation is *The Visitation of the Mother of God among the Torments (Khozhdenie Bogoroditsy po mukam)* where 'torments' refers to the sinners' sufferings. (Translator's note.)

16 This is precisely how it has been received by many readers in Russia – not only in Dostoevsky's time, but in the twentieth century as well, when, for example, the Symbolists saw Dante not so much as a poet proper, but as a teacher of life. See Lena Szilard and Peter Barta, 'Dantov kod russkogo simvolizma', *Studia Slavica Hungarica,* 35 (Budapest, 1989), 61–95.

17 On the essential influence of this peculiarity of Orthodox mentality on the poetics of the most important works of Russian literature see: I. A. Esaulov, *Kategoriia sobornosti v russkoi literature* (Petrozavodsk, 1995).

18 Iu. M. Lotman, *Kul'tura i vzryv* (Moscow, 1992), 257–70.

19 B. A. Uspenskii and Iu. M. Lotman, 'Rol' dual'nykh modelei v dinamike russkoi kul'tury do kontsa XVIII veka', *Izbrannye trudy,* 1 (Moscow, 1996), 339.

20 K. Mochul'skii, *Dostoevskii: Zhizn' i tvorchestvo* (Paris, 1980; first printed 1947), 518.

21 For a similar reading of this passage, see Diane Oenning Thompson, *The Brothers Karamazov and the Poetics of Memory* (Cambridge, 1991), 300–03.

22 For a more detailed discussion, see I. A. Esaulov, 'Iurodstvo i shutovstvo v russkoi literature: Nekotorye nabliudeniia', *Literaturnoe obozrenie,* 3 (1998), 108–12.

23 An important nuance is lost in English translation here. Instead of using *ee* (it) to designate the book, Dostoevsky used *ego* which, given the absence of an inanimate referent, has to mean 'him'. Hence, Smer-dyakov 'laid him [Isaac] aside'. (Translator's note.)

24 M. Bakhtin, *Estetika slovesnogo tvorchestva* (Moscow, 1979), 79, 319.

CHAPTER 7

'The Brothers Karamazov' as trinitarian theology

David S. Cunningham

The time is right, apparently, for a rebirth of trinitarian theology in the West.[1] From the Enlightenment until the mid-twentieth century, the doctrine had been largely left for dead; those who continued to affirm it often did so in merely formulaic ways, which did little to help anyone understand its significance. Nevertheless, while the doctrine has all too rarely been explicated in adequate ways, its claims have remained present – in ordinary Christian practice, in the European intellectual milieu, and even in the very air that was breathed in the (ostensibly antitrinitarian) Enlightenment. Hans-Georg Gadamer has argued that 'the Doctrine of the Trinity <. . .> has constantly stimulated the course of thought in the West as a challenge and invitation to try and think that which continually transcends the limits of human understanding'.[2]

So the soil was already fertile as the seeds of trinitarian theology were resown in the early twentieth century, by theologians such as Karl Barth and Hans Urs von Balthasar. These seeds are now producing a bumper-crop of thoughtful reflection on the Christian doctrine of God – much of it very good fruit (though not without the occasional weed).[3] The renaissance of trinitarian theology also owes a great deal to the East: to the early Greek fathers, to the ongoing Orthodox tradition, and – in general – to a region of theological discourse within which the doctrine did not fade from view (as it had in the West). It is difficult to find a significant work of recent Western trinitarian theology which does not cite names such as John Zizioulas, Vladimir Lossky and Alexander Schmemann – not to mention Saints John Damascene, Gregory of Nazianzus and Gregory of Nyssa.

However, there is, in my view, at least one other 'Eastern' source which the current generation of trinitarian theologians have not yet tapped: the writings of Dostoevsky. Even though Christian theologians have recently been more willing to turn to literary sources for illustrations (and explications) of doctrinal points, most theologians seem to view the doctrine of the Trinity as something far too esoteric, far too philosophically complex, to be explicated by means of literature. But I would suggest that for precisely these reasons – the complexity and obscurity of the doctrine – literature is one of the most appropriate vehicles for its explication.[4]

I

I begin with a few disclaimers about my method. I am not attempting to make claims about Dostoevsky's intentions in writing *The Brothers Karamazov*, whether conscious or otherwise. Those who know Dostoevsky's notebooks and correspondence better than I might be able to make such claims – or to refute them. But this would have little bearing on my argument, which is based on my particular reading of this novel. Not that I believe my reading to have been created *ex nihilo*; for regardless of Dostoevsky's personal intentions, trinitarian concerns certainly pervaded the 'region' from which he wrote. While I am highly dubious about efforts to reconstruct an author's psyche, I do recognise that all writing and speech has a source; I believe that we can legitimately inquire into the 'whence' of a text. But this source is never isolated; it is, rather, a larger network of relationships within which the text is written and read – what Calvin Schrag has called its 'space of subjectivity'.[5] The concept of such a 'space' provides a helpful way of thinking about the play of various forces that intersect and bring a text into being – that is, the forces that shape its writers and its readers. The sources of a text are pluriform and contingent; they are not exhausted by the isolated self of Romantic hermeneutics.[6] The sources of a text shape the space within which an author writes, and within which a reader reads – even if they seem different from, or even radically opposed to, the avowed 'intentions' of author and reader.

This seems especially significant in the case of Dostoevsky. He was an Orthodox Christian who held to his beliefs with a righteous fervour; and yet he was willing, in *The Brothers Karamazov* especially, to subject them to a severe test. Dostoevsky's views on religion – and on many other matters – may or may not align with those of his readers. As Victor Terras suggests, readers of the novel will endow it with a different 'subtext', depending upon their own frame of reference. And the most important element in this regard, he says, will be 'the reader's attitude towards religion. A reader whose external frame of reference includes a belief in the basic dogmas of Christianity – or perhaps in some other religion which accepts the notions of a transcendental God, immortality of the soul, and human free will – will read the novel quite differently from a reader who lacks these beliefs.'[7]

Thus, various readers will operate according to vastly different perspectives; and this will shape the range of possible readings of a text. In this chapter, I explore the ways that the range of readings of *The Brothers Karamazov* is shaped by a reader's acquaintance with the doctrine of the Trinity. I believe that certain trinitarian assumptions help to structure the 'space of subjectivity' within which Dostoevsky wrote this novel. However, these same assumptions are almost completely absent from its present-day culture of Western readers – even its Christian readers. This absence accounts, in part, for the failure of theologians to give an adequate place to *The Brothers Karamazov* within the canon of theological texts. In this chapter, then, I attempt to read 'against the grain' of much academic and theological method, and to suggest that we examine this novel as a work of trinitarian theology. In doing so, we discover not only an incisive critique of both monism and dualism, but also an explication of some of the most important claims of trinitarian doctrine. I will suggest that many of the novel's characters – and especially the three brothers – provide us with an 'icon' of the Trinity. It is, to be sure, an icon made with human hands; but it is an icon nonetheless.

II

In the theology of the early Church, the doctrine of the Trinity developed in opposition to two primary intellectual currents. The first of these was a philosophical monism, most apparent in some strands of Greek philosophy, which held that God is one and admits of no multiplicity. Among Christians, this monism tended to issue in either subordinationism, in which Jesus was a created being in God's employ (most acutely developed in early Arianism); or in modalism, in which the unity of God was emphasised by describing Father, Son and Spirit as mere 'masks' worn by the Deity at different moments. These movements generated reactions which eventually led to the emergence of trinitarian theology, as will be well known to students of the early Church.

But trinitarian theology was also a reaction against a harsh dualism of spirit and flesh – another significant intellectual current in ancient Greek thought. In early gnosticism, this had been given a specifically theological spin: the spiritual realm was ruled by God, whereas the realm of flesh was ruled by the devil, or by some minor deity (usually an incompetent or rebellious one). The divine, spiritual realm was good, and the human, fleshly realm was inadequate, corrupt, or just plain evil.

The acceptance of such dualism made it difficult to conceive of God taking on human flesh (and thus being soiled by the corrupt, carnal realities of human existence). Such anxieties produced a number of Christological heresies, such as docetism (in which Jesus only 'seemed' to be fleshly) and Apollinarianism (in which Jesus's flesh was declared 'divine', so that divinity might not be sullied by material finitude and corruption). This dualism also played a significant role in the fourth-century trinitarian controversies: It was used to justify the denial of the full divinity of the *logos* (since a truly divine being was thought by some to be incapable of taking on corrupt flesh), and hence to raise questions about the consubstantiality of 'the Father' and 'the Son'. As a result, the *homoousios* party (including St Athanasius and the Cappadocians) had to find a way to argue that the spiritual realm of divinity was not utterly incompatible with the fleshly realm of humanity.

In sum, then, early trinitarian thought was motivated by the desire to oppose both a radical monotheism and a gnostic dualism. These two enemies differed considerably, and those seeking to carve out a new doctrine of God often found themselves fighting a two-front war. The early trinitarian thinkers were most successful in developing a real alternative to both monism and dualism when they were able to discern (and attack) these two worldviews on the basis of their common elements. And what did radical monotheism and gnostic dualism have in common? Both operated with a certain 'either/or' method, constructing logical dilemmas that offered only two alternatives. Either God is one and simple, as we are told by Plato; or else God is multiple. Either God is spirit or God is flesh; God cannot be both. A human being is either under the control of God, or of the devil. The law of the excluded middle is absolute and universal.

Many early Christian writers found these logical 'either/or' dilemmas to be wholly inadequate for describing the will and power of God. They were not sure that the 'law of excluded middle' applied to God, nor even that it could apply universally in human affairs. St Gregory of Nazianzus, for example, complains loudly about the logical dilemmas proposed by the later Arians, calling his opponents 'logic-choppers'. In his *Third Theological Oration*, he proposes a series of three paradoxes – one involving time, one involving causality, and a third one – commonly known as the 'liar's paradox' ('I am now telling a falsehood') – to show that the so-called 'law of excluded middle' cannot be universally applied.[8]

This early Christian resistance to binary oppositions and 'either/or' logic pervades the early doctrinal debates; it also informs my treatment of Dostoevsky's novel. Specifically, I argue that *The Brothers Karamazov* offers a sustained polemic against binary oppositions and simplistic accounts of unity. I then show how these perspectives are resisted or expanded by Dostoevsky's *trinitarian* alternative. Finally, I will offer some initial indications about how some essential features of the Christian doctrine of God are reflected in the characters of the novel.

And now to business.

III

The first part of my argument – that Dostoevsky writes against simplistic accounts of unity and against binary oppositions – need not detain us long, since so much of the scholarly ground-clearing has already been done. Mikhail Bakhtin's description of the 'polyphonic' character of Dostoevsky's novels is widely known.[9] When we step into Dostoevsky's narrative world, we quite *expect* to find a polemic against monolithic claims and simplistic 'either/or' solutions. As Jostein Børtnes suggests, Dostoevsky's technique means that 'the author no longer so much aims at monological self-expression, as he is involved in a poetic activity in which the reader becomes a co-creator <. . .> In drawing upon the Orthodox tradition Dostoevskij overcomes what T. S. Eliot has called "the metaphysical theory of the substantial unity of the soul"'.[10] Let us consider, briefly, how this overcoming of substantialism and exclusivism plays itself out in the novel.

Ivan Karamazov is, of course, a consummate logical thinker. He is the brother with the most agile mind: the student, the free-thinker, the writer of polemical articles on Church–state relations. And it is precisely his logical mind that gets him into trouble. His chief reference point for his mode of thinking is Euclid: the formulator of perfectly logical, self-enclosed systems. That there may be a geometry beyond that of Euclid, Ivan admits; but he cannot understand it and therefore does not wish to think about it.

> If God exists and if he indeed created the earth, then, as we know perfectly well, he created it in accordance with Euclidian geometry <. . .> At the same time there were and are even now geometers and philosophers, even some of the most outstanding among them, who doubt that the whole universe, or, even more broadly, the whole of being, was created purely in accordance with Euclidean geometry; they even dare to dream that two parallel lines, which according to Euclid cannot possibly meet on earth, may perhaps meet somewhere in infinity. I, my dear, have come to the conclusion that if I cannot understand even that, then it is not for me to understand about God.[11]

A world in which parallel lines meet, like a world without the law of the excluded middle, is not Ivan's world. At the beginning of his discourse, Ivan says, 'I declare that I accept God pure and simple' (235). But we might rephrase his statement: he can accept *only* a 'pure' and 'simple' God – these terms here being understood in the philosophical sense of 'containing no non-Euclidean complexities'.

More broadly, throughout the novel, scientific reasoning and logical deduction are frequently associated with evil and with the devil, whereas a lack of logical clarity, and even contradiction, is associated with God. Dmitry worries that 'God gave us only riddles. Here the shores converge, here all contradictions live together' (108). Father Paisy says that 'the science of this world' has examined and analysed everything to the point that there is 'absolutely nothing left of what was once holy' (171). The Grand Inquisitor is a careful and logical thinker, whereas his prisoner is silent and enigmatic. Rakitin's obsession with science and logic is clearly one of his character flaws. We are even given evidence by the devil himself – Ivan's devil, that is. In his conversation with Ivan, the devil employs a great deal of French (the language of polite Russian society and of the pseudo-intellectual *poseur* of the salon); he even quotes Descartes ('je pense donc je *suis* – I'm sure of that', he says (642)). All in all, he greatly prefers the terrestrial realm that Euclid had brought under control; in this realm, he says, 'you have it all outlined, here you have the formula, here you have geometry'. He is much less enamoured of his own, 'metaphysical' realm: 'With us,' he laments, 'it's all indeterminate equations' (638). Even from early on, Ivan was vaguely aware that all this logic might lead one to despair or suicide. If he loves the world – if he has a longing for life – he recognises that this is somehow 'against logic' (230).

Furthermore, as V. E. Vetlovskaia has argued, logical proofs and refutations of evidence are constantly being circumvented in the novel.[12] Matters which should be irrelevant in logic – such as the moral character of the speaker – end up carrying the day. Morally dubious characters make claims which are logically accurate, yet unpersuasive. Consider, for example, the arguments of the defence attorney, or Ivan's claim that he played no role in the murder. And the devil himself knows that 'proofs are no help to faith, especially material proofs. Thomas believed not because he saw the risen Christ but because he wanted to believe even before that' (636). Dostoevsky, like St Gregory of Nazianzus before him (and many other Christian thinkers), believed that our routine logical deductions cannot be so easily carried over into the metaphysical realm. Victor Terras comments: 'Dostoevsky's notebook entries suggest that he was aware that a different logic applies to the material world and to the metaphysical or "other world".'[13] And I would add that Dostoevsky's other-worldly logic will necessarily make room for a specifically trinitarian mode of thought.

IV

When we approach Dostoevsky's fiction with specifically trinitarian concerns, the significance of Bakhtin's claims about 'polyphony' is heightened. The rebellion against monologic discourse, against the gravitation toward a single consciousness, is more than simply an aesthetic choice; it appears to spring from theological convictions. Dostoevsky's work is grounded in a metaphysical outlook in which the central point of focus is not individual consciousness, but *subsistent relationality*. According to this perspective, there are no fixed essences, but only fluctuations and displacements; personhood is thus not 'individuality', but is exhaustively constituted by relations to others.[14] These profoundly theological themes are carefully woven into Bakhtin's own work, as his biographers and commentators seem increasingly willing to admit. For example, as Katerina Clark and Michael Holquist observe, 'Two concepts that are bound up with the kenotic tradition [in Russian Orthodoxy] had a powerful effect on

Bakhtin's thought. The first of these is a radical communality (*sobornost'*); the second is a profound respect for the material realities of everyday experience.'[15]

Bakhtin's theological and metaphysical convictions were clearly at work in his evaluation of Dostoevsky's fiction. In fact, he sees the Christian belief in 'the communion of saints' as a type for Dostoevsky's theological and literary perspective:

If we were to seek an image toward which this whole world gravitates, an image in the spirit of Dostoevsky's own worldview, then it would be the church as a communion of unmerged souls, where sinners and the righteous come together; or perhaps it would be the image of Dante's world, where multi-leveledness is extended into eternity.[16]

Clearly, this perspective is radically different from the modern Western faith in the supposedly autonomous individual.[17]

Importantly, however, this notion of 'radical communality' or 'subsistent relationality' in Bakhtin's discussion of Dostoevsky's fiction is more than simply an assertion about the nature of humanity; it is also an assertion about the nature of God.[18] Indeed, the very term that I have employed to describe Dostoevsky's alternative to Western individualism – 'subsistent relationality' – calls forth the Christian doctrine of God, and the traditional claim that the *hypostases* of the Trinity are 'subsistent relations'. Are Dostoevsky's 'polyphonic discourse' and his critique of Western individualism related to the specifically Russian Orthodox understanding of God? An affirmative answer to this question is suggested by Julia Kristeva. After taking note of the strong pneumatologic and mystic tendencies of Russian Orthodoxy, she comments that:

It would be impossible to understand Dostoyevsky without it. His dialogism, his polyphony undoubtedly spring from multiple sources. It would be a mistake to neglect that of Orthodox faith whose Trinitarian conception (difference and unity of the three Persons within a generalised pneumatology inviting any subjectivity to a maximal display of its contradictions) inspires the writer's 'dialogism' as well as his praise of suffering *at the same time* as forgiving.[19]

I want to corroborate Kristeva's claim by building some bridges between Dostoevsky's Orthodox trinitarianism and the language of his novel.

To begin, of course, there is the number *three*. As many commentators have noted, triads dominate the novel. There are three 'strains' or 'ruptures' ('lacerations' in the Garnett–Matlaw translation), three 'confessions of an ardent heart', three temptations of Christ (mirrored by the three forces employed by the Inquisitor), three meetings with Smerdyakov, three 'torments of the soul'. The murder and the investigation focuses on Dmitry's need for 3,000 roubles, and the galloping troika is invoked at his trial (on three different occasions). Fyodor is murdered by being hit three times with a paperweight weighing about three pounds; the murderer takes from him an envelope (containing 3,000 roubles) which is sealed with 'large red wax seals' – yes, you've guessed – three of them.

To these more obvious references, scholars have added some that are more subtle: each of the three brothers experiences an epiphany of sorts (Alyosha during the reading of the story of the Wedding at Cana; Dmitry at Mokroe; Ivan with the devil). Alyosha also experiences three trials – by Father Ferapont, Rakitin and Grushenka – which places him in parallel to his brothers, who each experience a series of three trials as well.[20] The story of Zosima's life develops his character by means of three interrelated stories (those of Markel, the duel and the mysterious visitor).[21] Several times in the novel, Dmitry has to choose among three options that are open to him.[22] The epigraph of the novel occurs three times in the text. And on, and on. As William Rowe comments, although many additional instances of this 'triplicity' could be cited, 'the phenomenon seems to grade off – such is the weakness of this type of analysis – into a series of rather inconsequential details'.[23] All the same, he finds this structure sufficiently pervasive that he speaks of *The Brothers Karamazov* as marked by a 'triplicity' that is 'well in excess of Dostoevsky's customary fondness for tripartite patterning'.[24]

All this suggests that the number three holds, for Dostoevsky, much more than aesthetic and literary value. It is a mystical number, and has been considered such since ancient times. Its presence does not, by itself, make a case for reading the novel as trinitarian theology. But it does, I think, *invite* such a reading. And this invitation is underscored by our knowledge of Dostoevsky's activities and relationships while he was writing the novel. As a number of commentators have noted, the shape of *The Brothers Karamazov* was heavily influenced by Dostoevsky's relationship with Vladimir Solovyov.[25] This relationship may very well have helped to intensify the novelist's fascination with triads and triplicity.

Solovyov presented his *Lectures on Godmanhood* in 1878; they were attended by Dostoevsky and by many other prominent thinkers of his day. This is not the place for a full-scale explication of those lectures; suffice it to say that they are critical of the sort of isolating individualism that the West has come to take for granted.[26] While Solovyov advocated a philosophy of 'All-Unity', this unity did not dissolve differences but merely relativised them; as such, it allowed for the autonomy of particular spheres, but not for an absolute autonomy of separation and isolation.[27]

This philosophical conception in general, and many of the *Lectures on Godmanhood* in particular, are suffused with a trinitarian perspective.[28] For example, lectures six and seven argue that the Christian doctrine of the Trinity is in accord with human reason, and that the Triune God is made manifest in the very nature of human person-hood as relational. Solovyov's perspective is akin to that of St Augustine, whom he quotes with respect to the latter's trinitarian analogies. Solovyov's favourite Augustinian analogy, however, is not one of the frequently-cited ones from *De Trinitate*, but from the *Confessions*, in which Augustine speaks of the human psyche as 'being, knowing, and willing'. Solovyov comments that 'each of these three fundamental acts of the spirit is completed in itself by the other two, and thus becomes individualised into a full triune being'.[29]

None of this is meant to suggest that Dostoevsky's trinitarian perspective was developed only through his relationship with Solovyov. After all, Dostoevsky was an Orthodox Christian; the doctrine of the Trinity (and its implications for the nature of human existence) would have been part of the air that he had breathed throughout his life. Nevertheless, Solovyov's lectures may have helped Dostoevsky to develop his most obvious triad of all: the three 'brothers' who give his novel its title.

Many commentators have suggested that the three (legitimate) brothers provide an overall structure for the novel. Some have focused on Solovyov's triads, suggesting, for example, that 'being, knowing, and willing' are respective descriptions for Dmitry (driven by the passion of the moment, he simply 'is'), Ivan (the careful thinker) and Alyosha (who leaves the monastery and goes out into the world, to act).[30] But even without Solovyov's schema, the brothers can be seen as representing the three aspects of human nature (mind, body and spirit). Nathan Rosen sees them as responding, each in a different way, to the calculative, logical thinking of the Grand Inquisitor.[31]

I want to offer a more intentionally theological reading, in which the three brothers provide a very human reflection of the triune God. It is no accident that their number is three; even Smerdyakov's status as a possible fourth brother has the effect of emphasising the importance of the number *three*. (Smerdyakov's illegitimacy and his crime do not, in themselves, make him any less a reflection of God than his three half-brothers; indeed, as we observe below, even the greatest sinners reflect, however dimly, the *imago dei*. Nevertheless, like the thirteenth guest at the banquet, this fourth brother is the outsider who breaks open the already strained relationships and thereby implicitly draws attention to the significance of the number *three*.)

For the purposes of my argument, each brother need not represent a particular person of the Trinity. More significant is the way in which the three relate to one another; they do so in ways that illustrate the essential trinitarian concept of *perichoresis*, in which the specific characteristics of the three *hypostases* are understood to interpenetrate one another in a way that binds them in relationship.[32] And lest this seem too esoteric an aspect of trinitarian doctrine for it to have concerned the author, it should be noted that for Solovyov, it is one of the most important aspects of God's triune nature – and one with serious implications for the nature of *humanity*.[33]

Note how this phenomenon is emphasised in the novel: Ivan's anarchism is embraced by Dmitry and even, in various moments of crisis, by Alyosha himself (after the 'stink of corruption' following Zosima's death, and at the climax of Ivan's account of the tormentors of children in 'Rebellion'). Dmitry's quarrelsome and confrontational nature occasionally seems to be detectable, although usually well under the surface, in Alyosha (who sometimes responds harshly and then retracts or moderates his claim), and more obviously in Ivan (especially at the trial). And Alyosha's devoted faithfulness seems to lurk in the depths of his brothers as well: in Ivan, to whom Zosima attributes a 'higher heart', and whose passion for justice leads him finally to confess his own 'involvement' in the crime; and in Dmitry, who (for the most part) endures the humiliation of his accusation and trial with uncharacteristic calm. Bakhtin repeatedly points to double-voiced dialogues among the brothers, in which one character often responds externally to the 'internal' voice of the other, and in which the dialogue partners are woven together by their hidden rejoinders and unspoken replies.[34]

On one level, the relationships among the three brothers simply constitute an instance of the polyphonic character of Dostoevsky's work. But, as I noted above in quoting Kristeva, something more may be at work here. The 'plurality of independent and unmerged voices and consciousnesses'[35] of which Bakhtin writes is, in the case of this particular novel at least, clearly related to the plurality and non-identity of the triune God: the Three who are One. The very word polyphony suggests that these voices can never be completely isolated from one another; a true polyphony demands some semblance of mutually productive relationship, as well as a guarantee of diversity and difference.

The symphonic power of the three voices of this novel is secured by the fact that all three brothers are Karamazovs. Each brother provides us with a slightly different reading of what it means to be a Karamazov, but the family as a whole tells us more than does the sum of its members. As Boyce Gibson has pointed out, Dostoevsky's novel 'can be read as the story of Dmitry, or of Ivan, or of Alyosha: it has in fact been read in all these ways, naturally with different results'. He then goes on to argue for a reading which keeps 'the whole of the family in perspective the whole of the time'.[36] And if we follow him in this reading, we cannot elevate Alyosha to the status of an angel, nor simply dismiss Ivan as a devil. To be a Karamazov is to be angelic, and demonic, and many others things as well: indeed, to be possessed of all these elements – to differing degrees, to be sure – but possessed all the same.

Precisely because they are *three* brothers in *one* family, Dostoevsky is able to shift the reader's attention away from the individual consciousness of the 'hero', towards a simultaneous recognition of unity and difference. The three are truly 'persons' in the most profound sense of the word, in that their individuality is defined by their relationships to others (they are, to a degree, 'subsistent relations'). But the three are also truly one; just as their given names divide them, so their family name draws them together.

This point has been emphasised by Janine Langan. She focuses on the novel's closing lines, in which an answer to its most basic question

is proposed by Alyosha's disciples, in a statement not judging but eucharistic, beyond the closure of normative language: 'Hurrah for Karamazov.' This choral extolling of Alyosha under his family name – black smeared – brings to an end all deflated attempts at mythical egoism. Calling for joyful response to their common mirror-image, it demands of all present the ritual acceptance of their iconic vocation, the incarnation of God in fallen flesh, if only for an instant.[37]

Here we are asked to consider the rather outlandish claim that the Karamazov family bears the image of God. It is comparatively easy to believe that God might be manifest in one particular, historical, ultimately good human being. But that God might be manifest in the *Karamazov* family, with all its faults and failings, and that we are called to love *them* and bear responsibility for *them*: this is the true scandal of the Trinity, and that which Dostoevsky most thoroughly underscores in his work.

But why is 'the incarnation of God in fallen flesh' represented by human characters at all? Does not Christianity assert that the incarnation is a quite specific claim, referring only to the man Jesus? Why attend to an icon made with human hands, or made of fallen human flesh, when one can appeal to the one true 'image [Greek: *eikōn*] of the invisible God' (Col. 1:15), namely Jesus Christ? Here we see a difference in emphasis between Eastern and Western Christianity. In the West, we seem to be so severely tempted to idolatry – to think of the created order in terms appropriate only to God – that we have sought all sorts of measures to stave off this temptation. We have dramatically emphasised the uniqueness of the historical man Jesus as the unique locus of the incarnation, and we have been extremely nervous about any language of deification. In the East, where the distance between God and humanity has somehow been recognised as more obviously apparent, the language of *theosis* has a very prominent place; and the incarnate Christ is never understood in merely 'historical' terms.

In the novel, the 'Western' view is most clearly articulated by the Grand Inquisitor, for whom Christ is simply a past event whose memory the Inquisitor is actively seeking to erase (and whose reappearance causes him considerable consternation). In the words of George Panichas, the Inquisitor's concern is with 'the historical Christ, who had come and gone', in contrast to 'the *spiritual, or essential, Christ*, who has always been present in human souls', and who had become incarnate in order to manifest the fullness of God in bodily form.[38] The Inquisitor espouses a typical modern Western Christology, focusing primarily on historical questions. But in Eastern Orthodoxy, the significance of the incarnation can never be understood in such narrow terms. It is a cosmic event; Christ is the 'One of the Holy Trinity' who is made flesh and who suffers in the flesh – the One who takes up all of history into his act and transcends it. This should not be taken to deny the material reality of the incarnation, as abstract and mystical interpretations of Dostoevsky have sometimes tried to do.[39] It is, instead, a way of emphasising that the purpose of the incarnation is not simply to provide a role model for the ethically-minded. Christ is of *cosmic* significance precisely because of 'the intersection of the material and the divine' which is part and parcel of Christian theology, and which requires us to recognise the larger trinitarian context which surrounds the doctrine of the Incarnation. The Inquisitor, on the other hand, is concerned only

with the *visible* aspects of the Church: the externalities of material necessity and rational analyses of faith, and he symbolises the great gulf that exists between the visible and the invisible Church, since he cannot and will not accept the concept of the Holy Spirit and Christ Himself dwelling in both the visible (earthly) and invisible (eternal) Church, effecting a perfect harmony of the earthly and the heavenly, the human and the divine.[40]

Of course, Christ *is* the image of the invisible God; but through him, we also may be raised to divine glory. Even if we are Karamazovs.

v

Our final task, then, is to understand how the characters themselves bear the imprint of God, and thereby function as an icon of the Trinity. It is, as I have already said, a very *human* icon; it is therefore beset with all the shortcomings of the created order. Nevertheless, the power of any icon lies in its ability to transcend its humble origins, and to become the means by which its viewer is transfigured and brought into communion with God. And so it is with human beings – all of whom are icons, by virtue of the fact that they bear the *imago dei*. As Father Paisy reminds Alyosha, even 'those who renounce Christianity and rebel against it are in their essence of the same image of the same Christ, and such they remain' (171).

I make no attempt to distribute, among the three brothers, the various 'appropriated qualities' of the Trinity – that is, those aspects of God which are more frequently associated with one of the hypostases.[41] I attempt to suggest, however, that many of the characters – and especially the three brothers – help to illustrate some of the most prominent attributes of the Triune God, namely: love, suffering and communion.

The Triune God of Christian faith is a loving God and a forgiving God. The seeds of this claim are already planted in Ivan's parable, when he is prompted by Alyosha to give his 'poem' an ending. The contrast could not be greater: on the one hand, the talkative Inquisitor, with his supposed 'love' for humanity (but only in the abstract, of course; individual human beings he happily burns). On the other hand, we have the silent Christ, who 'suddenly approaches the old man in silence and gently kisses him on his bloodless, ninety-year-old lips' (262). And then Ivan speaks words loaded with irony: 'That is the whole answer.' The answer is *love* – love for one's enemies, which has the power to defeat them. The prisoner is let out into the dark squares of the city; and as for the old man, 'the kiss burns in his heart, but [he] holds to his former idea.' 'And you with him!' replies Alyosha to his brother. For Alyosha fears that Ivan has taken the side against love. Admittedly, Ivan will not join the Jesuits or become an inquisitor; but, for all his professed love of humanity, he will come to love actual, concrete human beings only after he has experienced great trials. Alyosha rightly asks him: 'And the sticky little leaves, and the precious graves, and the blue sky, and the woman you love! How will you live, what will you love them with?' (263)[42]

By the end of the novel, we sense that Ivan may have glimpsed the necessity of such love, even if this sight has shocked and devastated him. And the novel gives us many examples of those who do love humanity in all its fallenness. Of course, it is not one of the brothers, but Zosima, who provides the prototype of such love in the novel – a love which is all-encompassing.

Love man also in his sin, for this likeness of God's love is the height of love on earth. Love all of God's creation, both the whole of it and every grain of sand. Love every leaf, every ray of God's light. Love animals, love plants, love each thing. If you love each thing, you will perceive the mystery of God in things. Once you have perceived it, you will begin tirelessly to perceive more and more of it every day. And you will come at last to love the whole world with an entire, universal love. (318–19)

This is not 'rosy Christianity', nor an attempt to deny the realities of the created order (and the ways they have been abused). It is, rather, a self-discipline of love, in which we are trained by God to be like God – not by means of an egoistic overreaching, but precisely because God shows us the way.

No one is capable of perfection in this regard; even Zosima

laments of his failures. When he dies, his body proves itself to be as corruptible as any other. But the true miracle, as Alyosha finally realises, is not incorruptible flesh, but the incarnation of Zosima's love – or more precisely, of Christ's love – in the most unlikely places.[43] For this love is recognisable not only in Alyosha, but even, at times, in Dmitry and Ivan. Dmitry expresses his love often in the text – sometimes too carnally, to be sure, but often and unexpectedly in ways that resemble God's love (as in his dream of the 'babe'). And Ivan discovers that he is not, in fact, the devil – by meeting the latter face to face. In the process, he discovers that he is perhaps not as empty of love as he had professed himself to be.

Another central claim concerning the Christian doctrine of God is that 'one of the divine persons suffered in the flesh'. The doctrine of the Trinity describes God as having participated in human affairs and having suffered the slings and arrows of this mortal coil. Dostoevsky defends this notion as well, emphasising a kenotic Christology in which innocent suffering is actually redemptive. It can redeem precisely because it is paired with forgiveness. And because it is God's will for humanity, it must also be made the will of human beings. Kristeva writes, 'Confronted with that stay of time and actions within the timelessness of forgiving, we understand those who believe that God alone can forgive. In Christianity, however, the stay, divine to be sure, of crimes and punishments is *first* the work of human beings.'[44]

This idea, too, is present in the portrait of Christ in Ivan's parable, who suffers the Inquisitor's harangue and appears quite ready to suffer at the stake as well. It is also present in Zosima himself, as well as in the story of his brother Markel, and in the boy Ilyusha. But it is most markedly (and remarkably) present in the character of Dmitry, who eventually comes to consider the possibility that his own innocent suffering may be redemptive.

Dmitry's actions, from the time of the murder to the end of the book, clearly parallel the sufferings of Jesus – from his 'last supper' at Mokroe, to his arrest and apprehension (at which he is unjustly accused, questioned, mocked and stripped). He will later be tried; false witnesses will be brought against him, and he will be found guilty, much to the delight of the crowd assembled for the spectacle. But he will endure it, because he has come to believe what Zosima teaches – though he did not learn it from Zosima. He has learned that we are all responsible to all and for all, even to the cold and

hungry 'babe' about whom he has dreamed. Dmitry wakens from
that dream, and notices that someone has, out of compassion, placed
a pillow under his head. He then announces that he is willing to sign
the transcript of the arrest interview, even without reviewing it. He
knows that, even if he is not guilty of that of which he has been
accused, he is nevertheless guilty, and responsible.

Finally, the doctrine of the Trinity emphasises the notion of
mutual participation and communion. Each of the three brothers is
at his worst when he sees himself in isolation from others – whether
towering above them, fleeing from them or being abandoned by
them. This tendency towards romantic individualism and even
isolationism – so much a part of the intellectual furniture for those of
us in the West – leads only to alienation and violence. According to
Florovsky, Dostoevsky believed that 'the ultimate source of all social
ills is the spiritual disintegration and dissociation of human life, the
decay or decrease of brotherhood among men.'[45]

How is this alienation to be avoided? Dostoevsky believes that it
requires us to participate *in* and *with* the lives of others – not only in
the ultimate sense countenanced by Zosima in the novel ('responsibility to all and for all'), but also in our perichoretic relationships.
According to N. A. Zabolotsky, Dostoevsky insists that the human
being must learn to be, 'if we may use Christian terminology
(whether understood theologically or in a secular fashion), a "con-
ciliar person", a member of the Body of Christ <. . .> [This] implies
a movement from the personal, always somewhat egoistic, to the
social, in other words, from "I" to "we".'[46] Of course, one could
read all this as merely a lesson in social psychology, an invitation to
break free from the pervasive Western diseases of loneliness and
ennui and to recognise one's connectedness to the human race. But
something else may be at stake here – a harmony of the personal
and the social which is at the root of the Christian doctrine of God.
Zabolotsky continues: 'The trinitarian nature of God as recognised
in Christianity implies the ideal harmony of the personal attributes
of God in the Father, Son and Holy Spirit within the *koinonia* and the
dynamics of *symphonia* for the "unity of all in all".'[47]

Note that no *one* of the characters, not even Alyosha or Zosima,
can alone bear God's image. For the image of God belongs not to
any one human being, but – according to Genesis 1:27 – to human
beings. Thus, at the end of the novel, the gathered children do not
shout 'Hurrah for Alyosha' – as many commentators seem to have

done, but 'Hurrah for Karamazov.' This forces us to recognise how all three brothers – and even their father! – contribute to the essence of this name. And only then can we fully realise the novel's profound trinitarian implications. Boyce Gibson, again:

Any one of the three brothers, from a particular point of view, is the centre of the story. Dmitry commands the plot; Ivan is the ideological centre; Alyosha is the spiritual climax. As the novel has a plot, an ideology, and a destination, none of them can be neglected and all must be held together at every turn of the road.[48]

Few novels have been so successful in recognising the simultaneity of oneness and threeness as is this story of the three very different brothers, all of whom are still Karamazovs. It is not accidental then, that where the elements of love, suffering and community come together in the novel, God is there. Remember Dr Herzenstube, who showed compassion to Dmitry when the latter was just a child. When Dmitry returned to town, one of his first acts was to visit the doctor, to come back 'into communion' with this man who had loved him – in a very small way, of course – in the midst of his own suffering. It is no accident, I believe, that Herzenstube's gift of a pound of nuts was accompanied by a brief catechism: '*Gott der Vater, Gott der Sohn, Gott der heilige Geist*' (674).

Why have the trinitarian elements of *The Brothers Karamazov* typically been so difficult to discern? One explanation may be that critics have often focused on the human psyche as the primary object of Dostoevsky's interest. They have called him a 'psychologist' or an 'anthropologist'. But of course, psychology (in its true etymological sense) is the study of the *soul*; and, in the Orthodox tradition especially, an emphasis on the doctrine of the *imago dei* means that anthropology is inseparable from theology, inseparable from the doctrine of God. Human beings are created in the image of God, and they are also perfected in God, ultimately by becoming divine (the doctrine of *theōsis*). Thus, whenever Dostoevsky is described as having provided a particularly compelling portrait of concrete human beings, the astute reader will also be aware of the claims about God that are implicit in such portraits.

This is not to suggest that Dostoevsky collapses the distinction between God and humanity. Rather, in his novels, we find a radically *sacramental* worldview. He believes that God is signified by the mundane aspects of the created order as well as by its most glorious aspects. Again, Janine Langan finds this most clearly expressed at the end of the novel, when the boys gathered at the stone shout 'Hurrah for Karamazov.'

Beyond all Romantic judgmental aggression, it is a pledge of solidarity with all the Karamazov adolescents encountered in the book, not only Alyosha but his father and brothers as well. For they, too, are icons. However crippled, however involved in myth, they testify through their growing pains and twisted faces to the irresistible presence in them of an ineradicable seed: God's image and likeness.[49]

Even the most debased, 'black smeared' characters point us back to the perfect communion of the inner life of God: the communion that informs and underwrites our common bond of humanity, and the communion in which even we 'great sinners' are called to participate.

In the face of such a gift, we can only say: 'Hurrah for Karamazov!'

NOTES

1 Special thanks to Margaret Adam and A. K. M. Adam, who read early drafts of this chapter and helped give it shape. Thanks also to participants at the conference on 'Reading Dostoevsky Religiously' at the University of Glasgow for encouragement and suggestions, and to an anonymous reader for Cambridge University Press (particularly for further insights concerning Bakhtin and Solovyov). I develop some related themes in 'Trinitarian rhetoric in Murdoch, Morrison, and Dostoevsky', in *Literature and Theology at Century's End*, eds. Robert Detweiler and Gregory L. Salyers (Atlanta, GA, 1995), 189–213. Some parts of this chapter appear in a different form in *These Three Are One: The Practice of Trinitarian Theology* (Oxford, 1998).

2 Hans-Georg Gadamer, 'The relevance of the beautiful: Art as symbol, play, and festival', in *The Relevance of the Beautiful and Other Essays*, ed. Robert Bernasconi, trans. Nicholas Walker (Cambridge, 1986), 5.

3 For summaries of this work, see Catherine Mowry LaCugna, 'Philosophers and theologians on the trinity', in *Modern Theology*. 2, no. 3 (April 1986), 169–81; 'Current trends in trinitarian theology', in *Religious Studies Review*, 13, no. 2 (April 1987), 141–47; David S. Cunningham, 'Trinitarian theology since 1990' and 'What's [not] new in trinitarian theology', both in *Reviews in Religion and Theology*, 2, no. 4 (1995), 8–16 and 4, no. 1 (1997), 14–20. Some of the more important works of the past twenty years include Leonardo Boff, *Trinity and Society*, trans. Paul Burns (Tunbridge Wells; Maryknoll, NY, 1988); Colin Gunton, *The Promise of Trinitarian Theology* (Edinburgh, 1990); *The One, The Three, and the Many: God, Creation, and the Culture of Modernity* (Cambridge, 1993); Robert W. Jenson, *The*

Triune Identity: God According to the Gospel (Philadelphia, PA, 1982); Eberhard Jüngel, *The Doctrine of the Trinity: God's Being is in Becoming*, trans. Horton Harris (Edinburgh, 1976); *God as the Mystery of the World*, trans. Darrell L. Guder (Grand Rapids, MI, 1983); Walter Kasper, *The God of Jesus Christ*, trans. Matthew J. O'Connell (London, 1983); Catherine Mowry LaCugna, *God For Us: The Trinity and Christian Life* (San Francisco, CA, 1991); Jürgen Moltmann, *The Trinity and the Kingdom: The Doctrine of God*, trans. Margaret Kohl (New York, 1981); *History and the Triune God: Contributions to Trinitarian Theology* (New York, 1992).

4 Some helpful observations on the ways in which philosophical problems can be explicated by means of literature in general, and by *The Brothers Karamazov* in particular, may be found in Stewart R. Sutherland, *Atheism and the Rejection of God: Contemporary Philosophy and 'The Brothers Karamazov'*, ed. D. Z. Phillips (Oxford, 1977).

5 Calvin O. Schrag, *Communicative Praxis and the Space of Subjectivity* (Bloomington, IN, 1986).

6 See the helpful comments in Joseph C. Flay's 'Review of *Communicative Praxis and the Space of Subjectivity* by Calvin O. Schrag', *Philosophy and Rhetoric*, 21, no. 4 (1988), 294–304.

7 Victor Terras, *A Karamazov Companion: Commentary on the Genesis, Language, and Style of Dostoevsky's Novel* (Madison, WI, 1981), 97.

8 St Gregory of Nazianzus, 'Oration 29: On the Son', in *Faith Gives Fullness to Reasoning: The Five Theological Orations of Gregory Nazianzen*, ed. Frederick W. Norris, trans. Lionel Wickham and Frederick Williams, *Supplements to Vigiliae Christianae*, vol. 13 (Leiden, 1991), 245–61.

9 M. Bakhtin, *Problems of Dostoevsky's Poetics*, ed. and trans. Caryl Emerson, intro. Wayne C. Booth, *Theory and History of Literature*, vol. 8 (Minneapolis, MN, 1984), 6ff.

10 Jostein Børtnes, 'The function of hagiography in Dostoevskij's novels' (1978), in *Critical Essays on Dostoevsky*, ed. Robin Feuer Miller (Boston, MA, 1986), 192.

11 Fyodor Dostoevsky, *The Brothers Karamazov*, trans. Richard Pevear and Larissa Volokhonsky (New York, 1990), 235. All quotations of the text are from this translation; page numbers are hereafter given in brackets in the text.

12 E. Vetlovskaia, 'Rhetoric and poetics: The affirmation and refutation of opinions in Dostoevsky's *The Brothers Karamazov*', in Miller, ed., *Critical Essays on Dostoevsky*, 224–25.

13 Terras, *A Karamazov Companion*, 42–43.

14 The Russian word for 'personality' (*lichnost'*) never refers to an isolated, autonomous person; indeed, the root *lik* refers to the face on an icon (!), at which one gazes and through which one is connected with the community of believers and is thus transfigured. Russian has other words for 'individual human specimen', 'one of a species', and so on – some of which sound cold and even clinical.

15 Katerina Clark and Michael Holquist, *Mikhail Bakhtin* (Cambridge, 1984), 85.

16 Bakhtin, *Problems of Dostoevsky's Poetics*, 27.

17 For a further discussion of Dostoevsky's critique of (Western) individualism, see Sutherland, *Atheism and the Rejection of God*, 107.

18 More detailed attention to the specifically theological manifestations of these themes is provided in two recent studies of Bakhtin: Alexandar Mihailovic, *Corporeal Worlds: Bakhtin's Theology of Discourse* (Evanston, IL, 1997), and Ruth Coates, *Christianity in Bakhtin: God and the Exiled Author* (Cambridge, 1998).

19 Julia Kristeva, 'Dostoyevsky, the writing of suffering, and forgiveness', in *Black Sun: Depression and Melancholia*, trans. Leon S. Roudiez (New York, 1989), 214.

20 These latter two elements are summarised in Terras, *A Karamazov Companion*, 107.

21 Observed by Sutherland, *Atheism and the Rejection of God*, 110.

22 Robert Belknap, *The Structure of 'The Brothers Karamazov'* (The Hague, 1967), 112.

23 William W. Rowe, '*Crime and Punishment* and *The Brothers Karamazov*: some comparative observations', *Russian Literature Triquarterly*, 10 (1975), 339. Readers are referred to this article for a much more extensive list of triads.

24 *Ibid.*, 335.

25 See, for example, Konstantin Mochulsky, *Dostoevsky: His Life and Work*, trans. and intro. Michael A. Minihan (Princeton, NJ, 1967), 566; Hans Urs von Balthasar, *The Glory of the Lord: A Theological Aesthetics*, vol. 3, *Studies in Theological Style: Lay Styles*, ed. John Riches, trans. Andrew Louth, John Saward, Martin Simon and Rowan Williams (San Francisco, CA, 1986), 294–95, 343–44. In his *Legal Philosophies of Russian Liberalism* (Oxford, 1987), Andrzej Walicki comments that, according to Sergius Hessen (Sergei Gessen), 'Soloviev's influence penetrated the entire construction of Dostoevsky's *The Brothers Karamazov*' (p. 170, note 15).

26 See the comments of Peter P. Zouboff in the introduction to his translation: *Vladimir Solovyov's Lectures on Godmanhood* (n.p.: International University Press, 1944), 55–56. Later in his life, Solovyov would come to transfigure this critique into something that could ally itself with (what Dostoevsky would have seen as) the more monolithic and individualistic structures of Roman Catholicism. See Walicki, *Legal Philosophies of Russian Liberalism*, 171–75.

27 Walicki, *Legal Philosophies*, 176.

28 *Ibid.*, 176–79.

29 Solovyov, *Lectures on Godmanhood*, 157.

30 See, for example, Mochulsky, *Dostoevsky*, 598–99.

31 Nathan Rosen, 'Style and structure in *The Brothers Karamazov*', *Russian Literature Triquarterly*, 1 (1971), 352–65.

32 For more on this point, see Mihailovic, *Bakhtin's Theology of Discourse.*

33 Solovyov, *Lectures on Godmanhood,* 151–54.

34 Bakhtin, *Problems of Dostoevsky's Poetics,* 254–60.

35 Bakhtin, *ibid.,* 6.

36 Boyce Gibson, *The Religion of Dostoevsky* (London, 1973; reprint, Philadelphia, PA, 1974), 170.

37 Janine Langan, 'Icon vs. myth: Dostoevsky, feminism and pornography' *Religion and Literature,* 18, no. 1 (Spring 1986), 71–72.

38 George A. Panichas, 'Fyodor Dostoevsky and Roman Catholicism', *Greek Orthodox Theological Review,* 4 (Summer 1958), 22.

39 See the synopsis of this phenomenon in Colin Crowder, 'The appropriation of Dostoevsky in the early twentieth century: Cult, counter-cult and incarnation', in *European Literature and Theology in the Twentieth Century,* ed. David Jasper and Colin Crowder (London, 1990), 15–33.

40 Panichas, 'Fyodor Dostoevsky', 31.

41 However, it might be possible to do so; indeed, I suspect that the 'doctrine of appropriations' might be a fruitful avenue for further exploration of this theme. It may have been on Dostoevsky's mind as he wrote, since it was emphasised (and applied directly to human personhood) by Solovyov in his lectures. See *Lectures on Godmanhood,* 150–51.

42 On the contrast between Ivan's occasionally professed 'love' and his more consistent embrace of 'death', see especially Diane Oenning Thompson, *'The Brothers Karamazov' and the Poetics of Memory* (Cambridge, 1991), 179–86.

43 For some helpful comments on the ways in which the traditional concept of 'miracle' is refigured into 'love' in the novel, see Sutherland, *Atheism and the Rejection of God,* 118–20.

44 Kristeva, 'Dostoyevsky', 200; translation slightly altered.

45 Georges Florovsky, 'Three masters: Gogol, Dostoevsky, Tolstoy', *Epiphany: A Journal of Faith and Insight* 10 (Summer 1990), 51.

46 A. Zabolotsky, 'Fyodor Mikhailovich Dostoevsky today', *Scottish Journal of Theology,* 37, no. 1 (1984), 46–47.

47 *Ibid.,* 47.

48 Gibson, *The Religion of Dostoevsky,* 175.

49 Langan, 'Icon vs. myth', 72.

CHAPTER 8

Reading and incarnation in Dostoevsky

Eric Ziolkowski

'Only what on earth do I want here? Yes, to read!'
(Raskolnikov in *Crime and Punishment*[1])

Why do Dostoevsky's characters read? Over two decades ago, Ralph Matlaw called attention to Dmitryj Tschizewskij's 'seminal' 1929 essay on the influence of Schiller in *The Brothers Karamazov*: in his words, it emphasised 'Dostoevsky's extraordinary concern with the use of literature, the possibilities of characterization and deepening of portraits by citation of other literary works, a technical innovation of Dostoevsky's which has not yet been sufficiently investigated.'[2] Within the past twenty years, valuable investigations have been made of this area, not the least of which are Victor Terras's commentary on *The Brothers Karamazov*, which documents scores of literary allusions, quotations, and paraphrases; Nina Perlina's analysis of the aesthetic function of quotation in that same novel; and a convenient compilation of Gospel-related excerpts from Dostoevsky's fiction, issued by the Hutterian Brethren.[3] Nonetheless, a heightened awareness of the myriad citations in Dostoevsky's fiction will not alone lead to a full comprehension of his narrative employment of literature, hagiography and the Bible, or the role such citations play in his portrayal of characters. There is, of course, the formal question of how such citations fit into his broader poetics of polyphony, dialogism and carnival, as these hallmarks of his art were so notably fleshed out by Mikhail Bakhtin. An answer could probably be drawn from Bakhtin's discussion of Dostoevsky's creative renewal of the ancient menippean genre. With its characteristically wide use of various inserted genres (novellas, letters, speeches, newspaper articles and so forth), and its tendency to mix prose and verse,[4] the menippea would seem naturally conducive to incorporating literary, biblical and other citations. By the same token, Perlina has already performed a great service for students of *The Brothers Karamazov* by demonstrating from a Bakhtinian perspective that 'quotation organizes the whole architectonics of [that] novel'.[5]

However, even the critical contributions of Bakhtin and the further application of his theories by Perlina cannot exhaust the matter of literary and biblical citations in Dostoevsky. After identifying such citations, interpreting their bearing upon characterisation, and settling the question of their pertinence to narrative form, we would be left with a still more fundamental question. Citations of written texts presuppose reading. Why do Dostoevsky's characters read in the first place? Or, what is the significance of reading as an act in Dostoevsky's fiction?

In this chapter I suggest that the act of reading by Dostoevsky's protagonists, especially when they read or recite aloud, bears directly upon a constant compulsion of his narratives towards intimating and depicting the phenomenon of incarnation – a term I shall use primarily in a distinct literary sense adopted from Bakhtin's Brazilian-born Spanish contemporary, the Hispanist Américo Castro (1885–1972), but also, ultimately, in the theological sense bequeathed by the Gospel of John.[6] While Russian piety may be primarily rooted in the ocular reverence of the icon, the spirits and whole inner beings of Dostoevsky's protagonists often prove to be decisively affected or even shaped through some form of the act of reading, or through hearing some form of recitation or reading aloud.

For a reason that will soon become clear, I wish to begin by directing our attention back to a familiar figure from late antiquity.

AUGUSTINE, ZOSIMA AND THE QUESTION OF READING

In his *Confessions* (written 397–401 AD), St Augustine famously recalls having pondered as a young man why St Ambrose, the great Catholic bishop of Milan whom he sometimes observed reading, never read aloud. Perhaps, Augustine conjectures, Ambrose worried that if he read aloud, some difficult passage he recited might stir a listener's curiosity, and Ambrose might be asked to pause to expound it and thus be prevented from reading as much as he desired. Or perhaps he read to himself simply to preserve his voice (6,3). Whatever the case was, there can be no denying the extraordinariness of Ambrose's behaviour, given that it was evidently customary for educated adults to read aloud to themselves.[7] Augustine's initial conjecture may do less to illuminate Ambrose's habit of silent reading than to manifest Augustine's own concern with the hermeneutics of textual depths and obscurities, especially those of the holy scriptures. When he had first read the scriptures, before he met Ambrose, they had put him off: 'For my bulging pride', he tell us, 'shunned their style, and my sharpness of mind did not penetrate their inner meaning'. Only later – having come to appreciate them as 'humble in pace, lofty in manner, and veiled in mysteries' (3,5)[8] – did he formulate his theory of figurative expression, espousing in *De doctrina christiana* (written 396–426) that the divinely inspired meanings of scripture frequently lie concealed beneath textual obscurities and ambiguities but are perceptible through allegorical reading (2,6,7–8).

What caused Augustine such great concern in the late fourth century hardly troubled Dostoevsky's fictional Elder Zosima a millennium and a half later, as the Orthodox tradition to which Zosima adhered was less concerned with hermeneutic explication than was the Catholic tradition which Augustine had helped engender.[9] Alyosha's 'Biographical Notes' on Zosima in Book 6 of *The Brothers Karamazov* record the Elder's instruction that village priests should make a habit of reading the Bible aloud to the peasants once a week – hardly a surprising piece of advice, given that most of the peasants were illiterate and had no choice. Absent from his speech on this matter is even the slightest intimation of an Augustinian (or Ambrosian) concern about scriptural obscurities, or about the difficulties listeners might have in fathoming them. All a priest has to do, says Zosima, is 'open that book and begin reading it without grand words or superciliousness, without condescension to them, but gently and kindly, . . . only stopping from time to time to explain words that are not understood by the peasants. Don't be anxious, they will understand everything, the orthodox heart will understand all!' (272).[10]

Zosima's suggestion corresponds with Dostoevsky's own expressed convictions. Dostoevsky wrote that even if the Russian people of his time knew the Gospel poorly and were ignorant of basic principles of faith, they did 'know Christ' and had 'been carrying Him in their hearts from time immemorial'.[11] This notion seems far removed from Augustine's premise in *De doctrina christiana* that learning certain interpretive 'precepts' is a prerequisite for correctly understanding the scriptures and eschewing 'the absurdity of improper meaning' (prol. 9: *absurditas pravae sententiae*). In Augustine's view, the untrained mind could be afforded no instant recognition of Christ simply by reading or hearing the Gospel. According to the *Confessions*, his own serendipitous reading of a passage from St Paul was what finally triggered his conversion (8,12). Yet such a scripturally-induced experience would have been all but inconceivable had he not first learned from Ambrose how to interpret the scriptures 'spiritually' (6,4) and therefore to take them seriously. It is doubtful he would have agreed with Dostoevsky's proposal in a letter of 1878 that the best way to convert an unbeliever is by jettisoning discussion and arguments, and simply reading with the 'best possible attention' all of Paul's letters.[12]

This disagreement harks back to the momentous doctrinal divergence between the Western, Latin, Roman Catholic tradition which Augustine helped engender, and the Eastern, originally Cappadocian and Greek, Orthodox tradition whose Slavonic outgrowth furnished the religious context that formed Dostoevsky's beliefs and informed his art. For modern scholars, the writings of Augustine, who remained little known and exerted practically no influence in the East, help mark the initial bifurcation of Christian thinking into Eastern and Western doctrines on such basic matters as trinitarianism and the interpretation of Adam, the fall and original sin.[13] Dostoevsky, as an adherent to Orthodoxy, was certainly no heir of the Augustinian tradition. The difference between Zosima and Augustine in their hermeneutic assumptions about scriptures may therefore be illuminated by an observation by Georgy Fedotov regarding the distinct stances of Augustine and the early Russian Christians towards the cultures that inspired them: 'The wholehearted acceptance of culture, the freedom from obscurantism, is very often a sign of the barbarian youthfulness of a nation attracted mightily by a higher and "sacred" culture and unable to perceive the spiritual dangers inherent in every product of the human mind' – the 'product' referred to here being books. Augustine, Fedotov continues, 'is obscurantist in his relation to Plato or the ancient culture in general, but Bede and Columban are not. The first Christian generations in Russia worship the sacred Greek culture in the same way in which the Celtic or Saxon monks worshipped the Latin one.'[14]

The unquestioning attitude of the early Russian Christians

towards books and reading did not soon dissipate. Fedotov amply documents the veneration of books that found expression in the anonymous fourteenth-century 'collection' (*izbornik*) of devotional readings, *Izmaragd* ('Emerald'), which would remain the favourite compilation of its kind among the Russian laity for the next four centuries. Making no attempt to distinguish the divine revelation of the Bible from the theological writings of the Church fathers, Russians regarded all religious literature as 'sacred' and 'divine'. The *Izmaragd*, like most other *izborniki*, opens with a set of writings on 'books' and 'book reading', expounding that books are creations of the Holy Spirit; that God, in exhorting human beings to study His law, was referring to the study of books; that the person who holds books in hand will be unable to forget those 'terrible books' of Judgment which will be opened in the age to come; and that the person who blasphemes or fails to heed sacred books shall be judged and punished.[15] Books and reading are thus endowed with eschatological significance.

Dostoevsky's inheritance of such venerational attitudes towards books and reading is documented in his *Diary of a Writer*. If, for example, a Christian text of medieval Kiev can eulogise 'book learning' by praising books as 'the fountainhead of wisdom', 'the bridle of temperance', and by quoting from the Wisdom of Solomon to legitimate the authority of the wisdom books,[16] this eulogy anticipates a remark made by Dostoevsky in an entry of 1876. After expressing doubt that many Russians know about the saint Tikhon of Zadonsk, he asks: 'Why should one be so blankly ignorant; why should one promise oneself *not to read*? Is it for lack of time? Believe me, . . . you would be *learning beautiful things.*'[17] And if early Russian Christians deemed books to be eschatologically pertinent, this judgment renders all the more comprehensible Dostoevsky's rumination that if human beings were to be asked at the end of time whether they understood their life on earth, and what they concluded from it, their most adequate response could already be found in a book – not just any book, but a work of fiction that is widely regarded as the first modern novel: 'Man could silently hand over *Don Quixote*: "Such is my inference from life. – Can you condemn me for it?"'[18]

This apocalyptic valuation of Cervantes's classic, a valuation reiterated elsewhere in *Diary of a Writer*,[19] accords with Dostoevsky's pre-eminently Romantic view of the novel's hero.[20] In an oft-quoted letter, he compares Don Quixote to Christ, calling Christ the 'only one positively beautiful person [on earth]' and Don Quixote 'the most finished' of all 'beautiful characters in Christian literature'.[21] He surely perceived in the Knight of La Mancha six traits corresponding to his own notion of true religion: faith, compassion, suffering, a tendency towards humiliation, foolishness (à la 'holy fools'), and being childlike.[22] Moreover, he was evidently intrigued by the fact that the entire plot and narrative of the *Quixote* essentially revolve around the matter of books, reading and their effects. The protagonist, after all, is a man gone mad from obsessive reading of chivalry books, and his delusional career as knight stems from his ongoing effort to make reality conform to his book-derived fantasies.[23]

It is unclear whether Dostoevsky was aware of his own indebtedness to the *Quixote* for its having introduced into literature a special narrative phenomenon involving the act of reading by protagonists. Nonetheless, as we shall see, this phenomenon achieves full, transmogrified fruition in Dostoevsky, tending towards conjuring the Johannine vision of the Word-become-Flesh.

INCARNATIONAL READING IN DOSTOEVSKY

In an essay of 1947 – an essay easily as respected among *cervantistas* as Tschizewskij's is among Dostoevsky scholars – Américo Castro proposed that the *Quixote*'s 'supreme novelty' lay in its initiating a new form of literary creation, one that

> shows us that the reality of existence consists in receiving the impact of all that can affect man from without, and in transforming these influences into outwardly manifest life processes. The illusion of a dream, devotion to a belief – in short, the ardently yearned for in any form becomes infused in the existence of him who dreams, believes, or longs; and thus, what was before transcendency without bearing on the process of living becomes embodied into life.[24]

The overriding theme of the *Quixote* is thus 'the interdependence, the "interrealisation" of what lies beyond man's experience and the process of incorporating that into his existence' (26–27).

This creative life 'process' Castro calls incarnation (*encarnación*), which is closely akin to what Bakhtin has in mind when he speaks of the sway that quotations as 'authoritative' and 'internally persuasive' utterances have upon the 'ideological becoming of a human being'.[25]

And, he observes, the spoken, written and printed word stands pre-
eminent among all the external 'incitements' that become 'incarnated' in the lives of Cervantes's characters. The first of the *Quixote*'s
two parts essentially grows out of books read by Don Quixote. Part 2
grows out of part 1, as the life of the protagonist incorporates his
awareness of having already been the subject of a book. And the
Don Quixote of part 2 perpetuates himself and the literary interpretation of the fictive author (Cide Hamete Benengeli), appearing to
those who encounter him as both a living person and a 'human-
literary figure' (42). 'The traditional themes of literature', Castro
points out, 'are now fused with the living experience of those
themes; the book then becomes not only a book, but it also becomes
the reader who has incorporated its poetic material into his very life'
(43).[26]

Although considerable scholarly attention has been paid to Dostoevsky's literary relationship to Cervantes,[27] and although Castro
mentions Dostoevsky as one of the most important later novelists
whose stylistic innovations were affected by the 'various stimuli'
radiating from the *Quixote*,[28] the extraordinarily fruitful evolvement
of the incarnational phenomenon in Dostoevsky's fiction has yet to
be acknowledged. To be sure, Bakhtin does seem to touch upon this
phenomenon when he contends that 'at the center of Dostoevsky's
artistic world must lie dialogue', in which 'a person not only shows
himself outwardly, but he becomes for the first time that which he
is.'[29] The dialogic process whereby a person 'becomes that which he
is' might seem closely related to what Castro meant by 'incarnation'
through reading. Elsewhere, Bakhtin pertinently comments upon
that type of novel that concentrates its critique of literary discourse
around the hero as:

a 'literary man', who looks at life through the eyes of literature and who
tries to live 'according to literature'. *Don Quixote* and *Madame Bovary* are the
best-known exemplars of this type, but the 'literary man' and the testing of
that literary discourse connected with him can be found in almost every
major novel (to a greater or lesser extent these are the characters in Balzac,
Dostoevsky, Turgenev, etc.); they differ from each other only in the relative
weight accorded this feature in the novel as a whole.[30]

Nonetheless, in concentrating upon dialogism in Dostoevsky's
novels ostensibly as an ideological and epistemological mode in the
lives of those novels' characters, Bakhtin and consequently Perlina as
well stop short of fully acknowledging the existential, incarnational

import of the reading-act itself for those characters. Of course this is not to overlook that Bakhtin maintained his ostensible focus largely for political reasons, and that readers might in some instances read between his lines to glean possible religious implications. For during the years leading up to the initial publication of his Dostoevsky book (1929), he had, in response to the Soviet crack-down on religious institutions, practices and expression, 'reoriented his approach in his writings and largely abandoned his Neo-Kantian vocabulary for one that was more secular and sociological.'[31] Yet, as Ruth Coates has shown, Bakhtin remained, behind any appearance to the contrary, 'a philosopher whose work is fed by certain aspects of the Christian vision of and for the world'.[32]

Dostoevsky's fictive world is saturated with the ubiquitous trappings of the modern typographic culture – the Gutenberg galaxy, as Marshall McLuhan so memorably dubbed it – which helped make widespread literary incarnation possible in the first place.[33] Not surprisingly, the financial attraction of the publishing business itself is manifest: Dmitry Karamazov, in prison, states his ambition to start a newspaper (*BK*, 558), and peripheral characters such as Razumikhin and Rakitin also entertain plans of going into publishing (*CP*, 263; *BK*, 73). To be sure, the culture of print had developed very late in Russia, where more manuscripts were still in circulation than printed books until the mid-eighteenth century. In fact, the print business of Nikolai Novikov produced more books between 1775 and 1789 than had been published in Russia since the introduction of printing.[34] Nonetheless, the nineteenth-century Russian society depicted in Dostoevsky's novels is one whose intelligentsia and educated elite reveres the published word, as betokened by Raskolnikov's initial reaction when he sees his own article in the newspaper: he experiences 'the strange and painfully sweet sensations of the author who sees himself in print for the first time' (*CP*, 434). Given all the attention he receives for this article, he anticipates Ivan Karamazov, who achieves early recognition for his own published journalism, especially his article on ecclesiastical courts (*BK*, 11).

The phenomenon of literary incarnation born in the *Quixote* – a novel published less than a century and a half after the death of Johannes Gutenberg (c. 1400–68) – seems pervasively inherent in the more fully developed print culture of Dostoevsky's characters. The phenomenon seems most blatant when one character can interpret some trait in another character's personality by identifying that trait with an author whose qualities the latter may rightly or wrongly seem to incarnate as a result of reading. For example, Svidrigailov, who calls Raskolnikov 'a Schiller, a Russian Schiller, an absolute Schiller' tells him: 'The Schiller in you is always getting into a muddle' (*CP*, 408, 410). This identification of Raskolnikov with Schiller was earlier hinted at by a question put to him by Porphiry, who clearly assumed that Raskolnikov was familiar enough with Schiller to recognise when someone's speech resembled that of the German poet: 'What are you smiling at again – because I am talking like Schiller?' (389). At the same time, Dmitry Karamazov, having apparently committed numerous literary sources to memory (like Schiller, whom he had read 'till he knew him by heart' (*BK*, 176)), seems to have absorbed them so deeply that they are part of his self-identity and can well up into his consciousness whenever he happens to find himself in situations that call them to mind. On repeated occasions he spontaneously identifies himself with specific voices from works of great poets (Schiller, Pushkin, Shakespeare), grafting their personalities and roles onto his own existence by quoting verses from them that seem appropriate to his own immediate mood – as when he sadly tells Perkhotin: 'Do you remember Hamlet? "I am very sorry, good Horatio! Alas, poor Yorick!" Perhaps that's me, Yorick? Yes, I'm Yorick now, and a skull afterwards' (383).[35]

I cannot broach here the almost limitless array of more complex and subtler incarnational phenomena in Dostoevsky, or all the complexities involved in distinguishing exactly how each character views the particular texts which he or she might read, recite, or hear read aloud or recited. I conclude simply by indicating how a sequence of three familiar scenes, all of them involving characters reading aloud, reveals a progressive rejoining of the phenomenon of literary incarnation with its theological paradigm: the doctrine of the incarnate Word as set forth in Dostoevsky's favourite Gospel, the fourth. Observing that 'the indisputably authoritative word is the word of Holy Writ', Perlina notes that *The Brothers Karamazov* involves a complex 'hierarchy of quotations' on whose 'slopes' the 'words' of the different characters vie with each other dialogically, some progressing upwards 'from the internally persuasive to the authoritative', others degenerating downwards 'from persuasiveness to false authority.'[36] If this is true, then we should not be surprised that, within the hierarchy of Dostoevsky's works, it will be only in a single instant within that final novel that the phenomenon of literary incarnation and the doctrine of the incarnate Word symbolically touch.

The first scene is that in which Raskolnikov commands Sonya to read to him the account of the resurrection of Lazarus (*CP*, 274–75), an account which, as she has to remind him, occurs only in the fourth Gospel. The old and worn, leather-bound Russian New Testament in her possession, she informs him, was brought to her by Lizaveta, with whom she used to read. So even as she hesitatingly begins to oblige his repeated command, 'Read it!', by reading aloud from that copy, the irony is already clear (to us, as well as to Raskolnikov) that Sonya is unwittingly re-enacting with the killer the sacred reading-ritual which she formerly practised with his victim-to-be. This irony will be compounded at the novel's end, where it is disclosed that the convicted and imprisoned Raskolnikov now keeps that same copy of the New Testament under his pillow (as Dostoevsky himself kept a copy of it under his pillow during four years of penal servitude).[37] If this final disclosure will portend Raskolnikov's putatively impending regeneration, one aside regarding the present scene already hints in that direction: the narrator's remark that, upon reading the verse telling that Lazarus had 'been dead *four* days', Sonya 'strongly' emphasises the word 'four' (277). Four days have passed since Lizaveta and the pawnbroker were killed, and Sonya means to imply that Lizaveta, like Lazarus, will spiritually rise and – as Sonya said moments earlier – 'see God' (275). But *we* know that this occasion of Sonya's reading also marks a crucial initial stage in the spiritual resurrection of Raskolnikov.

In this scene, which would perfectly illustrate Zosima's advice on the value of reading aloud the Bible, the themes of divine incarnation and literary incarnation remain separate. The incarnate God is present as miracle-worker in the Lazarus story which is read aloud, while the human protagonist, the listener who recalls having read this tale 'a long time ago . . . When I was at school' (275), seems already to have begun incarnating an incitement he may recall (consciously or unconsciously) from elsewhere in the fourth Gospel: Jesus's distanciating remark to his mother at the wedding at Cana, 'Woman, what have I to do with thee? mine hour is not yet come' (John 2:4). Immediately following Sonya's reading, Raskolnikov announces abruptly and likewise: 'Today I deserted my family, my mother and sister. . . I have made a complete break' (278).

The second scene whose incarnational import I want to consider occurs in *The Idiot*, whose hero, as we know from Dostoevsky's letters and notebooks, was consciously conceived to blend the images of Don Quixote and the Johannine Christ. Just as there are indications in the novel's first part that Nastasia implicitly recognises Myshkin's saintly or Christlike nature, so Aglaya Epanchina explicitly recognises his quixotic nature in part 2. After reading a letter from the prince, she places it in a volume of Cervantes's novel and bursts out laughing.[38] Later, in the company of her family, the prince and others, she explains the link between Pushkin's ballad 'A Poor Knight' and Don Quixote (266), and then recites the ballad aloud from memory, slyly changing the letters inscribed on the hero's shield, A. M. D. (*Ave Mater Dei*), to A. N. B. (*Ave Nastasia Barashkova*) (2:7). Although the mocking association which Aglaya means to draw between the prince and the two literary knights escapes most of the persons present, the prince discerns it, and there is something strangely fatalistic about the way the content of the Pushkin poem becomes infused, or incarnated, in his subsequent life. (Noteworthily, he will later proceed to read all of Pushkin's works with Rogozhin (556)). His unflagging compassion for Nastasia, the 'fallen' woman, will recall not only Christ's refusal to condemn the adulterous woman (another story from John's Gospel) but also Aglaya's interpretation of the 'poor knight' as one who would still 'believe in' his lady 'even if she became a thief' (266). Aglaya will even hint at these associations when she later suggests to him that he is 'sacrificing' himself by refusing to marry Nastasia (445). By the end, when he winds up back in the Swiss sanatorium as a relapsed idiot, we will realise the extreme extent to which he incarnates the closing stanza of 'A Poor Knight': 'Returning to his distant castle, / There he lived and sighed, / Ever silent, sad, and cheerless, / Of reason bereft, he died' (quoted at 269).

While it was out of compassion and for Raskolnikov's spiritual benefit that Sonya read to him from the Gospel, Aglaya recites the Pushkin poem with her mocking insertions specifically in order to prick and embarrass the prince. Nonetheless, Sonya's reading and Aglaya's recitation end up having comparable effects, infusing the minds (and hence the actions and lives) of Raskolnikov and Myshkin with the images of the Johannine Christ and the Christlike knight. It is therefore left to Ivan Karamazov to be so bold as to as to retrieve from the Bible and, in effect, to *re-incarnate* the

Divine Logos in the character of Christ within the 'The Grand Inquisitor', the prose-poem of his own creation which he rehearses to Alyosha in the Metropolis tavern. It is significant that Ivan recites it extemporaneously with no text in hand; that, indeed, although he asserts that he 'composed' it a year earlier, he also claims to have 'never written' it down; and that therefore Alyosha is its 'first reader – that is, listener' (*BK*, 227). Suffice it for me to close by remarking the significance of what happens moments after the recitation of the poem is done. When the saintly listener kisses his rebellious brother on the lips, in precise emulation of the parting kiss Christ gave the Inquisitor in the poem, the act is more than simply 'plagiarism', which is what Ivan jokingly calls it, or 'a reaccented quotation', which is what Perlina calls it.[39] The kiss confirms that the conjured *exemplum* of the Incarnate God, the Christ of Ivan's tale, has hit its mark as an incitement in Alyosha's mind, and perhaps even his soul. A tremendous irony it may seem that this incitement was emitted from the imagination of a rebel-against-God. Yet the Word is the Word, or the Logos, the Logos, no matter by whom or in what spirit it is conveyed. And evidently for Dostoevsky, the Word, when recited aloud by a human – and Russian – voice, bears for the listener a force much profounder than the silence of Ambrose's study or of Don Quixote's reading room.

NOTES

1 Fyodor Dostoevsky, *Crime and Punishment*, trans. Jessie Senior Coulson, Norton Critical Edition with Backgrounds, Sources, and Essays in Criticism, ed. George Gibian (New York, 1964; 3rd edn 1989), 2:6, 135 (hereafter *CP*).
2 Preface to Fyodor Dostoevsky, *The Brothers Karamazov*, trans. Constance Garnett, revised by Ralph E. Matlaw, Norton Critical Edition with Backgrounds, Sources, and Criticism (New York, 1976) (hereafter *BK*), vii. See D. Tschizewskij, 'Schiller und *Die Brüder Karamazov*', *Zeitschrift für slavische Philologie*, 4 (1929), 1–42, excerpts from which are reprinted as 'Schiller and *The Brothers Karamazov*', trans. Matlaw, in *BK*, 794–807.
3 Victor Terras, *A Karamazov Companion: Commentary on the Genesis, Language, and Style of Dostoevsky's Novel* (Madison, WI, 1981); Nina Perlina, *Varieties of Poetic Utterance: Quotation in 'The Brothers Karamazov'* (Lanham, 1985); *The Gospel in Dostoyevsky: Selections from His Works*, ed. the Hutterian Brethren (Ulster Park, NY, 1988).

4 Mikhail Bakhtin, *Problems of Dostoevsky's Poetics*, ed. and trans. Caryl Emerson (Minneapolis, MN, 1984), intermittently throughout, but especially 112–22.

5 Perlina, *Varieties*, 39.

6 See Américo Castro, 'Incarnation in *Don Quijote*', in *An Idea of History: Selected Essays of Américo Castro*, trans. and ed. Stephen Gilman and Edmund L. King (Columbus, OH, 1977), 23–76.

7 Plutarch, interestingly, opines that reading aloud is good for the health. *Advice About Keeping Well*, par. 16, *Moralia*, 130C–D, in *Plutarch's Moralia*, 15 vols., with English translation by Frank Cole Babbitt, Loeb Classical Library (Cambridge, MA, 1927–69), 2:257–59. According to Leo C. Ferrari, Augustine's *Confessions* itself 'was written to be read aloud before an assembled audience' ('Beyond Augustine's Conversion Scene', in *Augustine: From Rhetor to Theologian* (Waterloo, ON, 1992), 97–108; here 102. See also Calvin L. Troup, *Temporality, Eternity, and Wisdom: The Rhetoric of Augustine's Confessions* (Columbia, SC, 1999), 48.

8 Translations of Augustine are mine.

9 Indeed, a century after Dostoevsky, an Orthodox priest like Georges Florovsky could still express wariness towards hermeneutics: 'We are in danger of losing the uniqueness of the Word of God in the process of continuous "reinterpretation". But how can we interpret at all if we have forgotten the original language?' (*Bible, Church, Tradition: An Eastern Orthodox View* (Belmont, MA, 1972), 10). This is not to suggest that Florovsky denies that scriptural revelation requires interpretation (see *ibid.*, 17–36). Yet, relative to Catholicism, the distinctly lesser concern with, or wariness towards, scriptural hermeneutics in Russian Orthodoxy may be attributable, at least in part, to the overbearing emphasis which the Orthodox always placed upon the seven Ecumenical Councils of 325–681 AD. As Timothy Ware (Bishop Kallistos of Diokleia) points out, the Councils 'defined once and for all the Church's teaching upon the fundamental doctrines of the Christian faith', doctrines that are hence to be accepted as 'absolute and unchanging' (*The Orthodox Church*, new edn (London, 1993), 20, 197).

10 References to *The Brothers Karamazov* are from the edition cited in note 2.

11 'Vlas' (1873), in F. M. Dostoievsky, *The Diary of a Writer*, trans. Boris Brasol (Salt Lake City, UT, 1985), 38.

12 To N. L. Osmidov, in *Letters of Fyodor Michailovitch Dostoevsky*, trans. Ethel Colburn Mayne (New York, 1964), 233.

13 For example, G. P. Fedotov, *The Russian Religious Mind*, 2 vols. (Cambridge, MA, 1966), vol. 1, 27, 221–22, 223; Jaroslav Pelikan, *The Christian Tradition: A History of the Development of Doctrine*, 5 vols. (Chicago, IL, 1971–89), vol. 2, 181, 260, 272.

14 *Russian Religious Mind*, vol. 1, 379.

15 *Ibid.*, vol. 2, 41–43.

16 *Ibid.*, vol. 1, 377.

17 *Ibid.*, vol. I, 377; Dostoevsky, *Diary*, 203, my emphasis.

18 *Diary, 260, quoted in Eric J. Ziolkowski, The Sanctification of Don Quixote: From Hidalgo to Priest* (University Park, PA, 1991), 114–15. On the view of the *Quixote* as 'the first and unsurpassed model of the modern realist novel' (M. Menéndez y Pelayo), see Ziolkowski, *Sanctification*, I, including note I.

19 See 'A lie is saved by a lie' (September 1877), in *Diary*, 836.

20 See Ziolkowski, *Sanctification*, 95–126.

21 Letter 1/13 January 1868 to Sofia (his niece), as quoted in Robin Feuer Miller, *Dostoevsky and The Idiot: Author, Narrator, and Reader* (Cambridge, MA, 1981), 74. As indicated by Ziolkowski, *Sanctification*, 113, note 41, Miller omits from her translation of the pertinent passage a parenthetical sentence that specifies 'the whole Gospel of St John' as Dostoevsky's source for the 'thought' of the beautiful as an 'ideal': 'John sees the wonder of the Incarnation, the visible apparition of the Beautiful' (quoted from Dostoevsky, *Letters*, 142).

22 See Ziolkowski, *Sanctification*, 120–25.

23 Dostoevsky's 'A lie is saved by a lie' (note 19 above), 835–38, conveys his fascination with the way Don Quixote overcomes a certain doubt that at one point threatens his belief in the truth of chivalry books. For discussion see Ziolkowski, *Sanctification*, 116–17.

24 'Incarnation', 23, 26. See viii–ix for references to the original 1947 sources, as well as a 1957 source in which this essay previously appeared (in both English and Spanish).

25 See Perlina, *Varieties*, 14–6.

26 Compare Carlos Fuentes, *Don Quixote, or the Critique of Reading* (Austin, TX, 1976).

27 For example, Wolfgango L. Giusti, 'Sul donchischiottismo di alcuni personaggi del Dostohevskij' in *Cultura*, 10 (1931), 171–79; Santiago Montero Díaz, 'Cervantes en Turguenief y Dostoyevsky' in *Revista de Estudios Políticos* (Madrid), vol. 15 (1946), 111–42; Ludmilla B. Turkevich, 'Cervantes in Russia', in *Cervantes Across the Centuries*, ed. Angel Flores and M. J. Benardete (New York, 1947; repr. with corrections, 1969), 353–81; Ludmilla B. Turkevich, *Cervantes in Russia* (Princeton, 1950; repr. New York, 1975), 115–30; Yakov Malkiel, 'Cervantes in nineteenth-century Russia', *Comparative Literature*, 3 (1951), 310–29; F. Maldonado de Guevara, 'Dostoievski y el Quijote' *Anales Cervantinos*, 3 (1953), 367–75; Z. I. Plavskii, 'Cervantes v Rossi', in *Miguel de Cervantes Saavedra: Bibliografiia russkikh perevodov i kriticheskoi literatury na nerusskom iazyke* (Moscow, 1959), 9–35; Segundo Serrano Poncela, 'Don Quijote en Dostoievski', *Insula*, 23 (1968), 19–20; George Soltys, 'Don Quijote en la obra de Dostoyevski', PhD dissertation, Middlebury College, VT, 1983; Anthony J. Cascardi, *The Bounds of Reason: Cervantes, Dostoevsky, Flaubert* (New York, 1986). The bearing of the *Quixote* upon Dostoevsky's *The Idiot*, especially the creation of Myshkin, is the subject of

part 2 of Ziolkowski's *Sanctification*, which cites numerous other studies that focus or comment upon this specific relationship.

28 Américo Castro, 'An Introduction to the Quixote', *Idea*, 83; compare 89, 90. For reference to the original source for this 'Introduction', see ix. Dostoevsky goes unmentioned in Castro's essay, 'Incarnation'.

29 Bakhtin, *Problems*, 252.

30 M. M. Bakhtin, *The Dialogic Imagination: Four Essays*, ed. Michael Holquist, trans. Caryl Emerson and Michael Holquist (Austin, TX, 1981), 413.

31 Katerina Clark and Michael Holquist, *Mikhail Bakhtin* (Cambridge, MA, 1984), 131.

32 Ruth Coates, *Christianity in Bakhtin: God and the Exiled Author* (Cambridge, 1998), 22.

33 Marshall McLuhan, *The Gutenberg Galaxy: The Making of Typographic Man* (Toronto, 1962; reprinted 1967).

34 As noted by D. S. Mirsky, *A History of Russian Literature from Its Beginnings to 1900*, ed. Francis J. Whitfield (New York, 1958), 5, 58.

35 Compare, for example, how a line about 'the whispering silence' from a poem by Pushkin 'for some reason rose to his mind' as he snuck around outside his father's house on the night of the murder (368).

36 Perlina, *Varieties*, 20–21.

37 'Old People' (1873) in *Diary*, 9.

38 Fyodor Dostoevsky, *The Idiot*, trans. David Magarshack (Harmondsworth, 1955; reprinted with new pagination, 1986), 2:1. All quotations are from the reprinted edition.

39 Perlina, *Varieties*, 48.

PART III

Reading Dostoevsky religiously: case studies

CHAPTER 9

Towards an iconography of Dostoevsky's 'Crime and Punishment'

Antony Johae

I take as my starting point the first of several dreams depicted by Dostoevsky in his novel *Crime and Punishment* (1866).[1] It is made to occur shortly before the protagonist, Raskolnikov, carries out his crime and, like the dreams which occur after the murder, is charged with violence. In his dream, Raskolnikov recalls the scene of his provincial childhood. He is on his way with his father to visit the grave of his grandmother and of his baby brother. But in the dream the progress of father and son is arrested by a violent incident which occurs outside the tavern on the road to the church. A crowd of drunken peasants has been invited to get on a huge cart to which a mare has been harnessed; but it is incapable of pulling such a load. Infuriated by this, the intoxicated owner, goaded on by the other peasants, proceeds to beat the horse to death. The boy tries to stop the onslaught himself, but his father pulls him away from the crowd saying: 'It's not our business. Come along!' The boy appeals to his father, but the father merely responds with: 'Come along, son, come along! <. . .> let's go home <. . .> They're drunk' (75). The dream narrative ends: 'He put his arms round his father <. . .> He tried to draw a breath, to cry out and – woke up' (78).

It has been suggested by W. D. Snodgrass in a well-known essay entitled 'Crime for punishment: The tenor of part one'[2] that Raskolnikov's history is mirrored in his dream: a return to the Christian faith (symbolised by his walk to the church and cemetery with his father) is interrupted by the murder of the pawnbroker and her half-sister (represented in the dream by the killing of the mare outside the tavern). In this interpretation the dream is not treated as though it were irrelevant to the final outcome, but rather is given the status of prediction or prophecy, so that the final outcome – Raskolnikov's salvation – appears to have been validated by the patterning of the dream. Images are not seen as picked-up residues

173

of the day disguising repressed wishes (Freud), but as archetypal figures which, when illuminated, verify the world as an ordered and meaningful whole (Jung).

To offer further support for this proposition, it is necessary first to piece the images together to form a system, a symbology, a theology even. Let us begin this process by examining part of the dream narrative or, to be precise, the descriptive passage which provides the context for the action outside the tavern.

Not far from the tavern was a road, a rough country road [which] stretched windingly away in the distance, and about three hundred yards farther on it turned to the right, skirting the town cemetery. In the middle of the cemetery was a stone church with a green cupola to which he used to go twice a year to morning Mass with his father and mother, when a service was held in memory of his grandmother <. . .> For the service they always used to take with them a special funeral dish on a white plate and wrapped in a white napkin, and the funeral dish was of sweetened rice and raisins stuck into it in the shape of a cross. He loved that church with its ancient icons <. ı .> and the old priest with the shaking head <. . .> [E]very time he visited the cemetery he used to cross himself over the grave religiously and reverently, and bow down and kiss it. (73)

If we are fully to appreciate the significance of this description, it will need to be visualised in more detail than has been directly represented here. We are told that the funeral dish of sweetened rice has been marked out by raisins in the form of a cross and that on each occasion the boy, Raskolnikov, visits the graveside of his baby brother, he makes the sign of the cross bowing down to kiss the grave. This duplication of cross imagery ought to draw our attention to the fact that the description is potentially replete with such images. The cemetery would be filled with crosses marking the numerous graves; the 'stone church with a green cupola' would certainly be crowned with a cross; and 'the old priest', intermittently crossing himself, would also be likely to be looked down upon by an icon representing the Crucifixion.

Apart from the shared communal value of such imagery, which would be transparently clear to many readers, it is also highly significant in terms of the protagonist's individual history, because the cross imagery may have been embedded in the text as a symbolic prefiguration of Raskolnikov's ultimate return to the faith of his childhood. But in order for the cross to carry such symbolic weight at a personal level (as distinct from the communal) we might first look for a further duplication of the primary image in one guise or another, treating each manifestation of it as signalling the way to Raskolnikov's ultimate redemption. To do this we need to pass over the threshold of dream (and of childhood) and to follow the trajectory of Raskolnikov's conscious (and adult) life. In doing so we are immediately be struck by the fact that, having killed the old pawnbroker, Raskolnikov discovers two crucifixes – 'one of cypress wood and another of copper, and in addition, a little enamelled icon' (97) – which are attached to a ribbon around the murdered woman's neck. There is also a purse bulging with money which he keeps for himself, but the crucifixes he throws on the body of the dead woman. Seconds later, the old woman's half-sister, Lizaveta, enters the flat and Raskolnikov is panicked into committing a second murder.

The action of throwing away the crosses would perhaps not have signified much beyond Raskolnikov's rejection of a Christian standard and his confirmed criminality – he commits a second murder and steals the purseful of money – had it not been revealed later that Lizaveta and the prostitute, Sonya, had exchanged similar crosses. 'She gave me her [copper] cross and I gave her my little icon', Sonya explains after Raskolnikov has made his confession to her (435). She then offers him the cross made of cypress wood, but Raskolnikov refuses the cross because Sonya has made it clear to him what its acceptance signifies: 'We'll suffer together', she tells him, 'so let us bear our cross together' (435). He must, in other words, confess his crime publicly and submit to the humiliation of punishment. Acknowledging that he is not yet ready to take the first step, Sonya says: 'When you go to accept your suffering, you will put [the cross] on. You will come to me and I'll put it on. We shall pray and go together' (436). Thus, when Raskolnikov eventually returns to Sonya and says to her: 'I've come for the crosses, Sonya' (533), the meaning is clear: he will make his public confession and accept the consequences.

It can be seen here how the cross as symbol works at both a private and public level. At first it is worn as a personal token of mutual relation (Lizaveta and Sonya support each other in their suffering) and of sacrifice (Sonya devotes her life to Raskolnikov). These, moreover, are affective exchanges and are quite different from the pecuniary exchanges negotiated between Raskolnikov and the pawnbroker or, even, between Raskolnikov and his mother.

A crucifix, furthermore, is usually worn hanging from the neck and is often hidden against the heart, thus betokening the private, affective nature of the gesture. But at the same time the cross symbol has the potential to make public: especially when displayed by the priest during the Divine Liturgy. Correspondingly, Raskolnikov's crime cannot remain a secret between him and Sonya: he must, as Sonya has told him, 'Go to the cross-roads, bow down to the people, kiss the earth <. . .> and proclaim in a loud voice to the whole world: I am a murderer!' (536).

One can observe here the way in which a macrocosmic dimension has been given to the cross symbol ('cross-roads <. . .> the whole world') as opposed to the small scale of the crucifixes and the 'little icon'. The effect of this enlargement of the symbol is to reinforce its function in the public domain. A similar correspondence may also be remarked between the behaviour of the child, Raskolnikov, as recorded in the dream – '[E]very time he visited the cemetery he used to cross himself over the grave religiously and reverently, and bow down and kiss it' (73) – and its virtual recurrence at the cross-roads before he goes to make his deposition to the police – 'He knelt down in the middle of the square, bowed down to the earth, and kissed the filthy earth with joy and rapture' (537). The circumscribed childhood experience, already breached by his witnessing the violent incident outside the tavern (and for readers in English translation the publicness of the place would be denoted in the name 'public house') has been enlarged into the adult experience of actually committing a crime and coming to the point of public confession – at the cross-roads.

Although psychological regression (i.e. a return to childhood in dream) seems here to form a paradigm of Raskolnikov's reversion to an amoral and primal violence (his murder of the two sisters), a prophetic projection into the future is made potentially possible by the symbols of the dream and, in particular, the recurring image of the cross, the shared communal value of which signals the way to Raskolnikov's return to Christian fellowship.

It can be understood more clearly here what Erich Auerbach meant when he asserted in his *Mimesis* that Dostoevsky had written his novels in the 'old-Christian' manner as opposed to modern occidental realism.[3] Although one could not deny a clearly deli-neated horizontal temporal continuum in Dostoevsky's fiction con-forming to occidental realism, the vertical figural dimension cannot be overlooked either. Auerbach's thesis may be more readily accepted if it is recognised that an iconographic mode of representation coming from Orthodox Church art was still endemic to Russian culture in the nineteenth century (as it had been in the European Middle Ages) and that the aesthetic principles upon which it was founded would likely have influenced the practice of a Russian novelist such as Dostoevsky for whom the tenets of an unqualified secular realism would have been alien. Thus, by implanting discrete metaphysical symbols into the literal representation, the author has effectively transcended the limitations of nineteenth-century secular realism (as indeed Mikhail Bakhtin has shown Dostoevsky to have overcome the limitations of nineteenth-century monologic narrative in the creation of his polyphonic discourse).[4]

It is perhaps not accidental that this combination of horizontal movement in time and space and the vertical and atemporal stasis of iconographic representation, when delineated, form the shape of a cross, a kind of watermark on the pages of the novel.[5] This would seem to support my contention that a resolution in *Crime and Punishment* is well founded and not simply a popular response to a surface reading of the text ('they lived happily ever after', or words to that effect).

The vertical dimension, furthermore, is not solely represented by religious symbol; the dream narratives are themselves synchronic breaks in the temporal progression of the plot and have as much potential for symbolic representation as do icons in a church. Dreams may signify in a condensed symbolic form the essential, or existential, core of the dreamer's being: a coalescence of his past life, his present dilemmas and his wishes for the future.

The symbolic thrust of Dostoevsky's fiction cannot, of course, be demonstrated on the strength of a single image; rather it has to be shown that a network of opaque signs resides in the text which, once acknowledged, calls for elucidation. Duplication may contribute to such an awareness as in the example of the recurring cross image; or hidden meanings may be stored in nomenclature (though less opaque to a reader of Dostoevsky in the original Russian than in translation). The name Raskolnikov, for example, is derived from *raskol'nik* meaning, in Russian, schismatic or heretic, thus giving a clue to the deeper functional level at which the naming process operates. Recognition of this kind of structure, furthermore, ought to alert us to the possibility of an internal network of nomenclatural symbols representing not merely the externality of the characters (the names they go by), but the hidden well-springs of their being. To illustrate: Porfiry, the name given to the examining magistrate in charge of the murder investigation, is also recognisably the name of a hard and highly-valued purple marble. Richard Peace has also observed that 'Porphyra' was the name given to 'the purple cloak which was the attribute of the Byzantine emperors',[6] all of which seems a far cry from the Porfiry who suffers from haemorrhoids (352) and who can say of himself: 'The good Lord has given me a figure that arouses nothing but comic ideas in people. A buffoon' (356). But Porfiry is here referring to his external appearance (as others see him) and not to his inner self from whence come his resourcefulness and integrity, qualities which in turn allow him to gain an insight into (or to 'see through') the split (*raskol*) psyche of the criminal who, with a hatchet, has 'split open' the heads of his two victims.

One could at this point set up a symbolic contrast between the (red) blood spilt by the criminal and the purple inherent in the examining magistrate's name, a proposition which would seem quite feasible if it is remembered how essential colour symbols are to the art of iconography. The purple in the name Porfiry ought to illuminate the text as it is hoped my exegesis of the cross symbol has done. Indeed, there is a direct relationship in ecclesiastical symbology between the image of the cross and the colour purple, for purple is the colour of the Passion when the sufferings leading up to the crucifixion of Christ are commemorated. During this period in the Church year the vestments worn are purple.

I am not intimating here that Porfiry's haemorrhoids represent the sum total of his suffering. These are only external signs of his discomfort, as his name is an external sign of his identity. On the other hand, the purple part of Porfiry establishes an ontological status for him: if he at first appears to be a mundane lawyer endeavouring to trick the criminal into revealing himself, he covertly, and figuratively, performs a sacred role as sage, or priest, whose function it is to hear the sinner's confession of guilt, to share his spiritual suffering, and to guide him towards the expiation of his crime through punishment. Thus, 'the purple cloak . . . of the Byzantine emperors' (who, incidentally, held semi-divine status) falls into place: Porfiry offers Raskolnikov protection (a reduction of his sentence) if he will 'go to the police and make a full confession' (469) (rather as the Imperial Tsar of Russia commuted Dostoevsky's sentence to hard labour as he was about to face the firing squad).

It is noteworthy in connection with the protective cloak of suffering which the examining magistrate, Porfiry, as it were, holds out to the criminal, that Sonya, about to accompany Raskolnikov to the police station to make his deposition, picks up a shawl and puts it over her head. We are told: 'It was a green drap-de-dames shawl . . . "The family shawl"' (534–35). And, at the penal settlement in Siberia, she is wearing the same shawl at the moment when Raskolnikov is finally reconciled to their union (557). The recurring image of the green shawl reinforces at an iconographic level what is already made explicit in the narrative: Sonya's protective influence over Raskolnikov. But we may go further than this by drawing on Richard Peace's additional observation that 'The full name of Sonya is Sofya (Sophia) which evokes the great Orthodox cathedral of Constantinople – Hagia Sophia (The Holy Wisdom of Orthodoxy).'[7] Nomenclature here, as elsewhere, harbours in it the potential for a radical transformation of surface representation (Sonya, the prostitute, but who is called 'little mother' by the convicts) into a profoundly metaphysical meaning (Sonya: Mother Church). This proposition can be supported by referring once again to our original paradigm: Raskolnikov's dream of childhood which, as has already been noted, appears to anticipate his eventual return to the Church: 'In the middle of the cemetery was a stone church with a green cupola, to which he used to go twice a year to morning Mass with his father and mother' (73). It will not have gone unremarked that the colour of the church cupola (that is, its protective vault) is green, and that green is also the colour of Sonya's shawl. This effectively illustrates how leitmotifs, whether colours, names or objects, converge on one another to give the imagery an illuminated status as symbol.

It could be argued, however, that what we are seeing here is no more than a coincidence of colour (green) with object (church and shawl) without any causal connection between them. This might be so if no repetition could be observed. But let us join Raskolnikov on the Nikolayevsky Bridge overlooking the River Neva the day after he has committed the murder. He has narrowly escaped being run over by a carriage, the driver of which has whipped him across the back (itself both a reflection of Raskolnikov's dream and presaging the way in which Sonya's father, Marmeladov, is to die). The people nearby mock him because they think that he is drunk (like Marmeladov, and like Raskolnikov himself when he goes to the cross-roads).

He then becomes aware that a coin has been placed in his hand: 'He looked up and saw an elderly, well-to-do woman of the merchant class, in a bonnet and goatskin shoes, accompanied by a young girl wearing a hat and carrying a green parasol, probably her daughter. "Take it, my dear, in Christ's name" '(132).

The green parasol (a kind of vault giving protection from the sun) might still be thought of as mere coincidence were it not for the descriptive passage which follows: 'The cupola of the cathedral, which nowhere appears to better advantage than when seen from <. . .> the bridge <. . .> glittered in the sunshine, and in the clear air every ornament on it could be plainly distinguished' (132). That the girl on the bridge holding the green parasol is not Sonya matters no more than that the rouged prostitute on the boulevard with a 'little shawl <. . .> thrown over her bare back' (64) is not Sonya (or that the red-lipped roué who pursues her is not Svidrigailov). The protective and life-giving principle remains constant: the mother with the daughter holding a green parasol gives money out of compassion. 'Take it, my dear, in Christ's name.' When Raskolnikov then turns his face in the direction of the Cathedral he realises what he has lost. 'His past seemed to be lying at the bottom of some fathomless cavern, deep, deep down, where he could only just discern it dimly, his old thoughts, problems, subjects, impressions, and that magnificent view [of the cathedral cupola], and himself, and everything, everything' (133).

The clear implication is that religion had been a part of his past (as is made explicit in the dream), but that now he is rejecting the protective wisdom of Mother Church as he now spurns the money given to him by mother and daughter: 'He opened his hand, stared at the silver coin, and, raising his arm, he flung it with a violent movement into the water <. . .> He felt as though he had cut himself off from everyone and everything at that moment' (133). It is problematic, too, whether or not the murderer will soon throw himself off the bridge into the shapeless water (in contradistinction to the clear forms of the cathedral cupola and the green parasol).[8]

One could perhaps imagine an iconographic representation of the scene, with the murderer standing on the bridge (an image itself charged with symbolic potential) looking at the cathedral and about to throw the coin into the river. There might be included a triad of buildings: the cathedral at the top with its glittering cupola; on the left, the classical façade of the university which Raskolnikov has also forsaken. 'On his way to his lectures at the university <. . .> he usually stopped here <. . .> on this very spot, and gazed intently at this truly magnificent panorama, and every time he could not help wondering at the vague and mysterious emotion it aroused in him' (132); and at the bottom of the picture the Palais de Crystal, the tavern in the prostitute quarter of St Petersburg to which Raskolnikov resorts in order to read in a newspaper of the crime he has committed.

The name of the tavern is not fortuitous, for it can be seen as an emblematic travesty of English Utilitarianism, a philosophy which proposed the greatest happiness for the greatest number but which, according to Raskolnikov, means that in practical terms a percentage of young women (Sonya, for example, and even his sister, Dunya) must fall into prostitution 'so that the others [the majority of women] should be kept fresh and healthy and not be interfered with' (69). The locale for such activity was, of course, the tavern – *pivnaia* – meaning in Russian literally 'the place of beer'. No doubt Dostoevsky, in naming his tavern, had in mind the Crystal Palace, the building constructed in London for the Exhibition of the Industry of All Nations in 1851, a monument, as it were, to industrialism and the Utilitarian system of thought which supported it. For the purposes of our iconographic representation, it is worth noting that the original Crystal Palace was largely constructed of glass – an extremely fragile material (as Dostoevsky regarded the entire Utilitarian system of thought) – whereas the cathedral was made of stone, a durable substance born out by the fact that the cathedral is still standing, whilst the Crystal Palace was destroyed by fire in 1936.[9]

Now it has already been noted that the name Porfiry contains within it the 'purple marble' and that the colour purple carries an iconographic value. Is it possible, also, that the 'hard and valuable stone' in the name conveys a similar religious import? Is Porfiry 'as solid as a rock' as the Church is in its ancient traditions (in contradistinction to the ephemeral modernity of the Crystal Palace)? It could be argued that I am overstating the liaison between concrete images and symbolic meanings. The cathedral is not, after all, described as made of stone (though clearly it is). On the other hand, if one looks again at the dream paradigm, it will be recalled that 'in the middle of the cemetery was a *stone* church with a green cupola' (73, my emphasis, A. J.). This does not, of course, confirm a definitive liaison between the examining magistrate and the Russian Orthodox

Church as religious institution; we need to look further at the texture
of the text and to continue to identify the connecting threads which
are often not seen individually when reading through impressionisti-
cally. It may have gone unnoticed that Porfiry's patronym is Petrovich (Peter's son) and that since Porfiry connotes 'stone', there may
be reason to suppose that 'Petrovich' signifies something more than
simply who his father is. Pyotr derives from the Latin *Petrus* ('stone'),
so there is a direct semantic association of the two names. It should
also not be forgotten that the very locale of Porfiry's criminal
investigation is St Petersburg, a city which although built of stone
was sited by the Tsar, Peter the Great, against all architectural logic
on marshland. But this hardly seems a promising route to establishing Porfiry as someone whose integrity is solidly based, for the
modern city of St Petersburg – topographically situated on marshland and philosophically modelled on a Western concept – would
appear to be as ill founded as the ultra-modernity of the Crystal
Palace in London.

St Petersburg is, of course, a German name (thus bearing out its
Western character) meaning literally 'St Peter's castle'. This reminds
us that within the city is the St Peter and St Paul Fortress, the prison
where Raskolnikov would most certainly have been taken before
being transported to Siberia (as Dostoevsky, after mock-execution,
was himself imprisoned and from where he was transported). Since
the St Peter and St Paul Fortress is going to play such a conspicuous
role in Raskolnikov's destiny (after he has confessed, it will be the
place of imprisonment, the prelude to penal servitude), a fourth
building might be added to our imaginary icon – the St Peter and St
Paul Fortress – placed on the right, or to the east (the direction of
Siberia), as the university (the Academy of Sciences) with its classical
portico has been placed on the left, or in the west.

The position of the Crystal Palace might be explained first of all
because it is morally the polar opposite of the cathedral and, also,
because on the religious plane the cupola of the cathedral, at the
top, extends into the vault of Heaven whilst the Crystal Palace is
engulfed in the formless waters of the River Neva (as analogously
Raskolnikov throws the coin given him 'in Christ's name' into the
water, or as the drunken woman throws herself off the bridge in an
attempted suicide; or, again, as Raskolnikov himself contemplates
such an act; and as Marmeladov dissolves in drink in the city
underworld; hence, the Palais de Crystal tavern).

It can be seen that as an iconographic representation of Raskolni-kov's spiritual journey at which stopping on the bridge is a moment of crux, the cathedral and the Crystal Palace have been placed in opposition to each other, the one leading 'upwards' (iconographically speaking) to salvation, the other 'downwards' to damnation. This does not necessarily imply that a choice has to be made by the criminal to repent or to remain obdurate. It is perhaps predestined (divinely planned, designed, drawn, painted or written) that he should lose his faith (the Church), dream up grandiose scientific ideas (at the university), commit murder to ensure the greatest happiness of the greatest number (the Crystal Palace), and that he should eventually submit to punishment (the St Peter and St Paul Fortress) before his ultimate return to the faith of his childhood (the Church). Here, there is no schismatic, or gnostic, pictorial denotation of, let us say, Good versus Evil or Heaven versus Hell, but an occult cyclical and symbolic unity which is concealed in the deep structure of the novel. The circle of experience has, as it were, been drawn around the four points of the cross of life's suffering, as there are four points of departure for Raskolnikov: the Church, the University, the Palais de Crystal, and the St Peter and St Paul Fortress.

It is possible to discern in this cyclical representation of the murderer's life at least a partial correspondence with the content of Raskolnikov's dream of childhood: his walk to the *church* where he used to go with his mother and father, is interrupted by the killing of the old mare outside the *tavern*; and in so far as there is a paradigmatic similarity between them, the dream does appear to anticipate, in a condensed form, the sequence of events that are recorded in Raskolnikov's history.

It may have been remarked that in the process of tracing the network of connecting threads in the novel, I have moved away from a consideration of the symbology of the patronym, Petrovich; and it is perhaps fitting, since we have returned to the childhood scene where the stone church with a green cupola stands, that our investigation should be resumed in that area. Attention has been drawn to the somewhat dubious status of St Petersburg in the iconography of the fiction: a city built of stone (unlike most Russian provincial towns where houses, up until the twentieth century, were built of wood) constructed on marshland. One is reminded here of Christ's parabolic injunction to build one's spiritual house on rock (Mt. 7: 24–25) and, furthermore, of his designation of the Apostle

Peter as the 'rock' upon whom the Christian Church would be founded (Mt. 16: 15–20). It is not, then, by mere chance that the Christian name, Porfiry (purple stone), is juxtaposed with the patronym, Petrovich (son of a 'rock'). Rather, what we are seeing here is a vivid example of Dostoevsky's iconographic method at work.

It has already been asserted that the colour purple in Porfiry's name signals a sacred role for him on the vertical axis. We might go further and suggest that, since the names have been juxtaposed, there ought to be a symbolic liaison between the stone in Porfiry's name and the potential 'rock' in Petrovich. This seems likely bearing in mind the canonical value of purple: if Porfiry symbolically wears the vestments of the Passion by taking on collective responsibility for Raskolnikov's crime and, hence, his suffering (an endemic part of Russian Orthodox-Church thinking), it would also be possible to see him symbolically as a son, or priest, of the Church; that is, 'St Peter's son'. Once this is accepted, Porfiry takes on the role of protector, or 'little father' as priests are called in the Orthodox tradition, thus providing a complement to Sonya's 'little mother' as she is known by the convicts in the penal colony. Seen iconographically, what we have here is a diptych, with Porfiry inscribed on one side and Sonya on the other.

However, if the name of the examining magistrate, Porfiry Petrovich, bears such an affirmative iconographic signification, how is one to interpret what Richard Peace has described as the embodiment of 'a new type of pettifogging legal expert' in, precisely, *Pyotr Petrovich* Luzhin?[10] If it is the case that Luzhin's Christian name, Pyotr, and patronymic, Petrovich, appear to function complementarily (as they do in Porfiry Petrovich), it is certainly not so when they are juxtaposed as a pair with his family name; for the name, Luzhin, comes close to the Russian word *luzha* – 'a puddle' – and, therefore, if inherent meaning is taken into account, must work antithetically to the stonelike properties of Pyotr and Petrovich. Since I have already posited the symbolic propensity of water as purporting formlessness, or loss of form, and 'stone/rock' as signifying substantive form, or the saving of human form, it will have become clear that the name, Pyotr Petrovich Luzhin, is invested with an irreconcilable duality similar to the disparate nomenclature given by Dostoevsky to the main protagonist of his novel, *The Idiot*: Prince Leo ('lion') Myshkin ('mousekin').[11]

The phonetic similarity of the name Luzhin with *luzha* ('puddle') also has relevance on a philosophical plane if it is remarked that Luzhin has been the 'student' of his former ward, Lebezyatnikov, whose adherence to the rationalistic values of Utilitarianism, symbolised by the Crystal Palace (and placed in the waters of the River Neva in our imaginary icon), is as unequivocal as was Raskolnikov's at the time of the murder. But Luzhin's avowal of the Utilitarian way of thinking learned from Lebezyatnikov is not born out of conviction, but because the notion of enlightened self interest suits his ruthless egoism; it is, in other words, a watered down philosophy – a mere puddle of an idea. Luzhin's actions have the effect of negating any altruistic moral value that his pseudo-Utilitarianism may purport to have: he merely seeks to profit by sowing discord, as when he falsely accuses Sonya of theft, or in his attempt to break up the Raskolnikov family by tempting Dunya to marry him so that she may be kept.

Clearly, the duality implicit in his names – Pyotr Petrovich, on the one hand, and Luzhin, on the other – is lived out in the divisiveness of his actions. Whereas Raskolnikov for all his schizoid behaviour did desire to put the world to rights – to bring it together again – Luzhin works at nothing but disuniting in the most petty and mean-spirited way; and it would not be too far-fetched, on a metaphysical plane, to call him 'diabolical' once we note that the word derives from the Greek *dia-bolos*, meaning literally 'to throw across', or 'to slander', a practice at which Luzhin is adept.[12] Contained within the word is the notion of division; Luzhin is diabolical precisely because he attempts to divide one person from another – Sonya from Raskolnikov, Dunya from her family – to break their integrity and to destroy their human solidarity with one another. Thus we can better understand the iconographic juxtaposition of the disparate nomenclature: Pyotr Petrovich (stone, son of stone) with Luzhin (*luzha*, 'puddle') which works counter to the fundamental integrity implicit in the name Porfiry Petrovich and, on a larger scale, the unifying symbol of the Christian cross. Again, seen iconographically, what we have here is a diptych with Pyotr Petrovich Luzhin placed on the left and Porfiry Petrovich on the right, but, unlike the spiritually complementary figures of Sonya the saint and Porfiry the sage, Luzhin and Porfiry are situated in opposition to each other on the moral scale.

If this once more seems to be in danger of overstating the case, let us counterbalance figurative stones in the name Porfiry Petrovich with the image of a literal stone:

[Raskolnikov] suddenly noticed <. . .> a huge unhewn stone, weighing about fifty pounds, and lying close against the outer stone wall <. . .> He bent down over the stone, caught hold of the top of it firmly with both his hands, and, applying all his strength, turned it over. There was a small cavity under the stone, and he at once started throwing everything [he had stolen from the murdered money lender] out of his pockets into it. (127)

It is noteworthy here that Raskolnikov had intended throwing the stolen things into a canal, or the river, thus destroying the evidence against him (symbolically rendering them formless), but that he suddenly decides to hide them in a safe place under the stone (thus preserving their form). This turns out to be fortunate because, later at the trial, the examining magistrates and judges are clearly impressed that the accused man 'should have hidden the purse and various articles from the flat under a stone without attempting to make any use of them' (543), a fact which partly contributes to a lessening of the severity of his sentence. The stone, then, has preserved the evidence which will save the condemned man from a life sentence (or total loss of human identity) just as, correspondingly, Porfiry Petrovich has offered Raskolnikov a degree of protection if he will reveal all, which in practical terms again means that the life sentence will be commuted to a few years penal servitude.

We have discovered here in what a complex way Dostoevsky's symbology works. On the one hand, the image of a stone is represented literally and does not appear, in its isolated form, to carry any symbolic weight; the image fits inconspicuously into the framework of secular realism. On the other hand, once the latent symbolism of the names Porfiry Petrovich and Pyotr Petrovich Luzhin becomes fully realised, the language of the text is itself illuminated in such a way that literal images are found to have a capacity for extra-literal meaning. This agrees entirely with religious iconography, the purpose of which is to express on a spiritual plane what it is not possible to attain through literal representation only. There has to be an in-built figural dimension, the foundation, as it were, of the discursive narrative. At a surface level, the polyphony which Mikhail Bakhtin has postulated for Dostoevsky's poetics – a technical innovation which has the effect of destabilising the text ('the world')[13] – is brought under control by, or is even arrested by, the vertical figural dimension which cuts through the diachronic, horizontal plane of the discourse.[14] Time is brought to a standstill to make way for an instant (or an eternity) of teleological certitude.

Symbology functions rather as the narrator might do in a monologic narrative, except that whereas the narrator may consciously know all, the symbols are hidden in the deep structure of the text, the realm of the text's unconscious. This difference can easily be accounted for by the fact that even if the voices are many, the visual perspective is limited: the world seen and experienced, for the most part, by one man: Rodion Romanovich Raskolnikov (*Crime and Punishment* was originally drafted as a first person narrative). It is natural, therefore, that with such a limitation imposed on him (as it is imposed on all of us) that the world should appear to the murderer chaotic, meaningless and absurd.

Conversely, once a network of symbols has been established and a hidden signification brought to light, it will be seen that symbols permeate the discourse with an attribute of what amounts to immanency, thus opening it up to inherent meaning. Moreover, this special status of symbol as the bearer of hidden meaning is metaphysical in thrust because it has the capacity to transcend the limitations of mundane discourse and to impose on it the stability which on the surface it seems to lack. As Mikhail Bakhtin has said: 'Dostoevsky destroys the flatness of the earlier artistic depiction of the world. Depiction becomes for the first time multidimensional.'[15]

NOTES

1 All quotations are from: F. M. Dostoevsky, *Crime and Punishment*, trans. D. Magarshack (Harmondsworth, 1970). Page references are given in brackets.
2 W. D. Snodgrass, 'Crime for punishment: The tenor of part one', *Hudson Review* 13, no. 2 (1960), 248.
3 E. Auerbach, *Mimesis: The Representation of Reality in Western Literature*, trans. W. R. Trask (Princeton, NJ, 1974), 521.
4 M. Bakhtin, *Problems of Dostoevsky's Poetics*, ed. and trans. C. Emerson (Minneapolis, MN, 1984).
5 See A. Johae, 'Idealism and the dialectic in *The Brothers Karamazov*', ed. L. Burnett, *F. M. Dostoevsky 1821–1881: A Centenary Volume* (Colchester, 1981), 111.
6 Richard Peace, *Dostoevsky: An Examination of the Major Novels* (Cambridge, 1975), 44.
7 *Ibid.*, 44–45.
8 See J. Catteau, *Dostoevsky and the Process of Literary Creation*, trans. A. Littlewood (Cambridge, 1989), 426.
9 For the significance of the Crystal Palace for Russians in the mid-

nineteenth century, see M. Berman, *All That Is Solid Melts Into Air: The Experience of Modernity* (London, 1983), 235–48. I have traced the Crystal Palace motif in Chernyshevsky, Dostoevsky and Zamyatin in 'The Russian sources of George Orwell's *Nineteen Eighty-Four*', *New Comparison*, 17 (1994).

10 See Peace, *Dostoevsky*, 23.

11 For an account of the ambiguities of name and character in Prince Leo Myshkin, see A. Johae, 'Retractive imagery: Dostoevsky and German Romanticism', *Germano-Slavica*, 8, no. 2 (1994), 10–12.

12 I am indebted to Hugh Drake for drawing my attention to the etymology of 'diabolical'.

13 Bakhtin, *Dostoevsky's Poetics*, 45–46.

14 Robert Louis Jackson in 'Bakhtin's Poetics of Dostoevsky' in *Dialogues with Dostoevsky: The Overwhelming Questions* (Stanford, CA, 1993), 283, has observed that Bakhtin 'projects <. . .> a horizontal plane to the Dostoevsky novel on which exist multiple "consciousnesses" <. . .> At the same time he [Bakhtin] suggests what we may term a vertical dimension in Dostoevsky's novelistic universe, a hierarchy of voices, orientations, or truths arising out of this sea of autonomous jostling truths.' On other religious readings of Dostoevsky's novels, see in the same volume, 'Chateaubriand and Dostoevsky: Elective affinities', 'Vision in his soul: Vyacheslav I. Ivanov's Dostoevsky' and 'Last stop: Virtue and immortality in *The Brothers Karamazov*'. None of these essays, however, give attention to the aesthetic sources of Dostoevsky's iconographic art in religious symbology.

15 M. Bakhtin, 'Towards a reworking of the Dostoevsky book', partly reproduced in Fyodor Dostoevsky, *'Crime and Punishment': The Coulson Translation: Backgrounds and Sources: Essays in Criticism*, ed. George Gibian, 3rd edn (New York, 1989), 655.

CHAPTER 10

Pavel Smerdyakov and Ivan Karamazov: The problem of temptation[1]

Vladimir Kantor

Literary reputations exist (of writers, of books, of fictional characters), which are to such an extent firmly established that they seem
almost givens of their age and are in any event unshakeable. At
times, this unshakeability can be explained solely by the inertness of
our perception. Thus does the interpretation of a certain character
or novelistic situation, laid down at some point in the past, migrate
from work to work, acquiring with time the appearance of an axiom
that requires no proof. This happens most often in those instances
when for some reason the character or situation seems to us
secondary or 'not the main thing' – and consequently the conception
of the whole does not depend upon its resolution. As regards other
situations, however, it is worth while pausing and considering
whether they are in fact secondary and of little importance. This is
especially the case with the novel under consideration, an artistic
work in which even secondary details can elucidate a great deal for
us about the writer's creative plan and position.

The opinion that Pavel Smerdyakov is nothing other than an
obedient tool in the hands of Ivan Karamazov, no more than the
executor of his evil will, was already voiced in the nineteenth century
by Orest Miller: 'Unfortunate Smerdyakov, having blindly subordinated himself to Ivan's ideal <. . .> committed the crime.'[2] Since
then, with various degrees of complexity and evidence but most
often simply in passing (for this is, after all, a secondary question;
what interests us in the novel is the conflict between Good and Evil,
the Grand Inquisitor, etc.), it is affirmed that 'Smerdyakov is only
the practical agent of criminality. Behind him in Dostoevsky's novel
the figure of Ivan Karamazov rises up, whose ideas and concepts,
the author assures us, prompted Smerdyakov to the crime, and
justified and even elevated the murderer in his own eyes.'[3] In this
way, laying the entire responsibility on one character, we utterly free

up the other from any responsibility at all. When we do this, the
direct unambiguous murderer turns out to be Ivan; pursuing the
logic of this thought, Ivan becomes the 'carrier of evil' in the poetic
world of the novel. In V. E. Vetlovskaya's profound and authoritative
study, this position is summed up in the following words: 'Thus
Alyosha (and the reader), in listening to Ivan, hear the devil
himself.'[4] But if this is the case, then Ivan's nature appears completely monosemantic – and all his torments, self-accusations, the
ambivalence and multiple meanings of his words and actions must
be considered insubstantial and unessential; the structure of his
image is thereby simplified, as is the understanding of guilt and
responsibility upon which Dostoevsky insisted. The entire figurative
structure of the novel is very noticeably disrupted. The genetic link
between Smerdyakov and the devil ('lackeydom') and the manifest
repetitiousness of the images that connect them are revealed as
accidental and artistically non-obligatory; the conversations between
Ivan and Smerdyakov, and later between Ivan and the devil who is
tempting him, become meaningless nonsense if the hero himself is
an unconditional force for evil ('the devil').

It should be kept in mind that the assessment of a given character
is important not in and of itself, especially with a writer like
Dostoevsky. Far more essential here is to glimpse behind these
characters the system of values that produces their worldview, a
system provided by the writer and necessary to understand his moral
and aesthetic credo.

If we endorse the point of view on Smerdyakov that he is a passive
murderer, a blind tool in someone else's hand, a person merely
carrying out Ivan's plan, then we will enter naturally into a
contradiction with the poetic and worldview-shaping concepts that
govern Dostoevsky's cosmos, a cosmos resting on the fact that each
person bears full responsibility for his or her own acts, regardless of
the social level from which he comes and no matter how undeve-
loped he may be. Speaking of the peasant who drove his wife to
suicide, Dostoevsky proclaims:

'Lack of development, dullness of mind – have pity, it's the environment!' –
this is what the peasant's lawyer has insisted. But millions of peasants live
like that and not all of them hang their wives by the feet! One must, all the
same, draw a line <. . .> Then on the other hand, here's an educated man,
and suddenly he hangs his wife up. No, you've prevaricated enough,
gentlemen lawyers, with your 'environment'! (21,23)

It is possible to forgive a person a great deal (Mitya). To forgive is possible, but one cannot remove responsibility from him, and not only for an act but also for an intention (Ivan). According to Dostoevsky, the 'environment', the external circumstances of a human being, do not define and do not justify. Yet here we end up with Smerdyakov having been forced into committing the murder by extraneous circumstances (for another person's will is an external cause), and he himself is not guilty.

It is also worth remembering that we have here a novel about the *brothers* Karamazov, where each possesses his own life motif and ideational motif, and that this novel is not about three brothers but four – since Smerdyakov, as we are given to believe at several points in the novel, is the illegitimate son of Fyodor Pavlovich and thus the half-brother of the central heroes. What is more, if Ivan and Mitya reveal themselves to be vacillating, inconstant natures, seeking good and truth but committing misdemeanours and crimes along the way, then Alyosha, from one side, and Smerdyakov, from the other, function like firm orientation points of good and evil. Immediately after Mitya's 'Confession of an Ardent Heart' (Book 3, 3–5) and long before Ivan expounds to Alyosha his understanding of how the world is made ('Pro and Contra'), Smerdyakov, in the chapter 'Disputation' (*Contraverza*) (that is, argument, conflict; it is characteristic that the Latin titles emphasise the closeness of the problems posed by the legitimate and the illegitimate brother, Ivan and Pavel) also sets forth his credo in a 'quarrel'. However, unlike Ivan, who tries to weigh and evaluate in his heart the pro as well as the contra, Smerdyakov is monosemantic and pronounces an apologia to perfidy, his own sort of 'justification of evil'.[5] It is not by chance (as I try to show below) that Ivan *swings* between Alyosha and Smerdyakov.

Smerdyakov is not a madman, not crazy; even less is he a 'weak-minded idiot', as he is called by the residents of the town – although he does have the falling sickness, he is an epileptic. It was he who thought out and subtly executed not only the plan with the envelope, which he ripped open and threw out just as someone would have done who didn't know whether there was money in it – thus strengthening suspicions against Mitya; he also successfully played through the performance of his epileptic fit. In endowing Smerdyakov with epilepsy, just as he did his favourite hero Prince Myshkin, Dostoevsky emphasises precisely his isolation and separateness from the sphere of the 'healthy' Rakitins (Rakitin,

incidentally, with his mediocrity and his strong worldly mind, recalls
Ganya Ivolgin), and takes him 'out of the ranks' of ordinary everyday
persons. But Smerdyakov is the opposite of Myshkin. In Dostoevsky's
view, epilepsy develops in a person, in certain instances, a heightened
keenness of mind and penetration, which can then be used for either
good or evil deeds. Everything depends wholly on the person's moral
foundation.[6]

We are always struck when an artist, in advance of his time, draws
with historical precision a type of person which, it would seem, he
could not himself have observed. 'Dostoevsky' – so wrote Robert
Musil – 'was able to detect in the nineteenth century the birth of
that socio-psychological danger which is fascism.'[7] In our literature
as well it has often been noted that the phenomenon of fascism and
Stalinism in the twentieth century confirmed the writer's tragic
insights.

The strength of Dostoevsky, that which permitted him to divine
the collisions of the future, lay in his moral maximalism, the fact that
he imposed on a person – especially as regards questions of life and
death – the entire fullness of moral responsibility, allowing no
transfer of it to another's shoulders. If we remember that Smerdyakov is intimately tied to the major problem of the novel, patricide,
it becomes clear that one can call him a secondary character only
with difficulty: he must be scrutinised more intently, in keeping with
the writer's own scale of values.

But at the same time he cannot be scrutinised separately, for he is
Ivan's double and thus becomes comprehensible only alongside him.
A 'double', however, is in no sense a 'hero of the second order'. A
double is of course more one-dimensional, more monosemantic, but
this does not at all mean he is subordinated to the hero; on the
contrary, as a rule it is the other way around. Recall Robert Louis
Stevenson's *The Strange Case of Dr Jekyll and Mr Hyde*, in which
Mr Hyde, created out of all the evil sides of the doctor's soul,
gradually gained the upper hand. Recall also that in Dostoevsky's
own Petersburg poem, *The Double*, Golyadkin Junior turns out to be
more decisive, more resourceful, more base, and in the end rubs out
Golyadkin Senior, who still preserved some elements of decency,
which in fact proved an obstacle to his 'success.' But in that short
novel, the double is a double in the full sense of the word,
duplicating not only the outer image but even the name and
patronymic of the hero. In *The Brothers Karamazov* the issue is more

complicated. But there too the double is vitally linked with the hero, with several of his desires that are unacknowledged even by the hero himself, yet he is linked not linearly, not in a 'frontal' way, and this creates difficulties in making sense out of their interrelations. Smerdyakov, Mikhail Bakhtin notes, 'gradually gains control over Ivan's voice, which the latter is concealing from himself. Smerdyakov is able to govern this voice precisely because Ivan's consciousness *does not look in that direction and does not want to look there*' [my emphasis, V. K.].[8] In any event and no matter what, the double is never identified with the author's lyrical hero (that is, with a hero whose task it is to resolve metaphysical problems of personality). If we declare Smerdyakov to be a simple executor of other people's ideas, then the entire complicated dialectic of the hero's interrelations falls away, the reason for Ivan's torments becomes incoherent or banal, and the conflict between two wills struggling over him disappears (the 'It's not you!' spoken by Alyosha and the 'But you are the main murderer!' spoken by Smerdyakov) – that is, what falls away is the internal tension that Mitya speaks of when he says: When 'the devil is struggling with God', then 'the field of battle is the hearts of men' (14,100).

'Ivan is a riddle', says Alyosha (14,209). It is impossible not to agree with him, because, beginning with his 'fateful arrival' in the town – 'which served as starting-point for so many consequences', as the narrator puts it – right up to his final 'fatal' deposition in court, the other characters and even more the readers try to figure Ivan out and get to the bottom of him (14,12). Ivan, it seems, feels more keenly than the others a hatred of 'Karamazovism', whose embodiment, for him, is his father and his brother Mitya: 'One reptile will devour another, and good riddance to them both!' (14,129). But is that the solution Dostoevsky himself accepts? And can we be sure that Ivan's desire to rid himself of the pollution of 'Karamazovism' by his father's death is his own actual final position?

The fact is that Ivan is a riddle not only for others but also for himself. He cannot define himself in any way, and this is the cause of his constant vacillation, inner turmoil, the absence in him of any precise position on life that so confused Smerdyakov. In the elder Zosima's cell (a visit that Ivan had insisted upon, during which he conversed with the elder 'in a modest and restrained manner, with visible courtesy'), Ivan first sets forth for the reader, although still in

compressed form, his own credo, as if awaiting the elder's advice
and evaluation both of his idea and of himself. At this point the elder
suddenly says to Ivan, apropos of his idea that if God and immortality do not exist then all is permitted, that Ivan has thought up this
idea 'from desperation':

  – This question is not yet resolved for you, and in this lies your great
grief, for it insistently demands resolution . . .
  – And can it be resolved in myself? Resolved in a positive direction? –
Ivan Fyodorovich continued to ask, somewhat strangely, looking at the
elder with an inexplicable smile.
  – If it cannot be resolved in a positive direction, then it will never be
resolved negatively either – for you yourself know this quality of your heart;
therein lies the whole of its torment. (14,65)

Apparently the elder's point of view coincided with Ivan's point of
view on himself, because after these words he 'suddenly rose from
his chair, went up to him, received his blessing, and, having kissed
his hand, returned silently to his place. His expression was firm and
serious' (14,65).

What sort of inner struggle is tormenting Ivan? In the chapters
'The Brothers Get Acquainted', 'Rebellion' and 'The Grand Inquisitor', Dostoevsky presents Ivan with the opportunity to develop his
understanding of God, the world, society, his own self, and possible
routes for restructuring the world.

Ivan begins his confession with the admission that at the basis of
his being lies an elemental, unreasoning 'Karamazovian' thirst for
life, which transcends all human derangements and disillusionments,
even despair, even the feeling that the whole world is a 'disordered,
accursed, perhaps even demonic chaos' (14,209). This feature, as
Ivan himself says, is 'in part Karamazovian', and in this thirst he
resembles his father. However, in Ivan the thirst for life emerges as a
consciously articulated force – and we begin to understand that this
'Karamazovian' elemental quality contains a life-creating potency of
incredible energy, but one not bounded by forms and not oriented in
a positive direction.

  – I'm terribly glad that you want to live so much, – Alyosha exclaimed. 'I
think that everyone should love life before all else in the world.'
  – Love life more than the meaning of it?
  – Absolutely, love it before logic, as you say, it must absolutely be before
logic, because only then will I grasp its meaning. I've long imagined this is
how it is. Half the deed is done, Ivan, and already acquired: you love to
live. Now you need only try at the second half, and you are saved. (14,210)

In contrast to old Fyodor Pavlovich, Ivan seeks this meaning, for he cannot reconcile himself with the world's disharmony: 'I want to see with my own eyes how the doe lies down with the lion and how the murdered man will rise up and embrace his murderer' (14,222). But the world is so cruel, and human sufferings so innumerable, tormenting, and without exit (especially the unjust and heart-rending sufferings of children), that Dostoevsky's hero demands vengeance and retribution. And this vengeance he refuses to cede to God, to the God who says: 'Vengeance is mine, and mine the retribution' (Deut. 32:35). Ivan paraphrases the utterance, turning it back on himself: 'I need retribution, otherwise I will put an end to myself. Retribution not in the infinite wherever and whenever, but here and now, on earth, so that I can see it myself' (14,222). According to Ivan, God cannot find – and does not have the right to find – a justification for human sufferings. This whole complex of ideas is formulated by Ivan in the aphorism with which he opened his conversation with Alyosha: 'It's not that I do not accept God, understand that, it is the world created by Him, it is God's world that I do not accept and will not agree to accept' (14,214). Since God was not able to establish the world on humane principles, Ivan takes upon himself full responsibility for this world. But can a person – alone – take upon himself such a responsibility? Does not such despotic individualism in fact signify a rejection of real – that is, human-scale – responsibility for one's own actions? This is one of the most important questions posed in the novel.

Ivan's theomachist zeal produced a very strong impression on Dostoevsky's contemporaries, even on those who did not accept the novel as a whole. Ivan Karamazov was entered into the ranks of such images of world literature as Job, Lucifer, Byron's Cain and Manfred, Lermontov's Demon.[9] Of all these parallels, perhaps the one that deserves the most attention is that between Ivan Karamazov and the Biblical theomach Job. In his novels Dostoevsky often provides distinctive hints to guide us towards those works of world literature meant to serve as commentary, as a tuning-fork to the events and heroes that he represents. For example, in *The Idiot*, Pushkin's verse about the 'Poor Knight' that Aglaya recites functions in this way, permitting the author to highlight the knightly, Don-Quixotic service of Prince Myshkin to his ideal. In *The Brothers Karamazov*, immediately after Ivan's confession to Alyosha (the chapters 'Rebellion' and 'The Grand Inquisitor') and his conversation with Smerdyakov ('It is always interesting to have a talk with a clever man') there follows the book 'A Russian Monk', where the elder Zosima names as the most important spiritual impact on his life the legend of Job, the righteous man 'who had cried out to God' after his countless sufferings but who in the end was forgiven by God. The elder not only recalls the legend but retells it, in his own interpretation, omitting, as if deliberately, the hero's theomachic speeches, which constitute three-quarters of the Book of Job. And most likely this is no accident, inasmuch as the utterances of Ivan Karamazov and those of the Biblical hero coincide to a striking extent. Just like Ivan, tempted by his own misfortunes and by the misfortunes of the world, so does Job accuse God:

He destroyeth the sinless and the guilty. If He suddenly strikes with the scourge, he will laugh at the torments of the innocent. The earth is given into the hand of the wicked; he covereth the faces of the judges thereof. If not He, then who?' (Job 9: 22−24)

He does not reject God, but enters into argument with him: 'Surely I would speak to the Almighty, and I desire to contend with God' (Job 13:3). The nineteenth-century reader (whom Dostoevsky addressed), who knew the Bible if only through the catechism in the secondary school curriculum, would inevitably have detected not only the omissions in the elder's version of the story but also, having recalled the words of Job − tempted, with God's permission, by Satan − he would correlate them with Ivan's words and understand that in this instance Ivan is not the tempter, but the tempted. The theme of Job, it should be noted, was of constant interest to Dostoevsky. As early as 1875, in a letter to his wife, he wrote: 'I'm reading the Book of Job, and it casts me into feverish ecstasy; I throw down my work, I pace my room for hours on end, almost weeping . . . this book, Anya, it's strange, this book was one of the first to make a deep impression in my life, when I was still a little child!' (29,i,43). The motif of Job is also heard in *The Adolescent*, in the teachings of Makar Dolgoruky (13,330). Doubtless too, while pondering 'The Life of a Great Sinner' (which in a way is a threshold for *The Brothers Karamazov*), Dostoevsky could not refrain from turning to what is almost the sole Biblical image of a theomachic righteous man. This parallel, in any case, demonstrates one of the reasons for the author's respectfully serious attitude towards his hero-rebel. Dostoevsky is writing his own variant of a man tormented by the Divine structure of the world, and that man's path to self-knowledge and to knowledge of the meaning of the world. A path that is far from easy.

In his 'poem' 'The Grand Inquisitor', Ivan affirms the feebleness of Christ (who had conceded to human beings freedom of choice in what they lived by) to correct people and to overcome their separateness through freedom: 'You have only the chosen ones, and we console all the others', so the Inquisitor tells Christ (14,235). For this reason Ivan wants to accept a violent annihilation of the world's evil for the sake of people's happiness, even if only of the herd-like and barrack-like sort represented by him in the poem, if – as it seems to Ivan – it proves impossible to organise humanity in any other way. But can a person, sincerely and even fervently thirsting after good and world harmony, accept not only the theoretical postulate of violence but also its practical conclusions? Can he, instead of honouring the freedom guaranteed to the *other*, impose *his will* on him? This is the question that occupied Dostoevsky. And although the ideas uttered by Ivan were alien to Dostoevsky, he allowed his hero to speak them out in full force in order to verify in earnest the principle of *despotic voluntarism*, and not write off his hero's shortcomings as the vices and shortcomings of a given individual. That is, Dostoevsky tries to solve the same question that so tormented Chernyshevsky: how to overcome our archetypical striving 'to do everything by the force of one's caprice, of one's uncontrolled decision.'[10]

But for that reason one can hardly assume that through this one self-utterance of Ivan's, in essence a vast lyrical poem (here all three chapters – 'The Brothers Get Acquainted', 'Rebellion' and 'The Grand Inquisitor' – come to a single point), Ivan's image is thereby finalised. After all, this is the hero of a novel and not some real-life thinker with his own set of thoughts, autonomous and independent of the will of an author. His fate finds its resolution in the further movement of the plot, in the poetic linking-up with other artistic images in the novel. Only within this complex artistic system is it possible to understand and evaluate the worldview and life position of Ivan Karamazov.

In contrast to the Grand Inquisitor, who is concentrated in his idea, Ivan is merely the author of a poem in which he analyses this idea artistically. He himself has not yet been defined, 'he has to get an idea straight', and he has not yet succeeded in doing so. It is this indefiniteness of Ivan's that prepares the ground for the appearance of a *double* (Smerdyakov), parasitically living off Ivan's inner struggle. It is not by chance that the Grand Inquisitor has no doubles. He himself is the best expounder of the worldview that he has suffered his way into endorsing. The best expounder of Ivan's worldview is what Ivan's double strives to become. In Ivan's conflict with Smerdyakov something like a reciprocal 'illumination' of both these persons takes place, and the meaning of the idea 'all is permitted' is clarified – along with the possible social and moral uses to which this idea might be put.

In his early novel *The Double*, Dostoevsky attempted to depict for the first time a situation where certain, albeit the very worst, wishes and feelings of the hero could appear to him as living an entirely autonomous and independent life. Dostoevsky himself considered the phenomenon of the double one of his most important artistic ideas – but one that he could not come to terms with in his youth. In particular it was difficult to resolve whether all these nasty feelings picked up by the double actually belonged to the personality-core of the hero, or whether they were somehow borrowed, alien, external. This problem received its ultimate socio-philosophical and artistic resolution in the writer's last novel.

I begin, therefore, with the double.

The first mention of Smerdyakov is made by Mitya, who because of him arrives late at the family gathering in the elder's cell: 'The servant Smerdyakov, who was sent by my father, to my persistent question about the time, answered me twice in the most decisive tone that the meeting had been set for one o'clock' (14,63). Thus, even before his first appearance in the pages of the novel, Smerdyakov is connected in the reader's mind with some sort of confusion, with the substitution of something false for what is real – and although it is still not clear whether this confusion is deliberate or accidental, in any event it has led to a certain tension. But for the nonce this is all only in passing. Then the author remarks about the birth of Smerdyakov in the second chapter of the third book ('Stinking Lizaveta'), albeit only in connection with the filthiest act of Fyodor Pavlovich. About Smerdyakov himself the narrator so far communicates no details at all, putting his trust in the fact that 'something about him will somehow come off by itself in the further course of the narrative' (14,93). Only in the sixth chapter of this same book does the narrator finally tell us about Smerdyakov. A secondary figure, clearly. Yet all the same, at a certain moment all our attention is focused on him. During his conversations with Ivan . . . But by that point Smerdyakov himself is already winning for himself a secondary role. He declares to Ivan: 'I was only your stooge, your faithful servant Licharda, I committed the deed according to your word' (15,59). With such persistence does he refuse for himself a primary role, which would carry with it responsibility, that – if only out of a feeling of contradiction – it is worth analysing this situation further.

Destructive and centrifugal forces exist in the common people. Dostoevsky knew this and did not conceal it. Recall the scene at 'Mokroe', recall Fedka the Convict from *Demons*, the sort of bandit on whom the Bakuninites placed their hopes, or the convicts from the *Notes from the House of the Dead*. There was yet another character-istically national type, in Dostoevsky's opinion, and that was the 'contemplator':

suddenly, having piled up impressions for many years, he would cast off everything and set out for Jerusalem, to wander and save himself; or perhaps he would suddenly burn down his native village, or perhaps both the one and the other would happen together. There are a good number of 'contemplators' among the people. One such contemplator was probably Smerdyakov. (14,117)

By his psychological makeup, then, Smerdyakov resembles similar types coming from the people. But Smerdyakov is not a moujik, not a peasant, he is a lackey. 'Lackeydom', in Dostoevsky's view, is spiritual spinelessness, a lack of autonomy accompanied by the remarkable ability to look after one's own material interests. Genetically, the lackey in Russia is a product of the serf-owning era: a person severed from the people, living in the noble's house but not on an equal footing with the nobleman, that is, a person occupying an ill-defined and degraded position, neither one thing nor the other. In the post-Reform period, so Dostoevsky believed, this phenom-enon became widespread. Inadequate education and its utilitarian bent gave rise to a mass of so-called 'half-educated people', torn from popular culture, from 'folk truth' ('Can a Russian peasant have a feeling against an educated person? Because of his lack of educa-tion, he cannot have any feeling at all' Smerdyakov mutters), but who at the same time were not elevated to higher spiritual questions (thus this same Smerdyakov reproaches Gogol: 'It's all about lies, what's written there') (14,205,116). A line can be drawn through the novel connecting a whole series of characters most unpleasant to the author, and all of them falling under the rubric of 'lackey' – beginning with Fyodor Pavlovich and ending with the devil. For Dostoevsky, the lackey is the embodiment of Russia's evil. It is characteristic that Smerdyakov, the illegitimate son of Fyodor Pavlovich, resembles him more closely than do the other children. Old Karamazov relies on him, does not acknowledge his paternity, but nevertheless, suspicious and not overfond of his two older legitimate children, 'somehow even loved him, although the young man looked at him just as askance as the others did, and was silent all the time' (14,116). And it is precisely Smerdyakov who bears the full patrilinear name (compare Fyodor Pavlovich and Pavel Fyodorovich), continuing the family tradition of lackeydom. After all, Fyodor Pavlovich in his youth was a hanger-on, that is, a lackey of the same sort. And Smerdyakov also dreams of amassing his own little capital, just like his father.

There is, however, an essential difference. If, for Fyodor Pavlovich, lackeydom is one of the facets of his external profile, then for Smerdyakov this concept emerges as a qualitative, pivotal characteristic of his personality. 'He is a lackey and a boor', Ivan lets drop about Smerdyakov, and the latter sensed that 'lackey' was not only the name of his position and duties but also that the word described him himself, his personality: 'And they refer to me as a stinking lackey' (14,122). Smerdyakov harbours a feeling of his own chosenness and superiority over the rest of the world: 'He was extremely unsociable and silent. Not because he was uncivilised or in any sense shy, no, on the contrary he was an arrogant character who seemed to despise everyone' (14,114). But a sense of having been thwarted in his rights draws a sharp boundary between him and the others: 'I could have done still otherwise, ma'am, I could have known still otherwise, ma'am, if it weren't for my fate since childhood' (14,204). For all his 'solitude', old Karamazov sometimes experienced the need for a 'trustworthy person'. Smerdyakov, however, experienced no need for any contact with another at all; he was 'unsociable', the narrator tells us, 'and felt not the slightest need for any society' (14,115–16). Here the boundary is drawn most sharply of all. For Dostoevsky takes Smerdyakov's aloneness, his isolation from the world, to the point of grotesque, raising it to a symbol. After Smerdyakov returned from studying in Moscow it was noticed that he 'had suddenly somehow aged extraordinarily, his face had wrinkled most inappropriately for his age, he had grown yellow and had begun to resemble a eunuch . . . He despised the female sex, . . . and held himself aloof from them, almost inapproachable' (14,115). In vain did Fyodor Pavlovich ask him: ' "Do you want me to find you a wife?" ' . . . But Smerdyakov only paled from vexation at such words and did not answer' (14,116). If 'Karamazovism', and especially old Karamazov himself, is an embodiment (for all the cruelty and spiritual emptiness of sensuousness) of the spontaneous and elemental, in its own way a natural life-creating principle which perhaps, in time, could be reined in morally, then against the backdrop of Karamazovian sensuousness, Smerdyakov appears symbolically sterile.

But Dostoevsky insists that 'Smerdyakovism' is a product of 'Karamazovism', its new stage; that death-bearing Smerdyakov is the result of elemental Karamazovian animal energies. Out of an elemental thirst for life which cared not one whit about another human being there is born, in the natural order of things, a merciless and calculating murderer. Smerdyakov is inseparably linked with the Karamazovs, and a sufficiently candid – symbolically candid – hint to that effect is provided by Rakitin. Speaking of the elder Zosima's bow to Mitya, Rakitin notes: 'In my opinion, the old man really is farseeing: he's sniffed a crime. Something stinks in your family' (14,73). The surname (Smerdyakov) signifying a bad smell, Ivan's words about a 'stinking lackey', and the emphasis given to Smerdyakov's own fastidious concern for his toilette (as if trying to cease being a 'stinking' lackey, 'Smerdyakov spent almost all his salary on clothes, pomade, perfumes and other such things') – all this involuntarily suggests associations with the odour of decay (the elder had 'sniffed it out') emanating from the 'nice little family' of Karamazovs (14,116). We add that, according to Dal', a *smerd* is a 'person from the mob, lowborn, a moujik, a special category or class of slaves, of unfree servants; later a serf'. The evaluative nuance of the word from which Dostoevsky produced the name Smerdyakov is easy enough to understand, and is linked with Russia's primary evil as most Russian writers saw it: the slavery of serfdom. Smerdyakov is a former slave who wants to straighten himself out. And as Konstantin Aksakov had warned, 'a slave in revolt is more dangerous than a wild beast, he exchanges his fetters for a knife. . .'

If the Karamazovs are constantly on view, then Smerdyakov is constantly in the shadows. A slave hides out before his time, before his rebellion begins; alien to him are the free word and the open act. Old Karamazov 'acts monstrously', Mitya boozes it up and creates scandal after scandal in the taverns, Ivan shocks society with his theories and Alyosha astonishes everyone by becoming a novice in the monastery, but through all this Smerdyakov is not noted for any reprehensible behaviour at all – on the contrary, all his negative qualities, which are well known in town, serve him as a justification and even work to his benefit. The reader, for example, firmly knows that Smerdyakov is a coward, an atheist, always ready to betray anyone out of fear for his own skin. But what is remarkable is that Smerdyakov doesn't hide this; quite the opposite, he tells it to everyone, even to the public prosecutor. Thus, during the trial the prosecutor, as if taking it for granted, says of him: 'In the capacity of domestic spy he betrayed his master, communicated to the accused both the existence of the packet with the money and the signs which were to be used to gain access to the master' (15,136). And all of that, they say, was done out of fear of Mityenka, who threatened to kill him. All this is taken to be the truth. But at the same time the reader knows that Smerdyakov tells the truth with the purpose of hiding it. Everyone sees his authentic face, which is the face of a coward and a scoundrel, and this turns out to be the most reliable guarantee that he will remain above suspicion. Which is to say, the face simultaneously turns out to be, as it were, a mask.

Smerdyakov usually speaks what he wants to say, sometimes in hints, sometimes straight out, at times even in such a way that one can understand and grasp his meaning fully. But one only has to seize him by the arm; he won't hide anything, he'll admit that he indeed did speak this or that, but then it will become clear that his truth was at the same time a mask, albeit a compulsory mask, which evil circumstances had forced him to put on. And he bears no responsibility for it.

It is no accident that when at last he lays all his cards on the table before Ivan ('The third and final meeting with Smerdyakov'), it is clear that he has communicated nothing new about himself to the reader at all. Moreover, not only has he communicated nothing to the reader but also nothing to the local society as well, even though it would have been shocked by this information had it been made public; they knew about all this unconsciously anyway. The defence attorney, who had gathered together all the town gossip and rumours, speaks thus in court about Smerdyakov:

Definitely an embittered being, exaggeratedly ambitious, vengeful and burning with envy. I collected some information: he hated his origins, was ashamed of his birth and gnashed his teeth whenever he remembered that he 'descended from Stinking Lizaveta'. He was disrespectful toward the servant Grigory and his wife, who had been his benefactors during his childhood. He cursed Russia and ridiculed her. He dreamed of emigrating to France in order to remake himself into a Frenchman. He spoke much and often about that earlier, saying that he lacked the means for doing so. It seems to me that he loved no one except himself, and that he held himself in strangely high regard. He saw enlightenment in good clothes, in clean shirt-fronts and in polished boots. Considering himself (and there are facts to support this) the illegitimate son of Fyodor Pavlovich, he might well have despised his position vis-à-vis the legitimate children of his master; everything goes to them, you see, and to him nothing, they had all the rights, they had the inheritance, while he was only a cook. (15,164–65)

The defence attorney even puts forth the hypothesis that Smerdyakov did the killing. But it remains a hypothesis, he does not insist on it, although he does exclaim: 'Is there anything untrue or unlikely in all that I have just now presented and described to you?' (15,166). But immediately afterwards, he all the same presumes that the murder was committed by Mitya.

The excessive hypothetical quality in this supposition that Smerdyakov was the murderer even spreads to an analysis of his face. His face again seems to be a mask, not his true face. Thus does the prosecutor object to the defence attorney in his final statement, and with full justification: 'The feebleminded idiot Smerdyakov, transformed into some sort of Byronic hero, avenging himself on society for his illegitimacy – isn't this really only a poem in the Byronic fashion?' (15,174).

Relevant here are humorous scenes like this: at carnival time, two masks meet; the people beneath the masks start a conversation and then, having decided to introduce themselves and get acquainted, they remove their masks. Under his stupid or terrifying mask one of them has a normal face; the other has the same mask. The mask was a *mould* of the face.

As V. E. Vetlovskaya has aptly observed, in his ideas Smerdyakov is very close to the Grand Inquisitor: 'The Grand Inquisitor says essentially the same thing as Smerdyakov. He also justifies his personal baseness and treachery before God, and does so on the same foundations, that is, resorting to conclusions about universal

human weakness, insignificance, and people's ineradicable sinfulness.'[11] But this observation speaks not only to the lackey-like
essence of the Grand Inquisitor and to a certain part of Ivan's soul
(for the Grand Inquisitor is his creation); it also speaks to the fact
that in Ivan's soul there is a mundane corroboration and intensifying
in evil's direction, evil not as his product but as his double, it is
independent of him although he feels its closeness to him, he feels
their mutual attraction.

Smerdyakov sets out his credo (in the chapter 'Disputation')
especially for Ivan's benefit, giving him, as it were, the first hints of
its existence and potentials ('Ivan!' Fyodor Pavlovich suddenly
shouted. 'Bend your ear down now. All this was concocted for you'
(14,118)). The independence and, in its own way, originality of
Smerdyakov's judgments on the legitimacy and legal inviolability of
treason is emphasised both by the narrator, when speaking of the
'contemplators', and by Fyodor Pavlovich, who comments on Smerdyakov's original way of thinking with some surprise: 'Here Balaam's
ass thinks, thinks, and the devil knows what he'll think himself up
to!' (14,122). Thus does he sum up the utterances of his illegitimate
son. Listening in to these words one must not forget that the devil is
one of the characters of the novel. Perhaps the power of evil does
indeed know about the lackey's evil intentions ('the devil knows . . .
what he'll think himself up to'), but so far Ivan Karamazov has not
guessed him out.

All the same, what is it that attracts this 'Jesuit' – this vain,
embittered, secretive, pettily envious and vengeful person – to Ivan,
who despises him? Smerdyakov is introduced into the action as it
were in passing, during dinner. Fyodor Pavlovich, Alyosha and Ivan
are at table. The narrator notes that for some time Smerdyakov had
very rarely been present at dinner, but 'from the time of Ivan
Fyodorovich's arrival in town he began to be present at dinner
almost every day' (14,117). Fyodor Pavlovich, a malicious person and
a sensualist but who, during apertures in his sensuality, could be a
very observant man, hit upon the true definition of Smerdyakov's
partiality for Ivan: 'Smerdyakov now slips in every day around
dinnertime, you are so *interesting* to him [my emphasis, V. K.], what
have you done to endear yourself to him? – Fyodor Pavlovich
added.' Ivan wants to give it another word: 'He's taken it into his
head to respect me' (14,122). But Fyodor Pavlovich, who has studied
Smerdyakov, does not agree: 'You see, I know that he cannot endure

me, as he cannot anyone, and just as he cannot endure you, although it seems to you that he's "taken it into his head to respect you". Alyoshka all the more, Alyoshka he despises' (14,122). This motif of the presumed respect that Smerdyakov bears toward Ivan stretches throughout the entire novel. The usual representation of the situation is that Smerdyakov began to respect Ivan and fell under his spiritual influence. Smerdyakov himself speaks of this, so that the prosecutor, quoting his words (and we already know that Smerdyakov was able to wind the prosecutor around his finger, for example, concerning the empty packet that was thrown on the floor, and most importantly concerning the murder itself), declares:

He [Smerdyakov], with hysterical tears, told me at the preliminary investigation how this young Karamazov, Ivan Fyodorovich, horrified him with his spiritual impudence. 'Everything, he says, in his view, is permitted, everything in the world, and nothing should be forbidden in advance – that's what he was teaching me.' It seems that he's become an idiot because of this thesis, which he was *taught*, and finally he went of his mind (15,126–27) [my emphasis, V. K].

As we noted earlier, this same idea is often encountered in the scholarship on Dostoevsky.[12] But is it in fact correct?

'They spoke about philosophical questions and even about why the earth was illuminated on the first day if the sun, moon, and stars were created only on the fourth day, and how one should understand that properly; but Ivan Fyodorovich was soon convinced that the sun, moon and stars, although these were interesting topics, were for Smerdyakov absolutely tertiary, and that he needed something absolutely other' (14,243). So, Smerdyakov is not interested in pure theory. What does interest him, then? 'Smerdyakov all the time inquired, asked indirect and apparently premeditated questions, but for what purpose he didn't explain, and during the most fervent moment of his questioning he would often either fall silent or suddenly pass over to something else altogether' (14,243). This does not suggest overall that Smerdyakov had studied any special topic – more likely he had not studied – but it does suggest that he *was studying* Ivan himself. And for his part he reacted very ironically to Ivan's ideas. 'They were of the opinion that I would rebel; they were mistaken, sir. If there had been such a sum in my pocket, I would have long ago been gone' – so Smerdyakov confesses frankly to the maid (14,205).

There is no way that Ivan could have failed to guess this. After all, Ivan knew about even these words of Smerdyakov, which Alyosha had accidentally overheard. (The chapter 'The Brothers Get Acquainted' follows the chapter 'Smerdyakov with a Guitar'.)

Alyosha told his brother quickly and *in detail* about his meeting with Smerdyakov. Ivan suddenly began to listen with a very concerned air, *even requestioning* him on some points [emphasis mine, V. K.]. <. . .> Ivan frowned and fell into thought.
   – Did you frown because of Smerdyakov? – asked Alyosha.
   – Yes, because of him. The devil take him. (14,211)

Something, apparently, has begun to trouble Ivan in his relations with Smerdyakov. He rejects him as evil ('the devil take him'). But he does not succeed in thinking his troubled state of mind through to the end. It is as if the lackey has cast a spell on him. After his conversation with Alyosha in the tavern, Ivan runs into Smerdyakov and wants to walk past him:

   – 'Out of my sight, you scoundrel, what sort of company am I for you, you fool!' – was about to fly off his tongue, but *to his great surprise* what came off his tongue was something quite different:
   – What's with father, is he sleeping or has he woken up? – he spoke quietly and with *unexpected* composure, *and suddenly, also wholly unexpectedly,* he sat down on the bench. For a moment he became almost terrified, he remembered it later. [my emphasis, V. K.] (14,244)

What's happening here? It is as if some irrational forces have entered into the action, and Ivan is not in a condition to resist them. Smerdyakov almost forces Ivan to give him a sanction for the murder.

   In a letter about the unfinished novel to one of his female correspondents, Dostoevsky explained the relationship between Smerdyakov and Ivan *as regards* the murder in the following way:

The servant Smerdyakov murdered old Karamazov. All the details will be explained in the further course of the novel. Ivan Fyodorovich participated in the murder *only indirectly* and *at a distance*, solely by the fact that he refrained (intentionally) from bringing Smerdyakov to reason during a conversation with him before departing for Moscow, he refrained from expressing to him clearly and categorically *his disgust at the evil deed being planned by him* (which Ivan Fyodorovich saw and clearly had premonitions of) and thus, *as it were, permitted* Smerdyakov to commit the crime. *Such permission* was indispensible for Smerdyakov, and again, it will be subsequently be explained why. (30,i,129)[13]

Let us assume that Smerdyakov heard Ivan's inner voice, a voice hidden from others and from his own self as well; let us assume that he guessed Ivan's desire for the death of his father, which reflected his theory that 'all was permitted'. But let us then consider carefully to what extent this theory corresponded, in Dostoevsky's artistic plan, to the core of that hero's personality, and whether or not the theory was adequate to his unselfish and passionate desire for world harmony.

Strictly speaking, the thesis 'all is permitted' reflects the essence of the behaviour of Fyodor Pavlovich Karamazov in the world, a man able to descend 'to the ultimate limit of any nastiness', fearing only 'those pranks which the court might punish' (14,80). But theory, of course, is more logically consistent.

It is probably no accident that, scattered throughout the novel, there are lines of dialogue emphasising the similarity between Ivan and Fyodor Pavlovich. Pointing to Ivan, old Karamazov himself, for example, exclaims: 'This is my son, flesh of my flesh, of my most beloved flesh' (14,66). But for precisely that reason does he fear Ivan more than he does Mitya ('I'm afraid of Ivan; I'm afraid of Ivan more than I am of the other one') (14,130). 'You, sir, of all the children most resemble Fyodor Pavlovich, your soul is the same as his, sir' – so Smerdyakov assures Ivan in their final conversation, and Ivan, struck by this, answers: 'You're not stupid' (15,68). Smerdyakov is both right and not right; he again, as it were, moves himself off into the shadows. But we can say that if Smerdyakov continued Fyodor Pavlovich's *practical* line, then Ivan gave sense to that practice *theoretically.* We recall that in his 'serious' questioning of God's world, Fyodor Pavlovich orients towards Ivan's position.

Ivan hopes, apparently, that the destructive force of the thesis 'all is permitted' will in the final analysis destroy 'Karamazovism' as well. But the coincidence of his theory with his father's practice is significant. In his notebooks for 1880–81, Dostoevsky wrote that 'the entire novel serves' as an answer to the torments of Ivan's idea (27,48). This aim is served by an explanation of the genesis of the idea 'all is permitted', the fact that it belongs 'to this world.'

But does Ivan himself endorse this idea to the end? There are good reasons to doubt that he does. All of Ivan's words, especially in his confession to Alyosha, are constructed in a tensely interrogative form, with maximal sharpness, as if the answer were intended to convince *him* of something and not only Alyosha; he himself is still in the process of deciding. What is more, one could say that the entire novel is structured as a struggle between Ivan and the evil that is tempting him. It is characteristic that the concluding idea of his theomachic torment – of which Dostoevsky wrote, not without pride: 'Even in Europe there is not and *has not been* such power of atheistic *expressions*' (27,86) – he accomplishes not in the indicative mood (that is, once having firmly decided), but in the subjunctive: 'There is no virtue *if* there is no immortality' [my emphasis, V. K.]. Recall the words of the elder Zosima, with which Ivan agreed: 'This idea is not yet resolved in your heart and is tormenting it' (14,65). 'In him there is a great and unresolved thought', Alyosha says of Ivan (14,76). And even Ivan himself emphasises the indeterminacy, the unfinalisability of his purely theoretical ideas, not realised in practice: 'The mind prevaricates and hides. The mind is a scoundrel' (14,215). However, this 'subjunctiveness' of the conclusion uttered by him is not noticed by other people. Others take his words as an affirmative, even as an imperative, utterance: '"You were bold back then, you kept saying back then that 'everything is permitted', sir; and now you're so frightened!" Smerdyakov murmured, marveling' (15,61). It is this absence of self-definition in Ivan that leads to the tragedy.

'Ivan Fyodorovich is deep', the writer noted about his hero (27,48). And the whole horror of Ivan's struggle with God, his rebellion, a horror acknowledged by him himself ('One cannot live by rebellion, and I want to live'), is that he has nothing upon which he can innerly rely for support (14,223). Facing him is emptiness. Thus the desire to hang on 'until thirty' and then 'fling the goblet to the floor' (14,209,239). No matter how much one reads into Ivan's words, and no matter how much one tries to read out of them, what is it, really, that he wishes to present to society in the sense of a higher truth? It's not revolution, of course, with its concrete social tasks for the reconstruction of the world. Dostoevsky found the exact word, *bunt*, rebellion, to which Pushkin in his time attached the epithets 'senseless and merciless'. And in reality, rebellion, vengeance, a denial of everything whatsoever without clear cognisance of the end result of one's actions, will take on a senseless and merciless character, 'creating anarchy in the realm of morality' (Karl Marx and Friedrich Engels), no matter how excellent and fine the feelings emanating from the rebel (*buntovshchik*). Precisely the absence in Ivan of a positive, life-structuring principle permits others not to notice the depth of his ethical questioning. For that reason, what for Ivan himself is a problem becomes for Smerdyakov an axiom – for the absence of theoretical clarity greatly facilitates the selfish utilisation of the idea Ivan utters. 'A slave in a rebellion is more dangerous than wild beasts . . .'

Ivan himself does not believe overall in the possibility of a practical realisation of the idea that 'all is permitted', which is linked, in his opinion, to 'anthropophagy', to the full-scale denial of the world. And when he informs Smerdyakov that he is going to Chermashnya, it is as if he is continuing (for himself) his own strange theoretical game, as if he is posing to himself the same question all the time: but is this possible in reality? It is Smerdyakov who provokes him to a seriousness that Ivan did not want to notice, but which in a strange way hypnotises him:

When he had already taken a seat in the carriage, Smerdyakov ran up to straighten the rug.
 – You see, I'm going to Chermashnya, – *somehow suddenly burst* from Ivan Fyodorovich, and *just as on the day before*, it flew out by itself, accompanied by a sort of nervous chuckle. He kept remembering it for a long time afterwards.
 – So it's true what people say, that it's always interesting to have a talk with an intelligent man, – Smerdyakov replied *firmly*, giving Ivan Fyodorovich a *penetrating* look [my emphasis, V. K.]. (14,254)

As soon as he had driven out of the courtyard and put some distance between himself and Smerdyakov, his internal battle begins with the 'lackey', the 'slave', the *smerd*, as if some charm had fallen off him. But it is a strange struggle . . . Proud and inflexible Ivan would like to prove to himself his independence from the lackey . . . But here, like a schoolboy before his teacher, what happens is precisely the opposite of what is promised.

 – And why did I announce to him that I was going to Chermashnya? – They pulled up to Volovya station, Ivan Fyodorovich got out of the carriage, the coachmen clustered around him. They haggled over the price to Chermashnya, twenty versts on a country road, in a hired carriage. Ivan gave orders to harness up. He entered the station, looked around, glanced at the stationmaster's wife and then suddenly walked back out on the porch.
 – I don't need to go to Chermashnya. Brothers, can I make it to the train station by seven o'clock? (14,255)

In place of a real act or confrontation, which would turn into a crime, he is simply running from Smerdyakov and his deeds, away, to Moscow, in order to cleanse himself more quickly. This is almost a physical need, for there is this feeling of moral filth; he has forgotten about his father. At first he doesn't even think that his words, his conclusions have now taken on the indisputability of a mathematical formula: Smerdyakov is no theoretician. And it seems to Ivan that everything that had happened was a nightmare, a dream, that he was theorising as before, that he had only to get away and to get a grip on himself, and then he would figure it all out at his leisure. 'At seven o'clock in the evening Ivan Fyodorovich boarded the train and flew toward Moscow. 'Away with the all the past, the old world is done with forever, and may I *never hear another word or echo* from it!' [Smerdyakov had hinted to him 'that from Moscow, sir, you can be bothered by telegraph from here, in any event, sir'] 'To a new world, to new places, without looking back!' [my emphasis, V. K.] (14,255).

But Ivan is already visited by the premonition that it will not be so easy to disentangle oneself from Smerdyakov and his deeds. And:

instead of delight there descended on his soul such terrible darkness, and such grief gnawed at his heart, such as he had never experienced in his entire life. He sat thinking the entire night; the train car sped on, and only at daybreak, already entering Moscow, did he suddenly come to.
– I am a scoundrel! – he whispered to himself. (14,255)

In these words we hear an acknowledgment that by his flight Ivan did not rid himself of Smerdyakov, did not save himself from the lackey who was pursuing him. On the contrary, having shamefully refused to be where his presence was required, he betrayed himself to another's will and, like a 'scoundrel', having avoided the responsibility of making a decision, escaped from the 'field of battle', from the field where a battle was being waged between good and evil. In these words Ivan's hidden conscience resounds, the voice of his personality-core that has not yet been eroded by evil; the lackey, the slave cannot conquer the hero and ideologist completely, the norms of morality do not permit the hero to accept as obligatory the conclusions of his theory 'all is permitted'.

For the narrator, telling the story, who is modelled in style and content after the Old Russian chroniclers,[14] Ivan's *bunt* is the rebellion of a person severed from his 'native or national truth' (for according to Ivan's idea, Christ is impotent 'in this world'); as a result, it enters into contradiction not only with higher idealism but also with itself. From the narrator's perspective, Ivan has tasted of scientific thought but has not been enlightened by its ideal, and for that reason he has been able to understand the shortcomings of the world without having glimpsed the paths to overcoming them. But here is a curious thing: that not for a single moment do we cease believing in Ivan, in the possibility of his overcoming the pollution which has surrounded him (if not now, then at some point in the future), and this despite the fact that it is precisely to him that the devil appears and it is he who succumbs to the temptation of Smerdyakov. It would seem that Ivan should call forth the narrator's most active dislike, but Ivan's thirst for world harmony is so sincere and all-encompassing that neither the narrator nor the elder Zosima, the author's ideal hero, can refuse sympathy to this atheist. 'A deep conscience' is what Alyosha says about him at the end of the novel (15,89). Quite possibly these words of Zosima refer directly to Ivan: 'Do not hate atheists, false preachers, materialists, even the malicious ones and not only the good ones, for there are many good ones even there, particularly in our times' (14,149). In this we hear above all Dostoevsky's own faith in the all-conquering force of good, especially in the young people 'of the most recent time', who for the official literature and state press were simply a swarm of 'godless atheists'. Dostoevsky himself saw the primary evil in the mass of 'semi-educated' people who had appeared in the post-reform transitional era, a sort of moral lumpenproletariat that was tempting Russia. It is no accident that as soon as Smerdyakov departs from the pages of the novel, the devil appears – who, as it were, plays the double to the 'lackey' who has committed suicide. It is this evil, which had led him astray in a maze as a wood sprite in the fairy tale leads travellers astray on the road, that Ivan must overcome. But how? Can he do it? To do this he must first solve the riddle of his own self.

The obstacle to this self-unriddling is Ivan's pride. Taking on himself responsibility for the entire cosmos, entering into a debate with God over the management of the universe, Ivan does not assume responsibility for the small, weak people nearby: 'So am I my brother Dmitry's keeper?' he remarks, in Cain-like hatred and indifference to his brother (14,211). 'If she's a child, then I'm not her nurse', is how he steps indifferently over the spiritual sufferings of Lise (15,38). And how much that symbolic scene is worth, where he flings away from him the drunken peasant who has turned up under his feet, so that the latter falls on the 'frozen ground'. Ivan passes by indifferently, although he knows that the little peasant will 'freeze'! In the same category one might locate his desire for the death of his father. It seems to him simpler to clear away 'Karamazovism' from the path then to spend the effort trying to awaken the human being in his father, as Alyosha tries to do, who urges his father to find a good principle in himself and who believes that an awakening is possible ('You're not a malicious person, but a corrupted one', he tells his father (14,158)). But for this, constant daily effort is necessary – and not only effort, but also an acknowledgment of the fact that he is the same as other people, weak and sinful, and not the proud lawgiver of the universe; for this it is necessary to love one's neighbour, the concrete living human being, and not all humanity as a whole. And such responsibility is heavier and more serious.

After the murder had been committed, Ivan says to Smerdyakov that he came 'to disentangle the mess you have made here', in this way placing himself outside the events that have occurred. It is as if he senses that if he turns out to be implicated, then he will have to admit that he is the same as the others, and perhaps even worse. 'If it wasn't Dmitry who killed, but Smerdyakov <. . .> then, of course, I am also a murderer' (15,54). But only by passing through this realisation, Dostoevsky suggests, can he overcome evil and break through to his own self, to what is best in him, to that genuine responsibility for one's neighbours that every person must bear. And only then will Ivan understand *who* the real murderer is, and his passionate dreams for world happiness will acquire a real-life ground, for they will be united with everyday life expressed in a constant pattern of behaviour.

It is apparently no accident that the unearthly, rather abstract and overly eloquent dream of Ivan's about universal happiness is perceived by Smerdyakov as a hidden desire of personal gain. To Ivan's question, why he (Ivan) wished the death of his father, Smerdyakov 'venomously and even vindictively' answered: 'And the inheritance, sir? . . . After all, then, after your parent, there would be coming to each of the three brothers maybe forty thousand or a little more' (15,52). Smerdyakov (like Rakitin, who also suspects Ivan of material greed) is one dimensional. He judges Ivan by his own measurement. As we have already noted, his face and his mask absolutely coincide, therefore he does not even suspect the multiple meanings possible for human personality and is capable of seeing in another person only the 'external crust', the socially conditioned features. Smerdyakov cannot hear Ivan's inner voice. And it is no accident that to no one but Alyosha did Ivan speak about his thirst for world harmony, whereas he frequently expressed aloud, and even 'on one local, largely female, social occasion', the idea that 'if God didn't exist, then all is permitted.' Thus Smerdyakov is repeating not some secret, hidden voice of Ivan's but that which had been turned outwards, to the surface. One might sooner say that Ivan expresses the hidden voice of post-reform Russian society, where families were disintegrating, where trade in human honour and dignity was continuing and even intensifying, where, just as before, everything was held in the servile fetters of a still-viable serfdom and high society and where, in essence, everything was permitted to the strong of this world, where in the hearts and minds the idea of 'arbitrary will' reigned supreme.

In other words: Smerdyakov repeats that which does not belong to the personality-core of Ivan, he repeats only those fixed ideas conditioned by society which the hero, as it were, has accumulated and releases to the surface. This is the meaning of 'doubleness' in the novel. The theory 'all is permitted' is like a chemically cleansed 'Karamazovism' that has received its theoretical expression, to the extent that 'Karamazovism' is the quintessence of the societal disintegration then underway. But Smerdyakov tries to persuade Ivan that he exists wholly and essentially in this theory, that he and Ivan are one – and Ivan, horrified at this circumstance, asks the lackey: 'What sort of alliance do you think I entered into with you, what is this, do you think I'm afraid of you?' (15,51). Smerdyakov is convinced that Ivan did enter in to such an alliance, for 'it is always interesting to have a talk with an intelligent man.' Thus Ivan faces a double task: to understand that his idea is itself lackey-like, secondary, non-autonomous, to see his fault in the fact that he shared this idea, spoke it out, and thereby took on his share of responsibility for murder; but, at the same time, he must understand that his potential is not exhausted by this idea.

At this point in the struggle for Ivan, two forces collide: from one side, Alyosha; from the other, Smerdyakov and then the devil. Alyosha is described in the novel as the antithesis of Ivan (Christ appears to him, the devil to Ivan), but it is precisely he who attempts to help Ivan cleanse himself from those foreign ideas which to Ivan have seemed like his own. If these words really express the essence of Ivan, then he is the real murderer of his father; if they do not, then somewhere there exists the real murderer. Alyosha confirms that the murderer is Smerdyakov – not Mitya and not Ivan. And what is most important, he tries to convince Ivan of this, in order, so to speak, to dis-identify him from Smerdyakov, from his double. As Bakhtin justly notes, 'Alyosha foresees that Ivan is by himself a 'deep conscience', that sooner or later he will give himself the categorical answer, 'I did the killing'. And according to Dostoevsky's creative plan, he could not give himself any other answer. And that is why Alyosha's word proves so useful, precisely as the word of the *other*'.[15] Alyosha's words, addressed to Ivan, are full of such force and energy that they constitute perhaps the most passionate utterance of Alyosha's in the novel.

Ivan Fyodorovich suddenly stopped.
– Then who is the murderer, in your opinion? – he asked for some reason with obvious coldness, and a certain arrogant note sounded in the very tone of the question.
– You yourself know who, – Alyosha said softly and with conviction.
– Who? You mean that fable about the crazy idiot epileptic? About Smerdyakov? –
Alyosha suddenly felt how he was trembling all over.
– You yourself know who,' escaped him helplessly. He was breathless.
(15,39)

And Ivan, mentioning Smerdyakov (let's even assume he was the murderer) as no more than a worthless plaything of his own will and passion, awaits the blow from his brother. He knows full well that Alyosha does not believe in Mitya's guilt. Which means only one person remains: he himself, Ivan.

– So who? Who? – Ivan cried out, almost fiercely. All his reserve suddenly vanished.
– I know only one thing, – Alyosha said, still in the same almost whisper.
– It was *not you* who killed father.
– 'Not you'! What do you mean by 'not you?' – Ivan was dumbfounded.
– It was not you who killed father, not you, – Alyosha repeated firmly.
The silence lasted for half a minute.
– But I know very well it was not me – are you raving? – Ivan muttered with a pale and crooked grin. He fastened his eyes on Alyosha. Both were standing under a streetlamp.
– No, Ivan, you've told yourself several times that you are the murderer.
– When did I say that? When I was in Moscow . . . When did I say that? – Ivan stammered, quite at a loss.
– You've said it to yourself many times while you were alone during these past terrible two months, – Alyosha continued, as softly and as distinctly as before. But he was now speaking not, as it were, out of himself, not of his own will, but obeying some sort of irresistible command. – You accused

yourself and confessed to yourself that the murderer is none other than you. *But it was not you who killed him, you are mistaken, the murderer is not you, do you hear me, not you! God has sent me to tell you that –* [my emphasis, V. K.] (15,40)

These words sound almost like an incantation intended to liberate and cleanse Ivan's soul from despair. Recall that he has been in despair from the very beginning of the novel. This had already been noticed by the elder. Alyosha appears at the optimally necessary moment for him, when not only Ivan but the reader too is definitively confused by all that has happened. And he speaks this not only to Ivan, but also to the reader and to all future criticism.

It is apparently again no accident that structurally in the novel, immediately after this discussion with Alyosha, there follows the three conversations with Smerdyakov, who, on the contrary, attempts to persuade Ivan that they, the two of them, are identical, and that Ivan is the real and only murderer:

– We're sitting here just the two of us, so what's the use of putting on an act, playing a comedy? Or do you still want to shift it all on to me alone, right to my face? *You killed him, you are the chief killer, and I was just your stooge, your faithful servant Licharda, and I committed the deed according to your word* [my emphasis, V. K.]. (15,59)

After almost every word of this retelling of the murder, Smerdyakov inserts, in diverse variations, the phrase: 'It was all done in the most natural manner, sir, from your very words.' And he carries out his story entirely from that point of view: 'I want to prove it to your face this very night *that in all this the chief murderer is you alone, sir, and I'm not the real chief one, although I did do the killing. But it's you who are the most lawful murderer!* [my emphasis, V. K.] (15,63).

But after Alyosha's words, part of Dostoevsky's intention is that it must at last become clear to the reader that Ivan is a spiritual cover-up for Smerdyakov, just as Mitya turned out to be a juridical cover-up. The lackey does not wish to bear any sort of responsibility. That is why he needed Ivan's *permission*, about which Dostoevsky had written. He had himself declared that nothing would have happened if Mitya hadn't come. But Ivan too entered into his plan. This plan had been too fastidiously, too autonomously worked out. When he told Ivan his actions and the counter-measures he had taken against possible suspicions towards his person, Ivan asked in horror:

– But is it really possible that you could have thought of all that right there on the spot? – Ivan exclaimed, beside himself with astonishment. Again he looked fearfully at Smerdyakov.

– Have pity on me, sir, how could I have thought all of that up, when everything was in such a flurry? *It was all thought out beforehand,* – Smerdyakov blurted out [my emphasis, V. K.] (15,66)

Smerdyakov is not only not a passive executor of Ivan's idea; he is also not an agitated, divided nature tormented by the evil surrounding him (as is Ivan). Smerdyakov is an active carrier of evil, which has drawn into the elemental forces of criminality not only Ivan. Remember how the young boy Ilyusha suffers because he thinks he has killed the dog Zhuchka. 'That's why I'm ill, papa, because I killed Zhuchka back then, for that God has punished me', he says over and over again to his father (14,482). There are many guilty parties in the illness and death of Ilyushechka, but only one who tried to destroy the pure soul of the boy by drawing him into a wicked deed – and that was Smerdyakov. 'He had somehow managed to make friends with the lackey of your late father, with Smerdyakov', Kolya Krasotkin explains the story to Alyosha (14,480). 'He taught the little fool a stupid trick, that is, a mean trick, a vile trick, how to take a piece of bread, the soft part, shove a pin into it, and then toss it to some mongrel, the kind of dog who's so hungry he'd swallow anything without chewing it, and then watch what happens. So they fixed up such a little piece and threw it to that same shaggy Zhuchka' (14,480). Ilyushechka suffers from that beastly act, but Smerdyakov, who in childhood had liked to hang cats in secret, doesn't even recall the episode. And for us, this temptation by Smerdyakov of a child (Ilyushechka) is in its essentials an enlightening parallel to the temptation of an adult (Ivan). The real criminal is Smerdyakov, but the entire weight of moral blame and responsibility falls on his accomplices. In this way they are linked by evil, and a great deal of spiritual strength is necessary to separate out oneself and one's participation in this evil act (the crime).

Smerdyakov, and then the devil (his new hypostasis) manage to convince Ivan that he is the authentic murderer of his father. Ivan communicates to Alyosha the devil's words:

– Oh, you are going to perform a virtuous deed, you will announce that you killed your father, that the lackey killed your father at your instruction'
– Brother, – Alyosha interrupted. – Stop. It wasn't you who killed him. That's not true!
– He says it, and he knows it, – Ivan repeated, as if mechanically. (15,87)

Ivan's soul is divided, and the devil, personifying the dark side of this soul, tries to persuade it that it too does not believe in good. 'You are going to perform a virtuous deed, but you don't even believe in virtue – that's what infuriates you and torments you; that's why you're so vindictive' (15,87). This is not quite true, but it is important to the devil to strengthen Ivan in evil, because Ivan's very approach to testify in court is already almost senseless, since Smerdyakov has hanged himself. Alyosha, who does not believe that Ivan is the murderer, nevertheless does not try to hinder Ivan from going to court and repenting, because to remain where he is means not only to hide from responsibility but also to be identified definitively with Smerdyakov. That's what Smerdyakov wanted from Ivan, and that's what the devil, speaking of the senselessness of any appearance at court, wants as well: 'Here Smerdyakov has died, hanged himself, so who is going to believe you in court on your own?' the devil remarks ironically, making fun of him because he cannot become a real murderer, that is, indifferently survive another's death ('it's not for such eagles to soar above the earth!') (15,88).

Ivan struggles with the devil with all his strength, but the deed of evil has gone so far he is no longer able to disentangle himself from his clutches. And although Ivan goes to repent, in order to master the devil, their struggle, one might say, finishes with a certain advantage accruing to the dark principle. The strength of autonomous will, of all-destroying arbitrary wilfulness, turns out to be helpless in a conflict with evil. Ivan mastered his pride by going to court, but by degrading his pride – as is often the case with Dostoevsky's heroes – he rages all the more angrily against the entire world and slandered himself more than was true or just, identifying himself with Smerdyakov, all exactly as Alyosha had feared. Having announced that Smerdyakov and not Mitya was the murderer, Ivan clarifies: 'He killed, and I instructed him to kill' (15,116). Ivan identifies himself with Smerdyakov and the truth of repentance becomes a demonic farce, definitively confirming Mitya in the murder. Because after Ivan's speech incriminating himself, Katerina Ivanovna, frightened for her beloved (Ivan), destroys Mitya with her own evidence. It is no accident that Ivan names as his single witness the *devil*.

– Who is your witness?
– He has a tail, your honour, you wouldn't allow him in! <. . . > Pay no attention to him, he's a wretched, petty devil, – he added, as it were confidentially. – He's probably here somewhere, under that table there, with the material evidence, where else would he be sitting if not there? (15,117)

Mastering his pride, Ivan declares that his idea is a vile, lackey-like one and as such belongs not to him but to all of vile society. This step was necessary. But Ivan is not yet strong enough to take one more step and to repudiate the idea. The effort to master his pride cost him his reason.

- Who doesn't wish the death of his father?
- Are you in your right mind? – inadvertently escaped from the judge.
- That's just it, I am in my right mind <. . .> and in a vile mind, the same sort of mind that you all have <. . .> you vile mugs! – He turned suddenly to the public. – A father's been murdered, and they pretend to be frightened, – he growled with savage contempt. – They'll make all sorts of faces at each other. Liars! Everyone wants his father dead! (15,117)

At the end of his speech he shouts out with the 'ferocious howl' of one possessed (as V. E. Vetlovskaya has observed). Here it is perhaps worth making one closing observation.

Ivan arrives at an idea that is very precious to Dostoevsky: that everyone is guilty for everything; but he arrives at it somehow strangely, as it were, from the other end. For him this is the possibility to lighten, or perhaps to remove altogether, his *personal* guilt and responsibility – because, by accusing himself, he can in no way *understand* his guilt. He refused to acknowledge spiritual 'Karamazovism' as a product of his own self, and consequently as part of his own essence, but to sever himself from it and to disidentify himself from Smerdyakov was something he could not manage to do. Thus Ivan's guilt in a certain sense turns out to be deeper and more difficult than if he had simply taught Smerdyakov his ideas; his proud mind, conditioned, in Dostoevsky's view, to despise people, did not give him the chance to look intently at those surrounding him, to understand them.

- You're not stupid, – Ivan muttered, as if struck by something; his blood rose to his face. – Earlier I thought you were stupid. But you're serious now! – he remarked, suddenly looking at Smerdyakov in a new way.
- It was from pride that you thought I was stupid. (15,68)

Such is the ending of the 'third, and final, meeting with Smerdyakov', and revelation came too late. That which is absolutely clear to Alyosha and on which he insists ('The lackey killed, but my brother is innocent') from the very beginning of this tragic murder is not at all clear to Ivan (15,189). The absence in his spiritual make-up of authentic inner freedom hinders him from breaking through to Alyosha's simplicity and clarity. Ivan's guilt and disaster is that in trying to find the path to an overcoming of the world's evil, he turns to the destructive elemental force of his thesis 'all is permitted', not realising that at the basis of this thesis lies a well-hidden *greed*. It is not accidental that the organiser of the destructive act is the greedy lackey Smerdyakov. Ivan falls from the frying pan into the fire, from 'Karamazovism' to 'Smerdyakovism'.

In his battle with repellent 'Karamazovism', Ivan does not expect that the external world contains anything capable of helping him: 'the people's truth'. Truth and goodness, according to Dostoevsky, are categories that function outside the bounds of the greed of the world. And the 'people's truth', contained in the image and idea of Christ, is not able to suppress the truth of personality, Dostoevsky believed; it can only come to its aid. The torments of a lonely mind lead the hero to madness. But in these torments there is a radiant force. They indicate to the reader Ivan's moral purity, which he cannot see in himself. Tyutchev (cited by Ivan in his tale of the Grand Inquisitor) wrote:

> It is not given to us to predict,
> How our word will resound,
> And we are given compassion
> As we are given grace.[16]

Ivan Karamazov's problem is the problem of a person's responsibility for a word uttered by him, a problem that has resounded tragically in the fate of Russia in the twentieth century. Ivan was not able to predict how his word would echo or resound. But the hero's spiritual torments give him the right, at least, to the reader's compassion and, perhaps, to the involuntary sympathy of the author. The realist Dostoevsky, whose 'hosannah' passed 'through a great crucible of doubts', decided all the same to sympathise secretly with his hero-theomach (27,86). Not by accident does Mitya say in the epilogue, 'Listen, brother Ivan will surpass all of us . . . He'll get well' (15,184). Alyosha is more cautious, but hope has not abandoned him either: 'And I too very much hope that he will get well' (15,185). And we must assume that in Dostoevsky, this means more than physical health. According to Dostoevsky, Christianity is the path to freedom. The Revolutionary-nihilists subordinate themselves to collective and party commands, for they are afraid of freedom and therefore they cannot take the path of Christ. Ivan, like Job, has a chance of reconciliation with God since he is free. Evidently, through the 'crucible of doubts' he too will arrive at his 'Hosanna'. Once he has renounced his egoism, he has only to look after others and pray for them. And then what is written in the Bible will take place: 'After Job had prayed for his friends, the Lord made him prosperous again and gave him twice as much as he had before' (Job 42:10). Only in this way can Ivan recover his spiritual health.

TRANSLATOR'S AFTERWORD *BY* CARYL EMERSON

In its 3–9 November issue for 1999, *Literaturnaya gazeta* published an interview with the philosopher, novelist and literary critic Vladimir Karlovich Kantor, entitled 'Forward to a cult of personality!' In the interview, Kantor gently refutes those doomsday journalists who see nothing but disaster for Russia, fore and aft. Russia's path has been difficult, he admits – but it *is* a distinctive path; and part of that distinction has been a tradition of seeking not just *freedom from* and *freedom for* (the familiar Western options) but a third type that has proved very attractive to the maximalist personality in crisis times: 'freedom in spite of' or 'in the teeth of' (*svoboda vopreki*). Fyodor Dostoevsky understood this impulse perfectly – so perfectly that he could provide both its ideal portrait and its necessary antidote.

That antidote is apparently also Kantor's own, what he calls 'Christian realism'. 'Only the devil deceptively promises us an ideal world', he remarks. He continues:

'Christian realism', which I follow both as a philosopher and as a writer, assumes that there are no such things as Holy Russia, the radiant future, developed socialism, ideal capitalism – each is sinful in its own way, and life is nowhere easy. One could not, of course, be charmed by perestroika, but one could draw up a priority list of expectations. I expected freedom; it arrived. There was no special prosperity then, and none now. But it became possible to see a world that had been closed. This is worth a great deal . . . Is it possible to defend our newly-received freedom under the new conditions? And what else? Again slavery? Again the Grand Inquisitor?

Kantor's contribution translated here, a chapter from his 1994 volume *In Search of Personality: The Experience of the Russian Classics*, reflects well these sensible, sober ethical priorities. For non-Russian readers, the most 'Christian' aspect of his treatment might well be its reduction of Ivan's 'sin of pride' to a reluctance to attend to 'the

weak and the small' within one's immediate reach. Ivan could be
arrogant and unobservant. But, it might be countered, Dostoevsky
himself took pride in those courageous spirits who could not (for all
their love of life) be distracted from human suffering, however
distant; and as regards human behaviour that lay within his heroes'
reach, the novelist was also troubled by the duty we owe the utterly
undeserving, the capricious, the genetically and socially irrespon-
sible. For all that his elder Zosima might counsel otherwise, the
writer would not condemn a refusal to serve such persons as simple
pride. Why, indeed, should such a man continue to live? Dostoevsky,
even granted his conviction that crimes against human life were the
only crimes that mattered, would not consider such a question
wholly monstrous or unmotivated.

In revisiting the paradoxes of the novel, Kantor combines some
conventional wisdoms in an often unconventional and highly suggestive way. Some merit further development here. Take, for example,
his linkage of 'doubles' and 'masks' with the phenomenon of
'lackeys'. Kantor notes the psychopathology of demonic Mr Hydes
destined to overpower the decent Dr Jekylls, citing Bakhtin's verdict
on debased or evil doubles, who succeed in gaining control of their
more benevolent 'originals' because those originals refuse to attend
consciously to ugly voices that are also part of their indwelling selves.
What is Bakhtin cautioning us against? Ignore your own inner
dialogue, he warns, and the most dangerous side of your personality
will become so hungry for interlocutors that it will court attention
from anywhere – and clamour to control the whole to the extent that
its point of view has been slighted. How does this dynamic work to
make Ivan the tool of Smerdyakov, and not the other way around? It
does so precisely by confirming the *strength* of unfinalisability (the
inherent breadth of Ivan's vacillating, indecisive moral position),
which at the same time is helpless before the self-confidence of a
limited, vengeful, servile nature. A lackey, like a double, is a spiritual
derivative. His authentic face is the mask of 'a coward and a
scoundrel', but he doesn't think to conceal this fact. He does not,
because – for all the outward vanity of his person – he has no inner
honour and does not care how he appears to others. He has no need
for, or interest in, others' opinions; he carries out tests on others for
his own purposes but does not submit his own self to change within
their zone. And thus, in a fateful paradox played out during Mitya's
trial, the lackey is considered 'honest'. Being of one dimension, he

can be obedient. No honourably open or receptive personality could hope to triumph over this simple agenda.

This is why, Kantor argues, we (and the narrator) admire Ivan in spite of everything. We wish him well until the end, and somehow we refuse to believe in his collapse. His is a mind of integrity (in Bakhtin's sense of that word): that is, it is a complex and *open* whole. But then Kantor proceeds to revise Bakhtin's rather conventional reading of the famous Smerdyakov–Ivan dialogue that takes place on the brink of the latter's leaving for Chermashnya. At a methodological level, Kantor will not endorse Bakhtin's basic unit for analyzing the great novels, which is a stretch of dialogic exchange – almost any exchange – that illustrates double-voicedness, usually severed from the surrounding plot. For Kantor, local dynamics can only make sense when characters are tracked from start to finish. A broad developmental view of Ivan suggests to him a different distribution of authoritative and internally-persuasive words than Bakhtin (or many other critics) have tended to see.

'Through Smerdyakov, Ivan's internal rejoinder [his wish for his father's death] is transformed from a desire into a deed', Bakhtin writes in Chapter 5 of *Problems of Dostoevsky's Poetics* (p. 259). 'Ivan's hidden will (hidden even from himself)' is boldly addressed by Smerdyakov's confident outer voice, which promises to make the deed come true and thus mesmerises its interlocutor. Not necessarily so, Kantor argues. There is little evidence that Smerdyakov is listening to Ivan's inner (i.e. 'repressed', more authentic, more honest) voice. Lackey that he is, Smerdyakov is attuned only to Ivan's exasperated public voice, the clichéd outer discourse of an irritated, impatient man, digusted by his gross parent and not above occasional drawing-room ostentation. Smerdyakov – who is not one to listen carefully to others in any event – does not hear Ivan's truly inner voice, that faintly sounding self which hungers for a rebirth of faith so acutely detected by the elder Zosima. For a true inner voice is identified as such because it always leaves a loophole towards the light. Kantor suggests that the standard, pathologically symbiotic reading of the verbal 'duel' between Ivan and Smerdyakov grants the former far too little moral credit and the latter far too much cunning. The lackey does not 'realise' the essence of our hero. He only muffles and dirties the zone. Thus can Ivan serve as spiritual cover-up for Smerdyakov, just as Mitya serves as juridical cover-up for the court. But one can go further: Ivan is not only a cover-up (*prikrytie*) for Smerdyakov, as Dmitry is for the court in search of a verdict; Ivan is also an invention or discovery (*otkrytie*) of Smerdyakov's, a fantasy or counter-double prematurely embodied. We see here the dark side of Bakhtin's dialogism, the openness that can be exploited as an emptiness.

Finally, what about Kantor's parenthetical subtitle, the 'problem of temptation'? Here is one of his most interesting moves. It would seem that Kantor means 'temptation' in several contexts. First there is the simple grammar of 'who tempts whom' in the Smerdyakov–Ivan exchanges, which Kantor resolves firmly on the side of Ivan: he is the tempted, not the tempter, for Smerdyakov is an active force for evil at work on a delicate, corruptible, still undecided soul. Then there is the subtext, much prized by Kantor, of the Book of Job. In passing, Kantor remarks that Job too had been tempted to his rebellion 'by his misfortunes and by the misfortunes of the world'. It is a telling phrase. It suggests that temptation of the truly crippling sort is not material or sensual – not Mitya's lust for Grushenka or Rakitin's for the goods of this world – but rather the temptation of our own suffering, the natural impulse to generalise and absolutise our own experience when in fact we are still working our life out as an idea and a practice. It is Ivan's *in*determinateness, his *lack* of self-definition in the presence of deeply felt convictions and a desire for intellectual closure that leads to the tragedy, for this openness left him vulnerable to unscrupulous manipulation by the determined and the defined. The murder was not his doing or his fault, it was Smerdyakov's fault and responsibility, but Ivan's openness was a factor and a temptation.

These thoughts suggest one last hypothesis. If that is temptation, how are we to protect ourselves against it? Dostoevsky, and with him the elder Zosima, would probably counsel us to live by our own experience – but by no more than our experience. Realise epistemological modesty, which is the best way to keep the devil at bay; do what you are able to do within your own immediate present. If, however, like the middle Karamazov brother, your worldview tends towards the vague and theoretical, learn from this novel: the only remotely safe vagueness is love, not vengeance or metaphysical rebellion. The lack of a positive principle in Ivan, his passionate interest in rebellion (*bunt*) as a self-justifying moral position, permitted Smerdyakov to utilise its energy for wholly selfish ends. In a word, Ivan allowed himself the exclusive luxury of *svoboda vopreki*, 'freedom in spite of'. Such freedom has many loopholes, almost all of them disastrous. At the end of his 1999 interview, Kantor remarked that 'nations live not by their mind but by reflexes' – and, although these reflexes take centuries to form and reform, they are, fortunately, responsive to historical memory. Re-reading Dostoevsky, Kantor intimates, will increase the odds that Russia's future will be wiser than the 'Smerdyakovian' moments of her past.

NOTES

1 This article is taken from: Vladimir Kantor, *V poiskakh lichnosti: Opyt russkoi klassiki*, (Moscow, 1994), 149–74.
2 O. Miller, *Russkie pisateli posle Gogolia*, vol. 1 (St Petersburg, 1900), 264.
3 Ya. S. Belinkis, *F. M. Dostoevskii* (Leningrad, 1960), 51. I deliberately cite a popular brochure to indicate the widespread prevalence of this point of view.
4 V. E. Vetlovskaya, *Poetika romana 'Brat'ia Karamazovy'* (Leningrad, 1977), 100.
5 T. S. Karlova, *Dostoevskii i russkii sud* (Kazan, 1975), 159.
6 Thomas Mann noted this double nature of illness in connection with his discussions of Dostoevsky. See T. Mann, *Sobranie sochinenii v 10–ti tt*, vol. 9 (Moscow, 1960), 509–11.
7 Cited in G. M. Fridlender, *Dostoevskii i mirovaia literatura* (Moscow, 1979), 370. Fridlender is citing from R. Musil, *Tagebücher, Aphorismen, Essays und Reden* (Hamburg, 1955). (Page reference not provided.)
8 M. M. Bakhtin, *Problemy poetiki Dostoevskogo* (Moscow, 1963), 427.
9 One of the prerevolutionary critics wrote: 'The grandiose figure of Ivan, who, like Job, declares: "O, if only man could enter into competition with God, as a human son with his nearest of kin"', eclipses the naive Alyosha and the seductively sweet teachings of the elder Zosima' (D. V. Filosofov, *Staroe i novoe* (Moscow, 1912), 182). Unfortunately, this similarity is only named and hinted at, not disclosed and explicated. Victor Shklovsky made reference to the link between Job and this novel in an equally transitory way; he writes only that Job 'rebelled against the structure of the world: this rebellion also helped the late Dostoevsky of *The Brothers Karamazov*' (V. Shklovskii, *Tetiva. O neskhodstve skhodnogo* (Moscow, 1970), 232).
10 N. G. Chernyshevskii, *Polnoe sobranie sochinenii* (Moscow, 1950), vol. 6, 616.
11 Vetlovskaya, *Poetika romana 'Brat'ia Karamazovy'*, 90.
12 See, for example, in N. Chirkov: 'The entire irresistible fatal nature of the relations between Ivan and Smerdyakov comes down to the fact that the latter is a spiritual product of Ivan' (N. M. Chirkov, *O stile Dostoevskogo* (Moscow, 1967), 273).

13 The letter to E. N. Lebedeva is dated 8 November 1879.
14 On this, see V. Kantor, *'Brat'ia Karamazovy' F. Dostoevskogo* (Moscow, 1983), 59–63.
15 Bakhtin, *Problemy poetiki Dostoevskogo*, 441.
16 These lines are from Tyutchev's lyric, 'It is not given to us to predict', dated 27 February 1869. F. I. Tiutchev, *Stikhotvoreniia: Pis'ma: Vospominaniia sovremennikov* (Moscow, 1988), 132.

CHAPTER 11

Beyond the will: Humiliation as Christian necessity 'Crime and Punishment'

Henry M. W. Russell

The most disturbing message of Dostoevsky's *Crime and Punishment* is its insistence that humiliation is the necessary precondition for Christian life. In a move that powerfully repels even the Catholic West, much more mainstream Protestantism or existentialism, Dostoevsky forces his characters far beyond a comfortable exercise in the virtue of humility to an abject state of humiliation. Only those individuals who admit the justice of being mocked and despised by all normal-minded people realise clearly enough the truth of human kind's fallen condition honestly to feel the necessity for grace. This theme binds into a remarkable unity characters as different as Marmeladov, Marmeladov's daughter Sonya, Raskolnikov and Svidrigailov. Each character must decide between an assertion of will and complete humiliated acknowledgment of his or her non-being without the creative power of God. The emphasis on true humiliation as true humility is a doctrinal commitment which should not be translated into any psychological category of masochism as a physical or psychic eros. Similarly the conception of humiliation pushes the reader beyond noble tragedy or transcendentalism. The doctrine of self-abnegation does not spring from a diseased psyche but from the Orthodox tradition of apophatic knowledge. It is within that tradition that Dostoevsky's meaning can best be grasped.

Apophatic knowledge, as Bishop Kallistos Ware explains, is a way of knowing that employs negative as well as affirmative statements, saying what God is not rather than what he is.[1] Through this method human beings can describe God's essence or their own only by a set of assertions and negations which admit the incomplete and distorting nature of the ideas asserted. In a tradition of theology best represented by Dionysius the Pseudo-Areopagite, St Gregory Palamas writes that 'The super-essential nature of God is not a subject for speech or thought <. . .> There is no name whereby it can be named, neither in this age or in the world to come, nor word found in the soul and uttered by the tongue, nor contact whether sensible or intellectual.'[2] St Gregory of Nyassa's Answer to Eunomius's Second Book asserts that the intellect is most useful when it give names that 'furnish a sort of catalogue and muster of evil qualities from which God is separate. Yet these terms employed give no positive account of that to which they are applied.'[3] Certainly this mystic way of negation is a major part of the Western Catholic tradition as well (whether we look at St Augustine, St Francis of Assisi, St John of the Cross, Margery Kemp or William Langland, among others). but that tradition of beatific illumination has been much obscured by the achievements of rational, discursive theology.

Lest apophatic knowledge be misunderstood, however, for its mute step-brother deconstruction, it is important to note that human inability to refer with full truth to God is a result of God's perfection which we, as sinful creatures, cannot know. Language about God refers then to a plenitude which it cannot contain, not to an absence. Gregory of Nyssa writes that God 'is named, by those who call upon Him, not what He is essentially (for the nature of Him Who alone is unspeakable), but He receives his appellations from what are believed to be His operations in regard to our life.'[4] But the cataphatic or positive and constructive side of Orthodox theology allows St Gregory to assert that 'in applying such appellations to the Divine essence, "which passeth all understanding", we do not seek to glory in it by the names we employ, but to guide our own selves by the aid of such terms towards the comprehension of the things which are hidden.'[5] Insofar as our words are said with a thorough awareness of their partial apprehension, then language can speak truly. 'The way of "unknowing" brings us not to emptiness but fullness', Bishop Ware explains, 'Destructive in outward form, the apophatic approach is affirmative in its final effects: it helps us to reach out, beyond all statements <. . .> towards an immediate experience of the living God.'[6] This experience, as for Gregory Palamas in *The Triads*, can become for the most holy a kind of 'durable vision of light, and the vision of things in the light, whereby <. . .> the future is shown as already existing', a state of being which is 'incomparably higher than negative theology, for it belongs only to those who have attained impassability.'[7]

What becomes interesting when the apophatic insight is applied to the human condition is that negations of the words said about persons might lead close to an almost overwhelming emptiness of spirit. If any single word is used about human virtues, and if we then examine to what extent a single virtue is truly within us, we come swiftly to a realisation of how tiny is our share in the plenitude of goodness, courage and gratitude. Here indeed a word may refer to a dwindling referent. The logical end of such examination is not a comfortable humility which retains a proud sense of our solid middle-class virtues or our pious religiosity.

In Dostoevsky, awareness of human insufficiency leads to an almost hysterical signalling of vice from characters who retain any vestige of social respectability, whether an old Karamazov, a Marmeladov or a Raskolnikov. These characters and many others intermittently seek exterior humiliation in the eyes of society while refusing to see the full contemptibility of their lives; thus they court punishment rather than mercy. They are honest enough to judge themselves harshly, but their pride in such self-condemnation – combined with an awareness that other people share their vileness without exercising a similar honesty of judgment – leads them to assume that they have seen the fullness of their debased condition. This is a false humiliation that, in the words of the old Russian proverb, is 'worse than pride'. This false humiliation, if maintained, will lead its bearer to seek extinction. Dostoevsky mercilessly pushes the reader onwards to see that anyone who fully understands the depths of his own sinful negations can have only the response of complete humiliation, one so profound that it cannot speak at all except to ask for grace or extinction. Filaret, Metropolitan of Moscow for much of Dostoevsky's lifetime, explains this vision: 'All creatures are balanced upon the creative word of God, as if upon a bridge of diamond; above them is the abyss of divine infinitude, below them that of their own nothingness.'[8]

This logic of personal abnegation propels R. P. Blackmur's eloquent and ignorant attack on Dostoevsky's vision of 'society with a drive toward collapse whether into the arms of God or the embrace of the devil', of which Blackmur writes further 'I cannot think of anything more repulsive; it is a fascist society in extremis' which reduces human life to 'the desperate virtue of idiots or of the damned'.[9] Here Blackmur ignores the fact that in Dostoevsky's world those who collapse in God's arms are then taught to stand anew; he obscures the fact that the great totalitarian societies have all been neo-pagan in their spirit; and finally he forgets that precisely such religious ideas as

Dostoevsky's supported the High Middle Ages and a large portion of later Western society whether Renaissance or Puritan. Certainly Blackmur ignores the fact that such humiliated recognition is only a first step towards Father Zosima's famous declaration of Christian responsibility: 'There is only one means of salvation, then take yourself and make yourself responsible for all men's sins, that is the truth, you know, friends, for as soon as you sincerely make yourself responsible for everything and for all men, you will see at once that it is really so, and that you are to blame for everyone and for all things.'[10] Does anyone seriously believe this is fascism?

Crime and Punishment presents us with at least four characters who have explored deeply into humiliation, although they form unlikely groupings. Marmeladov is the first to assent to the depths of his own shame; his appearance in the second chapter establishes his role as an emblem for all characters in the novel. As he often mentions, he takes pains to keep his shame visible and to obtain suffering. Yet in the weakness of his physical and moral nature, he does not move towards any proper response to his emptiness. Instead he seeks only the punishment and pity of a wife who beats him, even as she has forgiven him. Stubbornly, however, he refuses to change his life and ends by throwing himself under the feet of an aristocrat's horses. This fate is remarkably prefigured by Raskolnikov who himself is almost run down by a carriage after burying his loot and visiting Razumikhin. He 'had almost fallen under the horses' hooves, in spite of the coachman's repeated cries' [since] 'for some unknown reason he had been walking in the middle of the roadway' (96). This unconscious suicidal urge, a twisted form of the natural urge for expiation, is part of a larger set of false options to human unworthiness that includes the conscious suicide that Raskolnikov and Svidrigailov contemplate, the denial of guilt, the blaming of others, or false humiliation. Because Marmeladov will not go beyond the false humiliation which he insists on parading, he can choose only death, symbolically putting the blame for his fate on an unknown member of a higher economic class. Yet even death does not spare him the final agonised glimpse of his daughter Sonya in her trumpery costume as a prostitute. In this moment he does not know, at first, who she is. As he slowly realises her identity:

with unnatural strength he managed to prop himself on his arm. His wild unmoving gaze remained fixed for some time on his daughter, as though he

did not recognize her. Indeed he had never before seen her in such a costume. Suddenly he did recognize her, humiliated, crushed, ashamed <. . .> Infinite suffering showed in his face.
 – Sonya! Daughter! Forgive me!'

he cries, as he falls in his death.[11] Only at this point do his pleas for forgiveness seem to pass beyond ritual into true realisation and repentance.

Marmeladov is most clearly paired by Dostoevsky with Svidri-gailov; each chooses suicide over action based on a knowledge of his humiliated condition. These men also form the poles of a continuum between someone who almost cannot control his bestial desires to a man who will not control them as a matter of principle. Marmeladov refuses to act on his shame; Svidrigailov endures longer because he refuses to acknowledge that shame exists. The squire will calmly acknowledge that he has been a card-sharp, a bought husband, a seducer of children, and probably a murderer, several times over. His attraction to the sewer runs very deep and, unlike Raskolnikov, he has been able to maintain this crossing of moral boundaries for years. Indeed, he is the very Jacob of a false God. He labours for seven years to pay the price of his marriage to Leah (in the form of Marfa Petrovna), a bargain consummated in the best modern style by getting the goods first as a loan to be paid back. During that seven-year servitude he continues a life of debauching others by a cynical knowledge of their own hidden attractions to evil. Instead of seeing a community of suffering and wretchedness in this bondage to evil, he seizes it as an instrument of pure power, destroying any vestiges of innocence in his path.

His one great failure comes with Raskolnikov's sister Dunya. Totally smitten by her goodness he attempts to defile her in a lengthy philosophical seduction that suggests she should replace Christian humility with the will to power. So seriously does Dunya shatter his self-control that Svidrigailov, who hates overt violence, resorts to poisoning his wife and running like a spurned young lover to St Petersburg. Although he attempts to be subtle and Machiavellian, he ends up declaring: 'I love you so . . . I love you infinitely. Let me kiss the hem of your dress, let me! Let me!' (474). Finally he even gives his will completely over to her in a way that is perfectly sincere, if frenzied and momentary: 'Say to me, "Do this!" and I will do it. I will do anything. I will do the impossible. Whatever you believe in, I will believe in too' (474).

When Dunya resists this total surrender of herself to his cynicism, Svidrigailov reveals that he has locked the room, saying prophetically, 'I have lost the key and I shall not be able to find it' (474). What he has actually lost is the key to his own illusory world where his mind suavely reigns. Once he has been rejected by the one love which he cannot soil he must face his complete lack of power in the situation. And if there is a power acting through Dunya that does not submit to the sewer then his dominion, even over those whom he has dragged downwards, is as nothing compared to the power that can control him without such evil. In desperation Svidrigailov threatens ravishment and forces Dunya to draw a pistol she has hidden to defend herself. He believes this to be the perfect trap: either she will submit and join him or she will shoot him and prove that her goodness must use an evil instrumentality, if only once, in killing him. Of course, if his plot works, there is no way out for him either; he is still trapped in the sewer.

When Dunya almost kills him but then puts down the pistol, Svidrigailov feels some relief from his own huge fear of death but 'The relief he felt was from another emotion, gloomier and more melancholy, which he could not have defined in all its force' (477).[12] This relief is at the knowledge – which he will not fully face – that he is glad Dunya cannot fall into his trap and do evil for the sake of good. When she implores him with her eyes not to hurt her it is the force of his love and her innocence that wins out and makes him give her the key to the room. In this moment Dostoevsky's classically evil character is possessed by a pure love that overwhelms his whole world of nihilism, a love that could save him if he assented wholly to it. Such assent demands, however, a complete change of all his values for Dunya's, not for the sake of possessing her, but for the sake of that by which she is ruled. Svidrigailov seems to see and reject what Zosima says in *The Brothers Karamazov*, 'Loving humility is a terrible force; it is the strongest of all things, and there is nothing else like it' (298).

Svidrigailov's suicide is not best understood as a final bored choice of nothingness. It is the choice of nothingness over an honest recognition of his own humiliation. Throughout a long career of negation he was able to look at his shameful actions, see their evil, understand the obloquy they earned in others' eyes, and refuse to be shamed by them. Only when he has been brought to respect and love someone, as he does with Dunya, must he sense his own

unworthiness before her. Then he must choose whether to see his
actions as they are and seek grace, following her example, or to kill
himself and deny his knowledge. Dostoevsky created Dunya as a
Beatrice refused by an unfaithful Dante, one who is comfortable in
Hell but is ashamed to rise higher, convinced that it is she he seeks
rather than the God he sees reflected in her. Svidrigailov's disorien-
tation before his suicide beautifully enacts Gregory of Nyssa's words
about what a soul sees when it looks beyond the material world:

> Imagine a sheer steep crag with a projecting edge at the top. Now imagine
> what a person would probably feel if he put his foot on the edge of this
> precipice and, looking down into the chasm below, saw no solid footing nor
> anything to hold onto. This is what I think the soul experiences when it
> goes beyond its footing in material things, in its quest for that which has no
> dimension and which exists from all eternity. (page number not provided)

Svidrigailov's dreams before his death are some of the most
horrific emblems of the modern world found in literature because
they show the nature of his refusal to go beyond his will to control
the material world. Those dreams stem from his waking feelings of
love and pity for Dunya and the position in which he had placed her.
His first dream is of a potentially Edenic world: a Whit Sunday full
of warmth, cool breezes and abundant flowers. In an English-style
cottage he finds that 'The floor was strewn with fragrant freshly cut
hay, the windows were open, a cool, fresh, gentle breeze blew into
the room, birds were chirping under the windows, and in the middle
of the room, on tables shrouded in white satin, stood a coffin' (487).
In the coffin lies the young servant girl who drowned herself after
being seduced by Svidrigailov. Perhaps for the first time he sees that
she is 'savagely wounded by the outrage that had amazed and
horrified her young childish conscience, overwhelmed her soul, pure
as an angel's, with unmerited shame, and torn from her a last cry of
despair' (487). This dream is replaced by a vision of the waters rising
to flood St Petersburg, a flood into which Svidrigailov intends to
walk until he finds a shivering five-year-old girl, soaked to the skin.
When he attempts to help her, in pure charity and pity undressing
her from her drenched clothes and putting her to bed, she turns into
a seductive, suggestive child-prostitute. Svidrigailov is touched with
real horror at such corruption in the face of a child and calls her,
'Accursed creature!' before he awakes (490).

What the cynical man above the law sets loose on the world by his
destruction of the innocence of the young servant girl comes back,

like a flood over the social body, to haunt its creator. The amusing game of violating the peace and beauty of Eden comes to haunt him as the world is darkened into hovels where children know as much vice as he has ever practised. Yet he will not give up the world he has helped bring to birth. As he cuttingly remarks to Raskolnikov: 'If you are so sure that one can't listen at doors, but any old woman you like can be knocked on the head, then you'd better be off at once to America somewhere' (466). In the end it is he who repeats to the old guard, 'Achilles', the words 'I said I was off to America' as he puts a bullet in his brain (490). Svidrigailov, like Raskolnikov, finally finds himself weak, incapable of living in a world that his evil has darkened. For seven years he bears the images of dead servants and mistresses. Yet even he cannot bear the loss of his Rachel nor the image of the rising generation of children that he and his fellow corrupters have helped to fashion. He has been brought to see the weakness behind his assumed strength and can only submit to justice and grace or kill himself in a last denial.

Sonya, who lives out the humiliation of prostitution, is the only character who understands more fully than Svidrigailov that her human will is worth next to nothing unless turned towards God in a true humility. One by necessity and one by choice has lived out the destruction of all that society thinks noble. That Sonya's self-renunciation originates in her saintliness is a critical commonplace, but it is important to remember that her selling herself to support her family has left her feeling so dead in soul that she is a fit companion for Raskolnikov after he commits his murders. When she reads the story of the raising of Lazarus from the dead, Sonya is shaken by the same sort of feverish trembling and sense of guilt as Raskolnikov is when he thinks of the dead pawnbroker. Sonya requires the resurrecting power the Lord extended to Lazarus, just as does Raskolnikov.

For his part, if Svidrigailov is typologically linked to a false Jacob, then Raskolnikov is more firmly linked to Esau. Like many in Dostoevsky's modern world he gives up his inheritance in scorn. First he abandons his place in a Christian civil world by murder for a mess of roubles; then in a more noble-seeming but morally-suspect act he gives over his very family to Razhumikin. It is easy to mistake Svidrigailov as being truer to the type of Esau since he eagerly rejects the very idea of the good. Yet Svidrigailov is far more sinister since he lives out a secular religion based on defilement. Raskolnikov, like the thoughtless Esau, merely throws away by default all of the good which his culture offers him, thus leaving the role of Jacob to be filled by one whose type Yeats would come to call 'the worst <. . .> full of passionate intensity'.

Raskolnikov's own rebirth occurs in at least two movements. The first part of that conversion is affected, of course, when he is brought to confession in Sonya's dwelling at the Kapernaumovs. As at the Biblical Capernaum, where Christ brought the demoniac back to right reason (Mk. 1:21–28), Sonya is able to bring Raskolnikov to an awareness that he is not the Napoleonic superman who can trample all law and custom. At this point Raskolnikov achieves what Orthodoxy calls nepsis, a state of sobriety and watchfulness, of coming back to oneself. No longer will he fall into fever and delirium as if out of his mind. Previously Raskolnikov's constant self-doubt and self-contempt, based on his apophatic critique of his willpower, led him near to an almost hysterical humiliation. That period is over; but he refuses to think past the argument that others in the world – indeed, millions of others – are as evil as he. He clings to the delusion that recognising his transgression for what it is makes him superior to lesser men. Of course he defines his real transgression as weakness and cowardice, not as murder. Having looked at his own weakness, he turns that gaze into an occasion for vanity. In this act he is developing some of the same cynicism, even in prison, that moulds a Svidrigailov. He threatens to become the sort of Cathar who places himself above the world of the flesh by asceticism, just as Svidrigailov tried to become the sort who proves the irrelevance of the body by immersing himself in filth.[13]

But Raskolnikov's image of self-sufficiency is shattered when Sonya falls ill and he realises his need for her. In an image remarkably resonant with Hawthorne's Ethan Brand, Raskolnikov stops work as a lime burner to look out upon the freedom of the steppes and the tents of nomads who seem the children of Abraham. Then Sonya appears. This time he does not repel her but holds her hand and 'suddenly he seemed to be seized and cast at her feet' (526). This time he is hurled to his knees by the Spirit, not looking for justice but for the grace of love itself. Emptied out of himself he has rejoined the community as a fellow sufferer who is a wanderer in the hands of God. In his linkage with the tents of Abraham he approaches identification with the kind of people who, Sergy Bulgakov writes, 'are so characteristic of Orthodoxy, above all

Russian Orthodoxy: those who are not of this world and who have here "no abiding city"; pilgrims, the homeless "fools for Christ" who have renounced human reason, accepted the appearance of folly, voluntarily to experience outrages and humiliations for the love of Christ.'[14] Of course his motives are not yet fully understood or directed towards the God behind Sonya but, as Dostoevsky says, that is the beginning of another story.

Thus Raskolnikov is finally able to escape from his false self-image and from the deadly and deadened example of Svidrigailov who had offered himself as a false messiah, telling the young murderer, 'you shall see how easy-going I am. You shall see that it is possible to live with me' (419). These phrases, with their echo of Christ's pronouncement, 'My yoke is easy and my burden is light' (Mat. 11:30), once tempted Raskolnikov, but he follows the much more arduous path of Sofya/Sophia, Sonya's real name, which translates, of course, as Plato's Wisdom. The arrogant murderer who would not endure to be laughed at by the brilliant Porfiry Petrovich had allowed himself, at Sonya's urging, to confess to a man he found so insignificant as to call him 'The Squib'. At that moment Raskolnikov believed he was drinking fully of the cup from which Christ also drank. But Vladimir Lossky notes that in the deepest traditions of Orthodox thought 'If it is true that penitence is the beginning of this way, "the gateway of grace," this is not to say that it is a passing moment, a stage to be left behind. It is in fact not a stage but a condition which must continue permanently, the constant attitude of those who truly aspire to union with God.'[15] Raskolnikov's confession was only one step on the road to penitence, and it is a recognition of the intellect, not of the heart. So he is hated by his fellow prisoners in Siberia who sense his denial of the need for forgiveness even as he suffers the effects of justice. Only when he has submitted to Sonya's spiritual leadership, cast down at her feet by a power beyond him, can he begin to open himself to grace.

The Squib to whom Raskolnikov had confessed, for his part, was not so lowly that he could not scorn women, whom he thinks below him, as he shows in his foolish yet meaning-laden joke about women as midwives 'Who push themselves into the Academy and study anatomy; well, tell me, if I fall ill am I going to call in a girl to cure me? He, he!' (509). Of course Dostoevsky is both criticising the 'New' woman and also recalling that Socrates described himself as a midwife in Plato's *Symposium*. As the wise woman from Mantinea, Diotima, helped Socrates bring forth his soul in beauty and reach

Sophia or wisdom, so Sonya serves as a midwife for the soul of Raskolnikov, even as a spiritual physician who helps cure him of his madness, pace the Squib.

If Svidrigailov insists on using women as objects in a game of power disguised as liberation, the intellectual Raskolnikov must submit to the humiliation of being healed by an uneducated woman who has herself known the depths of shame. What must be done in the eyes of Dostoevsky is so radically unacceptable to the modern world that we are glad Raskolnikov is so grotesque a sinner. Otherwise the words of St Mark the Monk might be applicable to us: 'Unless a man gives himself entirely to the Cross, in a spirit of humility and self-abasement; unless he casts himself down to be trampled underfoot by all and despised, accepting injustice, contempt and mockery. . . he cannot become a true Christian'.[16]

NOTES

1 Kallistos Ware, *The Orthodox Way* (London, 1981), 12–32.
2 V. Lossky, *The Mystical Theology of the Eastern Church* (New York, 1976), 37.
3 Gregory of Nyssa, *Select Writings and Letters*, trans. William Moore and Henry Wilson, *The Nicene and Post-Nicene Fathers of the Christian Church*, 5, 2nd series 1892 (Grand Rapids, MI, 1979), 264.
4 *Ibid.*, 265.
5 *Ibid.*, 265.
6 Ware (1981), 17.
7 Lossky (1976), 65.
8 Ware (1981), 57.
9 R. P. Blackmur, '*Murder in Your Own Room*', *Eleven Essays in the European Novel* (New York, 1964), 151.
10 F. M. Dostoevsky, *The Brothers Karamazov*, ed. Ralph Matlaw, trans. Constance Garnett (New York, 1976), 299.
11 F. M. Dostoevsky, *Crime and Punishment*, trans. Jessie Coulson, ed. George Gibian (New York, 1975), 179.
12 *Ibid.*, 477.
13 The Cathars were a Gnostic heresy of great power from the tenth to the fifteenth century that had adherents all over Europe, but who are best known from sects like the Bogomils and Albigensians. Calling themselves 'the pure' or 'Cathari', they saw all flesh as Satan's domain. They were reported to show their contempt for all but pure spirit by living lives either of extreme asceticism or vicious sensualism. They also advocated suicide, especially by starvation, as an act of purity.
14 S. Bulgakov, *The Orthodox Church*, trans. T. Hopko (New York, 1988), 151.
15 Lossky (1976), 204.
16 Reference not provided.

CHAPTER 12

Freedom's dangerous dialogue: Reading Kierkegaard and Dostoevsky together

George Pattison

In the days when existentialism was fashionable, the names of Kierkegaard, Dostoevsky and Nietzsche were frequently linked as the three great nineteenth-century precursors of existentialist thought. In contrast to Nietzsche, Kierkegaard and Dostoevsky had one further element in common: that they were both *Christian* writers. They could therefore serve both to illustrate the extent – I think the enormous extent – to which religious concerns were central to existentialism and how faith could respond to the challenge posed by existentialism that, in the popular imagination at least, was strongly identified with the atheism of Nietzsche, Sartre and (many claimed) Heidegger.[1] Nor were Kierkegaard and Dostoevsky thought of merely as two separate historical sources of subsequent intellectual development. Again and again we find them virtually identified *as saying essentially the same thing*. I shall therefore begin by taking three examples of writers who, from distinct but not unrelated perspectives, saw them as being joined in this way.[2]

Karl Barth's commentary on St Paul's Letter to the Romans was one of the defining works of European intellectual life in the 1920s. In the preface to the second edition of this commentary, Barth lists the most significant areas of difference between this and the first edition. Amongst these he mentions the influence of 'what may be culled from the writings of Kierkegaard and Dostoevsky that is of importance for the study of the New Testament'.[3] The importance of this 'culling' may be deduced from a further comment in the same preface, when he says: '. . . if I have a system, it is limited to a recognition of what Kierkegaard calls the "infinite qualitative distinction" between time and eternity. . .'[4]

In the body of his text Barth quotes or alludes to Kierkegaard and Dostoevsky in a wide range of contexts although he only occasionally cites them together, as when commenting on Chapter 4, verse 1

'What shall we say then of Abraham?': 'Jesus would not be the Christ if figures like Abraham, Jeremiah, Socrates, Grünewald, Luther, Kierkegaard and Dostoevsky remained, contrasted with Him, merely figures of past history, and did not rather constitute in Him one essential unity; if their positions were merely dissolved by the negation He proclaimed and were not at the same time established.'[5] These names constitute what Barth calls 'the crimson thread' running through history, by virtue of which we can know that the revelation of God in Jesus Christ is not just an arbitrary event, unconnected with anything else in history, but the fulfilment of the Law, 'the meaning and substance of the whole history of religion'. They are, as it were, the chosen representatives of a sacred history hidden within the course of secular history but secretly judging it and pointing to its final meaning.

Still later, in the discussion of Chapter 7, verses 9–11, he speaks of the ambiguity of humanity's relation to God's commandments. In conventional religion this ambiguity is concealed, but in the men of the crimson thread it is disclosed in its perilous risk – so perilous that we may well want to draw back from the precipice thus revealed. 'We may, however, judge the relentlessness of Calvin, the dialectical audacity of Kierkegaard, Overbeck's sense of awe, Dostoevsky's hunger for eternity, Blumhardt's optimism, too risky and too dangerous for us. We may therefore content ourselves with some lesser, more feeble possibility of religion.'[6]

In such ways Kierkegaard and Dostoevsky are portrayed as united in depicting the human situation *in extremis*, as it appears at those boundaries where normal rules, normal ways of thinking and judging and acting, break down and where the human being's inability to stand in the presence of God is revealed without reserve or pretence.[7] In such boundary-situations the human subject is revealed as profoundly resistant to incorporation in any rational system or any universal framework of understanding.

An extreme statement of this view is to be found in the works of Lev Shestov (1866–1936), the idiosyncratic but influential Russian critic and philosopher, who left Russia in 1920, settling in Paris the following year. Straddling the worlds of philosophy and literary criticism, Shestov may be read as a profoundly anti-philosophical philosopher, decrying the claims of rationalism to explain human life which, he believes, is always life lived on the edge of the abyss. Dostoevsky and Kierkegaard (the latter of whom he only 'discovered' in the later part of his career, reading him on the advice of Husserl,[8] with whom he struck up a somewhat improbable friendship) feature as two of the writers who most honestly and completely reveal this situation. Shestov was himself well aware of the charge that he read his own views into his favourite authors, telling his friend Benjamin Fondane how Berdyaev teased him for 'Shestovising' his sources.[9]

Shestov's study *Kierkegaard and the Existential Philosophy* was to prove highly significant for the French reception of Kierkegaard when it was published in 1936, and in many ways it created the portrait of Kierkegaard that was subsequently accepted amongst French existentialists. In his introduction Shestov sought to demonstrate the connection between Kierkegaard and Dostoevsky. Taking Hegel as the representative of a line of philosophy that privileges knowledge over existence and systematic thought over the contingencies and particularities of life, Shestov comments that '. . . both Dostoevsky and Kierkegaard (the first without realising it, the second fully aware of it) saw their life work as a struggle with, and victory over, that system of ideas embodied in Hegelian philosophy . . .'[10] For both of them, 'Faith is above and beyond knowledge',[11] and both oppose Job to the complacency of rationalism. Knowledge, as Shestov sees it (and as he believes both Dostoevsky and Kierkegaard saw it too), is the cause of humanity's original fall: knowledge reveals to human beings their subjection to necessity. 'But for God all things are possible. This constitutes *the struggle of faith: a mad struggle for possibility.* For only possibility reveals the way to salvation.' And, he adds (famously), 'here [Kierkegaard] comes so close to Dostoevsky that one may say . . . that Dostoevsky is Kierkegaard's double.'[12]

According to Shestov the Underground Man speaks with Dostoevsky's own voice, entering the lists on behalf of man's abyssal freedom: 'Will you still maintain', Shestov asks rhetorically, 'that Dostoevsky and his underground hero are not one and the same man?'[13] Yet, like Barth, Shestov regards this freedom as profoundly problematic in the face of the human being's situation before God. Indeed, he regards both Dostoevsky and Kierkegaard as ultimately failing to live up to or to think consistently in the light provided by their most profound insights. The truth is almost too unbearable for human beings.

Colin Wilson's *The Outsider* was one of the most influential works of literary criticism in Britain in the 1950s. Despite its many flaws it remains a good example of how existentialism was received in the post-war period outside the precincts of the academy. Once more, Dostoevsky and Kierkegaard share centre stage. In his discussion of Dostoevsky's novella *Notes from the Underground*, whose anti-hero he refers to as the 'beetle-man', Wilson remarks that 'Kierkegaard's *Unscientific Postscript* . . . is the beetle-man's case extended to several hundred pages.'[14] And what is this 'case'? Essentially, Wilson says, it is a belligerent 'reaction against something, and that "something" is rational humanism'. 'And suddenly, Dostoevsky's beetle-man starts up, with his bad teeth and beady eyes, and shouts: "To hell with your System. I demand the right to behave as I like. I demand the right to regard myself as *utterly unique*."' In this protest, the beetle-man becomes a pure representative of 'the Outsider'-type, to whom Wilson's study is devoted, and whom he also regards as central to the work of such other writers as Blake, Nietzsche and Kierkegaard.

> We have here a strange group of men – Blake, Kierkegaard, Nietzsche, Dostoevsky: two violently unorthodox Christians, one pagan 'philosopher with a hammer', and one tormented half-atheist-half-Christian [I'm not sure if that's meant to be Blake or Kierkegaard or Dostoevsky!], all beginning from the same impulse and driven by the same urges . . . *these men held basically the same beliefs* . . . the basic idea is the same in all four.[15]

Following in the footsteps of Barth and Shestov, Wilson sees Kierkegaard and Dostoevsky as representing the *im*possibility of enclosing or comprehending human existence within the limits of any conventional human system of thought or ethics. More humanistically inclined than either Barth or Shestov, however, Wilson believes that although the path of the Outsider through history is littered with tragedy and failure, that is merely the preliminary result of an effort that may yet lead to better things. 'The individual begins the long effort as an Outsider', he concludes, 'he may finish it as a saint.'[16]

Three views, then, that despite their differing lines of vision present a common picture of Dostoevsky and Kierkegaard as prophets revealing to 'modern man' the abyssal freedom, the wild frontiers and the midnight cries that threaten both the rational system-building of philosophers and social engineers as well as the moral complacency of a bourgeois world that is only too happy to believe that 'all is well'.

Unfortunately, this image is deeply flawed and relies on serious misreadings of key texts. It is certainly true that both Dostoevsky and Kierkegaard are critical of totalising rational systems and bourgeois complacency – but they are equally critical of the kind of arbitrary, capricious and individualistic protest that Dostoevsky portrays in the Underground Man and Kierkegaard in his various aesthetic characters. Both recognise that such protest is reactive and ultimately incapable of challenging the system against which it cries out so passionately. Indeed, so strong is the critique both writers make of such outsider protesters that some have interpreted them as apologists for ecclesiastical and political conservatism. But that, I suspect, is another misreading.

The point is this: that both see the outsider syndrome as representing a vitally and fundamentally important event in the spiritual, moral, social and intellectual life of modernity. The outsider is the inevitable shadow of modern rationalism, such that both rationalist and outsider are mutually interdependent, symbiotic life-forms that, in their mutually destructive rivalry, threaten to obliterate altogether the integrity of the human being and destroy the bases of authentic sociality. Nihilism, in short, is not to be identified simply and solely with the voice of the outsider, the voice of protest, the negation of rationality: nihilism is the denial of authentic humanity that both rationality and the protest against rationality conspire to bring about. So where can we find deliverance from this sterile and destructive conflict between two equal and opposite forces that are between them grinding the human image back into the dust from which it was made?

Can we find a way of reading Dostoevsky and Kierkegaard together that not only does justice to the radicality with which they give expression to the voice of the outsider, 'man in revolt', but also helps us to link the ways in which they envisage a possible exodus from the nihilism of which the outsider is the immediate precursor?

What I shall do in the remainder of this chapter is to experiment with a critical perspective that might enable such a reading to take place.

Crucial to this perspective is the contemporary French critic and cultural theorist, René Girard. Girard has come to prominence in recent years in religious studies as a theorist of violence and the sacred, offering a profound and polymathic exploration of the common origins of violence and religion. At the heart of religion and of culture alike – indeed, embedded in the most fundamental evolutionary processes of hominisation – Girard sees the problem of violence, a problem that arises for human beings from their uniquely imitative nature. The imbalance between imitation and instinct brings it about that human beings can only establish their identity as selves through imitation. But this means desiring what the other desires, so that the object of imitation, the one from whom I have learned my desires, becomes the prime obstacle to my fulfilling them. The resultant violence can then – fuelled by the power of imitation – proliferate throughout society until the point is reached at which the very survival of the community is itself threatened. At this point, he suggests, the characteristically human response is to channel or focus the violence arbitrarily onto one individual: the scapegoat, whose resultant death re-unites the community in the complicity of blood-guilt. The sacrificial representation of such primal murder is then established as the basis of religion. On the one hand this 'solves' the problem of violence, but only by perpetuating the mind-set of violence itself: 'the culture born of violence must return to violence', Girard says.[17] Only in the gospels, in the narrative of the passion, do we find an adequate critique of such sacrificial religion, for the gospels take the standpoint of the scapegoat himself, the innocent victim of society's violence who refuses to allow the justice of his death and who, in that death and against those who condemn him, is identified as the bearer of God's cause. Of course, this means reading the gospels against the grain of those ecclesiastical traditions that require a sacrificial understanding of Christ's work. For, in Girard's view, the passion narrative is essentially anti-sacrificial; indeed, it is the ultimate repudiation of sacrifice and of the social processes that engender sacrifice.

Much of Girard's work since *Violence and the Sacred* (1972) seems to be drawing on the data of anthropology, psychology and the study of ancient texts (e.g. Sophocles). However, his earlier work centred on Dostoevsky, in his studies *Dostoevsky: From the Double to Unity* and *Deceit, Desire and the Novel: Self and Other in Literary Structure*. I would suggest that although Dostoevsky is rarely (if at all?) referred to in the presentation of his mature theory of violence, many of the elements of this theory can be found in the earlier studies.

His *Dostoevsky* portrays Dostoevsky as undertaking 'la recherche de l'Absolu', a quest begun 'in anguish, doubt and deceit' but ending 'in certitude and joy'. As Dostoevsky both experienced and described the human situation, we are typically caught in a double-bind of attraction and repulsion in our relation to the other: 'The presence of the rival, the fear of being checked, the obstacle, exercised on Dostoevsky, as on his heroes, an influence at one and the same time paralyzing and exciting.'[18] In contrast to more recent existentialist thinkers such as Sartre, Girard states, Dostoevsky understands that 'In the world structured by the gospel revelation, individual existence is essentially imitative, even, indeed especially, perhaps, when it rejects the thought of imitation with horror.'[19] Dostoevsky's fictional universe is thus peopled by characters whose 'pride' impels them to assert their own claims to stand at the centre of their universe, to determine their own values and their own identity – and yet who are unable to break free from their idolised role models or who are dragged back and down by their 'abhorred rival'.

Most ambivalent of all such rivalrous relationships is that of father and son; not because (as Freud believed) the son has some kind of instinctual sexual desire for the mother that condemns him to being his father's rival, but because it is from the father himself that he learns his desires: the father is the supreme example of 'the hated rival who is equally the venerated model'. The theme of parricide in Dostoevsky is therefore pre-eminently suited to expose the mechanisms of mimetic rivalry.

In *Deceit, Desire and the Novel*, Girard develops further the concept of what he is now calling the triangular model of desire: triangular because the subject does not simply relate to the desired object immediately or instinctually, but because he is directed to the object by the mediator: the role model who so easily becomes the rival and obstacle to the fulfilment of desire. This relationship is particularly acute in what Girard further specifies as 'internally mediated desire', when both the subject and the mediator share the same objects. It is – we are not surprised to read – Dostoevsky who represents novelistically 'the highest level of internal mediation': '. . . in Dostoevsky there is no longer any love without jealousy, any friendship without envy, any attraction without repulsion . . . [the hatred thus generated] finally "explodes", revealing its double nature, or rather the double role of model and obstacle played by the mediator. This adoring hatred, this admiration that insults and even kills its object, are the paroxysms of the conflict caused by internal mediation.'[20]

That the revelation of this structure is already latent within Christian teaching itself – and that Christianity implicitly 'demythologises' the pretensions of desire – is also shown in Dostoevsky's novels, especially in his later works which '. . . provide a coherent

interpretation of the very strict analogies and of the radical difference between Christianity and imitative desire.'[21] Dostoevsky has
learned from Christianity and now passes on to his readers that 'the
truth of metaphysical desire is death . . .'[22] For 'to perceive the
metaphysical structure of desire is to foresee its catastrophic conclusion'.[23]

Girard sees the event of the Dostoevskian novel – the ability to
reveal and to name the machinations of desire – as an overcoming of
the compulsiveness of desire itself and, a such, a triumph over
metaphysical desire. The religious 'meaning' of Dostoevsky's novels
is not imposed upon them, but is invested in the very form of the
novel, so that 'the last distinctions between novelistic and religious
experience are abolished.'[24] The demons are cast out. Resurrection
is attained.

Importantly, and against those views which see the Underground
Man as a mouthpiece for Dostoevsky himself, Girard asserts that
Dostoevsky is far removed from the Underground Man and from the
existentialist apotheosis of radical spontaneity and unpredictability,
and the cult of freedom, understood as arbitrary and individualistic
caprice. Dostoevsky does not endorse the protest of the Underground Man: he represents it – and in doing so explains it precisely
as a mark the underground man's lack of freedom, his domination
by a structure of mimetic desire that is mechanistic in essence and
that effects the frustration of self-attainment. True freedom is to be
found through the transformation of social experience – and not in
the mere denial of that experience. The fundamental problematic of
freedom has not merely to do with the transcendental constitution of
the self but with the self in relation to others: the self in dialogue –
and here we might understand Girard as complementing the
dialogical understanding of the person as formulated by that most
influential of Dostoevsky readers: Mikhail Bakhtin. Bakhtin believes
that dialogue is founded in the situation that 'I am conscious of
myself and become myself only while revealing myself for another,
through another, and with the help of another' and that 'A person
has no internal sovereign territory, he is wholly and always on the
boundary; looking inside himself, he looks into the eyes of another or
with the eyes of another.'[25] But this is precisely the situation that
grounds Girard's analysis of the subject as determined by the
mimetic relation to the other, that I am what I am through the
desires that I learn from the other. For both, the question is whether

that situation is capable of issuing in a situation of reciprocal affirmation, or whether we abandon the demands of dialogue and take a route that ends in violence, death and ultimate silence.

Whereas Bakhtin, however, is primarily concerned with rescuing dialogue from subjugation by the monological voice of absolutising worldviews, Girard is acutely concerned with the way in which dialogue itself always runs the risk of disintegrating into violence: or, more precisely, the way in which the structure of the self that grounds the possibility of dialogue is the same structure that grounds the possibility of violence. In a powerful passage in *Violence and the Sacred* Girard discusses how the dialogue in Greek drama effectively re-enacts the violent exchange of blows between duelling warriors: words fly back and forth like sword blows. The question that Bakhtin and Girard together confront us with, then, is this: how can the basic dialogical structure of the human subject be rescued from the threat of violence and transformed into a model of mutual affirmation and liberation?

This is not to say that Bakhtin and Girard can simply be conflated. There are real differences between them, and what I am aiming at here is not a synthesis but a critical dialogue in which each serves as the other's 'corrective' (to use a Kierkegaardian expression). For if Girard helps us to see the seriousness of failing to arrive at an affirmative and liberative way of dialogue, Bakhtin can help us to guard against Girard's sometimes irritatingly inflated claims to provide an all-embracing and exhaustive explanatory account of human culture. For if we take to heart Bakhtin's insistence on the essential unfinishedness of all genuine dialogue, Girard may well seem to be offering what Bakhtin refers to as 'an externalizing secondhand definition'.[26] Against Girard, and with Bakhtin, we must insist that the issue of violence must always, over and over again, be returned to and resolved through the situation of humanity's being-in-dialogue.

But what about Kierkegaard?

Certainly, the Girardian motif of the scapegoat is central to Kierkegaard's writings and is especially dominant in the writings of his later years. Take Kierkegaard's account of what he calls a genuine Christian witness to the truth, whom he describes as:

a man who is scourged, maltreated, dragged from one prison to the other, and then at last – the last promotion, whereby he is admitted into the first

class as defined by the Christian protocol, among the genuine witnesses to
the truth – then at last . . . crucified, or beheaded, or burnt, or roasted on a
gridiron, his lifeless body thrown by the executioner, in an out-of-the-way
place . . . or burnt to ashes and cast to the four winds, so that every trace of
the 'filth' (which the Apostle says *he* was) might be obliterated.[27]

Although he himself did not suffer any of the afflictions he lists as
characterising such a witness to the truth, one of the pivotal events
in his life was his run-in with a satirical journal, *The Corsair*, in which
he was extensively lampooned – a literary exchange that ended in
his being subject to abuse and to what he experienced as the threat
of violence on the streets of Copenhagen – an event he later
described as 'a martyrdom of laughter'.

Kierkegaard, then, had a keen sense of the violence lurking under
the surface of society: but was this sense more than that of the
morbid attraction of a religious melancholic towards the shadow-
side of life? The martyr complex of a natural-born victim? Is
Kierkegaard mystified by the mechanisms of violence or is he – like
Dostoevsky – able to analyse and demystify them?

I can do little more here than indicate some of the ways in which,
I believe, Kierkegaard not merely expresses his own experience of
being scapegoated but also offers an analysis of the dynamics that
precipitate such scapegoating congruent with that of Girard and
with that which Girard reads out of Dostoevsky.

One of the fundamental characteristics that Kierkegaard observed
in his contemporaries was the longing to be just 'like the others',[28] a
characteristic that culminates in the triumph of 'the numerical' that,
Kierkegaard says, 'transfers mankind to an exalted state just as
opium does' so that we are 'tranquillized by the trustworthiness of
millions'.[29] But what does the majority mean when all have been
degraded to 'copies' of each other?[30] The social conformity of the
crowd is a product of the dialectic of 'comparison'. Unlike the world
of nature, where everything is just what it is and doesn't aspire to be
anything else, the human world is a world of comparisons in which:

One man compares himself with another; one generation compares itself
with another; and thus the accumulated multitude of comparisons really
grows above a man's head. As everywhere ingenuity and busyness increase,
there come to be in every generation more and more men who toilsomely
labour throughout their whole life far down in the deep subterranean
regions . . .[31]

These subterranean regions, in which 'comparison' has generated

dare contribute to levelling and by the same suffering act . . . pass judgment on [it] . . . in suffering he will defeat it and thereby experience in turn the law of his existence, which is not to rule, to guide, to lead, but in suffering to serve, to help indirectly.'[38]

The suffering of the Christian, then, is undertaken as a means of revealing the latent violence of a society built on levelling, i.e. envy, i.e. mimetic rivalry. The suffering of the witness to the truth is a revelation of the true nature of the social compact: the compact of sacrificial violence.

Naturally, in all this the believer sees in the suffering of Christ an exemplary instance of such demystificatory suffering and it is no coincidence that many of Kierkegaard's later religious writings are dominated by the theme of the imitation of Christ's sufferings. However, this is not a sign that he is thereby locking himself in to the mechanisms of mimesis, since, as Girard says with regard to Dostoevsky's later works, the analogies between the Christian imitation of Christ and imitative desire do not mean that there are not also 'radical differences': the imitation of man (the kind of imitation that generates envy) is not the same as the imitation of God, because the imitation of God breaks the cycle of reciprocity by which one act of envy generates another and one violent act leads on to another. In this context we might consider Kierkegaard's essay 'Has a man the right to allow himself to be put to death for the truth?' in which it is argued that *only* the God-man has such a right, because only He can truly offer forgiveness to his killers and thereby break the cycle of guilt and retribution. Yet it may also be possible for the believer, by imitation, to share in that work of liberation.[39]

But not only does Kierkegaard show a grasp of the dynamics of violence and scapegoating similar to that found in Dostoevsky by Girard. His work also cries out for a Bakhtinian reading.[40]

Recall at this point Bakhtin's comment about the typical Dostoevskian hero: that 'he is not only a discourse about himself . . . but also a discourse about the world; he is not only cognizant but an ideologist as well' – although, equally, he is not a mere vehicle for an idea, since 'the truth about the world, according to Dostoevsky, is inseparable from the truth of personality.'[41] A similar aim with respect to integrating ideological functions and personal existence lies at the heart of Kierkegaard's authorship. As Kierkegaard put it in his unpublished Lectures on Communication, the pseudonyms are 'designed' as 'poetized personalities who say *I*' and who at the same time represent possibilities of 'ethical and ethical-religious truth'.[42] On the other hand, many would claim that Dostoevsky's characters – despite their 'ideological' function of representing particular views on life – stand out as authentically flesh and blood human beings, expressing a range and depth of passions that is fully (and more than fully) three-dimensional, whereas Kierkegaard's pseudonyms and other characters are more purely ideological and humanly unconvincing, two-dimensional puppets who are no more than ciphers for the 'ideas' they represent. Also, Dostoevsky's novels include elements of adventure and drama that are only minimally present even in Kierkegaard's most novelistic works.

Is this, however, saying anything more than that – whereas Dostoevsky is first and foremost a novelist – Kierkegaard is a religious and philosophical writer who makes use of novelistic forms? Yet, even if such a distinction (whatever it means!) has some value, it must admit of variation and qualification, since ideological functions, critical questioning and concrete personality are present in the works of both authors. In other words, it is not the case that Dostoevsky provides us with novelistically drawn descriptions of the human predicament which Kierkegaard, the Christian philosopher, is then able to explain.[43] Although there may indeed be a significant difference in balance between Dostoevsky and Kierkegaard in this respect, there are elements of novelistic form *and* ideological evaluation in both their writings.

It is in this respect worth recalling Bakhtin's comment that in a period when the novel becomes the dominant literary form, other genres are assimilated into the novel just as the novel itself expands to incorporate elements from other genres. There thus occurs what Bakhtin calls 'the novelisation of other genres'.[44] If this is, in a sense, already happening in Hegel's evocation of the *bildungsroman* tradition (by the way in which he writes philosophy as the narrative of spirit's journey to itself) then it is even more the case in Kierkegaard – so that the boundaries between what is philosophy and what is literature are radically destabilised and rendered permeable such that the one is readily transposed into the other. Recalling also Bakhtin's comments on the ultimate debt owed by the novel, via satire, to the Socratic dialogues, we may well suspect that it is no coincidence that the novelisation of philosophy in Kierkegaard takes place through the pen of one who was thoroughly steeped in the Platonic dialogues and who never ceased to acknowledge the extent to which Socrates served him as an exemplary model of how a thinker should be.

The value of reading Dostoevsky and Kierkegaard together, then, is that they are mutually-supporting writer-philosophers who describe and analyse for us freedom's dangerous dialogue, a dialogue bounded by the extreme sub- and super-dialogical moments of violence and faith?

Almost, but not quite.

The mention of Socrates enables me to make one further specification. Kierkegaard understood his own project as the Socratic and indirect communication of Christianity: meeting his readers where they were, trapped and blinded by their aesthetic illusions, unmasking the hollowness of their life-views and preparing the way for them to become receptive to the image and voice of Christ. It is striking how susceptible the works he produced in pursuit of this end are to Bakhtinian analysis in purely formal terms – think of *Either/Or*; the Assessor and 'A'; Constantin Constantius and the young poet; Johannes Climacus and his interlocutor, and so on.

My point is not, however, simply to draw attention to this dialogical structure, but to issue a reminder that, for Kierkegaard, the dialogue could not be concluded within the body of the text. The dialogue constituted in and by the text is an appeal to the reader to join in, to decide which of the represented possibilities is for him (or her), to choose. Even if we take the view that Kierkegaard's own hope is quite clear: that the reader chooses faith and the imitation of Christ, it is no less clear that he believed that the ideological personalities of his pseudonyms and the dialogue to which they invited the reader provided the most appropriate means by which that choice could be elicited. Only so could the reader's freedom of choice be honoured and maintained. The finding and vindication of truth was subject to or could only emerge through the full play of the competing voices and views that constituted the social and intellectual world he wrote in and for and that, in its most significant traits, he sought to represent in his writings.

Kierkegaard's programme of indirect communication can therefore remind readers of Dostoevsky that they are not merely spectators at a tragedy, no matter how powerful the emotional catharsis such an experience may offer. In Dostoevsky, as in Kierkegaard, the account of freedom's dangerous dialogue does not lead to final indeterminacy but requires choices that neither author can make for us, because we can only make them for ourselves.

And yet – indeed necessarily – in making this point through Kierkegaard, I do not believe that I am saying anything alien to Dostoevsky. Let me, then, conclude by offering one small example of how such an understanding of the author–text–reader relationship informs a piece of Dostoevskian writing.

My example is 'A little boy at Christ's Christmas tree', a short story from Dostoevsky's *Diary of a Writer* for January 1876. The story describes how a small boy dies of cold and hunger, alone on the streets of St Petersburg, while all around him Christmas is being celebrated and the rich boys and girls are getting their presents from beautifully-adorned Christmas trees. As he dies, he is transported to heaven, where Christ himself gives presents from his own Christmas tree 'for those little children who have no Christmas tree of their own'. The story returns suddenly and harshly to earth:

Next morning, down in the courtyard, porters found the tiny body of a little boy who had hidden behind the piles of kindling wood, and there had frozen to death . . . And why did I invent such a story, one that conforms so little to an ordinary, reasonable diary – and especially a writer's diary? And that, after having promised to write stories pre-eminently about actual events! But the point is that I keep fancying that all this could actually have happened – I mean, the things which happened in the basement and behind the piles of kindling wood. Well, and as regards Christ's Christmas Tree – I really don't know what to tell you, and I don't know whether or not this could have happened. Being a novelist, I have to invent things.[45]

I suggest that Dostoevsky's deliberately laboured point about the mutual limits of novelistic writing and 'reality' shows a literary irony that requires the communication of faith's eschatological hope to be undertaken and understood 'indirectly', as Kierkegaard would have put it.

With these words, Dostoevsky makes clear the limits of his own capacity as a writer. As one, like Kierkegaard, 'without authority', he can only represent the ultimate issues in the oblique medium of literature. The radical freedom that is indeed (as an earlier generation of commentators perceived) vital to the writings of Dostoevsky and Kierkegaard is not a 'message' contained within the body of their writing, but an appeal to the reader that the writing constitutes. This freedom is and can only be actualised in the measure that readers actualise their own freedom by taking responsibility for their own interpretation of the text. Moreover, as this particular Dostoevskian text makes ineluctably clear, the process of interpretation cannot easily be separated from our moral orientation in a world where children die of cold and hunger. To respond appropriately to the appeal of the text is thus to embark upon an ethical and not just an aesthetic education. Naturally, it would require an extensive discussion to justify this claim in the context of an overall reading of our authors, but these remarks may be sufficient to suggest the lines along which I would hope to argue my case. Thus contextualised in the labour of interpretation, the free faith to which both Dostoevsky and Kierkegaard summon us cannot be labelled arbitrary or capricious: it is necessarily difficult, responsible and profoundly moral.

NOTES

1 For a fuller discussion of religion and existentialism see George Pattison, *Anxious Angels: A Retrospective View of Religious Existentialism* (Basingstoke, 1999).

2 The first person to work on developing a substantial link between them seems to have been George Lukács who was planning a book on Dostoevsky in the period immediately preceding the outbreak of the First World War. Lukács used Kierkegaard, about whom he had already written an important essay in the collection *Soul and Form*, to provide several of the key interpretative categories for his study of Dostoevsky. These categories included what he called 'Second Ethics' (i.e. ethics that, following the example of Kierkegaard's Abraham, break with the Kantian requirement of universalisability) and the challenge to a form of Christianity that had aligned itself with the State. The onset of war led to Lukács breaking off this project. However, the notes are published in G. Lukács, *Dostojewski: Notizen und Entwürfe* (Budapest, 1985). Martin Buber, who spoke of Kierkegaard and Dostoevsky 'as the two men of the nineteenth century who will . . . "remain" in the centuries to come'. Maurice S. Friedman in *Martin Buber: A Life of Dialogue* (London, 1955, 35), also seems to have been reading them together in the years prior to the First World War. Perhaps the geographical situation of Austro-Hungary (Buber was based in Vienna) made it the natural site for this meeting of East and West. It is, of course, scarcely coincidental that, despite Lukács's subsequent 'conversion' to Marxism, *Soul and Form* has often been regarded as a proto-existentialist text and that Buber was at this time arriving at the ideas that were to identify him as, in some sense, an 'existentialist' figure.
The only book-length comparative study of which I know is J. Mølle-

have, *Kaerlighed og Daemoni: Hvorfor Fejladvikler Kaerligheden sig?* (Copenhagen, 1992); Møllehave takes as his leitmotif the 'gaze' or manner of looking of various Dostoevskian characters and Kierkegaardian pseudonyms. Although of interest it is not a serious academic study. For other comparative studies see notes 40 and 43 below.

3 Karl Barth, *The Epistle to the Romans*, trans. E. C. Hoskyns (Oxford, 1968), 4.

4 *Ibid.*, 10.

5 *Ibid.*, 117. It is highly characteristic of Barth's rhetoric in *Romans* to 'argue' by means of producing long lists of witnesses to the point of view he is putting forwards – a concrete example of the theological tradition of appealing to authority as a supplement to reason and revelation!

6 *Ibid.*, 252.

7 It is perhaps relevant to note that Barth mentions his indebtedness to his friend Eduard Thurneysen for his knowledge of Dostoevsky and that Thurneysen's book on Dostoevsky (published in 1920) is prefaced with a motto from Kierkegaard's journals!

8 Although he first heard of Kierkegaard shortly before that, when he visited Martin Buber in Frankfurt, where, he reported, Kierkegaard was very much the topic of the day. Benjamin Fondane's memoir suggests that Shestov discussed Kierkegaard with Berdyaev in the early 1900s. Kierkegaard was known to some in Russia at that time, but it seems more likely that Fondane's account, based on conversations with Shestov in the 1930s, is not entirely accurate. See note 9.

9 See N. Baranova-Shestova, *Zhiizn' L'va Shestova po perepiske i vospominaniiam sovremennikov* (Paris, 1988), 58.

10 L. Shestov, *Kierkegaard and the Existential Philosophy* (Athens, OH, 1969), 12. For comment on this as an interpretation of Kierkegaard, see J. M. McLachlan, 'Shestov's reading and misreading of Kierkegaard' in *Canadian Slavonic Papers*, 18, no. 2, 174–86.

11 *Ibid.*, 15.

12 *Ibid.*, 21.

13 *In Job's Balances* (London, 1932), 47.

14 C. Wilson, *The Outsider* (new edn, London, 1978), 172.

15 *Ibid.*, 173.

16 *Ibid.*, 295. Essentially Wilson seems to be returning to the interpretation of Dostoevsky offered by Middleton Murry (see the Editors' Introduction to this volume) and extending it to Kierkegaard.

17 R. Girard, *Things Hidden from the Foundation of the World*, trans. Yvonne Freccero (London, 1987), 148.

18 R. Girard, *Dostoïevski: du double à l'unité* (Paris, 1963), 27.

19 *Ibid.*, 49f.

20 R. Girard, *Deceit, Desire and the Novel*, trans. Stephen Bann and Michael Metteer (Baltimore, MD, 1965), 41–42.

21 *Ibid.*, 59.

22 *Ibid.*, 282.
23 *Ibid.*, 288.
24 *Ibid.*, 314.
25 M. Bakhtin, *Problems of Dostoevsky's Poetics*, ed. and trans. Caryl Emerson (Minneapolis, MN, 1984), 287.
26 *Ibid.*, 58.
27 S. Kierkegaard, *Attack upon 'Christendom'*, trans. Walter Lawrie (Princeton, NJ, 1968), 7.
28 S. Kierkegaard, *Journals and Papers*, trans. and ed. Hong and Hong, vol. 3 (Bloomington, IN, 1975), 333.
29 *Ibid.*, 338.
30 See *ibid.*, 333.
31 S. Kierkegaard, *Edifying Discourses*, trans. Walter Lawrie (London, 1958), 225–26.
32 I have elsewhere written about the vital role played by art – and above all the theatre – in this process. See G. Pattison, *Kierkegaard: The Aesthetic and the Religious* (Basingstoke, 1992; 2nd edn London, 1999), especially Chapter 4.
33 S. Kierkegaard, *Two Ages*, trans. Walter Lawrie (Princeton, NJ, 1978), 83.
34 Kierkegaard, *Journals and Papers* vol. 4, 139.
35 *Ibid.*, 149.
36 S. Kierkegaard, *Gospel of Sufferings*, trans. A. S. Aldworth and W. S. Ferrie (London, 1955), 134–35.
37 *Ibid.*, 133.
38 Kierkegaard, *Two Ages*, 109.
39 D. McCracken, *The Scandal of the Gospels* (New York, 1994) is the most complete interpretation of Kierkegaard in the light of Girardian ideas to date. McCracken also connects his reading of Kierkegaard/Girard with Bakhtin.
40 For an excellent summary of Bakhtin's own reading of Kierkegaard and the connections between Bakhtin's dialogism and Kierkegaardian indirect communication see A. Fryszman, 'Kierkegaard and Dostoyevsky seen through Bakhtin's prism' in *Kierkegaardiana*, 18 (1996). See also his articles ' "Teoria kommiunikatsii" Seriona K'erkegora i dialogicheskoe mishlenie Bakhtina' in *Wiener Slawistischer Almanach*, 31 (1993), 39–55; 'Ia i Drugoi: Kritika romanticheskogo soznania y Bakhtina i K'erkegor' in *Russian Literature XXXVIII* (1995), 273–94; and 'Dostoevskii i K'erkegor: Dialog i molchanie' in A. Fryszman (ed.) *Mir Kierkegorda* (Moscow: Ad Marginem, 1994). See also G. Pattison 'If Kierkegaard is right about reading, why read Kierkegaard' in N.-J. Cappelørn and H. Deuser (eds.) *Kierkegaard Revisited: Kierkegaard Monograph Series I* (Berlin, 1997); and T. V. Shitzova, 'Ekzistentsial'nyi analiz esteticheskogo sposoba bitiia y K'erkegora' in T. V. Shitzova, *K'erkegor i sovremennost'* (Minsk, 1996).

41 Bakhtin, op. cit., 78.

42 *Journals and Papers* vol. 1, 302.

43 As, for example (and with varying qualifications), in Geoffrey Clive, 'The sickness unto death in the underworld' in *The Harvard Theological Review*, 51 (1958), 133–67; John L. Greenway, 'Kierkegaardian doubles in *Crime and Punishment*' in *Orbis Litterarum*, 33 (1978), 45–60; Cyrena Pondrom, 'Two demonic figures: Kierkegaard's Merman and Dostoevsky's Underground Man' in *Orbis Litterarum*, 23 (1968), 161–77; Einar Thomassen, 'Kierkegaard og Dostojevskij' in *Edda*, 55 (1955), 246–65.

44 M. M. Bakhtin, *The Dialogic Imagination*, ed. Michael Holquist, trans. Caryl Emerson and Michael Holquist (Austin, TX, 1989), 5–6.

45 F. M. Dostoevsky, *The Diary of A Writer*, trans. Boris Brasol (Haslemere, 1984), 172.

Bibliography

This bibliography contains all the sources cited in this volume as well as a selection of recommended studies relating to the religious dimension in Dostoevsky's works.

I   PRIMARY SOURCES

Dostoevskii, F. M., *Polnoe sobranie sochinenii v tridtsati tomax* (Leningrad, 1972–90)

Polnoe sobranie sochinenii: Kanonicheskie teksty, ed. V. N. Zakharov (Petrozavodsk, 1995–)

Neizdannyi Dostoevskii: Zapisnye knizhki i tetradi 1860–1881, ed. V. R. Shcherbina, *Literaturnoe nasledstvo*, 83 (Moscow, 1971)

Dostoevsky, F. M., *Crime and Punishment*, trans. D. Magarshack (Harmondsworth, 1970)

The Brothers Karamazov, trans. David Magarshack (Harmondsworth, 1958)

The Brothers Karamazov: The Garnett Translation, Revised by Ralph E. Matlaw: Backgrounds and Sources, Essays in Criticism, ed. Ralph E. Matlaw (New York, 1976)

The Brothers Karamazov, trans. Richard Pevear and Larissa Volokhonsky (New York, 1990)

Crime and Punishment, trans. Jessie Senior Coulson, Norton Critical Edition with Backgrounds, Sources and Essays in Criticism, ed. George Gibian (New York, 1975, 3rd edn, 1989)

The Demons, trans. Richard Pevear and Larissa Volokhonsky (London, 1994)

Devils, trans. and ed. Michael R. Kate (Oxford, 1992)

The Diary of a Writer, 2 vols., trans. and ed. Boris Brasol (New York, 1949), reprinted (Salt Lake City, UT, 1985)

The Gospel in Dostoyevsky: Selections from His Works, ed. Hutterian Brethren (Ulster Park, NY, 1988)

The Idiot, trans. David Magarshack (Harmondsworth, 1955; reprinted with new pagination, 1986)

Letters of Fyodor Michailovitch Dostoevsky, trans. Ethel Colburn Mayne (New York, 1964)
Notes from Underground, trans. Richard Pevear and Larissa Volokhonsky (London, 1993)
A Raw Youth, trans. Constance Garnett (New York, 1950)
The Gospel in Dostoevsky: Selections from His Works, ed. the Hutterian Brethren (Ulster Park, NY, 1988)
Terras, Victor, *A Karamazov Companion: Commentary on the Genesis, Language and Style of Dostoevsky's Novel* (Madison, WI, 1981)
Dostoevskaia, A. G., *Vospominaniia* (Moscow, 1971)
Bible, Russian Testament, *Gospoda nashego Iisusa Khrista Novyi zavet*, 2nd edn (St Petersburg, 1823)
The Jerusalem Bible (Garden City, NY, 1966)
Kniga khvalenii ili Psaltir', 3rd edn (St Petersburg, 1822)
Molitvoslov (St Petersburg, 1908)
Dal', Vladimir. *Tolkovyi slovar' zhivogo velikorusskago iazkya*, 4 vols., 4th edn, ed. I. A. Boduen-de-Courtene (St Petersburg–Moscow, 1912)
New Catholic Encyclopedia, 17 vols. (New York, 1967–74)

Anthologies

A Treasury of Russian Spirituality, ed. G. P. Fedotov (New York, 1950)
Medieval Russia's Epics, Chronicles, and Tales, ed. Serge A. Zenkovsky (New York, 1963)
A History of Russian Literature: 11th–17th centuries, ed. Dmitry Likhachev (Moscow, 1989)
An Anthology of Russian Literature from Earliest Writings to Modern Fiction: Introduction to a Culture, ed. Nicholas Rzhevsky (London, 1996)
Vlastitel' dum: Dostoevskii v russkoi kritike kontsa XIX – nachala XX veka, ed. N. Ashimbaeva (St Petersburg, 1997)

2 SECONDARY SOURCES

Abramovich, D. I., ed., *Kievo-Pechers'kii paterik* (Kiev, 1930)
Afanasiev, Nikolai, 'Vlast' liubvi: K probleme prava i blagodati', *Trudy Pravoslavnogo Bogoslovskogo Instituta v Parizhe*, 14 (Paris, 1971), 5–23
Allain, Louis, *Dostoïevski et Dieu: La morsure du divin* (Lille, 1981)
Andreyev, Nikolay, 'Literature in the Muscovite Period (1300–1700)', *An Introduction to Russian Language and Literature*, eds. Robert Auty and Dimitri Obolensky (Cambridge, 1980), 90–110
Antonovich, M. A., *Izbrannye stat'i* (Leningrad, 1938)
Arseniev, Nicholas, *Russian Piety*, trans. Asheleigh Moorhouse (London, 1964)
Auerbach, Erich, *Mimesis: The Representation of Reality in Western Literature*, trans. Willard R. Trask (Princeton, NJ, 1974)

'Figura', *Scenes from the Drama of European Literature*, Theory and History of Literature, 9 (Minneapolis, MN, 1984)

'*Sermo Humilis*', *Literary Language and its Public in late Latin Antiquity and in the Middle Ages*, trans. Ralph Manheim (Princeton, NJ, 1993), 27–66

St Augustine, *Confessions*, trans. Vernon J. Bourke (Washington DC, 1953)

Averintsev, Sergei, 'Zhan Mariten, neotomizm i katolicheskaia teologiia iskusstva', *Religiia i Literatura* (Ann Arbor, MI, 1981), 121–38

Bakhtin, Mikhail, *Problemy tvorchestva Dostoevskogo* (Leningrad, 1929)

Voprosy literatury i estetiki (Moscow, 1975)

Problemy poetiki Dostoevskogo, 4th edn (Moscow, 1979)

Estetika slovesnogo tvorchestva (Moscow, 1979)

The Dialogic Imagination, ed. Michael Holquist, trans. Caryl Emerson and Michael Holquist (Austin, TX, 1981)

Problems of Dostoevsky's Poetics, ed. and trans. Caryl Emerson (Minneapolis, MN, 1984)

Speech Genres and Other Late Essays, trans. Vern M. McGee, eds. Caryl Emerson and Michael Holquist (Austin, TX, 1986)

Balthasar, Hans Urs von, *The Glory of the Lord: A Theological Aesthetics*, vol. 3, *Studies in Theological Style: Lay Styles*, ed. John Riches, trans. Andrew Louth, John Saward, Martin Simon and Rowan Williams (San Francisco, CA, 1986)

Baranova-Shestova, N., *Zhizn' L'va Shestova po perepiske i vospominaniiam sovremennikov* (Paris, 1988)

Barth, Karl, *The Epistle to the Romans*, trans. E. C. Hoskyns (Oxford, 1968)

Beckwith, John, *Early Christian and Byzantine Art* (Harmondsworth, 1979)

Belinkis, a. S., *F. M. Dostoevskii* (Leningrad, 1960)

Belinsky, Vissarion Grigorovitch, *Izbrannye sochineniia* (Moscow, 1941)

Polnoe sobranie sochinenii (Moscow, 1953–59)

Belknap, Robert L., *The Structure of The Brothers Karamazov* (The Hague, 1967)

The Genesis of The Brothers Karamazov: The Aesthetics, Ideology, and Psychology of Making a Text (Evanston, IL, 1990)

Bely, Andrei, *Tragediia tvorchestva: Dostoevskii i Tolstoi* (Moscow, 1911)

Bem, A. L., 'Dramatizatsiia breda (*Khoziaika* Dostoevskogo)', *O Dostoevskom*, 1 (Prague, 1929), 77–124

'*Skupoi rytsar'* v tvorchestve Dostoevskogo', *O Dostoevskom: sbornik statei*, vol. 3 (Prague, 1936), 115–17

'*Faust* v tvorchestve Dostoevskogo', Fascicle 5, *Russkii Svobodnyi Universitet v Prage: Zapiski nauchno-issledovatel'skogo ob'' edineniia* (Prague, 1973), 109–43

Berdiaev, Nikolai, *Mirosozertsanie Dostoevskogo* (Prague, 1923)

Berdyaev, Nicholas, *The Russian Revolution* (London, 1931)

Dostoievsky, trans. Donald Attwater (London, 1934), reprinted as *Dostoevsky* (New York, 1957)

Berman, M., *All That Is Solid Melts Into Air: The Experience of Modernity* (London, 1983)

Besançon, Alain, *L'image invisible* (Paris, 1984)
Bethea, David M., *The Shape of Apocalypse in Modern Russian Fiction* (Princeton, NJ, 1989)
Billington, James H., *The Icon and the Axe: An Interpretative History of Russian Culture* (New York, 1970)
Bitsilli, P. M., 'K voprosu o vnutrennei forme romana Dostoevskogo', *O Dostoevskom: Stat'i*, ed. Donald Fanger, Brown University Slavic Reprints, 4 (Providence, RI, 1966), 1–72
'Pochemu Dostoevskii ne napisal "Zhitia velikogo greshnika"', *O Dostoevskom: sbornik statei*, vol. 2, ed. A. L. Bem (Prague, 1933), 25–30
Bocharov, S. G., 'Ob odnom razgovore i vokrug nego', *Novoe literaturnoe obozrenie*, 2 (1993), 70–89
Boff, Leonardo, *Trinity and Society*, trans. Paul Burns (Tunbridge Wells, Maryknoll, NY, 1988)
Bolshakoff, Sergius, *Russian Mystics* (Kalamazoo, MI, 1977)
Børtnes, Jostein, 'The Function of Hagiography in Dostoevskij's Novels', *Scando-Slavica*, 24 (1978), 27–33
'The last delusion in an infinite series of delusions: Stavrogin and the symbolic structure of *The Devils*', *Dostoevsky Studies*, 4 (1983) 53–67
'Polyphony in *The Brothers Karamazov*: Variations on a theme', *Canadian–American Slavic Studies*, 17 (Fall, 1983), 402–11
Visions of Glory (Oslo, 1988)
'The Literature of Old Russia, 988–1730', *The Cambridge History of Russian Literature*, rev. edn, ed. Charles A. Moser (Cambridge, 1992), 1–44
'Dostoevskij's idiot or the poetics of emptiness', *Scando-Slavica*, 40 (1994), 5–14
'Russkii kenotizm: k pereotsenke odnogo poniatiia', *Evangel'skii tekst v russkoi literature XVIII–XX vekov*, ed. V. N. Zakharov (Petrozavodsk, 1994), 61–65
'Dostoevskian fools: holy and unholy', *The Holy Fool in Byzantium and Russia* (Bergen, 1995), 18–34
'"Khristos-otets": k probleme protivopostavleniia ottsa krovnogo i ottsa zakonnogo v *Podrostke* Dostoevskogo', *Evangel'skii tekst v russkoi literature XVIII–XX vekov*, 2, ed. V. N. Zakharov (Petrozavodsk, 1998), 409–15
'Religion', *The Cambridge Companion to the Classic Russian Novel*, ed. Malcolm V. Jones and Robin Feuer Miller (Cambridge, 1998), 104–29
Braun, Maximilian *Dostojewskij: Das Gesamtwerk als Vielfalt und Einheit* (Gottingen, 1976)
Bulgakov, S. N., 'Ivan Karamazov kak filosofskii tip', *Ot marksizma k idealizmu* (St Petersburg, 1903), 83–112
Bulgakov, Sergy, *The Orthodox Church*, trans. Thomas Hopko, revised Lydia Kesich (Crestwood, NY, 1988)
Cascardi, Anthony J., *The Bounds of Reason: Cervantes, Dostoevsky, Flaubert* (New York, 1986)
Cassedy, Steven, 'The formal problem of the epilogue in *Crime and Punish-*

ment: the logic of tragic and Christian structures', *Dostoevsky Studies*, 3 (1982), 171–90

Castro, Américo, 'Incarnation in *Don Quijote*', *An Idea of History: Selected Essays of Américo Castro*, trans. and eds. Stephen Gilman and Edmund L. King (Columbus, OH, 1977), 23–76

'An Introduction to the *Quixote*', *An Idea of History: Selected Essays of Américo Castro*, trans. and eds. Stephen Gilman and Edmund L. King (Columbus, OH, 1977)

Catteau, Jacques, *La Création Littéraire chez Dostoïevski* (Paris, 1978)

'The paradox of the legend of the Grand Inquisitor in *The Brothers Karamazov*', *Dostoevsky: New Perspectives*, ed. Robert Louis Jackson (Englewood Cliffs, N J, 1984), 243–54

Dostoevsky and the Process of Literary Creation, trans. A. Littlewood (Cambridge, 1989)

Cervantes, Miguel de, *Don Quixote*, trans. J. M. Cohen (Harmondsworth, 1950)

Chernyshevskii, N. G., *Polnoe sobranie sochinenii* (Moscow, 1950)

Chirkov, N. M., *O stile Dostoevskogo* (Moscow, 1967)

Chizhevski, D., 'Schiller und die Brüder Karamazoff', *Zeitschrift für Slavische Philologie*, 6 (Leipzig, 1929), 1–42

'The theme of the double in Dostoevsky', *Dostoevsky: A Collection of Critical Essays*, ed. René Wellek (Englewood Cliffs, NJ, 1962), 112–29

Clark, Katerina and Holquist, Michael, *Mikhail Bakhtin* (Cambridge, MA, 1994)

Clive, Geoffrey, 'The sickness unto death in the underworld', *The Harvard Theological Review*, 51 (1958) 133–67

Coates, Ruth, *Christianity in Bakhtin: God and the Exiled Author* (Cambridge, 1998)

Cornwell, Neil (ed.) *Reference Guide to Russian Literature* (London, 1998)

Cox, Roger, *Between Earth and Heaven: Shakespeare, Dostoevsky and the Meaning of Christian Tragedy* (New York, 1969)

Crowder, C., 'The appropriation of Dostoevsky in the early twentieth century: Cult, counter-cult, and incarnation', *European Literature and Theology in the Twentieth Century: Ends of Time*, eds. D. Jasper and Colin Crowder (London, 1990), 15–33

Cunningham, David S., 'Trinitarian rhetoric in Murdoch, Morrison, and Dostoevsky', *Literature and Theology at Century's End*, eds. Robert Detweiler and Gregory L. Salyers (Atlanta, GA, 1995), 189–213

These Three Are One: The Practice of Trinitarian Theology (Oxford, 1997)

'Trinitarian theology since 1990', *Reviews in Religion and Theology* 2, no. 4 (1995), 8–16

'What's [not] new in trinitarian theology', *Reviews in Religion and Theology* 4, no. 1 (1997), 14–20

Díaz, Santiago Montero, 'Cervantes en Turguenief y Dostoyevsky', *Revista de Estudio Políticos*, 15 (Madrid, 1946), 111–42

Dudkin, V. V. 'Dostoevskii i Evangelie ot Ioanna', *Evangel'skii tekst v Russkoi literature XVIII–XX vekov*, 2, ed. V. N. Zakharov (Petrozavodsk, 1998), 337–48

Durylin, Sergei, 'Ob odnom simvole u Dostoevskogo: Opyt tematicheskogo obzora', *Dostoevskii* (Moscow, 1928), 163–98

Egeberg, E., 'F. M. Dostoevskii v poiskakh polozhitel'no prekrasnogo cheloveka. *Selo Stepanchikovo* i *Idiot*', *Evangel'skii tekst v russkoi literature XVIII–XX vekov*, 2, ed. V. N. Zakharov (Petrozavodsk, 1998), 385–90

'How should we then read *The Idiot?*', *Cultural Discontinuity and Reconstruction: The Byzanto-Slav Heritage and the Creation of a Russian National Literature in the Nineteenth Century*, eds. Jostein Børtnes and Ingunn Lunde (Oslo, 1997), 163–69

Ermilov, V., *F. M. Dostoevskii* (Moscow, 1956)

Esaulov, I. A., *Kategoriia sobornosti v russkoi literature* (Petrozavodsk, 1995)

'Paskhal'nyi arkhetip v poetike Dostoevskogo', *Evangel'skii tekst v russkoi literature XVIII–XX vekov*, 2, ed. V. N. Zakharov (Petrozavodsk, 1998), 349–62

'Iurodstvo i shutovstvo v russkoi literature: Nekotorye nabliudeniia', *Literaturnoe obozrenie*, no. 3 (1998), 108–12

Evdokimov, Paul, *Gogol et Dostoïevsky ou la descente aux enfers* (Bruges, 1961)

Fanger, Donald, *Dostoevsky and Romantic Realism* (Chicago, IL, 1974)

Fasting, Sigurd, 'Transformacija filantropičeskix epizodov u Dostoevskogo', *International Dostoevsky Studies*, 1 (1980), 65–72

Fedorov, N. F., *Filosofiia obshchego dela* (Moscow, 1906)

Fedotov, George P., *The Russian Religious Mind*, 2 vols. (Cambridge, MA, 1966)

The Collected Works of George P. Fedotov, 3 vols. (Belmont, MA, 1975)

Sviatye drevnei Rusi (Paris, 1985)

Fennell, J. and Stokes, A., *Early Russian Literature* (London, 1974)

Ferrari, Leo C., 'Beyond Augustine's conversion scene', *Augustine: From Rhetor to Theologian* (Waterloo, ON, 1992), 97–108

Figes, Orlando and Boris Kolonitskii, *Interpreting the Russian Revolution: The Language and Symbols of 1917* (New Haven, CT, 1999)

Filosofov, D. V., *Staroe i novoe* (Moscow, 1912)

Flay, Joseph C., Review of 'Communicative praxis and the space of subjectivity, philosophy and rhetoric', by Calvin O. Schrag, *Philosophy and Rhetoric*, 21, no. 4 (1988), 294–304

Florovsky, Archpriest Georges, *Bible, Church, Tradition: An Eastern Orthodox View* (Belmont, MA, 1972)

Ways of Russian Theology, Part 1, *Collected Works of Georges Florovsky*, vol. 5, ed. Richard S. Haugh, trans. Robert L. Nicholas (Belmont, MA, 1979)

'Three masters: Gogol, Dostoevsky, Tolstoy', *Epiphany: A Journal of Faith and Insight*, 10 (Summer 1990), 43–58

Florovskii, Archpriest Georges, *Puti russkogo bogosloviia*, 2nd edn, intro. Archpriest Meiendorf (Paris, 1981; 1st edn Paris, 1937)

Frank, Joseph, *Dostoevsky: The Seeds of Revolt, 1821–1849* (Princeton, NJ, 1976)
Dostoevsky: The Years of Ordeal, 1850–1859 (Princeton, NJ, 1983)
Dostoevsky: The Stir of Liberation, 1860–1865 (Princeton, NJ, 1986)
Dostoevsky: The Miraculous Years, 1865–1871 (Princeton, NJ, 1995)
Fridlender, G. M., *Dostoevskii i mirovaia literatura* (Moscow, 1979)
'Ot *Podrostka* k *Brat'iam Karamazovym*', *Dostoevsky Studies*, 7 (1986), 3–10
Friedman, Maurice S., *Martin Buber: A Life of Dialogue* (London, 1955)
Frye, Northrop, *The Great Code: The Bible and Literature* (London, 1982)
Fryszman, A., ' "Teoria kommiunikatsii" Seriona K'erkegora i dialogiches-koe mishlenie Bakhtina', *Wiener Slawistischer Almanach*, 31 (1993) 33–55
'Dostoevskii i K'erkegor: Dialog i molchanie', ed. A. Fryszman, *Mir Kierkegorda* (Moscow, 1994), 106–122
'Ia i drugoi. Kritika romanticheskogo soznania y Bakhtina i K'erkegor', *Russian Literature XXXVIII* (1995), 273–94
'Kierkegaard and Dostoyevsky seen through Bakhtin's prism', *Kierke-gaardiana*, 18 (1996), 100–25
Fuentes, Carlos, *Don Quixote, or the Critique of Reading* (Austin, TX, 1976)
Gadamer, Hans-Georg, 'The relevance of the beautiful: Art as symbol, play, and festival', *The Relevance of the Beautiful and Other Essays*, ed. Robert Bernasconi, trans. Nicholas Walker (Cambridge, 1986)
Gerigk, Horst-Jürgen, 'Der Mörder Smerdjakow: Bemerkungen zu Dosto-jewskijs Typologie der Kriminellen Persönlichkeit', *Dostoevsky Studies*, 7 (1986), 107–22
Gertsen, A. I., *Sobranie sochinenii v deviati tomakh* (Moscow, 1955–58)
Gessen, S. I., 'Tragediia dobra v *'Brat'iakh Karamazovykh* Dostoevskogo', in *O Dostoevskom: Stat'i*, ed. Donald Fanger (Providence, RI, 1966), 197–229
Gibson, A. Boyce, *The Religion of Dostoevsky* (London, 1973)
Girard, René *Dostoïevski: du double à l'unité* (Paris, 1963)
Deceit, Desire and the Novel, trans. Stephen Bann and Michael Metteer (Baltimore, MD, 1976)
Things Hidden from the Foundation of the World, trans. Yvonne Freccero (London, 1987)
Resurrection from the Underground, trans. James G. Williams (New York, 1997)
Giusti, Wolfgango L., 'Sul *donchischiottismo* di alcuni personaggi del Dosto-hevskij', *Cultura*, 10 (1931), 171–79
Golubov, Alexander, 'Religious imagery in the structure of *The Brothers Karamazov*', *Russian and Slavic Literature: 1700–1917*, ed. Richard Free-born (Bloomington, IN, 1976), 113–36
Gornostaev, A. K., *Rai na zemle: K ideologii tvorchestva F. M Dostoevskogo* (Harbin, 1929)
Gorodetzky, Nadejda, *Saint Tikhon of Zadonsk: Inspirer of Dostoevsky* (Crest-wood, NY, 1976)
Greenway, John L., 'Kierkegaardian doubles in *Crime and Punishment*', *Orbis Litteratum*, 33 (1978) 45–60
St Gregory of Nazianzus, *Faith Gives Fullness to Reasoning: The Five Theological*

Bibliography

Orations of Gregory Nazianzen, ed. Frederick W. Norris, trans. Lionel Wickham and Frederick Williams, *Supplements to Vigiliae Christianae*, vol. 13 (Leiden, 1991)

Gregory of Nyassa, *Select Writings and Letters*, trans. William Moore and Henry Wilson, *The Nicene and Post-Nicene Fathers of the Christian Church*, 5, 2nd series 1892 (Grand Rapids, MI, 1979)

Grossman, Leonid, *Poetika Dostoevskogo* (Moscow, 1925)

'Put' Dostoevskogo', *Tvorchestvo Dostoevskogo, Sbornik statei i materialov*, ed. L. P. Grossman (Chicago, IL, 1970), 83–108

Guevara, F. Maldonado de, 'Dostoievski y el *Quijote*', *Anales Cervantinos*, vol. 3 (1953), 367–75

Gunton, Colin, *The Promise of Trinitarian Theology* (Edinburgh, 1990)

The One, The Three and the Many: God, Creation, and the Culture of Modernity (Cambridge, 1993)

Hackel Sergei, 'F. M. Dostoevsky (1821–1881): Prophet Manqué', *Dostoevsky Studies*, 3 (1982), 5–25

'The religious dimension: Vision or evasion? Zosima's discourse in *The Brothers Karamazov*', in *New Essays on Dostoevsky*, ed. M. V. Jones and G. Terry (Cambridge, 1983), 139–68

Hamilton, W., 'Banished from the land of unity: Dostoyevsky's religious vision through the eyes of Dmitry, Ivan and Alyosha Karamazov', *Radical Theology and the Death of God*, eds. T. J. J. Altizer and W. Hamilton (Harmondsworth, 1968), 65–94

Hick, John, *Evil and the God of Love* (London, 1968)

Hilarion (Ilarion), Metropolitan of Kiev, *Slovo o Zakone i Blagodati* (Moscow, 1994)

Hollander, Robert, 'The apocalyptic framework of Dostoevsky's *The Idiot*', *Mosaic*, 6 (1974) 123–39

Holquist, Michael, *Dostoevsky and the Novel* (Princeton, NJ, 1977)

Hutchings, Stephen C., *Russian Modernism: The Transfiguration of the Everyday* (Cambridge, 1997)

Ivanov, Viacheslav, 'Dostoevskii i roman-tragediia', *Borozdi i mezhi* (Moscow, 1916)

Freedom and the Tragic Life: A Study of Dostoevsky, trans. Norman Cameron (New York, 1960)

Po zvezdam, Bradda Rarity Reprints, 25 (Letchworth, 1971)

Ivanov, V. V., 'Iurodivyi geroi v dialoge ierarkhii Dostoevskogo', *Evangel'skii tekst v russkoi literature XVIII–XX vekov*, ed. V. N. Zakharov (Petrozavodsk, 1994), 201–9

Jackson, Robert Louis, *Dostoevsky's Quest for Form: A Study of His Philosophy of Art*, 2nd edn (New Haven, CT and London, 1966)

'The triple vision: The peasant Marey', *Yale Review* (Winter, 1978), 225–35

The Art of Dostoevsky, Deliriums and Nocturnes (Princeton, NJ, 1981)

Dialogues with Dostoevsky: The Overwhelming Questions (Stanford, CA, 1993)

Jakobson, Roman, 'Quest for the essence of language', *Selected Works II* (The Hague, 1971), 345–59

'Two aspects of language and two types of aphasic disturbances', *Selected Works II* (The Hague, 1971), 239–59

Jarrett-Kerr, Martin, *Studies in Literature and Belief* (London, 1954)

Jasper, D., *The Study of Literature and Religion: An Introduction* (Basingstoke and London, 1989)

Jenson, Robert W., *The Triune Identity: God According to the Gospel* (Philadelphia, PA, 1982)

Johae, A., 'Idealism and the dialectic in *The Brothers Karamazov*', *F. M. Dostoevsky 1821–1881: A Centenary Volume*, ed. Leon Burnett (Colchester, 1981), 109–17

'Dostoevsky's Walls and Holbein's Paintings', *Germano-Slavica*, (1992–93), 102–5

'Expressive symbols in Dostoevsky's *Crime and Punishment*', *Scottish Slavonic Review* 20 (1993), 17–22

'Retractive imagery: Dostoevsky and German Romanticism', *Germano-Slavica*, 8, no. 2 (1994), 3–15

'The Russian Sources of George Orwell's *Nineteen Eighty-Four*', *New Comparison*, 17 (1994), 138–49

'Groundwork for a comparative study of Dostoevsky and Kafka', *Germano-Slavica*, 10, no. 1 (1997)

Jommi, Goffredo, *Realität der irrealen Dichtung: Don Quijote und Dante* (Hamburg, 1964)

Jones, John, *Dostoevsky* (Oxford, 1983)

Jones, Malcolm V., *Dostoyevsky: The Novel of Discord* (London, 1976)

'"The Legend of the Grand Inquisitor": The suppression of the second temptation and dialogue with God', *Dostoevsky Studies*, 7 (1986), 123–34

Dostoevsky After Bakhtin: Readings in Dostoevsky's Fantastic Realism (Cambridge, 1990)

'Silence in *The Brothers Karamazov*', '*Die Brüder Karamasow*': Dostojevskijs letzter Roman in heutiger Sicht*, ed. Horst-Jürgen Gerigk (Dresden, 1997), 29–46

'The death and resurrection of Orthodoxy in the works of Dostoevskii', *Cultural Discontinuity and Reconstruction, the Byzanto-Slav Heritage and the Creation of a Russian National Literature in the Nineteenth Century*, eds. Jostein Børtnes and Ingunn Lunde (Oslo, 1997), 143–67

Jüngel, Eberhard, *The Doctrine of the Trinity: God's Being is in Becoming*, trans. Norton Harris (Edinburgh, 1976)

God as the Mystery of the World, trans. Darrell L. Guder (Grand Rapids, MI, 1983)

Kant, Immanuel, 'Degrees of responsibility', *Readings in the Problem of Ethics*, ed. Rosalind Ekman (New York, 1965), 234–40

Kantor, Vladimir, *Brat'ia Karamazovy F. Dostoevskogo* (Moscow, 1983)

V poiskakh lichnosti: Opyt russkoi klassiki (Moscow, 1994)

Kariakin, Iu., *Dostoevskii i kanun XXI veka* (Moscow, 1989)

Karlova, T. S., *Dostoevskii i russkii sud* (Kazan, 1975)

Kasper, Walter, *The God of Jesus Christ*, trans. Matthew J. O'Connell (London, 1983)

Kaye, Peter, *Dostoevsky and English Modernism 1900–1930* (Cambridge, 1999)

Khrapovitskii, Metropolitan Antonii, *Pastyrskoe izuchenie liudei i zhizni po sochineniiam F. M. Dostoevskogo* (Kazan, 1898)

Kierkegaard, S., *Gospel of Sufferings*, trans. A. S. Aldworth and W. S. Ferrie (London, 1955)

Edifying Discourses, trans. Walter Lawrie (London, 1958)

Attack upon 'Christendom', trans. Walter Lawrie (Princeton, NJ, 1944, 1968)

Two Ages, trans. Walter Lawrie (Princeton, NJ, 1978)

Journals and Papers, vol. 3, eds. Hong and Hong (Bloomington, IN, 1975)

Kiiko, E. I., 'Iz istorii sozdaniia *Brat'ev Karamazovykh*: Ivan i Smerdiakov', *Dostoevskii: Materialy i issledovaniia*, 2 (Leningrad, 1976), 125–29

'Dostoevskii i Renan', *Materialy i issledovaniia*, 4, ed. G. M. Fridlender (Leningrad, 1980), 106–22

Kjetsaa, Geir, *Dostoevsky and his New Testament* (Oslo, Atlantic Highlands, NJ, 1984)

Fyodor Dostoyevsky: A Writer's Life, trans. Siri Hustvedt and David McDuff (New York, 1987)

Klyuchevsky, V. O., *Drevnerusskiia zhitiia sviatykh kak istoricheskii istochnik* (Moscow, 1871)

'Velikie minei chetii, sobrannye vserossiiskim Mitropolitom Makariem', *Sbornik statei*, 3 vols. (Petrograd, 1918)

Knapp, Liza, 'Myshkin through a glass, guessingly', *Dostoevsky's 'The Idiot': A Critical Companion*, ed. Liza Knapp (Evanston, IL, 1998), 191–215

Komarovich, V. L., 'Dostoevskii i Geine', *Sovremennyi mir* (1916), no. 10, 100–04

Kovács, Arpád, 'The narrative model of the novel of *Awakening*: Dostoevsky', *Acta Litteraria Academiae Scientiarum Hungaricae*, 25 (1983), 359–73

Kovalevsky, Pierre, *Saint Sergius and Russian Spirituality* (Crestwood, NY, 1976)

Kristeva, Julia, *Black Sun: Depression and Melancholia*, trans. Leon S. Roudiez (New York, 1989)

Kunilsky, A. E., 'Problema "smekh i khristianstvo" v romane Dostoevskogo *Brat'ia Karamazovy*', *Evangel'skii tekst v russkoi literature XVIII–XX vekov*, ed. V. N. Zakharov (Petrozavodsk, 1994), 192–200

'O khristianskom kontekste v romane F. M. Dostoevskogo *Idiot*', *Evangel'skii tekst v russkoi literature XVIII–XX vekov*, 2, ed. V. N. Zakharov (Petrozavodsk, 1998), 391–408

LaCugna, Catherine Mowry, 'Philosophers and Theologians on the Trinity', *Modern Theology*, 2, no. 3 (April 1986), 169–81

'Current trends in trinitarian theology', *Religious Studies Review*, 13, no. 2 (April 1987), 141–47

God For Us: The Trinity and Christian Life (San Francisco, CA, 1991)

Langan, Janine, 'Icon vs. myth: Dostoevsky, feminism and pornography', in *Religion and Literature*, 18, no. 1 (Spring 1986), 63–72

Lapshin, I. I., 'Kak slozhilas' legenda o Velikom Inkvizitore', *O Dostoevskom: sbornik statei* I, ed. A. L. Bem (Prague, 1929), 125–39

Lawrence, D. H., 'Preface to Dostoevsky's *The Grand Inquisitor*', *Dostoevsky: A Collection of Critical Essays*, ed. René Wellek (Englewood Cliffs, NJ, 1962), 90–97

Leatherbarrow, W. J., 'Apocalyptic imagery in Dostoevsky's *The Idiot* and *The Devils*', *Dostoevsky Studies*, 3 (1982), 43–51

Leontiev, K., *Sobranie sochinenii*, 9 vols. (Moscow, 1912)

Likhachev, D. S., *Chelovek v literature drevnei Rusi* (Moscow–Leningrad, 1958)

'"Predislovnyi rasskaz" Dostoevskogo', *Poetika i stilistika russkoi literatury: Pamiati adademika Vitora Vladimirovicha Vinogradova* (Leningrad, 1971), 189–94

'"Nebrezhenie slovom" u Dostoevskogo', *Materialy i issledovaniia*, 2 (Leningrad, 1976), 30–41

'Tezisy doklada o staroi orfografii: 1928', *Stat'i rannikh let* (Tver', 1993), 6–14

Linnér, Sven, *Starets Zosima in 'The Brothers Karamazov': A Study in the Mimesis of Virtue* (Stockholm, 1975)

Losskii, N. O., *Dostoevskii i ego khristianskoe miroponimanie* (New York, 1946)

Bog i mirovoe zlo (Moscow, 1994)

Lossky, V., *The Mystical Theology of the Eastern Church* (London, 1957)

The Vision of God, trans. A. Moorhouse (London, 1963)

In the Image and Likeness of God, eds. J. H. Erickson and T. E. Bird (London, 1975)

Lotman, L. M., 'Romany Dostoevskogo i russkaia legenda', *Russkaja literatura*, 15, no. 2 (1972), 129–41

Lotman, Yuri M., *Universe of the Mind: A Semiotic Theory of Culture*, intro. Umberto Eco, trans. Ann Shukman (London, New York, 1990)

Kul'tura i vzryv (Moscow, 1992)

Lubac, H. de, *The Drama of Atheist Humanism* (London, 1949)

Lukács, Georg, 'Dostoevsky', *Dostoevsky: A Collection of Critical Essays*, ed. René Wellek (Englewood Cliffs, NJ, 1962), 146–58

Dostojewski: Notizen und Entwürfe (Budapest, 1985)

Lunde, I., 'Ot idei k idealu: ob odnom simvole v romane Dostoevskogo *Podrostok*', *Evangel'skii tekst v russkoi literature XVIII–XX vekov*, 2, ed. V. N. Zakharov (Petrozavodsk, 1998), 415–23

McCracken, D., *The Scandal of the Gospels* (New York, 1994)

McLachlan, J. M., 'Shestov's reading and misreading of Kierkegaard', *Canadian Slavonic Papers*, 18, no. 2, 174–86

McLuhan, Marshall, *The Gutenberg Galaxy: The Making of Typographic Man* (Toronto, 1962; reprint 1967)

Malkiel, Yakov, 'Cervantes in Nineteenth-Century Russia', *Comparative Literature*, 3 (1951), 310–29

Mann, T., *Sobranie sochinenii v 10–ti tt* (Moscow, 1960)

Marmeladov, Iu. I. (pseudonym of Robert Mann), *Tainyi kod Dostoevskogo: Il'ia-prorok v russkoi literature* (St Petersburg, 1992)

Mathewson, Jr., Rufus. W., *The Positive Hero in Russian Literature* (Stanford, CA, 1975)

Matlaw, Ralph E., *'The Brothers Karamazov': Novelistic Technique* (The Hague, 1957)

  'Recurrent Imagery in Dostoevskij', *Harvard Slavic Studies*, 3 (The Hague, 1957), 201–25

Meerson, Olga, 'Ivolgin and Holbein: Non-Christ risen vs. Christ non-risen', *Slavic and East European Journal*, 39 (1995), 100–13

Merezhkovskii, D. S., 'O *Prestuplenii i nakazanii* Dostoevskogo', *Russkoe obozrenie*, 2, no. 3 (1890), 155–86

  L. Tolstoi i Dostoevskii: Khristos i antikhrist v russkoi literature 1 (St Petersburg, 1901)

  'Khristos i Antikhrist v russkoi literature', *Mir iskusstva*, no. 7 (1901), 85–128

Meyendorff, John, 'L'iconographic de la sagesse divine dans la tradition Byzantine', *Byzantine Hesychasm* (London, 1974), 259–77

Mihailovic, Alexandar, *Corporeal Words: Mikhail Bakhtin's Theology of Discourse* (Evanston, IL, 1997)

Miller, O., *Russkie pisateli posle Gogolia*, vol. 1 (St Petersburg, 1900)

Miller, Robin Feuer, *Dostoevsky and 'The Idiot'* (Cambridge, MA, London, 1981)

  'The Brothers Karamazov': Worlds of the Novel (New York, 1992)

  'Dostoevsky's "The Dream of a Ridiculous Mann"': Unsealing the Generic Envelope', *Freedom and Responsibility in Russian Literature: Essays in Honor of Robert Louis Jackson* (Evanston, IL, 1995), 86–104

  'Dostoevskii's parables: Paradox and plot', *Cultural Discontinuity and Reconstruction, the Byzanto-Slav Heritage and the Creation of a Russian National Literature in the Nineteenth Century*, eds. Jostein Børtnes and Ingunn Lunde (Oslo, 1997), 168–84

Milosz, Czeslaw, 'Dostoevsky and Swedenborg', *Emperor of the Earth* (Berkeley, CA, 1981), 120–43

Mirsky, D. S., *A History of Russian Literature: From Earliest Times to the Death of Dostoevsky (1881)* (London, 1927)

Mochul'skii, K., *Dostoevskii: Zhizn' i tvorchestvo* (Paris, 1947, reprinted 1980)

Mochulsky, K., *Dostoevsky: His Life and Work*, trans. and intro. Michael A. Minihan (Princeton, NJ, 1967)

Møllehave, J., *Kaerlighed og Daemoni: Hvorfor Fejladvikler Kaerligheden sig?* (Copenhagen, 1992)

Moltmann, Jürgen, *The Trinity and the Kingdom: The Doctrine of God*, trans. Margaret Kohl (New York, 1981)

  History and the Triune God: Contributions to Trinitarian Theology (New York, 1992)

Müller, Ludolf, 'Der Einfluss des liberalen Protestantismus auf die russische Laientheologie des 19. Jahrhunderts', *Kirche im Osten*, 3 (1960), 21–32

Dostojewskij (Munich, 1982)

'Die Religion Dostojewskijs', *Von Dostojewskij bis Grass: Schriftsteller vor der Gottesfrage*, ed. Wolfgang Bohne, Herrenalber Texte, 71 (Karlsruhe, 1986), 30–59

'Obraz Khrista v romane Dostoevskogo *Idiot*', *Evangel'skii tekst v russkoi literature XVIII–XX vekov*, 2, ed. V. N. Zakharov (Petrozavodsk, 1998), 374–84

'Die Werke des Metropoliten Ilarion', *Forum Slavicum*, no. 37 (Munich, 1971)

Murav, Harriet, *Holy Foolishness: Dostoevsky's Novels and the Poetics of Cultural Critique* (Stanford, 1992)

Murry, J. Middleton, *Dostoevsky: A Critical Study* (London, 1916)

Musil, R., *Tagebücher, Aphorismen, Essays und Reden* (Hamburg, 1955)

Neuhäuser, Rudolf, '*The Landlady*: A new interpretation', *Canadian Slavonic Papers*, 10, no. 1 (1968), 42–67

'*The Brothers Karamazov*: A Contemporary Reading of Book VI, "A Russian Monk"', *Dostoevsky Studies*, 7 (1986), 135–51

Nicholl, Donald, *Triumphs of the Spirit in Russia* (London, 1997)

Obolensky, Dimitri, 'Early Russian literature (1000–1399)', *An Introduction to Russian Language and Literature*, eds. Robert Auty and Dimitri Obolensky (Cambridge, 1980), 56–89

Ollivier, S., 'Polemika mezhdu Polem Klodelem i Andre Zhidom po povodu obraza Iisusa Khrista v tvorchestve Dostoevskogo', *Evangel'skii tekst v russkoi literature XVIII–XX vekov*, eds. V. N. Zakharov (Petrozavodsk, 1994), 210–21

'Dostoevskii's *The Landlady* and the icon of the Mother of God', *Cultural Discontinuity and Reconstruction: The Byzanto-Slav Heritage and the Creation of a National Literture in Nineteenth-Century Russia*, eds. Jostein Børtnes and Ingunn Lunde (Oslo, 1997), 202–16

'Dostoevskii i Shatobrian', *Evangel'skii tekst v russkoi literature XVIII–XX vekov*, 2, ed. V. N. Zakharov (Petrozavodsk, 1998), 328–56

Onasch, Konrad, *Dostoejewski als Verführer* (Zürich, 1961)

Der verschwiegene Christus: Versuch über die Poetisierung des Christentums in der Dichtung F. M. Dostojewskis (Berlin, 1976)

Ouspensky, Leonid, *Theology of the Icon* (Crestwood, NY, 1978)

Palamas, Gregory, *The Triads*, ed. John Meyendorff (New York, 1983)

Panichas, George A., 'Fyodor Dostoevsky and Roman Catholicism', *Greek Orthodox Theological Review*, 4 (Summer 1958), 16–34

Parker, Alexander A., *Literature and the Delinquent: The Picaresque Novel in Spain and Europe, 1599–1753* (Edinburgh, 1967)

Pascal, Pierre, *Dostoevski* (Paris, English edn 1963; French edn 1969)

Pattison, George, *Kierkegaard: The Aesthetic and the Religious* (London, 1999)

'If Kierkegaard is right about reading, why read Kierkegaard', eds. N.-J.

Cappelørn and H. Deuser, *The Meaning of Meaning It: Kierkegaard Monograph Series I* (Berlin, 1997), 291–309

Anxious Angels: A Retrospective View of Religious Existentialism (Basingstoke, 1999)

Peace, Richard, *Dostoyevsky: An Examination of the Major Novels* (Cambridge, 1971; paperback edn 1992)

Pelikan, Jaroslav, *The Christian Tradition: A History of the Development of Doctrine*, 5 vols. (Chicago, IL, 1971–89)

Perlina, Nina, *Varieties of Poetic Utterance: Quotation in 'The Brothers Karamazov'* (Lanham, MD, 1985)

'Herzen in *The Brothers Karamazov*', *Canadian-American Slavic Studies*, 17, no. 3 (1983), 349–61

Peters, Ted, *God as Trinity: Relationality and Temporality in Divine Life* (Louisville, KY, 1993)

Picchio, Riccardo, 'The function of biblical thematic clues in the literary code of *Slavia Orthodoxa*', *Slavica Hierosolymitana*, 1 (Jerusalem, 1977), 1–31

Plavski, Z. I., 'Cervantes v Rossi', *Miguel de Cervantes Saavedra: bibliografiia russkikh perevodov i kriticheskoi literatury na nerusskom iazyke* (Moscow, 1959), 9–35

Pletnev, R., 'Ob iskushenii Xrista v pustyne i Dostoevskom', *Russian Language Journal*, XXXVI, nos. 123–24 (1982) 66–74

'"Serdtsem mudrye": (O "startsakh" u Dostoevskogo)', *O Dostoevskom*, 2, ed. A. Bem (Prague, 1933), 73–92

Plutarch's Moralia, 15 vols., with English trans. by Frank Cole Babbitt, Loeb Classical Library (Cambridge, MA, 1927–69)

Poncela, Segundo Serrano, 'Don Quijote en Dostoievski', *Insula*, 23 (1968), 19–20

Pondrom, Cyrena, 'Two Demonic Figures: Kierkegaard's Merman and Dostoevsky's Underground Man', *Orbis Litterarum*, 23 (1968), 161–77

Pospielovsky, Dimitry V., *A History of Soviet Atheism in Theory and Practice, and the Believer*, vols. 1–3 (London, 1987, 1988)

The Russian Church Under the Soviet Regime, 1917–1982, 2 vols. (Crestwood, NY, 1984)

Pumpianskii, L. V., *Dostoevskii i antichnost'*, Studien und Texte, vol. 1 (Bremen, 1973)

Pushkin, A. S., 'O russkoi istorii XVIII veka', vol. 7, *Sobranie sochinenii* (Moscow, 1962)

Pyman, Avril, 'Dostoevskii's influence on religious thought in the Russian Silver Age', *Canadian American Slavic Studies*, 17, no. 3 (Fall 1983), 287–324

Renan, Ernst, *Renan's Life of Jesus*, trans. William G. Hutchison (London, 1898)

Rosen, Nathan, 'Style and structure in *The Brothers Karamazov*: The Grand Inquisitor and the Russian Monk', *Russian Literature Triquarterly*, 1 (1971), 352–65

Rötzer, Hans Gerd, *Picaro-Landtstörtzer-Simplicius* (Darmstadt, 1972)

Rowe, William W., '*Crime and Punishment* and *The Brothers Karamazov*: some comparative observations', *Russian Literature Triquarterly*, 10 (1975), 331–42

Rozanov, V. V., *Legenda o Velikom Inkvizitore F. M Dostoevskago: Opyty kriticheskogo kommentariia* (St Petersburg, 1906)

Rozov, N. N., 'Sinodal'nyi spisok sochinenii Ilariona: russkogo pisatelia XI veka', *Slavia*, 32 (Prague, 1963), 141–75

Sandoz, Ellis, *Political Apocalypse, Dostoevsky's Grand Inquisitor* (Baton Rouge, LA, 1971)

Schrag, Calvin O., *Communicative Praxis and the Space of Subjectivity* (Bloomington, IN, 1986)

Seduro, Vladimir, *Dostoevsky in Russian Literary Criticism 1846–1956* (New York, 1958)

Dostoevsky's Image in Russia Today (Belmont, MA, 1975)

Seeley, Frank Friedeberg, 'Ivan Karamazov', in *New Essays on Dostoevsky*, eds. Malcolm V. Jones and Garth M. Terry (Cambridge, 1983), 121–26

'Smerdiakov', *Dostoevsky Studies*, 7 (1986), 99–105

Setchkarev, V., 'From the Golden to the Silver Age (1820–1917)', *An Introduction to Russian Language and Literature*, eds. Robert Auty and Dimitri Obolensky (Cambridge, 1980), 133–84

Shestov, L., *In Job's Balances* (London, 1932)

Kierkegaard and the Existential Philosophy (Athens, OH, 1969)

Shitzova, T. V., *K'erkegor i sovremennost'* (Minsk, 1996)

Shklovskii, V., *Tetiva: O neskhodstve skhodnovo* (Moscow, 1970)

Shul'ts, O., fon, 'Russkii Khristos', *Evangel'skii tekst v russkoi literature XVIII–XX vekov*, ed. V. N. Zakharov (Petrozavodsk, 1998), 31–41

Snodgrass, W. D., 'Crime for punishment: The tenor of Part One', *Hudson Review*, 13, no. 2 (1960), 202–53

Solov'ev, V. S., 'Tri rechi v pamiat' Dostoevskago, 1881–1883', *Sobranie sochinenii V. S. Solov'eva*, vol 3, St Petersburg, 1901, 169–205

Solovyov, V. S. *Lectures on Godmanhood*, trans. and introduced by Peter P. Zouboff (n.p.: International University Press, 1944)

Soltys, George, 'Don Quijote en la obra de Dostoyevski' (Ph.D. dissertation, Middlebury College, VT, 1983)

Stepanian, Karel, ed., *Dostoevskii v kontse XX veka* (Moscow, 1996)

Stern, J. Peter, *On Realism* (London, 1973)

Sutherland, Stewart R., *Atheism and the Rejection of God: Contemporary Philosophy and 'The Brothers Karamazov'* (Oxford, 1977)

'The philosophical dimension: Self and freedom', in *New Essays on Dostoyevsky*, eds. Malcolm V. Jones and Garth M. Terry (Cambridge, 1983)

God, Jesus and Belief (Oxford, 1984)

Szilard, Lena and Barta, Peter, 'Dantov kod russkogo simvolizma', *Studia Slavica Hungarica*, 35 (Budapest, 1989), 61–95

Terras, Victor, *The Young Dostoevsky, 1846–1849* (The Hague, 1969)
'Turgenev and the Devil in *The Brothers Karamazov*', *Canadian–American Slavic Studies*, 6 (Summer, 1972), 265–71
'The art of fiction as a theme in *The Brothers Karamazov*', *Dostoevsky: New Perspectives*, ed. Robert Louis Jackson (Englewood Cliffs, NJ, 1984), 193–205
Thomassen, Einar, 'Kierkegaard og Dostojevskij', *Edda*, 55 (1955), 246–65
Thompson, Diane Oenning, 'Poetic transformations of scientific facts in *Brat'ja Karamazovy*', *Dostoevsky Studies*, 8 (1987), 73–85
'The Brothers Karamazov' and the Poetics of Memory (Cambridge, 1991)
'Lise Khokhlakova: *shalunia/besenok*', *O Rus!: Studia Litteraria Slavica in Honourem Hugh McLean* (Oakland, CA, 1995), 281–97
'Motifs of compassion in Dostoevskii's novels', *Cultural Discontinuity and Reconstruction: The Byzanto-Slav Heritage and the Creation of a Russian National Literature in the Nineteenth Century*, eds. Jostein Børtnes and Ingunn Lunde (Oslo, 1997), 185–201
'The problem of conscience in *Crime and Punishment*', *Celebrating Creativity: Essays in Honour of Jostein Børtnes*, eds. Knut Andreas Grimstad and Ingunn Lunde (Bergen, 1997), 190–204
'Problemy sovesti v *Prestuplenii i nakazanii*', *Evangel'skii tekst v russkoi literature XVIII–XX vekov*, 2, ed. V. N. Zakharov (Petrozavodsk, 1998), 363–73
Thurneysen, E., *Dostoevsky*, trans. K. R. Crim (London, 1964)
Tikhonravov, N., 'Khozhdenie Bogoroditsy po mukam', *Pamiatniki otrechennoi russkoi literatury*, 2 (Moscow, 1863), 23–30
Tiutchev, F. I., *Stikhotvoreniia. Pis'ma. Vospominaniia sovremennikov* (Moscow, 1988)
Toporov, V. N., *Sviatye i sviatost' v russkoi dukhovnoi kul'ture*, vol. 1 (Moscow, 1995)
Tracy, David, 'Metaphor and Religion: The test case of Christian texts', *On Metaphor*, ed. Sheldon Sacks (Chicago, IL, 1979), 89–104
Traversi, Derek, 'Dostoevsky', *Dostoevsky: A Collection of Critical Essays*, ed. René Wellek (Englewood Cliffs, NJ, 1962), 159–71
Troubetskoy, Eugéne, *Trois études sur l'icône* (Paris, 1965)
Troup, Calvin L., *Temporality, Eternity and Wisdom: The Rhetoric of Augustine's Confessions* (Columbia, SC, 1999)
Tschizewskij, Dmitrij, ed., *Das Paterikon des Kiever Hohlenklosters*, 2nd edn (Munich, 1964)
'Schiller und die Brüder Karamazov', *Zeitschrift für slavische Philologie*, 4 (1929), 1–42
Turgenie, I. S., *Polnoe sobranie sochinenii i pis'em v tridtsati tomax* (Moscow, 1982)
Turkevich, Ludmilla B., *Cervantes in Russia* (Princeton, NJ, 1950; reprint NY, 1975)
'Cervantes in Russia', *Cervantes Across the Centuries*, eds. Angel Flores and

M. J. Benardete (New York, 1947; reprinted with corrections, 1969), 353–81

Tynianov, Iu., *Problema stikhotvornogo iazyka: stat'i* (Moscow, 1965)

Uspenskii, B. A. and Lotman, Yu. M., 'Rol' dual'nykh modelei V dinamike russkoi kul'tury do kontsa XVIII vekav', *Izbrannye trudy* (Moscow, 1996), 338–80

Uzhankov, A. N., 'Kogda i gde bylo prochitano Ilarionom', *Slovo o Zakone i Blagodati: Gemenevtika russkoi literatury,* Sbornik 7, chast' 1 (Moscow, 1994), 75–106

Valentinov, N., *Vstrechi s Leninym* (New York, 1953)

Vetlovskaia, V. E., 'Simbolika chisel v *Brat'iakh Karmazovykh*', *Drevnerusskaia literatura i ee traditsii v russkoi literature XVIII–XIX vv.* (Leningrad, 1971), 143–61

   'Dostoevskii i poeticheskii mir drevnei Rusi: (Literaturnye i fol'klornye istochniki *Brat'ev Karamazovykh*)', *Trudy Otdela Drevnerusskoi Literatury*, 28, ed. D. S. Likhachev (Leningrad, 1974), 296–307

   Poetika romana 'Brat'ia Karamazovy' (Leningrad, 1977)

   'Pater Seraphicus', *Dostoevskii: Materialy i issledovaniia*, vol. 5, ed. G. M. Fridlender (Leningrad, 1983), 163–78

   'Alyosha Karamazov and the hagiographic hero', *Dostoevsky: New Perspectives*, ed. Robert Louis Jackson (Englewood Cliffs, NJ, 1984), 206–26

   'Rhetoric and poetics: The affirmation and refutation of opinions in Dostoevsky's *The Brothers Karamazov*', ed. Robin Feuer Miller, *Critical Essays on Dostoevsky* (Boston, MA, 1986), 223–33

Vivas, Eliseo, 'The two dimensions of reality in *The Brothers Karamazov,* Dostoevsky: A Collection of Critical Essays*, ed. René Wellek (Englewood Cliffs, NJ, 1962), 71–89

Volynskii, A. L., *Tsarstvo Karamazovykh* (St Petersburg, 1901)

Vysheslavtsev, B. P., *Etika preobrazhennogo erosa* (Moscow, 1994)

Walicki, Andrzej, *A History of Russian Thought from the Enlightenment to Marxism*, trans. Hilda Andrews-Rusiecka (Stanford, CA, 1979)

   Legal Philosophies of Russian Liberalism (Oxford, 1987)

Ward, Bruce K., *Dostoevsky's Critique of the West: The Quest for Earthly Paradise* (Waterloo, ON, 1986)

Ware, Archimandrite Kallistos, *The Orthodox Way* (London, 1981)

Ware, Timothy, *The Orthodox Church* (London, 1986)

Wasiolek, Edward, *Dostoevsky: The Major Fiction* (Cambridge, MA, 1973)

Wellek, René, 'Introduction: A history of Dostoevsky criticism', *Dostoevsky: A Collection of Critical Essays*, ed. René Wellek (Englewood Cliffs, NJ, 1962), 1–15

   'Bakhtin's View of Dostoevsky: "Polyphony" and "Carnivalesque"', *Dostoevsky Studies*, 1 (1980), 31–39

Williams, Charles, *The Descent of the Dove* (London, 1939)

   The Image of the City and Other Essays (Oxford, 1958)

Wilson, C. *The Outsider* (London, 1978)

Wilson, Henry, *The Nicene and Post-Nicene Fathers of the Christian Church* 5, 2nd series, 1892 (Grand Rapids, MI, 1979)

Zabolotski, N. A., 'Fyodor Mikhailovich Dostoevsky today', *Scottish Journal of Theology*, 37, no. 1 (1984), 41–57

Zakharov, V. N., 'Russkaia literatura i khristianstvo', *Evangel'skii tekst v russkoi literature XVIII–XX vekov*, ed. V. N. Zakharov (Petrozavodsk, 1994), 5–11

ed., *Novye aspekty v izuchenii Dostoevskogo* (Petrozavodsk, 1994)

'Umilenie kak kategoriia poetiki Dostoevskogo', *Celebrating Creativity: Essays in Honour of Jostein Børtnes*, eds. Knut Andreas Grimstad and Ingunn Lunde (Bergen, 1997), 237–55

Zander, L. A., *Dostoevsky* (London, 1948)

Zen'kovskii, V. V., 'Dostoevsky's religious and philosophical views', *Dostoevsky: A Collection of Critical Essays*, ed. René Wellek (Englewood Cliffs, NJ, 1962), 130–45

Zenkovsky, Basile, *Histoire de la philosophie russe*, vol. I (Paris, 1953). Translated as Vassili Zenkovsky, *A History of Russian Philosophy* (London, 1967)

Zernov, Nicolas, *Eastern Christendom* (London, 1961)

Ziolkowski, Eric J., *The Sanctification of Don Quixote: From Hidalgo to Priest* (University Park, PA, 1991)

Ziolkowski, Theodore, *Fictional Transfigurations of Jesus* (Princeton, NJ, 1972)

Zvoznikov, A. A., 'Dostoevskii i pravoslavie: predvaritel'nye zametki', *Evangel'skii tekst v russkoi literature XVIII–XX vekov*, ed. V. N. Zakharov (Petrozavodsk, 1994), 179–91

Index

MAIN INDEX

Christ *see* Jesus Christ
Christology (see also Incarnation, kenoticism)
   31–40, 44–9, 50, 76, 136–8, 146–7, 149
Church Slavonic   9, 27n., 83
Clarke, K.   140, 154n., 170n.
Clive, G.   255n.
Coates, R.   154, 163, 170n.
Colour, symbolism of   178–84
Columban, Saint   159
Communism   4, 5–6
Cross   174–6
Crowder, C.   27n., 28n., 155n.
Crucifixion   73, 174–6, 178
Crystal Palace, the   181–3, 187n., 188n.
Cunningham, D. S.   25, 152n.
Cyril, St.   105

Dante   11, 103, 121–2, 132n., 141, 232
Decembrists   42–3
De Lubac, H.   16–17, 27n.
Death of God, the   19
Demonic, the   234
Derzhavin, G. R.   3
Descartes, R.   139
Detweiler, R.   152n.
Devil, the   58, 88, 126, 139, 191, 195, 196,
   200, 211, 216–17, 220
Diaghilev, S.   110
Dialogue, dialogism   83–4, 99n., 111, 144,
   156, 162, 164, 221–2, 248
Diaz, M.   169n.
Dickens, C.   107
Dionysius *see* Pseudo-Dionysius
Dobrolyubov, N. A.   4
Dolinin, A. S.   7
Don Quixote   75, 80–2, 97n., 98n., 160–2,
   163, 166, 169n., 195
Dostoevsky, A. G. (second wife of F. M.
   Dostoevsky)   108
Dostoevsky, F. M.
   Biographical references   41–3, 46
   Works discussed or cited:
   The Adolescent see The Raw Youth
   Bobok   82–4
   The Brothers Karamazov   3, 4, 5, 6, 7, 8, 9,
      17, 18, 20, 23, 27n., 31, 36, 41, 43, 49, 58,
      63–4, 75, 77, 87–95, 97n., 99n., 111, 112,
      119–20, 122–31, 133n., 134–55, 156–8,
      163–4, 166–7, 168n., 189–225, 231 [The
      Grand Inquisitor   9, 17, 58, 91, 92, 120,
      143, 146, 167, 197, 203–4, 220]
   Crime and Punishment   20, 24, 47, 49, 71–3,
      95, 120–1, 127–8, 156, 163–5, 173–88,
      226–36
   The Devils   6, 7, 8, 23, 27n., 31, 35, 36, 46,

48, 52, 59, 66n., 76–7, 86, 95, 111, 131,
   199
The Diary of a Writer   40, 44, 48, 65, 106,
   160, 168n., 169n., 170n., 252, 256n.
The Double   53, 192, 198
The Dream of a Ridiculous Man   85–6
The Idiot   21, 49, 57, 58–9, 73–6, 95, 96,
   97n., 166, 169n., 170n., 184, 191, 195
The Landlady   3, 53–8, 65, 66n., 67n.
The Meek One   60, 62, 67n., 84–5
Mr. Prokharchin   53
Notes from the House of the Dead   8, 42, 108,
   199
Notes from the Underground   8, 20, 239–40,
   241, 244
Poor Folk   53
The Possessed see *The Devils*
The Raw Youth   41, 51, 60–2, 67n., 86,
   108–9, 196
A Weak Heart   66n.
Letters   31, 42, 43, 45, 107, 108
Notebooks   41
D's orthography   9
Dostoevsky, M. M. (brother of F. M.
   Dostoevsky)   107
Double, phenomenon of   192–3, 198–9, 221
Double-voiced discourse   70, 95
Doubt   103
Drake, H.   188
Dreams   173, 176, 177, 232

Early Russian Literature   2, 4
Eliot, T. S.   138
Emerson, C.   11, 24, 89, 96n., 98n.
Engels, F.   208
Enlightenment   2–3
Envy   247–8
Epilepsy   191
Ermilov, V. V.   8, 26n.
Esaulov, I. A.   10, 23, 98n., 99n., 132n.
Eschatology   160
Euclid *see* Rationality
Eunomius, Saint   227
Evil   139, 190, 191, 200, 211, 216–17, 230, 233
Evdokimov, P.   64
Existentialism   12, 15, 18, 19, 237–41, 244

Faith   116, 239
Fall   239
Fascism   192, 228
Fear   248
Fedotov, G.   32, 40n., 159–60, 168n.
Fennell, J.   132n.
Feodosy of Pechersk   33, 34, 35, 40n.
Ferrari, L.   168n.

BIBLE REFERENCES

CAMBRIDGE STUDIES IN RUSSIAN LITERATURE

General editor CATRIONA KELLY

Editorial board: ANTHONY CROSS, CARYL EMERSON,
HENRY GIFFORD, BARBARA HELDT, MALCOLM JONES,
DONALD RAYFIELD, G. S. SMITH, VICTOR TERRAS